BRITISH RAILWAYS WAGONS

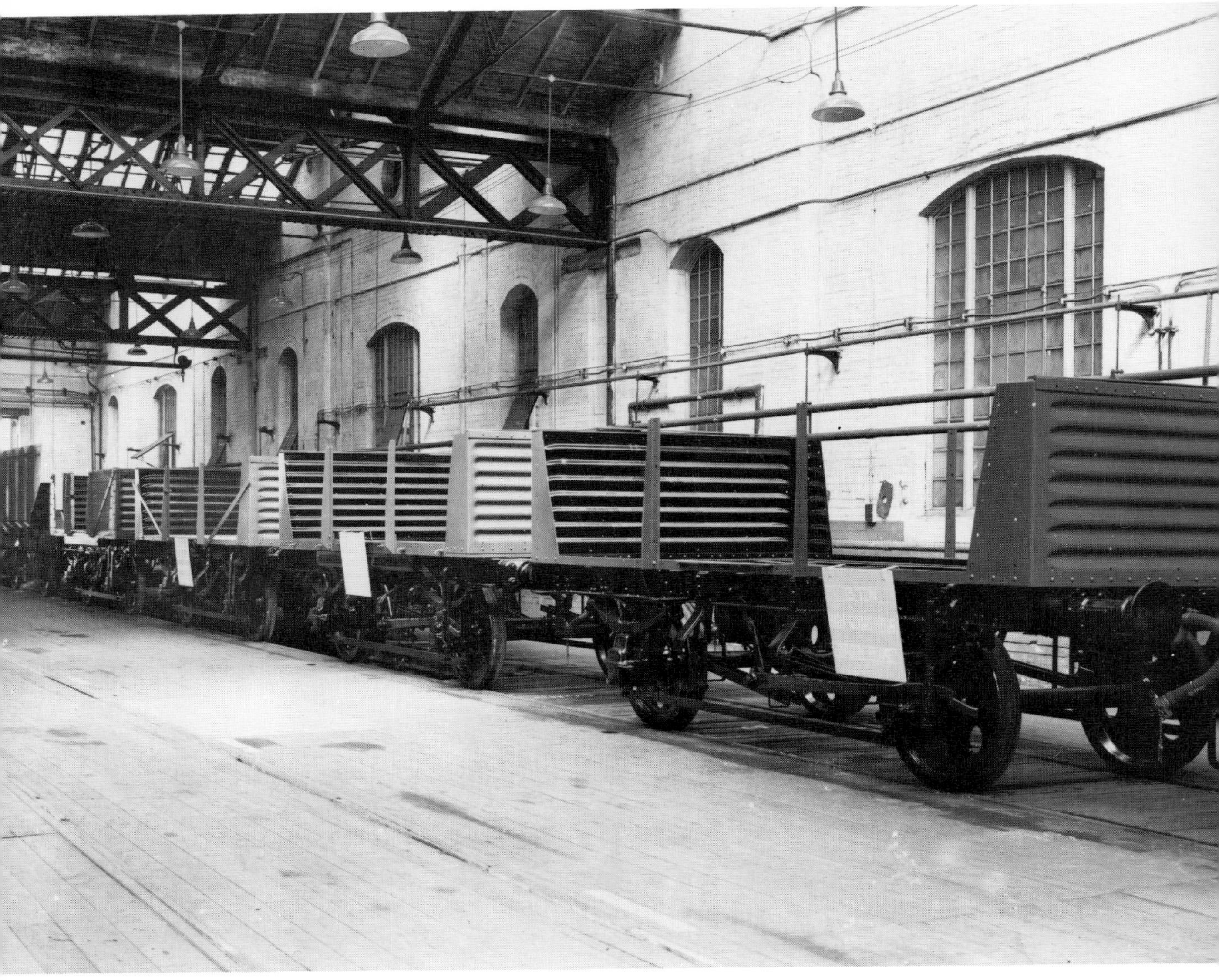

Plate 1. *This picture of wagons under construction typifies the British Railways approach to freight stock during the early years of nationalisation. The four wagons nearest the camera all use the BR standard four-wheel underframe 17ft 6in long over headstocks with a 10ft wheelbase and wheels 3ft 1½in diameter. Axleboxes are the split type and Instanter couplings are used, while automatic vacuum brake and Morton handbrake are fitted. The first three wagons are 13ton high goods and await the fitting of wooden floors, sides and end planking — the latter going inside the corrugated ends. Sheet support apparatus will be fitted to the wagon nearest the camera. All this indicates a vehicle to diagram 1/039. The next wagon appears to be the shock-absorbing version to diagram 1/040. The photograph was probably taken at Derby in the early 1950s.* (Author's collection).

BRITISH RAILWAYS WAGONS

the first half million

DON ROWLAND

This edition published in 1996
By Leopard, a division of Random House UK Ltd
20 Vauxhall Bridge Road London SW1V 2SA

First published in 1985
by David & Charles Ltd

ISBN 0 7529 0378 0

Printed in Great Britain by
Butler & Tanner Ltd, Frome
for David & Charles (Publishers) Limited,
Brunel House, Newton Abbot, Devon.

Publishers note: The wagon diagrams have all been reproduced as far as possible to the modelling scale of 4mm – 1ft, unless shown otherwise in the captions to the figures or alongside the drawings concerned. It should be noted that reproduction limitations in one or two cases have prevented an exact scale reproduction and the drawing dimensions shown should be checked for modelling use.

Contents

Introduction

While engaged on research for this book, I was privileged to visit the Railway Technical Centre at Derby to examine rolling stock records. During the visit I was taken to sidings at the rear of the complex to see tangible evidence of the Centre's development work in the shape of the High-Speed Train and the Advanced Passenger Train. At that time both trains had done trial runs only, but the former had shown itself capable of speeds of 125mph while the latter was confidently expected to reach 150mph in service. Both trains were designed to run at these speeds on standard British Railways tracks, and to do this the Advanced Passenger Train especially embodied many technical innovations.

Later that afternoon, working away amongst lot numbers, diagrams, amendments to building programmes and similar detail, the full impact of what had been seen slowly dawned. Looking out of the office window, across London Road and into the yard of the wagon repair shops, the contrast was quite unbelievable. There, not two hundred yards away from the Advanced Passenger Train, the wagons awaiting repair were all simple vehicles, mostly four-wheeled and many with but hand lever brakes for control. For every wagon in that yard 125mph, let alone 150mph, was definitely taboo. Some were permitted a maximum speed of just *45mph*, one-third that of the Advanced Passenger Train. What was remarkable was not just that they should exist side by side but that in service they should use the very same tracks.

To be sure, there are plans to eliminate the older types of wagon. Larger, heavier air-braked wagons are appearing in greater numbers on British Railways. The demise of the traditional small simple wagon is confidently forecast — and has been for many years. Although these two paragraphs were drafted a few years ago they have been allowed to stand. The HST is in fleet service even if the APT has still to run regular services. Yet the contrast is still there — there are still unbraked wagons in use on British main lines today.

This book is mainly about the older wagons — in fact all wagons, and containers, built by or for British Railways from 1948 until production of traditional wagons finally petered out, plus a few more besides. For although such wagons still exist, to the embarrassment of railwaymen and the amazement of visiting Americans, production of the time-honoured British wagon, three-link couplings and all, finally ceased some years ago. New wagons are a much different breed, and in the final chapter we take a quick look at some of the more recent developments, including the advent of air-braked stock.

British Goods Wagons, by Essery, Rowland & Steel (David & Charles, 1970) traced the steady if unspectacular development of the British goods wagon from the first attempts at standardisation in 1887 up to the emergence of modern air-braked vehicles 80 years later. This book looks in detail at the last phase when the multitude of railway companies had merged into British Railways. There was now a single design authority and, for wagon builders, just a single customer. For the railways, the change brought a peculiar mixture of challenge and frustration. Being a nationalised industry they were to experience the full force of change in policy. Stop, go, mark time, even about turn, became the order of the day as governments changed, policies were revised, and one Transport Act followed on the heels of another. Through all these changes British Railways was expected to soldier on, providing a service and making a profit.

It is against this background that we must view the development of freight wagons by British Railways. Neither must we forget the effect on the railways of similar changes of government policy in other fields. Thus a decision to halt the decline in coal production meant that not only did the railway authorities have to stop the scrapping of what had previously been surplus mineral wagons, but they were virtually forced into rebuilding some obsolete wagons to cope with increased traffic. So if some of our strictures at times seem critical of those responsible for the wagon stock it must be remembered that the Railway Executive, British Transport Commission or the British Railways Board have never been really masters in their own house. Since 1948 a constant succession of Ministers responsible for transport has ensured, if nothing else, a variety of policies.

This book would not have been possible without the co-operation of British Railways and I readily acknowledge my indebtedness to them. Facilities accorded at the Railway Technical Centre have already been referred to, and I am especially grateful to Mr T. J. Edgington, lately of the British Railways Public Relations Office at Euston, for arranging them, and to Mr A. T. Scrivenor (now retired) and his staff at the Central Rolling Stock Registry there for all their assistance and for answering my many questions. Since then Mr Edgington has moved to the National Railway Museum, where he continues to be unfailingly helpful. In the first instance this book was only made possible because of the lineside photographic facilities accorded to me over the years by the British Railways Public Relations Office in Glasgow. Through their ready co-operation I have been able to record much that is now just history. Many of the photographs in this book are my own, and the reader may note how many were taken in Scotland.

There are also numerous friends who have provided information, Ray Chorley, Mike Hall, David Larkin, Stuart Sellar and Peter Tatlow especially. I am particularly grateful to David Larkin for help with the final chapter and the use of his photographs. I should also like to thank British Rail Engineering for permission to use Plates 108, 116 and 171 taken in Ashford Works, and John Davenport for his help in the preparation of Appendix 4. I would finally like to thank my wife Olive and our daughter Elaine for oft times waiting patiently whilst I went off to photograph yet another interesting wagon espied in some distant siding.

Throughout the text, other than in Chapter 13, I have spoken of British Railways in preference to the currently approved British Rail. This is quite deliberate, as for most of the events covered it was the correct title. For consistency also the past tense has been used in almost every instance, the final chapter again excepted. This too was a conscious decision, albeit a more difficult one, because although thousands upon thousands of the wagons built by and for British Railways have been scrapped some still remain, even if the wagon stock today is one-tenth the figure it was when British Railways was born. Most which still remain belong obstinately to an older age when British Railways carried nigh on one million tons of freight every working day. Maybe we should have called this book *Twilight of the Goods*.

D. P. ROWLAND
Dalkeith
August 1982.

Chapter 1

Review

Inheritance

On 1 January 1948 the newly-formed British Railways became the owner of some 1,279,543 wagons and containers inherited from the four main line companies. These self-same wagons had worked hard throughout the war years carrying a prodigious tonnage of freight. Although loadings had dropped a little from the heights of 1943, the railways still handled massive quantities of merchandise and mineral traffic. The wagons used to carry this traffic were showing signs of age. By 1946 for example 92,724 LMS wagons, nearly one-third of all stock, had been built in 1922 or earlier. At the beginning of 1947 some 71,247 railway-owned wagons were under or awaiting repair.

Between them, these two figures probably illustrate better than anything else the task facing the new owners so far as freight stock was concerned. What they do not indicate is just how few modern refinements were present throughout the wagon fleet. Automatic brakes and screw couplings were fitted to very few vehicles, so that the number of fully-fitted freight trains was pitifully small. Even on railway-owned vehicles the oil axlebox was far from universal, with many wagons still retaining the older greaseboxes, thus making them unsuitable for express freight trains. A few wagons fitted with shock-absorbing apparatus were in traffic but such things as hydraulic buffers, roller-bearing axleboxes and disc brakes were unheard of.

Alongside the railway wagons there were also over half-a-million privately-owned wagons operating on the main lines. About 20,000 of them, used principally for carrying petroleum products, salt, lime and other special traffics, were to remain privately-owned and are outside the scope of this book. The remaining wagons, some 544,694, were all mineral wagons. Although remaining the property of their owners, they had been requisitioned by the government in 1939. After the war they were never handed back and were taken into British Railways stock in 1948. We shall consider them again in Chapter 3, but here it will suffice to say that if in 1948 the condition of railway-owned goods stock was less than ideal it was definitely superior to that of the privately-owned wagons. The result was an unduly high proportion of ill maintained antiquated low capacity wagons fitted with greaseboxes, the veritable *bêtes noires* of the railwayman's life. On top of all this they, like the railways' wagons, had suffered from shortage of labour and materials for maintenance. Not surprisingly against such a background, attention to the wagon fleet was high on British Railways' long list of priorities.

Reaction

British Railways' reaction to this situation they had inherited was to repair those wagons which had a reasonable life expectancy and scrap those which did not, building as replacements larger, more modern vehicles. So successfully was this policy pursued and so rapidly did the situation change that, as we shall see, before the state system had reached its majority there was a surplus of wagons and relatively modern vehicles were being scrapped. Table 1 gives details of wagon stocks. But that is to anticipate our story.

At first wagons continued to be built to the designs of the old railway companies. Each company had wagon orders which were not completed by nationalisation. In some cases it is believed that these were completed as ordered but in other instances — and this is especially true of wagons ordered by the LMS — the original lot numbers were cancelled and BR lot numbers substituted with the relevant diagram being issued in the BR series. As an example, the first British Railways lot, No 2001, issued on 8 December 1948 for 1,300 12ton goods vans to be built at Wolverton to BR diagram 200, was originally LMS lot 1456 to that company's diagram 2108.

Table 1 British Railway Wagons — Traffic Stock

Year	*Opening stock*	*Additions*	*Withdrawals*	*Closing stock*	*Fitted vehicles*	*Unfitted vehicles*	*Average Capacity (Tons)*
1948	1,223,634	39,464	83,694	1,179,404	131,965	1,047,439	12·50
1949	1,179,404	31,929	98,190	1,113,143	136,207	976,936	12·75
1950	1,113,143	33,638	41,816	1,104,965	143,014	961,951	12·97
1951	1,104,965	40,651	36,383	1,109,233	154,392	954,841	13·16
1952	1,109,233	43,770	32,885	1,120,118	160,889	959,229	13·34
1953	1,120,118	40,882	38,956	1,122,044	169,898	952,146	13·51
1954	1,122,044	54,553	51,887	1,124,710	176,819	947,891	13·76
1955	1,124,710	58,734	58,632	1,124,812	181,424	943,388	14·02
1956	1,124,812	61,479	68,827	1,117,464	190,826	926,638	14·27
1957	1,117,464	59,690	72,263	1,104,891	227,033	877,858	14·54
1958	1,104,891	36,293	120,987	1,020,197	269,698	750,499	14·90
1959	1,020,197	16,514	76,358	960,353	296,253	664,100	15.09
1960	960,353	14,179	12,585	961,947	311,754	650,193	15·14
1961	961,947	8,421	14,084	956,284	320,162	636,122	15·24
1962	956,284	8,729	102,373	862,640	319,969	542,671	15·55
1963	862,640	3,001	143,475	722,166	298,805	432,361	16.01
1964	722,166	769	72,853	650,082	249,102	400,980	16·26
1965	650,082	2,061	41,145	610,998	241,291	369,707	16·36
1966	610,998	1,701	61,277	551,422	214,428	336,994	16·60
1967	551,422	1,590	86,389	466,623	190,853	275,770	16·94

Notes on the Tables

Table 1

The details are taken from the Annual Reports of the British Transport Commission or its successor, the British Railways Board, except for the average wagon capacity, which after 1961 has been calculated from figures in the reports. The figures for additions to stock cover new construction by railway workshops and contractors, vehicles purchased second hand, and transfers from other categories, together with vehicles previously withdrawn and later reinstated. Likewise the figures for withdrawals cover not only condemnations but also transfers and conversions to other categories. As an example, the 43,770 wagons added to stock in 1952 include 15,960 locomotive coal wagons transferred from service stock.

The figures for unfitted and fitted vehicles relate to all wagons, including brake vans. A fitted vehicle is defined as one fitted with continuous brakes or with through pipe only.

The average wagon capacity is obtained by taking the total carrying capacity and dividing it by the total number of wagons, excluding brake vans. This figure and those for fitted and unfitted vehicles refer to the year-end position.

This first phase gave way fairly quickly to the second, where designs originated from British Railways rather than the companies. There was no sudden change of policy and it is sometimes very difficult to say if a design was 'pure' British Railways. If one considers say the 20ton coke hopper wagons to diagram 150, they are found to be almost identical to the LMS version except that in the latter the coke raves were of wood, whereas the BR type used steel. Generally speaking, new designs began to show less and less company parentage.

The most outstanding feature of this second phase was probably the sheer volume of new con-

Table 2 British Railway Wagons — Service Stock

Year	*Opening Stock*	*Additions*	*Withdrawals*	*Closing Stock*
1948	36,551	2,069	1,334	37,286
1949	37,291	1,309	1,391	37,209
1950	37,220	583	844	36,959
1951	36,960	1,036	1,301	36,695
1952	36,695	697	16,692	20,700
1953	20,731	1,119	752	21,098
1954	21,098	1,114	727	21,485
1955	21,485	1,486	878	22,093
1956	22,093	2,068	1,004	23,157
1957	23,157	3,029	1,004	25,174
1958	25,174	1,422	817	25,779
1959	25,779	1,834	864	26,749
1960	26,749	1,855	746	27,858
1961	27,858	1,324	756	28,426
1962	28,426	1,020	974	28,472
1963	28,472	7,478	1,338	34,612
1964	34,612	8,959	2,399	41,172
1965	41,172	3,656	2,789	42,039
1966	42,039	1,550	3,531	40,058
1967	40,058	1,177	3,995	37,240

Table 2

The details are from the same source as those for Table 1. The definitions are the same as in that table. The apparently heavy withdrawals in 1952 include the 15,960 locomotive coal wagons transferred to traffic stock.

It will be noted that in some instances the figure for opening stock differs from that for closing stock at the previous year end. These same discrepancies appear without explanation in the official statistics. As an example, the number of travelling cranes quoted as being in stock on 1 January 1949 was three greater than the figure for 31 December 1948.

struction. Reading Appendix 4 will show that as yet there had been no reduction in the number of wagon works which the railway owned that were engaged on new work. Alongside the demands made on railway workshops, extensive orders were placed with outside contractors. Orders for 1,000 wagons became quite common, and often it seemed that the lack of workshop capacity was the limiting factor which controlled the amount of cash spent on freight rolling stock construction.

But if output in these earlier years was prodigious it still consisted of largely traditional types and designs of wagon. Certainly wooden underframes were out, as were grease axleboxes and for general traffic no vehicles of less than 12tons capacity were built, with 16tons or more being standard for minerals. But the oil axlebox was still looked on as being quite adequate, while vacuum brake equipment was generally confined to covered vans and some open merchandise wagons. The relaxation of restrictions on road haulage operators increased competition and this, coupled with a general demand for even faster transits, made the railways stop and take stock. The result was the 1955 Modernisation Plan. For freight traffic it envisaged faster trains vacuum-braked throughout (air brakes were eschewed on the grounds of expense) with the demise of 'Emmett-like trains clanking across the country'. Universal vacuum brakes of course spelled the end of the three-link coupling, with screw or Instanter couplings in use on all trains.

The report paved the way for a third phase when all new construction had automatic brakes as standard and existing wagons were systematically updated. It was the conversion of mineral wagons in this latter group which gave rise to such problems as to cause a certain amount of re-thinking and to this day not all mineral wagons have automatic vacuum brakes. This is why a quarter of a century later we still see goods trains with the typically British guard's van dutifully bringing up the rear.

Even if in the event vacuum brakes were not fitted to all wagons the story does not end there. A downturn in railway freight loadings meant that the railways, instead of having a wagon shortage, found themselves with a surplus. Furthermore, a new financial approach decreed that surplus wagons should now be scrapped rather than stored until needed. In terms of wagon stocks this change in commercial approach ushered in a fourth phase which was marked by heavy withdrawals of redundant wagons, often relatively new, with construction of wagons confined to specialist types such as pallet vans and conflats. Where traffic potential was seen, existing wagons were converted to cater for a known or hoped-for flow. An example of this latter approach is shown in Plate 3.

This phase turned out to be the swan-song of the traditional wagon. Conversions continued, principally of redundant passenger coaches into carflats, but all new construction was of air-braked vehicles, which as defined previously are considered outwith the scope of this work. Yet so massive was the scale of new construction in the early years of British Railways that, despite the cessation of new construction and heavy withdrawals, there still remain some thousands of what are now very old-fashioned goods wagons in service up and down the land.

Diagrams and lots

Reference to diagrams and lots calls for explanation of the classification systems initially used by British Railways. Following in the steps of the Big Four companies, British Railways set up three diagram books to cover freight stock. A diagram was issued for each design of wagon or container which was referred to by its page number. Thus the 16ton end door wagon, 'to diagram 108', refers to page 108 of the Wagon Diagram Book. The three books initially issued were Book 1 for ordinary wagons, Book 2 for specially-constructed wagons and Book 3 for containers. The pages in each were numbered from 1. The introduction of the TOPS (Total Operations Processing System) system of wagon control caused a complete change of approach, but as this is outwith the time scale of this book we shall refer to diagrams by their former numbers throughout.

Unlike the GWR and LMS railways which used lot number systems, construction of new wagon stock on the LNER was to annual programmes. British Railways combined both features, although as will be seen the use of annual programmes was to be superseded. A series of British Railways lot numbers starting at 2001 was allocated for the construction of all wagons and containers. Passenger vehicles were allotted a separate series beginning at lot 30001. The system used in the lot registers records the date of issue of

Table 3 British Railways — Container Stock

Year	*Opening Stock*	*Additions*	*Withdrawals*	*Closing Stock*
1948	19,358	943	335	19,966
1949	19,966	2,758	561	22,163
1950	22,163	2,003	599	23,567
1951	23,567	1,507	788	24,286
1952	24,286	3,400	2,019	25,667
1953	25,667	5,246	1,802	29,111
1954	29,111	4,261	969	32,403
1955	32,403	3,684	1,864	34,223
1956	34,223	3,492	1,882	35,833
1957	35,833	5,871	1,492	40,212
1958	40,212	8,549	1,340	47,421
1959	47,421	3,951	1,221	50,151
1960	50,151	637	1,717	49,071
1961	49,071	1,197	1,972	48,296
1962	48,296	218	1,979	46,535
1963	46,535	217	5,286	41,436
1964	41,436	118	5,064	36,490
1965	36,490	354	3,428	33,415
1966	33,415	419	1,865	31,969
1967	31,969	2,855	3,786	31,038

The sources and definitions are the same as those for Table 1. Until 1956 the great majority of containers were classified as 'freight' with a very small number described as 'coaching'. From 1956 onwards all were classed simply as 'container', so for consistency the figures for 1948-55 above include the coaching containers.

Plate 2. *20ton brake van. Diagram 1/505. The first British Railways wagons were to existing company designs. Although B950022 was one of BR lot 2025, it is very obviously to an LMS design. It was actually ordered as part of that company's lot 1557 which was taken over and amended after nationalisation. Millerhill, 15.11.64.* (Author).

Figure 1. *This drawing of the proposed standard designs of wagon appeared as Appendix B of the Ideal Stocks Committee's 'Report on Design, Capacity and Types of Railway Freight Rolling Stock'. It may have been included after the report had been issued for some time, as the copy from which it was taken was dated March 1950 and yet it illustrates, for example, the 24½ton mineral wagon to diagram 1/115 which was not ordered until June 1952.*

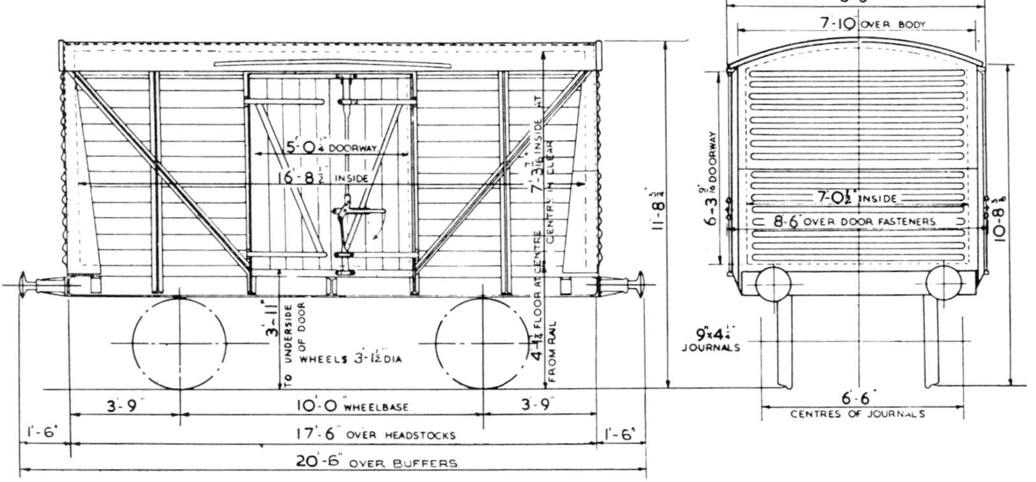

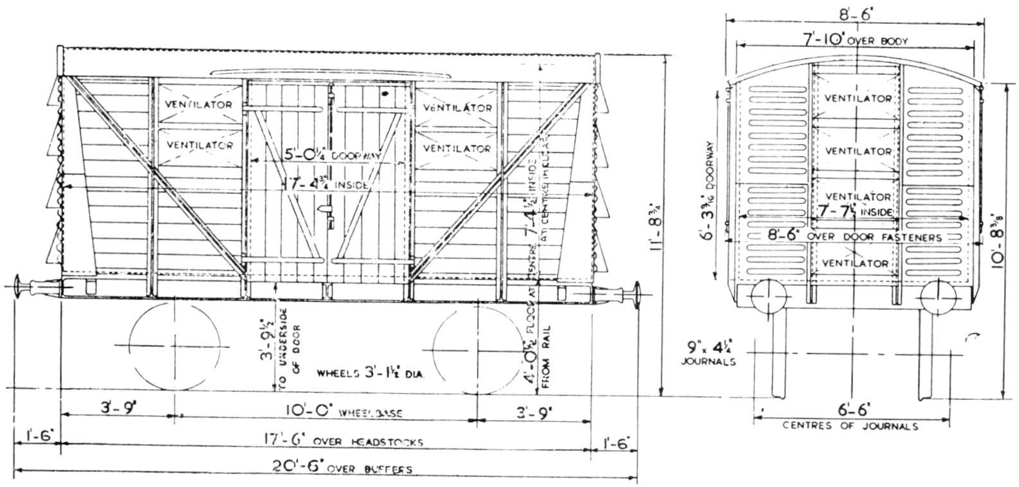

10 TON VENTILATED MEAT VAN FOR FRESH MEAT

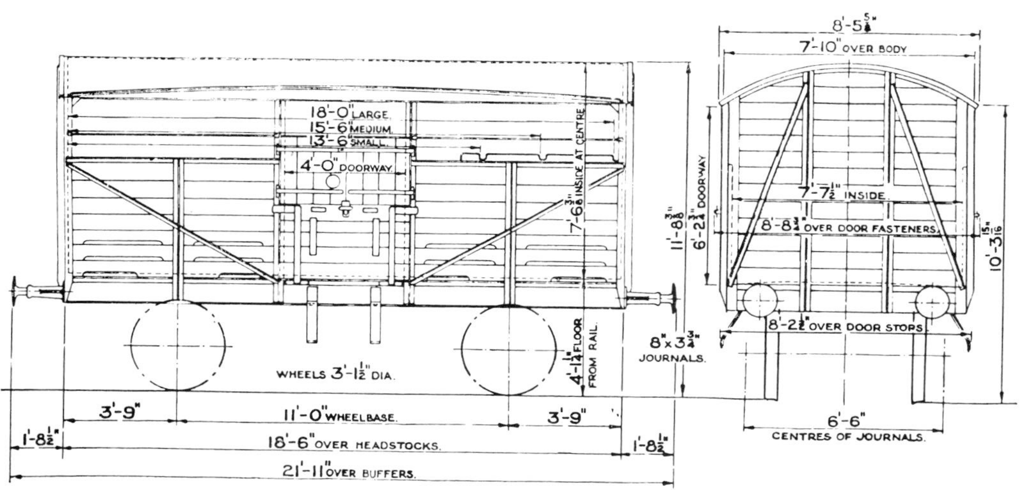

8 TON CATTLE WAGON

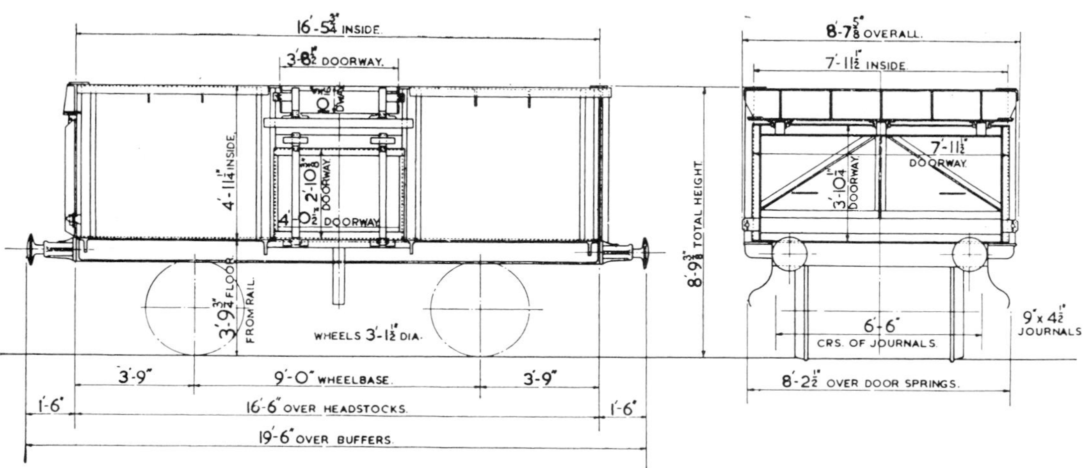

16 TON ALL-STEEL MINERAL WAGON

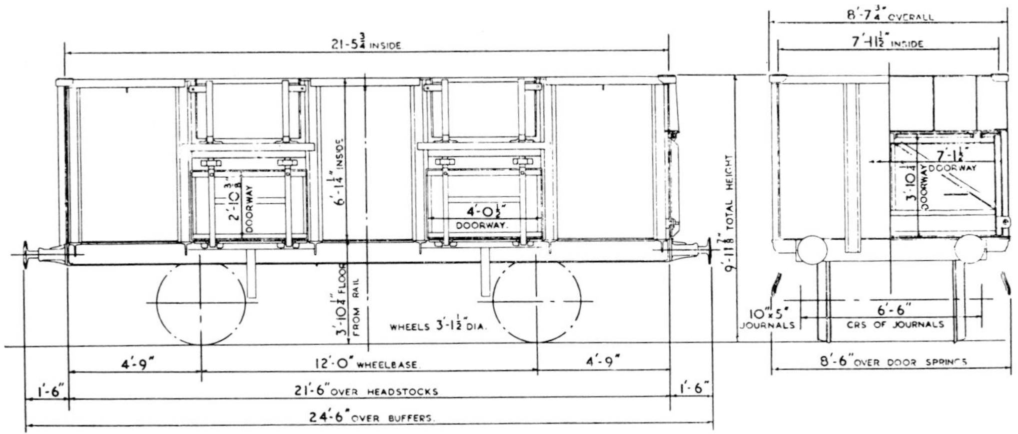

24½ TON ALL-STEEL MINERAL WAGON

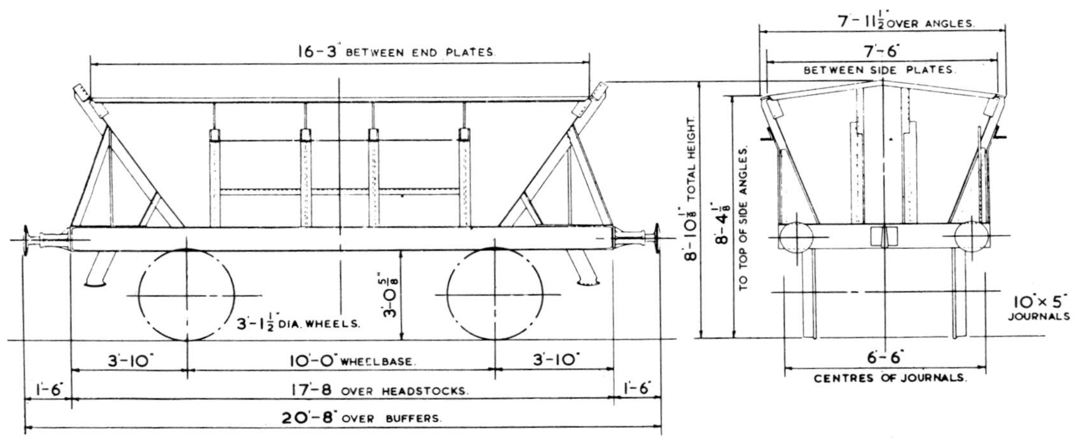

25 TON IRONSTONE WAGON

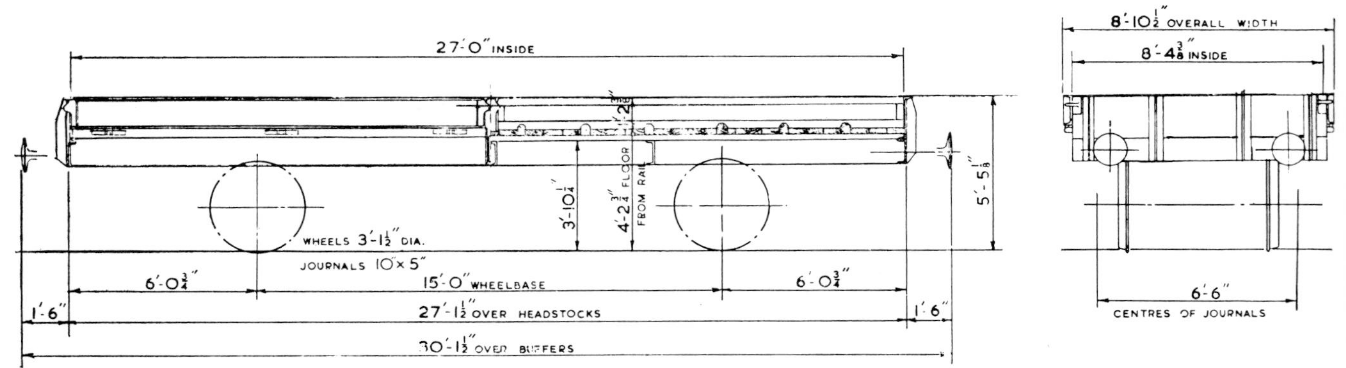

22 TON PLATE WAGON

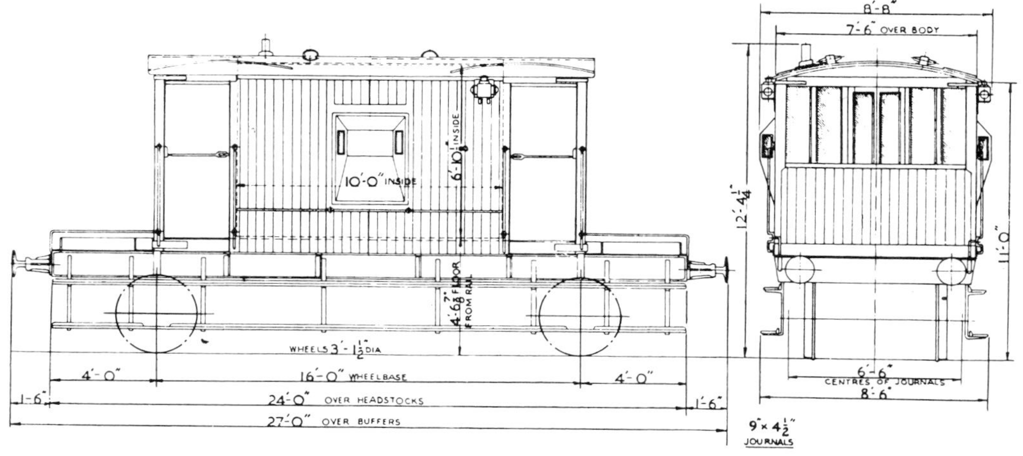

20 TON GOODS BRAKE VAN

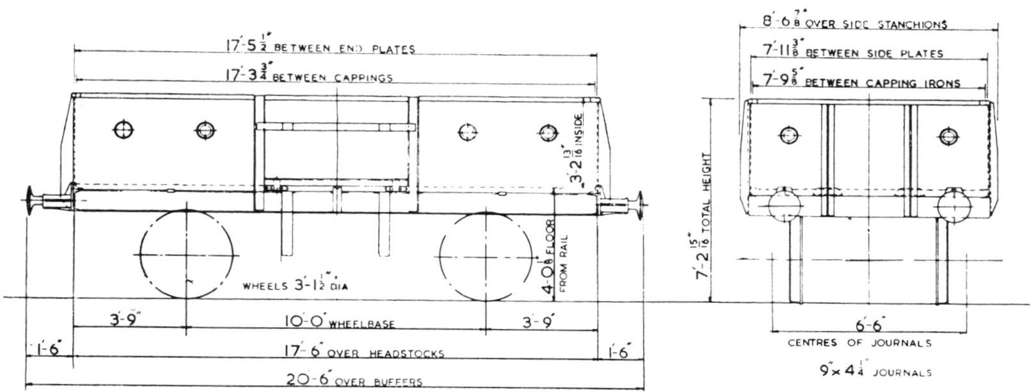

13 TON ALL-STEEL HIGH GOODS WAGON

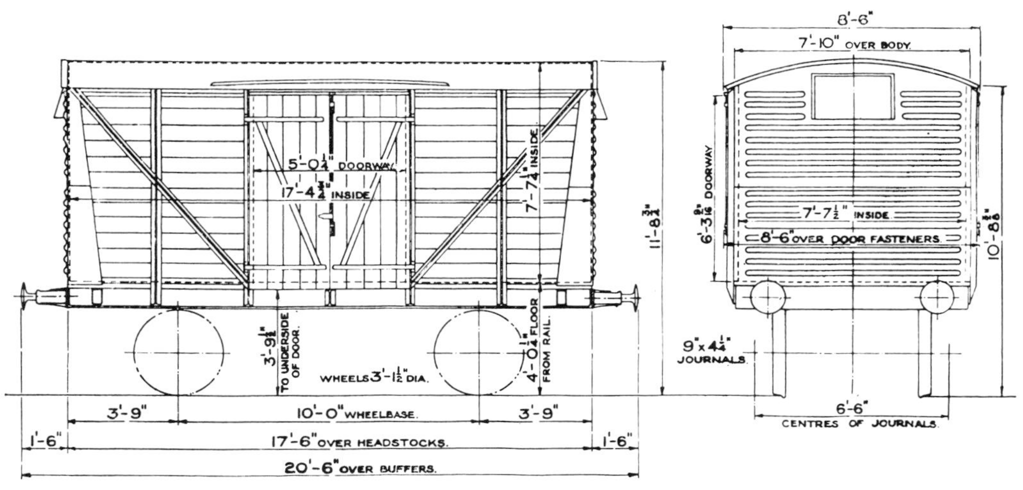

12 TON COVERED GOODS VAN

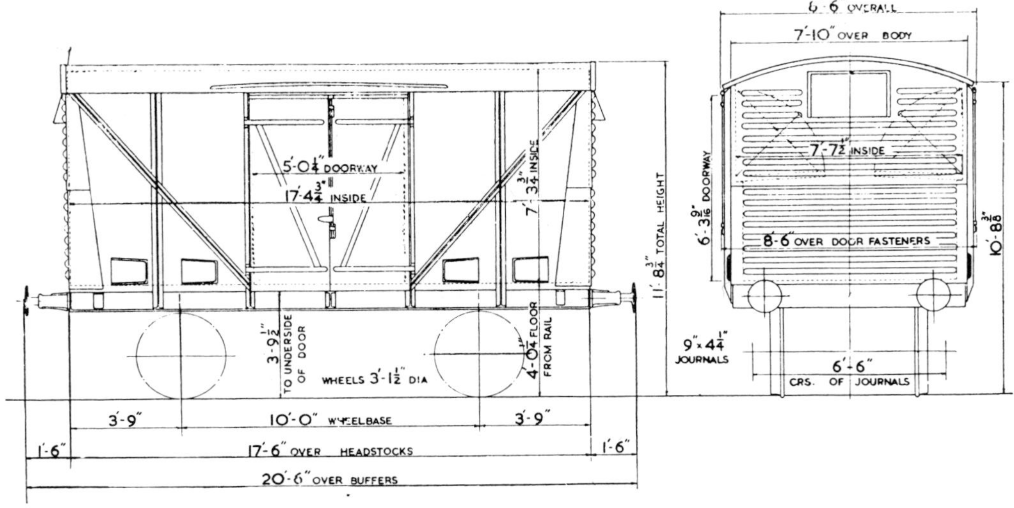

12 TON FRUIT AND VEGETABLE VAN

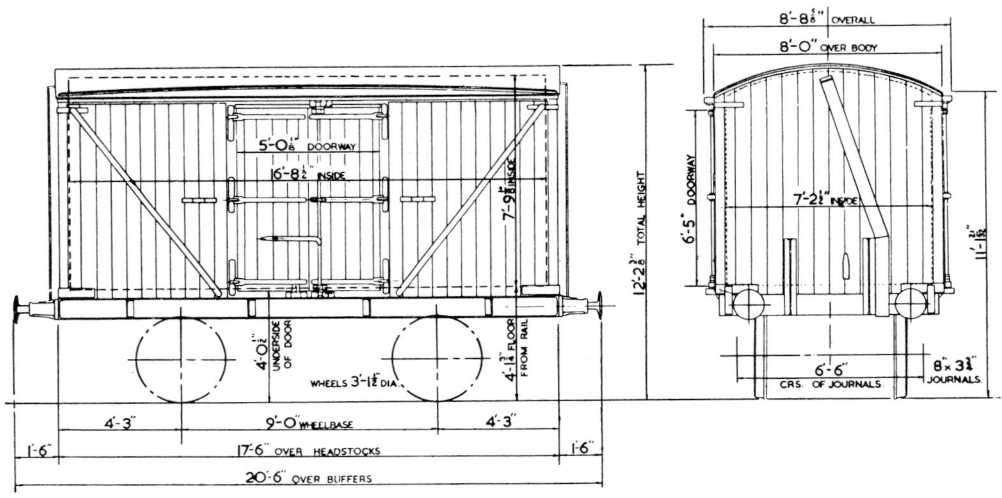

8 TON BANANA VAN

the lot number, quantity and description of wagons or containers involved, capacity, diagram, programme, builder and running numbers. The date the last vehicle entered traffic is also recorded, as are any amendments with the dates they were effective. Details of works costs are also given but have not been considered for this book.

A lot number may be issued to cover anything from the building of a large batch of new wagons to the conversion of a single existing vehicle. Generally speaking, over the years as financial controls have been extended, the quantities in a lot have grown smaller. In the early 1950s lots of 1,000 wagons were quite common, the high point being reached in 1955 when an order was placed with Pressed Steel Limited for four lots of 16ton mineral wagons (lots 2920, 2921, 2922 and 2923) for 6,500, 7,000, 7,000 and 7,000 wagons respectively.

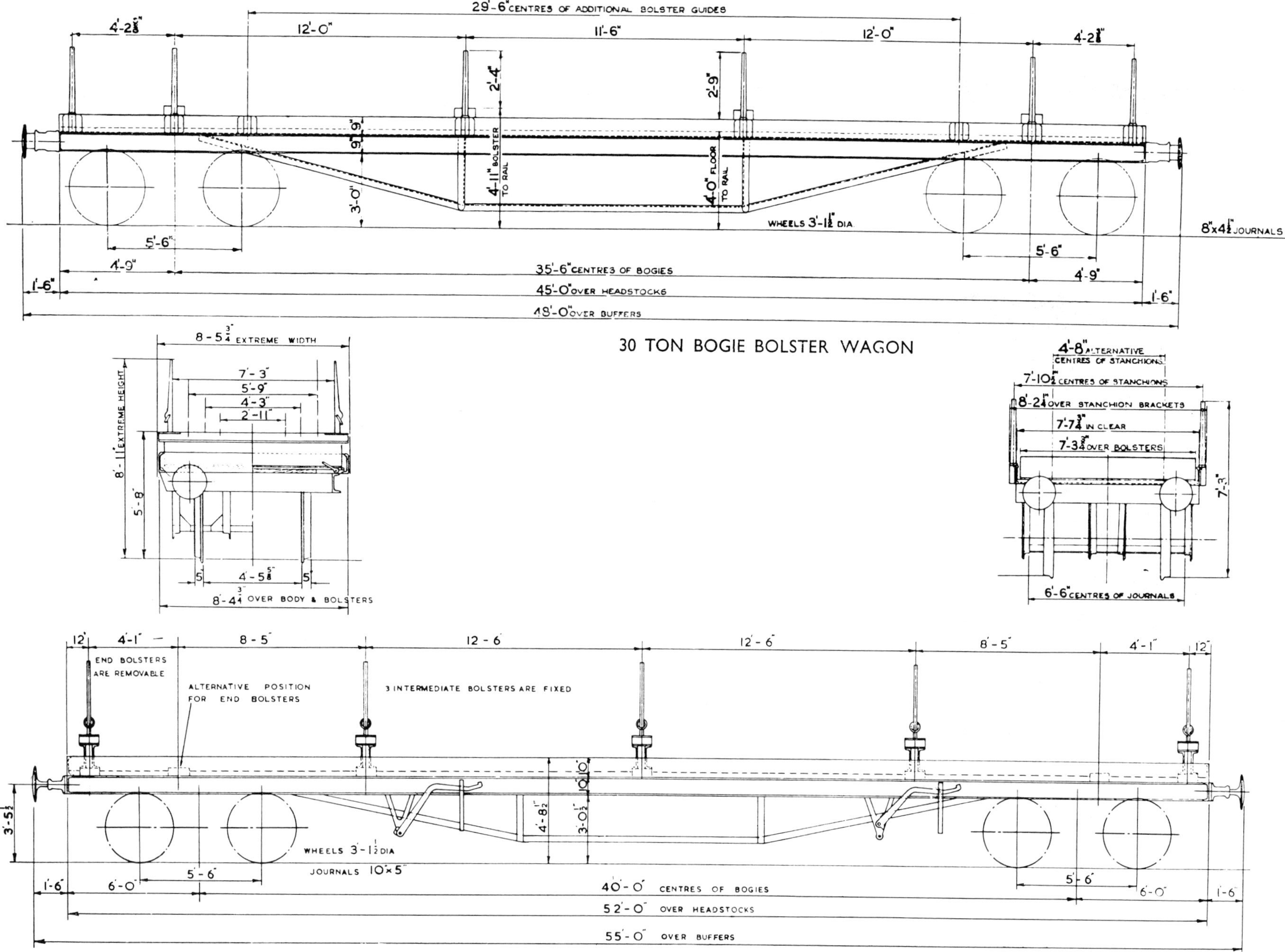

30 TON BOGIE BOLSTER WAGON

42 TON BOGIE BOLSTER WAGON

In later years a lot number would solemnly be issued for a single fuel tank wagon purchased second-hand from an oil company.

A study of the lot book reveals that various regions would sponsor proposals for the provision of new wagons or containers for a particular year's programme. One can see evidence of batches of lots being issued for ordinary wagons, special wagons and containers, with construction being spread over all sources. By the mid-1950s the actual performance of most builders, be they railway workshops or private firms, had got so out of step that delivery dates bore little or no relation to programme dates. There was an extensive revision of programme dates, affecting special wagons in particular, but soon afterwards we find references to Committee or Board minutes being quoted as authority for construction, rather than an annual programme.

On issue of a lot number it was customary to allocate a block of consecutive running numbers for all vehicles or containers covered. When an amendment reduced the quantity ordered it was normal practice to use only the lowest numbers. If, as sometimes happened, the next series of running numbers had already been allocated when the amendment took place this would result in a gap in the numbering which was not filled. Apart from this, the British Railways numbering system resulted in large blocks of consecutively-numbered wagons and containers with all examples of one type being together. To distinguish them from stock inherited, all British Railways wagons received a B prefix to their running numbers or a DB prefix in the case of service vehicles. For containers a separate series of numbers was set up, with containers of each type running consecutively within blocks. The system differed slightly from that used for wagons in that the British Railways B was a suffix, while an alphabetic prefix indicated the container type.

When former privately-owned wagons were taken into British Railways' stock they were given numbers in a separate series with a P prefix. The former Ministry of Transport or Ministry of War Transport mineral wagons were treated differently in that they received B prefixes to their Ministry numbers. More detail on the numbering systems can be gleaned from Appendices 1, 2 and 4.

Plate 3. *22ton timber wagon. Diagram 1/439. B932869 began life as a vacuum-fitted Plate wagon to diagram 1/432, one of lot 2734. It was one of sixty wagons later modified to take one BD and one A container and as such re-classified 'Conflat P'.* (See Plate 24.) *They were allotted diagram 1/433, later changed to diagram 1/060, and saw use on the* Condor *service, forerunner of the freightliners. When this was phased out a number of Conflat Ps were again converted, this time to Timber P wagons for carrying timber to the Corpach pulp mill near Fort William. Photographed at Crianlarich Lower, 19 September 1970* (Author).

Development

It is well known amongst those interested in locomotives that British Railways decided as the LMS had done before that a range of standard locomotive designs, few in number, would meet all motive power requirements. The BR standard steam locomotives were the fruit of this policy. What is not so well known is that the range of standard wagon designs produced by British Railways stemmed from a similar policy decision on freight rolling stock.

The Ideal Stocks Committee was appointed by the Railway Executive in February 1948 with the remit to 'Consider and report, having regard to probable traffics in 1950, on the approximate 'ideal' stocks and types of locomotives, carriages and wagons under conditions of unified working so as to cater efficiently for anticipated traffics and to yield the maximum reduction in costs; to consider these 'ideals' in relation to actual stocks and to make recommendations as to how the 'ideal' . . . may be achieved. . . .'. In typical railway parlance the last sentence of the remit contained no verb, only infinitives. It ran 'Interim reports to be submitted from time to time, to deal first with wagons'. The Committee's 'Report on Design,

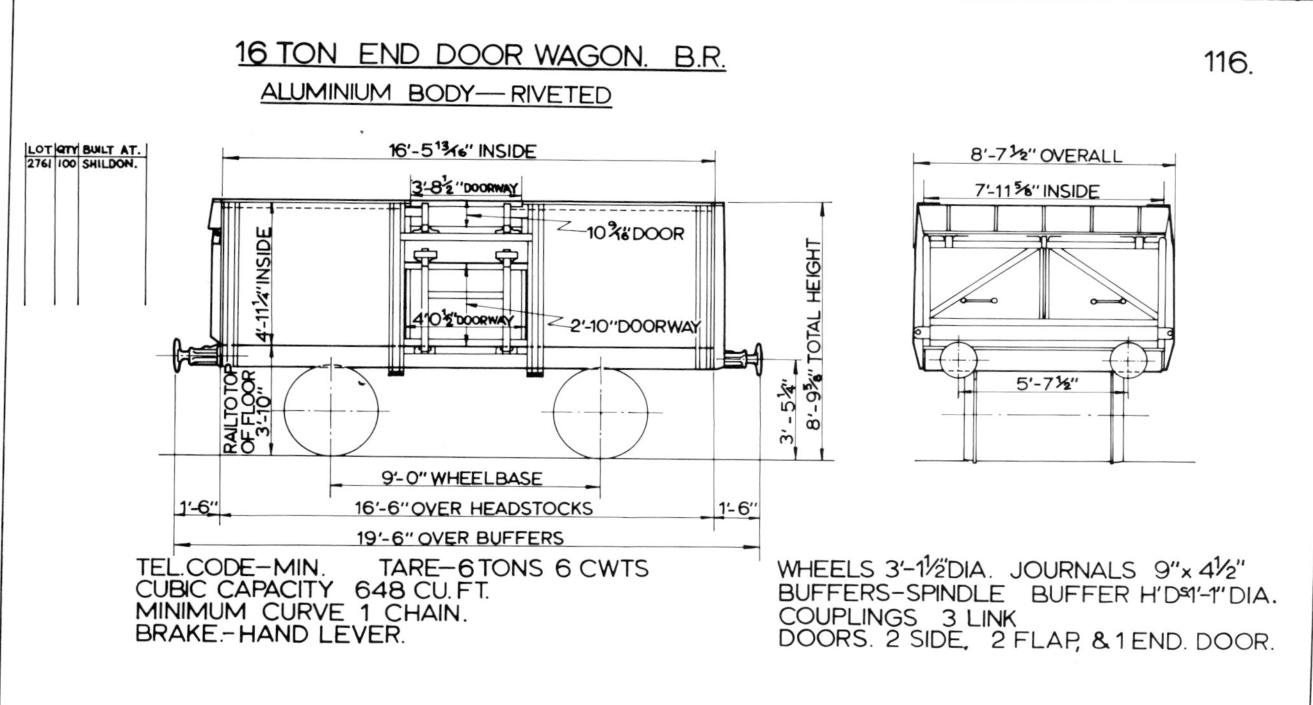

Figure 2. *Typical diagram. As explained in the text this book is written around the orginal three British Railways freight diagram books. The drawings are reproductions of actual diagrams and apart from omitting text the originals have been followed as closely as possible. This 16ton end door wagon (the BR often appears on early diagrams to make sure they were not mixed up with the previous company diagram books) is fairly typical. While body detail is reasonably full and accurate, that below the solebar (brakes, suspension, etc) is never given. Here stencils have been used for all the lettering, whereas on the original the lettering of dimensions was freehand.*

Capacity and Types of Railway Freight Rolling Stock' appeared in March 1950. Although, as the authors anticipated, it was modified by events, nevertheless it formed the basis of freight stock development in this country for the next decade and more.

The Committee seemed to have a goodly complement of former LMS men, and not surprisingly they began by considering mineral wagons. Equally unsurprisingly they recommended the elimination of grease axleboxes, which was a nice way of saying old private-owner wagons. This they hoped to complete by 1956. The members then considered what their ideal mineral wagon should be and came to the conclusion that a 24½ton wagon was to be preferred rather than the previously favoured 20ton or 40ton types. Luckily, they added a rider that 'Meantime, until terminal and other conditions permit . . . the 16ton wagon . . . should be built'. For carriage of iron ore they recommended the adoption of two types of wagon, namely the 25½ton hopper and a 27ton vehicle without doors, for tippler discharge.

For general merchandise traffic it was considered that the 12ton van and the 13ton open wagon were ideal. The LNER design of steel open wagon with wooden floor found favour with the Committee, although it was agreed that for some traffics a wooden body was more suitable and some wagons of this type would still be required. Rather surprisingly perhaps in view of the strong LMS influence and the efforts made by that company to develop container traffic, no construction of container wagons was proposed, neither does such a vehicle appear amongst the standard designs suggested in Appendix B of the Committee's report (Figure 1). It merely spoke of '. . . possible developments of specific types, e.g. "dual purpose" wagons for containers etc.'. The fitting of sheet support bars and shock-absorbing gear were both considered to have advantages, and it was recommended that 10% of high-sided open goods wagons should be fitted with sheet support bars and that the number of shock-absorbing wagons should be increased by an unspecified number.

When dealing with covered vans the Committee's principal recommendation, made on the grounds of operating and cost, was that all vans should have hinged rather than sliding doors. Since the Grouping the two largest companies (LMS and LNER) had used sliding doors on almost all their vans, whereas the two smaller lines (GWR and SR) had favoured hinged doors. Official policy had now swung, if one may be forgiven the pun, round to the smaller companies' viewpoint so much that when considering fruit traffic the Committee recommended that 'Fruit vans in the future should be built to the latest London Midland Region design, with slight modifications'. Among these modifications was the substitution of the sliding doors of diagram 230 by hinged doors on diagram 233.

The same region's design of banana van was also favoured with the proviso that it be altered to give a minimum of 10ft wheelbase. In the event the change was not incorporated until the 1952 programme. Looking at meat van design the Committee felt itself unable to suggest a standard until future requirements became more clearly defined. As things turned out, this caution was justified in that most meat came to be carried in containers rather than in vans. For meat on the hoof it decided on the Western Region 8ton design fitted with continuous brakes but without steam heating.

When it came to looking at iron and steel traffic the Committee was much less positive, speaking rather vaguely it seems about continuing cooperation with the British Iron & Steel Federation. Its only definite recommendation was that no more single bolster wagons should be built, bogie bolster wagons being considered more satisfactory. In direct contrast it recommended that one standard design of brake van should be built, having come to the conclusion that 'There is no justification for any variation between regions in the weight, fitments or equipment of the freight brake van'.

Determination of ideal stocks of service vehicles was made much easier by the fact that a Civil Engineers' committee had recently reviewed the matter and proposed six standard types of wagon. The Committee adopted the recommendations of its civil engineering counterpart and also added one of its own, namely that locomotive coal wagons should be transferred to traffic stock.

Apart from actual vehicle designs the Committee also considered and subsequently made recommendations on certain technical matters. It looked at couplings and decided that the three-link loose coupling was 'the cheapest and most satisfactory coupling for unfitted wagons'. For brake fitted stock, and here one assumes that it meant the automatic vacuum brake, it came down in favour of the 'Instanter' coupling for all except cattle wagons. In passing it is interesting to note that in 1950 the cost of an Instanter coupling was quoted as £1 9s 2d (£1.46) whilst that of a screw coupling was given as £3 2s 1d (£3.10) so that adoption of the Instanter saved £3 5s 10d (£3.29), actually quoted as £3 6s 0d (£3.30) per wagon.

Next the Committee turned its attention to wagon brakes. It quickly came to the conclusion that for hand-braked vehicles the two-wheel brake was quite adequate where the wagon capacity was less than 20 tons. For larger vehicles the four-wheel brake was recommended. The possibility of an improved type of brake using tension rigging, then at the experimental stage, was also considered. Presumably this was Bulleid's design noted in Chapter 3.

Finally the Committee deliberated on the use of continuous brake on freight stock. The cases for and against were both presented in some detail. Assuming that *all* trains ran as fitted freights it reckoned that there would be a saving of between 3.4 and 5.0 million freight train engine hours on the 1948 figure of 16.8 million, equivalent to a reduction in stocks of between 1,000 and 1,500 locomotives. Numerous other advantages (covering over eight pages of foolscap) were also put forward. Against these many contra arguments were put forward, the principal one being that it would cost over £31 million to equip the wagon fleet. In financial terms it was felt that the result of fitting all wagons would be somewhere between an annual loss of £1,229,000 and an annual gain of £1,335,000. In best committee fashion it was therefore recommended that '. . . further investigation should be made into the fitting of continuous brake on all freight stock'.

Throughout this review of continuous brakes it

was accepted that 'continuous' was synonymous with 'vacuum'. At one point the Committee did consider the relative efficiency of vacuum versus air brake and admitted there was some doubt whether the vacuum brake would be satisfactory for controlling heavy freight trains. The superiority of the air brake was tacitly admitted, but reading the report one gets the impression that it was felt that the railways were too far committed even then to consider changing to air brakes.

After giving its recommendations, the Committee concluded that their effect would be to reduce the number of types of wagon, including special types, from 480 to about 150. Unfortunately there is no indication, other than that in Figure 1, of how these 150 types might be made up, so we cannot say how far the recommendations were put into practice. We do know that in the early years many of them were: grease axleboxes were eliminated, the new designs appeared, and so on. No doubt as the years wore on and conditions changed other committees reviewed the situation. Even so this report seems to have been a good foundation for British Railways freight stock development.

Livery

Many railway enthusiasts and railway modellers in particular place great emphasis on liveries. It is for this reason as much as out of a desire to complete the record that British Railways wagon liveries find a place in this book. In general, while they are and always have been neat and functional in concept, their maintenance in service has been quite poor. As a result the appearance of a British Railways freight train, its wagons coated with a mixture of rust, dust and grime, has never been such as to convey the impression of a reliable, let alone speedy, service to the onlooker. Over the years appearance has tended to deteriorate as complete repainting of repaired wagons has become rare.

If style and execution have done little to excite the railway enthusiast, then as a consolation for the railway historian liveries have been reasonably simple and changes relatively few. The basic styles were laid down shortly after nationalisation and remained virtually unaltered until the TOPS system and air-braked wagons came on the scene. In all cases running gear (ie below the solebars) has been painted black. In contrast, and unless otherwise stated, lettering has been white, as have

Plate 4. *13ton high goods wagon. Diagram 1/041. The use of steel bodies for merchandise wagons wherever possible was favoured by the Ideal Stocks Committee. B490563, seen here at Shildon in April 1952, was such a wagon and was based on an LNER design. It was one of lot 2366, the only ones to that diagram to be built unfitted. In contrast to the brake van in Plate 6, note that solebars, headstocks and buffer shanks are all black. The wooden blackboards beside the number panel were intended for use by shunters and loaders, but an examination of wagons in service as shown throughout this book indicates how little they were used.* (Author's collection).

Plate 5. *22ton creosote tank wagon. Diagram 1/636. As well as the types built for traffic stock many new designs were evolved for departmental wagons, one of which was the creosote tank, used for carriage of creosote for treatment of wooden sleepers. Diagram 1/636 was an improved version of the previous design (diagram 1/633, Plate 117) with increased capacity, roller-bearings, hydraulic buffers and automatic vacuum brake. As such it may be taken as typical of the third phase of British Railways wagon development. Date probably February 1959.* (British Railways).

symbols such as stripes.

For unfitted wagons the body colour was a light grey. In most cases solebars and sometimes headstocks also have been black but sometimes, especially when mineral wagons have been completely repainted in later years, the body colour has also been applied to solebars and headstocks. To make the lettering stand out black patches have been applied over the relevant areas as seen in Plate 6. For end-door wagons the white stripes at the door end have not been simularly backed. The body colour chosen for most fitted wagons was red bauxite. Again, the treatment of solebars and headstocks has not be consistent. If anything, the solebars especially have more often been painted body colour than was the case with unfitted wagons but even a light covering of rust, brake dust and oil on a solebar makes it very difficult to determine just what the base colour actually is. No backing patches are used, lettering being applied to the body colour direct.

It is with fitted vehicles that most of the livery variations have arisen. Insulated vans and refrigerated vans were at first painted white with black lettering but this was later changed to a mid-blue with white lettering. Banana vans, though insulated, were painted red bauxite. In the earlier years of nationalisation some meat vans were given a light stone body colour while the first batch of ventilated meat vans, and probably the second batch as well, were given passenger livery of crimson lake bodies with yellow lettering. A similar livery was at first applied to uninsulated containers, only to be phased out later in favour of red bauxite. Insulated containers followed insulated vans in changing from white to mid-blue.

The first official livery for service vehicles was black all over with yellow lettering. In more recent times some such wagons have appeared in an olive green livery. In general, service vehicles even more than those in revenue service present a decidedly motley picture with partial repaints, the addition of strange symbols such as green triangles, and wagons transferred from capital stock but still in original livery all appearing side by side.

Despite these apparent variations it should be emphasised that in practice the general picture was of two liveries. First there were the unfitted wagons, usually all-steel minerals, in faded grey with numerous areas of rust, and second the fitted vehicles. Here the general covering of grime has often made it difficult for the writer to decide whether red bauxite, white or blue was the body colour. On one occasion a gentle rub with a wet rag was necessary only to reveal not white, blue or red bauxite but the original crimson lake of a meat van. If this sounds dull and depressing it can only be pleaded that the writer finds it so, and despite the great advances made by British Railways in freight rolling-stock design their goods trains look decidedly shabby.

Plate 6. *This particular photograph is used to give an idea of the early wagon livery. It was taken in 1950, probably August, and shows an unfitted 20ton brake van to diagram 1/503 (lot 2026) with a train of demountable tanks for silicate of soda to diagram 1/329, (lots 2077 & 2277). All are ex-works. The brake, in light grey unfitted livery, shows its regional allocation. Note that solebars and headstocks are body colour. The tank wagon underframes are all black with white lettering. Plates 2 and 75 show similar vehicles after some years in service.* (British Railways).

Chapter 2

Open Merchandise Wagons

In this chapter we cover all the open merchandise wagons built by British Railways for general service. Excluded are the steel-carrying wagons which are dealt with in Chapter 8 and the special wagons, almost exclusively open wagons, which are covered in Chapter 11. Open wagons designed from the start as service vehicles are also omitted, being considered in Chapter 10. Concerning service vehicles we have had to make a rather arbitrary distinction. With a reduction in traffic some vehicles withdrawn from capital stock have been transferred to departmental use where they continued in service, even sneaking back into occasional revenue service at times. In general such wagons have not been re-numbered into the service vehicle range (DB964000-999999) but had the D prefix applied to the existing numbers. (Note that we are talking here of pre-TOPS days, as defined in the Introduction.)

Even with such a formidable list of exclusions there are still a large number of types to be dealt with. The British Railways diagram book allocated pages 1-99 to open merchandise wagons but recently the last two pages have been re-used for re-bodied mineral wagons. Within the range there are five major sub-groups, the low, medium and high goods wagons (referring to the height of the sides), the container flat wagons and the carriage trucks, each group with its derivatives.

Low Goods

The first low goods wagons to appear were some produced by Wolverton to page 1 of the diagram book. With single plank sides and ends all hinged, plus full automatic brake, the design's LMS parentage was obvious. Subsequent construction of the type was undertaken entirely by Shildon works which produced 2,750 wagons, all to diagram 2. They were very similar to the Wolverton type but the original wood-planked sides and ends were replaced by ones of steel. Shildon's construction of all

Plate 7. *13ton Lowfit — lettered Lowfit. Diagram 1/001. B450092 was one of the solitary batch of 400 wagons to this diagram. The lot book suggests they were originally to be built unfitted, in spite of the J-hangers to the springs. Drop sides and ends are of wood. Millerhill, 27 July 1968.* (Author).

examples of this design was actually by default, a combination of circumstances resulting in the transfer of the work from Derby.

The principal derivative of the low goods was the pig iron wagon. Four different designs were produced, these being respectively the 13ton version to diagram 3, two 20ton designs to diagrams 4 and 7 plus the 30ton hot pig iron wagon to diagram 5. All were open wagons with relatively shallow sides. The first ones built were to diagram 3 and strongly resembled the low goods wagon.

One can suspect that these original pig iron wagons suffered from overloading as the next design, the 20ton version, turned out to be a stockier vehicle, more robust and shorter with heavier journals. It was allocated diagram 4. Apparently even this was not considered ideal because as part of the 1958 programme lot 3085 appeared. It was designated diagram 7 and was basically a modernised version of its predecessor. Whilst Derby was

Plate 8. *13ton Lowfit — lettered Lowfit. Diagram 1/002. All the remaining Lowfits had drop sides and ends of steel as seen above. The 'Not to be loaded with Containers' branding was seen on all Lowfits as there was no adequate means of securing a loaded container. This design used the LNER style of brake gear with double Vee hangers on the one side. Shildon works, January 1951.* (British Railways).

Plate 9. *30ton hot pig iron wagon. Diagram 1/005. An even more substantial design. The journals, for example, are 12in x 6in compared with the 9in x 4¼in of the standard 17ft 6in underframe. Note in particular the sloping floor and the painting of the body sides. B744620 was the prototype, photographed at Shildon, probably on 21 May 1955.* (Author's collection).

building the 20ton pig iron wagon Shildon was busy with the 30ton design. After a prototype, given lot number 2835, a further 139 were built, all to diagram 5. Like the 20ton version it was a robust all-steel open wagon, but with fixed sides and ends, and a floor which sloped to the centre. So far as is known, diagram 6 was never issued.

Medium Goods

Four different designs of medium goods wagon have been produced by British Railways. All had a common underframe length of 17ft 6in with a 10ft wheelbase with 1ft 9in deep fixed ends and drop sides. Capacity was 13tons. As with the low goods wagons initial construction featured planked wood for sides and ends, later replaced by steel.

The first foray into the medium goods field was a little unusual. It was lot 2061 issued in December 1948 for 200 wagons built at Ashford. The design seems to have originated at Eastleigh. Diagram 16 was issued, but in the event it covered only 100 vehicles. The other 100 had their sides and ends increased to five planks to give an inside height of 3ft 2¾in, for which diagram 33 was issued. The remarkable feature was that the whole side still dropped and it must have required at least two men to raise such a weight. So far as we are aware these 100 are the only standard gauge examples of five-plank drop-side wagons ever to appear in this

Figure 3. *20ton pig iron wagon — lettered Pig Iron. Diagram 1/004. In spite of its similarity with the medium goods wagon the pig iron wagon was of much more substantial construction, with heavier journals. Steel sides and ends were fixed and double brake was fitted.*

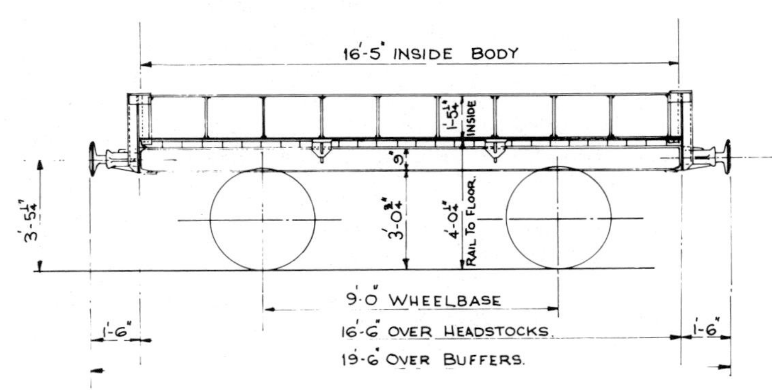

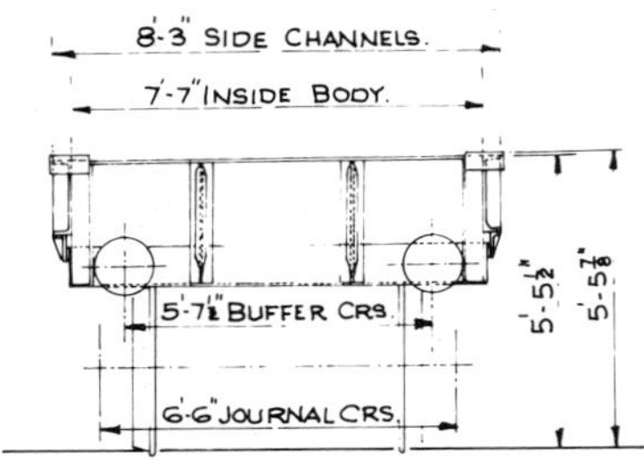

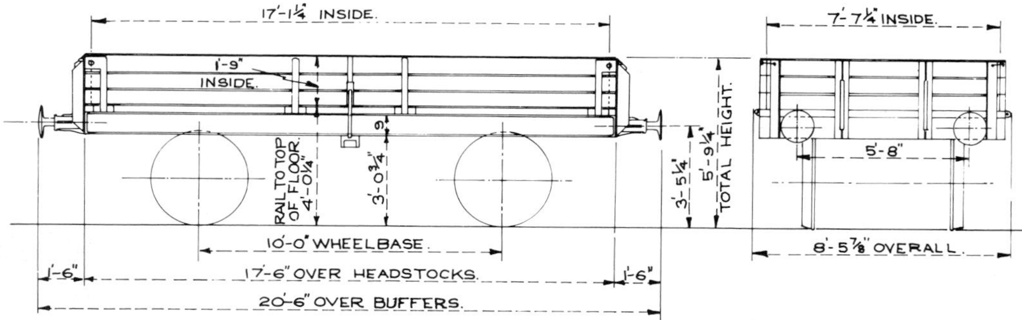

Figure 4. *13ton medium goods wagon. Diagram 1/017. A three-plank dropside wagon design, this lot being built unfitted. Ends are fixed. The bar joining the wagon side to the bracket below the solebar is a door controller to assist anyone lowering the side, and to prevent injury.*

country. No further examples of either diagram were ever built.

The next medium goods design was diagram 17 consisting of one lot, No 2108, of 397 wagons produced by Wolverton in the first months of 1950. The order was for 400 but the last three were never built, probably due to material shortages. At the same time Shildon was building the first variant of the medium goods design, a shortened body (16ft 6in) mounted on a shock-absorbing underframe. Limited end movement, controlled by springs, was allowed and they were fully-fitted. Diagram 18 was issued to cover the 25 vehicles. Their lot number was 2152 and they were intended to convey glass, for which cradles were provided if needed. The design appears to be identical to the former LMS diagram 2152.

Subsequent construction of medium goods wagons was concentrated at Ashford where some 4,000 such vehicles were produced between the middle of 1951 and December 1955. These later Ashford examples were to a newer design covered by diagram 19. The planking on sides and ends was replaced by steel sheet and in consequence internal dimensions were increased. Vacuum brake and Morton hand brake were now fitted.

So far the story of the medium goods is straightforward, but once we come to consider the principal variant the plot thickens. This was the Palbrick, as its name suggests, designed for the conveyance of bricks on pallets which are side loaded. The load is kept in place by removable side panels with end movement controlled by screw adjusters. An example is shown in Plate 12.

From lot book evidence it seems that lot 2668 was issued on 5 January 1954 for 400 medium goods wagons to diagram 19. It was variously amended until on 22 February 1957, twenty-seven days after the last wagon had left the shops, it covered a mere eight wagons to diagram 20, 'converted from diagram 19' and referred to lots 3138 and 3140. These eight wagons, of 13tons capacity and classed Palbrick A, were the only examples officially built to diagram 20. Lot 3140, issued 22 February 1957, comprised 380 Palbrick A to a slightly different design for which diagram 23 was allocated. The remaining twelve wagons from the original 400 were produced as lot 3138, 16ton Palbrick Bs and the only examples of diagram 21.

Plate 10. *13ton medium goods wagon. Diagram 1/019. The steel-bodied version of the medium goods wagon. It compares with diagram 1/017, just as diagram 1/002 compared with the wooden-bodied version of the Lowfit, diagram 1/001. The door controller can be seen here. Millerhill, 6 April 1963.* (Author).

Plate 11. *13ton medium goods wagon. Diagram 1/019. B459553 no doubt began life as a medium goods but by 28 March 1970 had been converted to a pallet brick wagon as seen here, and was coded Palwag. Although both wagons have fully-fitted brake gear the springs here are not supported on J-hangers as they are on B457881 in Plate 10. Photographed at Falkirk (Springfield).* (Author).

Plate 12. *16ton pallet brick wagon — lettered Palbrick B. Diagram 1/024. Compared with the Palbrick A the B had a wider body which allowed an extra three tons of payload, as can be seen in this photograph. The wagon in question is actually B462507 branded for return to Manuel (Sc R), with the sides of B462194 originally branded for return to somewhere on the Western Region. Millerhill, 15 November 1964.* (Author).

As if the Palbrick story were not already confused enough personal observations make things worse. We have for example seen wagons from lot 2236 coded PALBRICK (no suffix) together with others from lot 2235 coded PALWAG, a code name apparently unknown to the lot books and diagram books. What probably happened was that a commercial requirement for wagons to handle palletised brick traffic was at first met by ad hoc conversions of existing wagons which were not immediately given lot or diagram numbers. Once the requirement was formalised suitable provision was made but it was then too late for the lot books to tell the full story, thus proving if nothing else that such situations are not the sole prerogative of the pre-group researcher.

The next batch of Palbrick wagons to be built also began life, in theory at least, as medium goods wagons with drop sides. Lot 2724 was issued on 29 March 1954 for 450 such wagons but was later

Figure 5. *13ton pallet brick wagon — lettered Palbrick A. Diagram 1/020. The rather confused story of the Palbrick wagons is dealt with in the text. This diagram covers eight wagons converted from diagram 1/019, but it can be seen that compared with the Palwag conversion in Plate 11 the original body ends have been completely removed. Later Palbrick As were to diagram 1/023, which is very similar.*

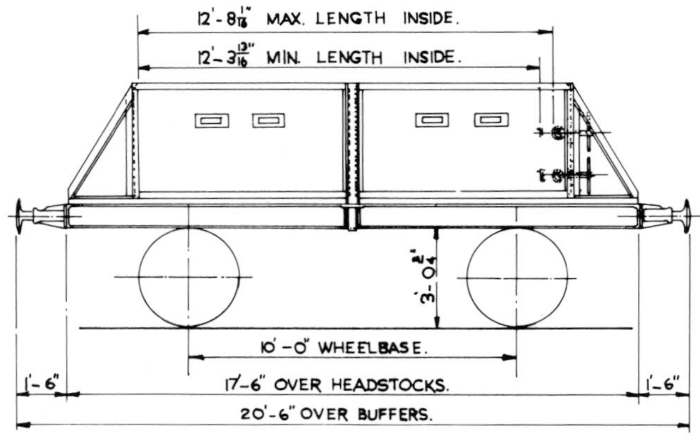

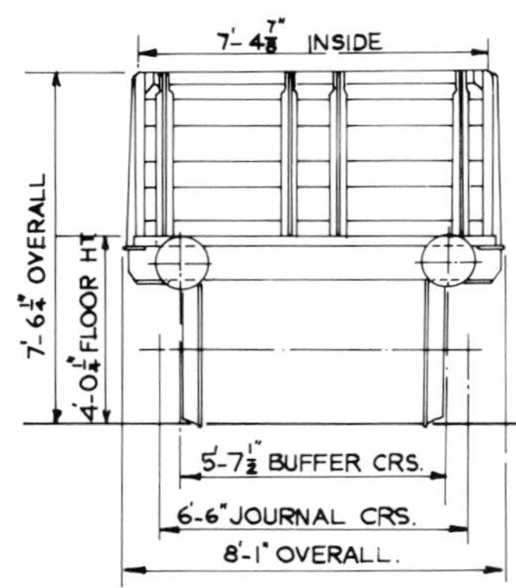

amended to Palbrick B, 120 to diagram 24 and the remainder to diagram 22. For later construction diagrams 25 and 26 were issued but apart from the 13ton capacity of the Palbrick A as opposed to the 16tons of the B and C versions differences between diagrams were minor consisting mainly of variations in internal dimensions. Later lots were equipped with roller-bearings and oleo buffers but all had automatic vacuum brake.

If the emergence of the Palbrick went largely unrecorded its demise too was inadequately chronicled in the lot books. First, some twenty-two were converted into Shellcase wagons. So far as is known no lot number was issued but diagram 27 was allocated. Whether prints of the diagram were issued is not known — certainly we have never seen a copy. The same is true of the following diagram, page 28, allocated to fifty-four vehicles converted from tube wagons (diagram 448) to ale pallet wagons. Finally an unknown number of Palbrick Bs from lot 3243 were converted from their original role to act as match wagons for Freightliner vehicles. Thus to these Palbrick wagons fell the honour of bridging the gap between the traditional British four-wheeled wagon with its three-link couplings and the air-braked, centre-coupled, bufferless Freightliner wagons.

Plate 13. *Shell case wagon. Diagram 1/027. Twenty-two Palbrick B wagons were converted at Currock wagon shops, Carlisle, for carrying shell cases between ordnance depots. This photograph of B462140 is believed to have been taken outside the shops in November 1967.* (British Railways).

High Goods

The development of the low goods wagon was relatively straightforward as was that of the medium one, in spite of the diversions over the Palbricks. With the high goods the story is less straightforward. In retrospect this section of the book was the hardest to write, for instead of there being a slowly evolving mainstream design we find that in fact several designs were being produced simultaneously. The reasons behind this state of affairs were many and some are set out below, but from the reader's point of view the result was a welter of apparently unrelated diagrams, all based on a standard 17ft 6in underframe with 10ft wheelbase. Bodies were a standard 8ft wide (approximately) with sides more-or-less standard 3ft 2in deep. Midway along each side a single drop door was provided to give a 4ft 9in opening. The other principal

Figure 6. *13ton high goods wagon. Diagram 1/032. This diagram covered fifty fully-fitted wagons built at Swindon to lot 2082. They seem to be the same as GWR diagram O42 and were probably a Great Western order taken over by British Railways.*

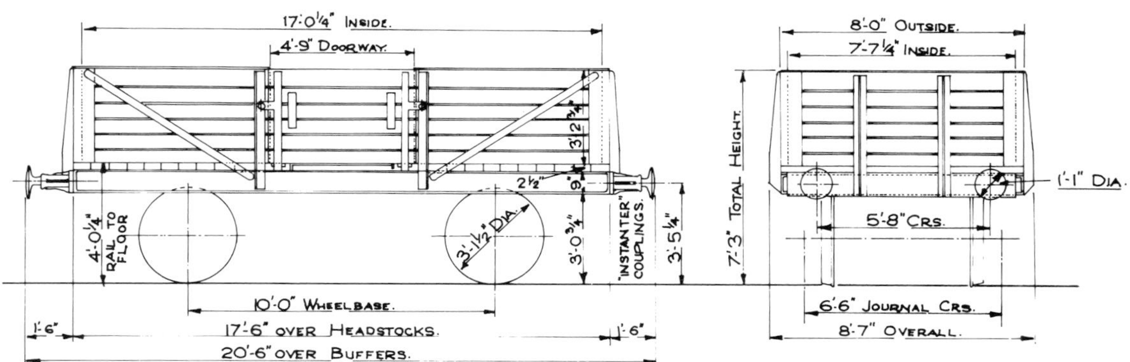

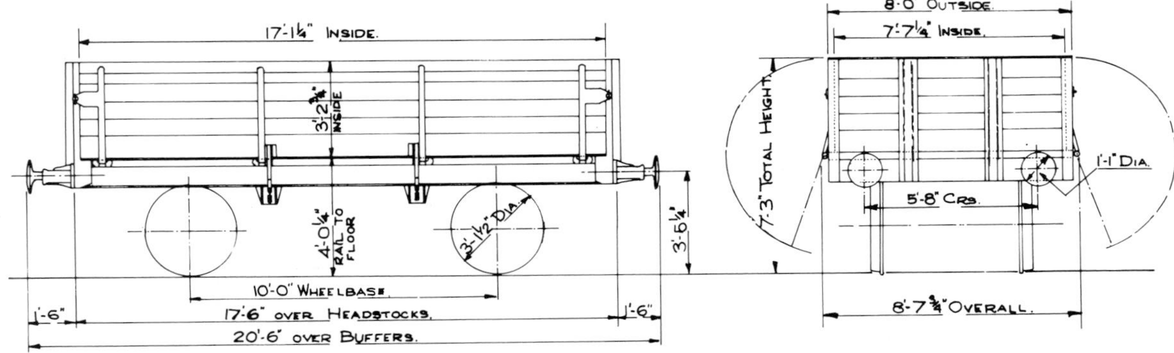

Figure 7. *13ton high goods. Diagram 1/033. One hundred wagons (half of lot 2061) were built at Ashford works as five-plank dropside wagons. Not surprisingly, bearing in mind the weight of a five-plank full length side door, two door controllers were provided. The corner stanchions were welded to the solebars and curb rails to give a box-like structure for added strength. Beyond these first hundred wagons the design was not repeated.*

features of each design are summarised in the table opposite.

Probably the reason behind so many variations was one of history. Being the main type of merchandise wagon it was only logical that each main line company should be equipped to produce its own design and more-or-less continued to do so for a time. The Ideal Stocks Committee found that there was an annual saving of £3.14 (£3 2s 10d) per wagon if the steel-sided wooden-floored 13ton LNER design were adopted. It considered that although it was unsuitable for some traffics, principally foodstuffs, nevertheless '. . . in future . . . regard should be had to this potential economy consistent with the requirements of traders for particular types of wagons'. By this admission that despite its reduced cost the steel-bodied merchandise wagon could not be universally introduced, the Committee was allowing for the existence of at least two types from the outset.

Plate 14. *13ton high goods wagon. Diagram 1/034. This was in effect the unfitted version of diagram 1/032. Although built as an unfitted wagon, when photographed at Granton on 12 February 1966 B477352 had been fitted with automatic vacuum brake. On the nearside buffer at the right-hand end can be seen one of the 2½in collars which were welded to the buffer shanks to give the 1ft 8½in necessary with screw couplings on such conversions. Many previously unfitted wagons were dealt with in this way.*

Over and above the different constructional methods employed the Committee also recommended that a number of wagons be built with shock-absorbing apparatus to reduce damage to goods in transit, and that others be equipped with sheet support rails. For any constructional style four possible variants existed, namely ordinary open wagon, with shock-absorbing apparatus, with sheet support rail and with both shock-absorbing apparatus combined with sheet support rail. The potential for variety was enormous.

As if this were not enough, the shortage of materials could also give rise to a variant. Of the 500 wagons of lot 2409 for example, some 350 were built with steel ends to diagram 44 but the remainder, and a shortage of steel seems the most likely reason, had wooden ends and were to new diagram 45. If we also consider the differences in braking systems, since of many of the earlier designs both fitted and unfitted types were built, and the presence or absence of curb rails, the reason for so many different diagrams is obvious.

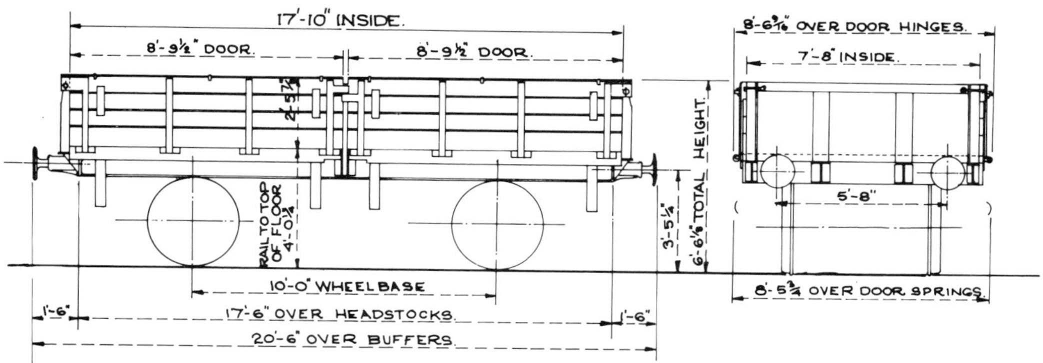

Figure 8. *13ton brick wagon. Diagram 1/038. The three wagons to this diagram were lettered 'Experimental Brick Wagon' and no further examples were built. The last one entered traffic in December 1950 and it seems reasonable to assume that it was then decided to develop the Palbrick design instead.*

High Goods Wagons — Comparison of Main Features

Diagram	*Sides*	*Ends*	*Curb rail*	*Shock-absorbing*	*Sheet support*		*Brakes*	*Related diagram*
31	s	s	x	x			AVB	37
32	p	p				Fully-fitted	AVB	34
33	p	p	x			Full drop sides	Double	
34	p	p					Hand	32
35	p	s	x	x		Fitted and unfitted		36
36	p	s	x	x	x		Hand	32
37	s	s	x				AVB	31
39	p	c	x		x		AVB & M	40
40	p	c	x	x	x		AVB & M	39
41	s	s	x			Fitted and unfitted		
42	p	m	x				Hand	43
43	s	s					Hand	42
44	p	c	x				Hand	45
45	p	p	x				Hand	44
46	s	s	x		x	Soda ash	Hand	
47	s	s					Hand	41
48	p	c	x	x			AVB & M	
49	s	s			x		AVB & M	
50	p	c	x	x			AVB & M	
52	p	c	x	x	x		AVB & M	
55	p	c	x	x	x		AVB & M	

NOTES
Sides & ends: p = planked; s = steel; c = corrugated steel; m = planked with two steel channel sections at the foot.
Brakes: Hand = Morton handbrake only; Double = double independent lever handbrake; AVB = Automatic vacuum brake with shoes on all four wheels; AVB & M = As above but with Morton handbrake.

Plate 15. *13ton high goods wagon with sheet support rail — lettered High-Bar. Diagram 1/039. With planked sides and corrugated steel ends. Some 5,650 wagons were built to this diagram and all were vacuum-fitted from the outset. The spelling and hyphenation of Hybar is unusual. Note that this particular wagon has fabricated axleboxes with opening fronts. This type and the split-casting type seem to have been used interchangeably with the standard 9in x 4$\frac{1}{4}$in journal and it is not unknown for both types to be on the same wagon. Millerhill, 5 April 1969.* (Author).

The first high goods wagons to appear under the BR aegis were some shock-absorbing opens from Shildon works. In May 1945 this establishment had produced the first steel-bodied wagons for the LNER, a very clean-looking design which as seen above found official favour. The shock-absorbing version became British Railways diagram 31 and three consecutive batches of 50, 200 and 175 wagons were built as lots 2031, 2032 and 2033. Further construction at Shildon was of the ordinary open to diagram 37, which was basically the LNER design.

These first opens had LNER design fully-fitted brakework, but for subsequent construction it was decided to modify the design to use the simpler Morton brake. Both fitted and unfitted examples were built, although all were considered to be to diagram 41. Some 5,970 examples were ordered in all of which 1500 were sub-contracted. In fact only 5,969 were built since a decision was taken to modify the design and one example of lot 2366 was chosen. This wagon was built without curb rail, allowing the ends of the floor planks to be seen. The change was obviously considered worthwhile as this single wagon, together with future batches, was built to the new diagram 47.

Around the time it was being decided to do away with curb rails there emerged from Shildon some eighty soda ash wagons. To all intents and purposes they were diagram 41 fitted with sheet support rail and improved door fastenings and lettered 'Soda Ash'. The final Shildon high goods design was in fact this diagram 46 without curb rail, door modifications and special lettering. It was given diagram number 49 and 1,000 were built under lot numbers 2469 and 2704.

The first and only batch of high goods wagons built by Swindon for British Railways was one lot of fifty vehicles, lot 2082, completed on 10 September 1949. More than likely it was a remnant of the Great Western wagon programme and was certainly in complete contrast to LNER ideas. Sides and ends were planked, no curb or side rails were fitted and the sides were secured by substantial cranked stanchions attached to the solebars.

Looking at the medium goods wagon we referred to Ashford's opening attempt at a high goods wagon (diagram 33). On 22 August 1949 authority was given for Ashford to built 600 wagons, lot

Plate 16. *13ton high goods wagon diagram 1/041. This one diagram was used to cover both fitted and unfitted versions of the same design, the latter having already been illustrated in Plate 4. B487135 had vacuum brakes when built, but later had sheet support rail and modified doors fitted for soda ash traffic. Even so, when photographed at Granton on 28 May 1960 it seemed to have carried general merchandise. Note in particular the Morton brake and tie-bar joining the axleguards.* (Author).

Plate 17. *13ton high goods wagon. Diagram 1/041. B482575 was built in 1951 to the same diagram as B487135 in the previous illustration, but has no tie-bar to the axleguards and is fully-fitted with LNER style brake gear rather than Morton pattern. As well as drawing attention to contrasting designs within the one diagram, it also shows the sheet support rail in use. Like B487135 it also has been modified for the conveyance of soda ash. There was in fact a diagram (1/046) issued for eighty wagons built new for this traffic, but it does not show the lower securing bar to the doors. Probably photographed at Darlington in November 1956.* (British Railways).

2153, to a new diagram 34 which was to all intents and purposes an unfitted version of the Swindon high goods. These were immediately followed by 800 13ton shock-absorbing wagons, 500 fitted with vacuum brake, lot 2154, and 300 unfitted, lot 2155. Diagram 35 was used to cover all 800. In turn they were followed by one hundred similar wagons fitted with sheet support rail, lot 2156, diagram 36. We now had the situation that up in the North-East of England Shildon was producing steel-bodied high goods wagons and fitting tarpaulin rails and shock-absorbing apparatus as required, while in the deep south Ashford was carrying on the Swindon tradition and building bodies in wood, offering the same optional extras.

Between these two sets of ideas lay the option of a compromise. Between these two centres lay Derby, and Derby would provide the best of both worlds. There would be wooden body sides and steel ends (corrugated this time) with the same optional extras if desired. And that was exactly what happened! Diagrams were drawn and Derby set about construction with a will. After a few years Ashford was let into the club, and two private contractors.

In numerical order the first diagram to be issued was page 39 for a five-plank wagon with curb rails and corrugated ends. A sheet support rail was fitted; the wagons had vacuum brake and Morton handbrake. This design was followed by a shock-absorbing version, diagram 40, again with sheet support rail. Some 7,850 examples were built in total, 5,650 to diagram 39 with the balance to diagram 40. It would seem that Derby did not consider itself irrevocably wedded to the corrugated ends idea because in 1952 it began producing high goods wagons with wooden sides and wooden ends, the only difference being that the bottom two planks of the ends were replaced by steel channels. They were to diagram 42 except for one wagon which managed to get a steel body, no curb rails and diagram 43 all to itself. However this phase turned out to be short-lived and there was a reversion to corrugated ends with diagram 44. A shortage of materials could well have been behind these changes because at this time the first 150 wagons of the 500 of lot 2409 were given wooden ends and allocated diagram 45, of which they were the sole examples.

The history of lot 2445 as revealed by the records

Plate 18. *13ton high goods wagon. Diagram 1/042. This photograph shows an example of the third high goods body style with planked body except for the two lower end planks which are replaced with steel channels. It also shows that these wagons were originally turned out with woodwork unpainted except for lettering patches. Photographed at Derby, probably early in 1952.* (British Railways).

Plate 19. *13ton high goods wagon. Diagram 1/044. B493898 is an example of the high goods body style having planked sides and corrugated steel ends. It has fully-fitted brake gear, J-hangers to the axlebox springs and no tie-bar to the axleguards, all as per the high goods in Plate 17 but has Morton type brake — the dog clutch can be clearly seen. Axleboxes are split pattern. Note that the number is* not *out of focus; both it and the numberplate had been rather crudely repainted. Haymarket, 2 January 1968.* (Author).

Plate 20. *12ton high goods with sheet support rail — lettered Shock. Diagram 1/052. The idea of having body springs to absorb shunting shocks was adopted by three of the old companies and continued by British Railways. B724032 is an example of such a wagon. The body control springs have been covered to prevent accidents, a modification that was to be applied to all such wagons. As with all shock-absorbing wagons, the body is painted with three vertical white stripes but they have not been applied over renewed planks. Haymarket, 2 January 1968.* (Author).

gives some idea of how commercial thinking may influence rolling stock design. Construction of 250 shock-absorbing wagons to diagram 48 was authorised on 20 May 1952. On 22 October 1952 it was decided to build them as ordinary wagons with oleo buffers. Then some six months later the decision was reversed, whether on grounds of cost or on the basis of experience with oleo buffers is not known, and they finally emerged as shock-absorbing wagons as originally intended. They were given corrugated ends and were the only examples of diagram 48. For some reason, again not readily apparent, later shock-absorbing wagons were rated at 12tons capacity rather than the previous 13tons, thus giving rise to another diagram, page 50, otherwise identical to page 48.

From this point onwards very few open merchandise wagons were produced, and with two exceptions all that were had shock-absorbing apparatus. The exceptions were two lots of 21ton

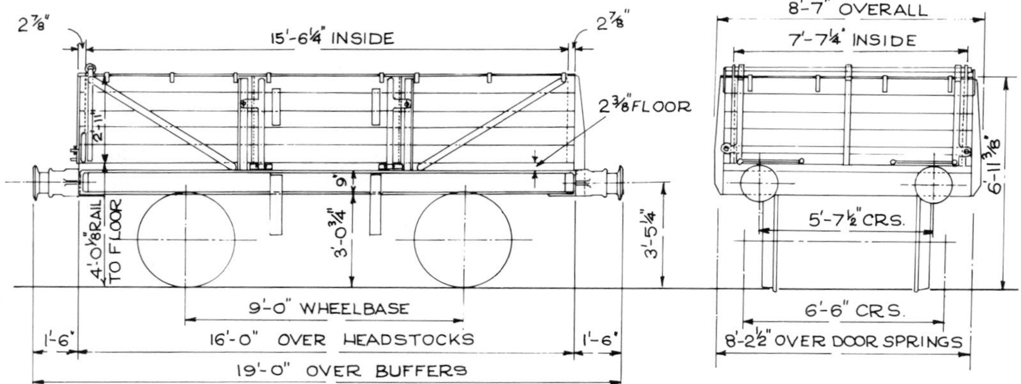

Figure 9. *13ton china clay wagon. Diagram 1/051. This, the sole design of china clay wagon, has obvious Great Western parentage, probably stretching back to 1913. The wooden body was retained to prevent the load being stained by rust, while the end door allowed unloading by end tippler, generally into coastal vessels.*

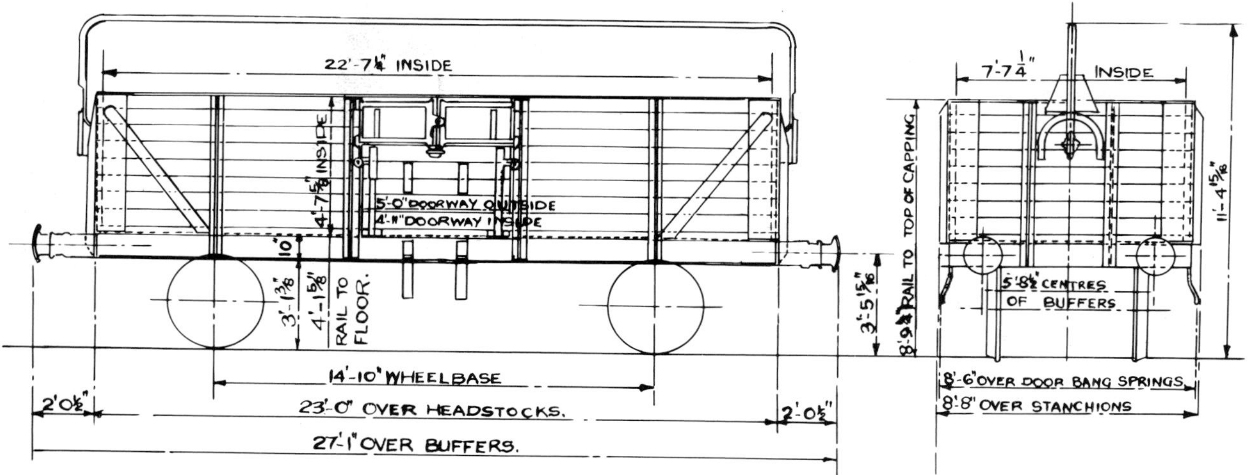

Figure 10. *21ton high goods wagon with sheet support rail. Diagram 1/055. With its increased capacity and Westinghouse through pipe in addition to automatic vacuum and hand brakes this design is in complete contrast with all the previous high goods designs and was built for continental traffic. Wheels were one metre diameter rather than the usual 3ft 1½in. Only forty examples were built.*

high goods wagons for continental traffic, to diagram 55. After them, three lots of shock-absorbing wagons with sheet support were built to diagram 56, the final one appearing in November 1959. They were followed in their turn by a batch of one hundred shock-absorbing wagons fitted with the MacGregor-Comarin rolling roof, to which diagram 57 was allocated. The final development presaged the appearance of the long-wheelbase air-braked merchandise wagon in that wheelbase was increased to 12ft, length over headstocks rose to 21ft 6in, the body was correspondingly lengthened and a nylon hood was fitted. Capacity was increased to 20tons and the code Shochood B was applied. Three hundred were built to lot 3429 and diagram 58.

Apart from these last two groups of wagons there was really precious little difference between B726124, the last traditional high goods wagon when it entered traffic in November 1959, and B720000, the first British Railways example which had emerged from Shildon ten years before. The reader could therefore be excused if he feels somewhat confused by a lot of changes, principally in body styles, which apparently led nowhere in particular.

China clay and sand

Strictly speaking, these two groups of wagons should be considered with the mineral wagons, but British Railways included them among the merchandise types so we shall follow that lead. One diagram, No 51, was issued for the 13ton china clay wagon, with Swindon responsible for all con-

Plate 21. *12ton high goods shock-absorbing — lettered Shocroof A. Diagram 1/057. The development of open wagons with a sliding roof, of which B726137 is an example, is referred to in the text. The roof mechanism apart, other noteworthy features are that body control springs have now been placed inside the solebars and also that the wagon has been branded 'Condor Service'. Townhill, 5 July 1974.* (Author).

Plate 22. *According to the lot books B494481 seen here should be a 13ton high goods with planked sides and corrugated-steel ends to diagram 1/044, yet obviously this is not the case. It was probably converted on a New Works Order as a prototype to test the sliding roof idea. The photograph has been included to show that wagon research, even relatively soon after the event, is not always straightforward. Probably photographed at Doncaster, date unknown.* (British Railways).

Plate 23. *20ton shock-absorbing wagon. Diagram 1/058. This design, coded Shochood B, was ordered on 11 August 1961, and represents a move away from the standard 13ton goods on a 17ft 6in underframe towards the larger air-braked wagons which were to follow. The frame is 4ft longer, and the wheelbase is increased by 2ft, with capacity 7tons greater. The hood folds to one side for loading. Probably photographed at Derby in 1962.* (British Railways).

struction. Beginning with lot 2590 in the 1954 programme a batch was included every year up to the 1960 programme to give a total of 875 wagons.

A companion type, the 13ton sand wagon, featured a similar 9ft wheelbase, and at 16ft 6in a body six inches longer than that of the china clay wagon. Three very similar designs were produced, to diagrams 71, 72 and 73, but in contrast to the china clay wagons the bodies were all steel without any doors. For each diagram one lot was produced, making a total of 850 wagons.

Container Flats

In the previous chapter we have already remarked that the Ideal Stocks Committee made no provision for a container flat amongst the standard wagon types. This is rather surprsing when one considers the energetic efforts made by the railways pre-war to develop container traffic and British Railways inherited substantial stocks of both containers and suitable flat wagons. As things turned out many thousands more such wagons were turned out by and for British Railways, the high point being reached in 1959 when the Pressed Steel Company produced a single lot (3153) of 5,550. There were six main types of container flat, each given the code name Conflat with a suffix to denote the particular type.

By far the most numerous was the Conflat A for which six different diagrams were issued. All exhibited a common body length of 17ft 6in, wheelbase was a standard 10ft and automatic vacuum brake was fitted to all. Atop the underframe the only vestige of bodywork was a planked floor with end baulks, edged along most of the sides and all the ends by a shallow lip. Pockets for the container securing chains were prominent features secured to the solebar sides with access by means of lids in the wagon floor. One of the most noticeable features of the Conflat A has always been the admonition to 'Replace Chain Pocket Lids' painted on the sides of these pockets.

In appearance there is so very little difference between one Conflat A and another that one wonders why so many diagrams were necessary. The answer seems to lie in the steady improvement of details becase dimensionally and descriptively the diagrams are identical. In the records there is evidence of some policy changes regarding the rating of the Conflat A because we have quoted capacities of 11, 12, 13 and 14tons. The smaller journal size of

Plate 24. *22ton wagon for conveyance of BD and A type containers. Diagram 1/060. In the caption to Plate 3 and in the text we have referred to the conversion of some plate wagons for the* Condor *service, one of which is shown here. The improved suspension, hydraulic buffers, roller-bearings and full-fitted brake gear were all added at this conversion. The paint date on B933249 is 5 September 1958. The containers — which unlike the wagon have received little attention — are a BD type to British Railways diagram 3/050, and an A type to LMS container diagram 18.* (British Railways).

Figure 11. *13ton container flat wagon — lettered Conflat A. Diagram 1/061. As the text relates, there were several different Conflat A designs with 11ton, 12ton and 13ton capacities but all having the same basic body design. Diagram 61 here is typical of the early design (it is in fact the earliest) where the low sides extend the full length of the body. On later types there was a gap in the centre.*

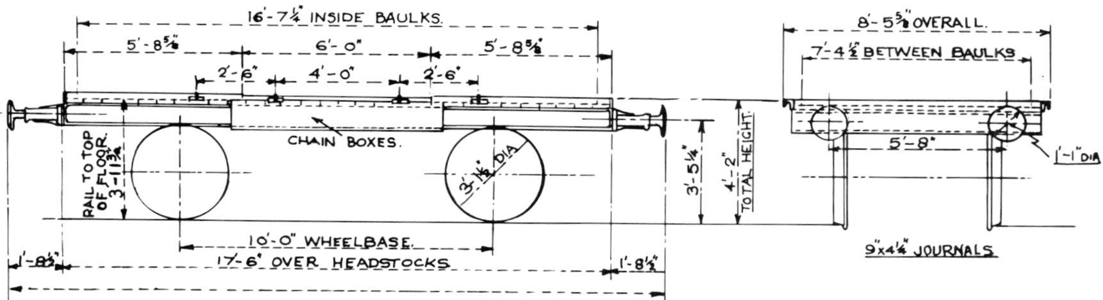

diagram 67 could account for the lower figure but the answer is not quite so clear-cut as that. On the evidence available we can only surmise that perhaps the riding qualities of the earlier designs may have given reason for some re-appraisal. There seems little point in merely listing a host of lots and diagrams and the reader is referred to Appendix 4 for details. It will suffice here to say that with 20,089 examples built in twenty-seven lots the Conflat A made a significant contribution to the British Railways wagon fleet.

Apart from the 'A' the only other Conflat to be built in anything like large numbers was the Conflat L, designed for carrying L or LC type containers. There were two designs, both of which could take three containers of either type, as opposed to the single A or B type which the Conflat A carried. The first design of Conflat L to diagram 64 was very similar in appearance to a Lowfit. 373 were built in one lot, No 2489. Later construction was to diagram 68 and here any semblance of

Plate 25. *14ton container flat wagon — lettered Conflat L. Diagram 1/069. Apart from its being designed specifically to carry three L type containers, the Conflat L differed from the Conflat A in having shallow hinged sides and ends. Hindlow, 1 July 1962.* (Author).

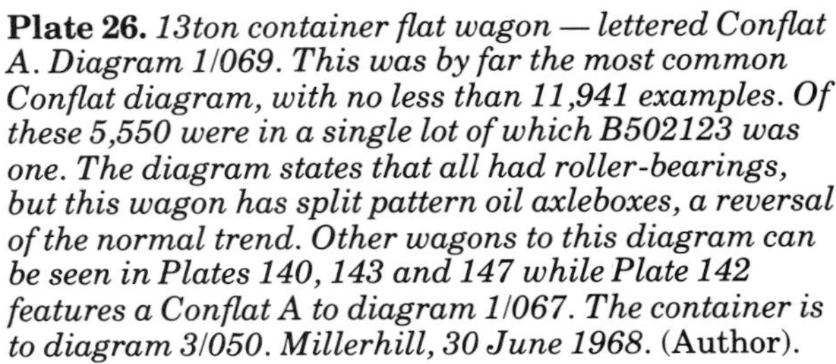

Plate 26. *13ton container flat wagon — lettered Conflat A. Diagram 1/069. This was by far the most common Conflat diagram, with no less than 11,941 examples. Of these 5,550 were in a single lot of which B502123 was one. The diagram states that all had roller-bearings, but this wagon has split pattern oil axleboxes, a reversal of the normal trend. Other wagons to this diagram can be seen in Plates 140, 143 and 147 while Plate 142 features a Conflat A to diagram 1/067. The container is to diagram 3/050. Millerhill, 30 June 1968.* (Author).

Plate 28. *35ton container flat — Condor. Diagram 1/075. The fifty wagons to this diagram bridge the divide between the older vacuum-braked short wheelbase designs and the later air-braked wagons; visually they are obviously very akin to the latter. One official source refers to them as bogie vehicles, the lot book refers to them as being 35ton wagons and yet the photograph shows 25ton capacity. The order for their construction was placed on 3 March 1964 and they were completed on* (sic) *22 March 1964. Together all these facts suggest that if the way ahead in wagon design was not then completely clear, then at least the end of the traditional wagon was in sight.* (British Railways).

Plate 27. *13ton open sand wagon. Diagram 1/072. Amongst all the Conflats come three diagrams for sand wagons, all sharing the same body design. B746736 was originally unfitted, but with Morton brake. Again the collars on the buffer shanks indicate a later conversion to vacuum brake. Portobello, 5 March 1960.* (Author).

bodywork was abandoned in favour of a simple three sets of corner supports and the usual chain pockets.

Despite its similar name the Conflat LD was quite a different vehicle, of 21tons capacity, longer and heavier, and used for the carriage of dolomite containers. Fifty-five examples were built, in two lots and all to diagram 63. Likewise the six vehicles of diagram 78, the Conflat LS, were again dissimilar, being modified plate wagons. Photographic evidence indicates that both the wagons and their containers were re-coded LT. The remaining types of Conflat were also conversions.

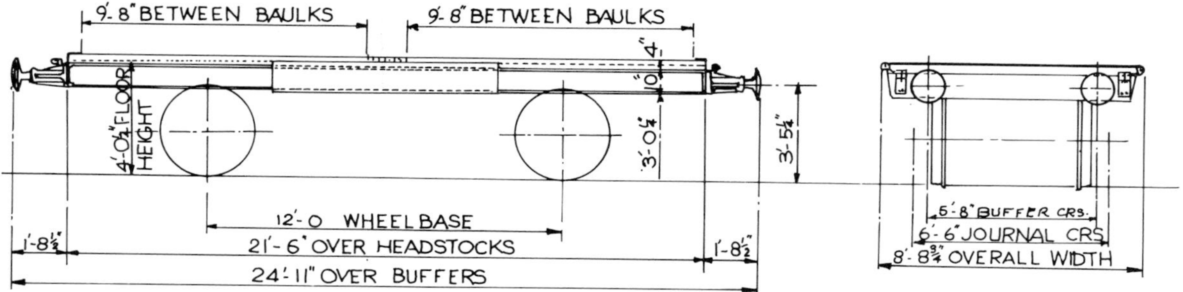

Figure 12. *12ton container flat wagon — lettered Conflat B. Diagram 1/076. This diagram covered the modification of fifty pipe wagons (see Plate 86 and Figure 47). The precise reason for this modification is not known, but it may have been to carry two A type containers (possibly for frozen food or ice cream traffic) on one wagon.*

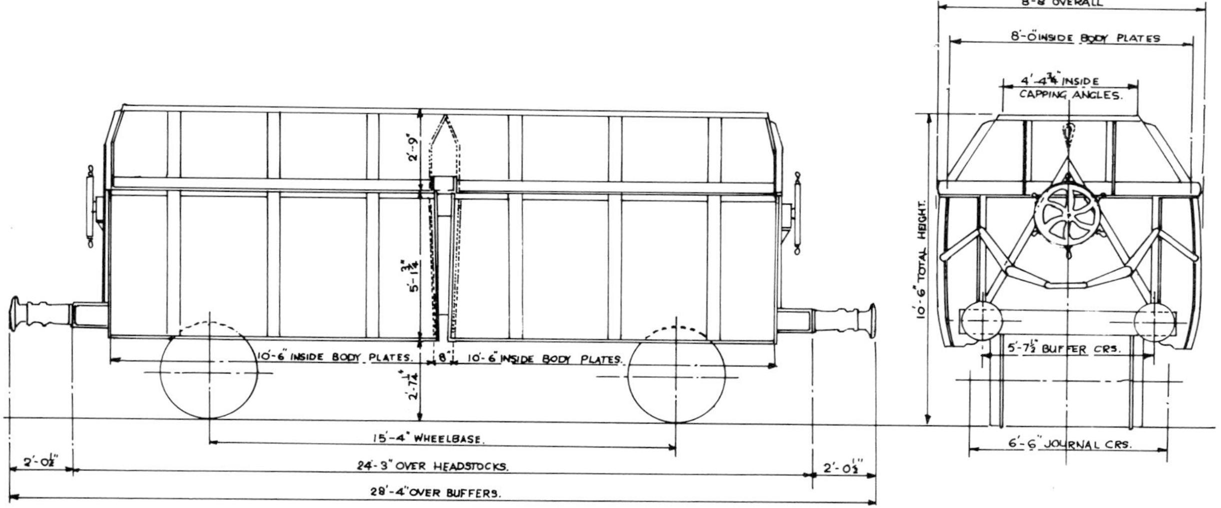

Figure 13. *20ton salt wagon. Diagram 1/085. The fifteen side discharge hoppers built to this diagram were originally considered to be to diagram 1/274, hence their running numbers in the same series as the hopper grain wagons. It is believed the design originated at the instigation of ICI Ltd.*

The 60 examples of diagram 60, the Conflat P, were plate wagons converted to carry one B type container plus one A type whereas the 100 Conflats ISO were a mixture of LMS, LNER and BR Lowmacs modified to carry ISO containers. Finally there are the fifty pipe wagons modified to become the sole examples of the type Conflat B and looking in effect like an elongated Conflat A.

Carriage Trucks

Without wishing to be derogatory in any way it may be said that the remaining group of open wagons are something of a mixed bag. They can be split into two groups, the four-wheeled and the bogie types. The latter group are basically redundant passenger carriages shorn of their bodies and provided with lashing rings or other securing devices, to be used for car transport. The varying lengths and designs of carriage underframe have given rise to many variations resulting in turn in a multitude of diagrams. Reference to Appendix 4 will show that lots have tended to consist of a few vehicles each, lot size being governed no doubt by the number of coaches being available at any one time. Furthermore, conversions have taken place in some unusual locations.

Plate 29. *12ton open carriage truck — lettered Carfit A. Diagram 1/091. Before the widespread conversion of redundant bogie passenger carriage underframes for motor cars two designs of four-wheeled wagons were produced especially for the traffic. This is the one for domestic traffic. The extensions over the buffers are for end loading, and at the right-hand end it is just possible to see that the ends of the floor slope towards the centre. Millerhill, 12 April 1964.* (Author).

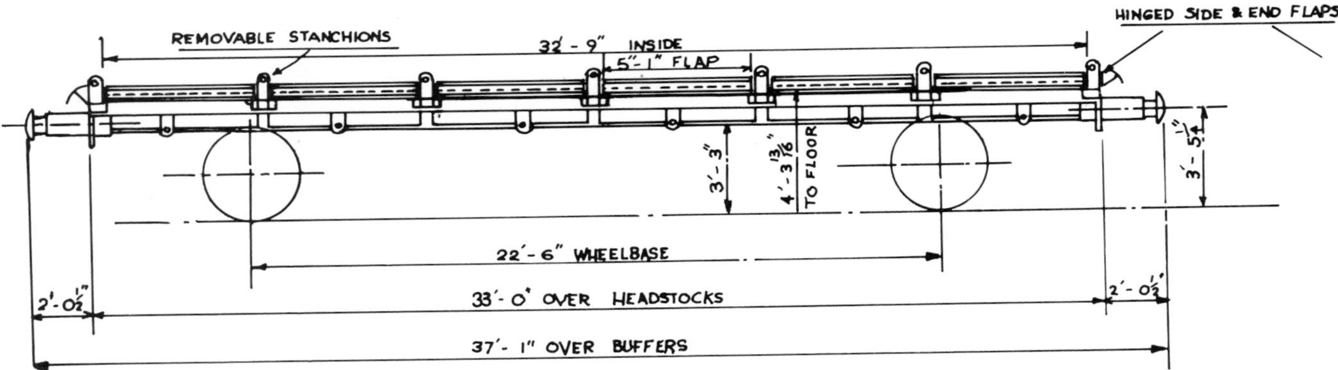

Figure 14. *20ton open carriage truck — lettered Carfit C. Diagram 1/092. The other four-wheeled design for an open carriage truck was the version for continental traffic shown here. They were originally ordered as 'low goods' wagons. A later issue of the diagram states that full Westinghouse brake was fitted rather than simply the usual through pipe.*

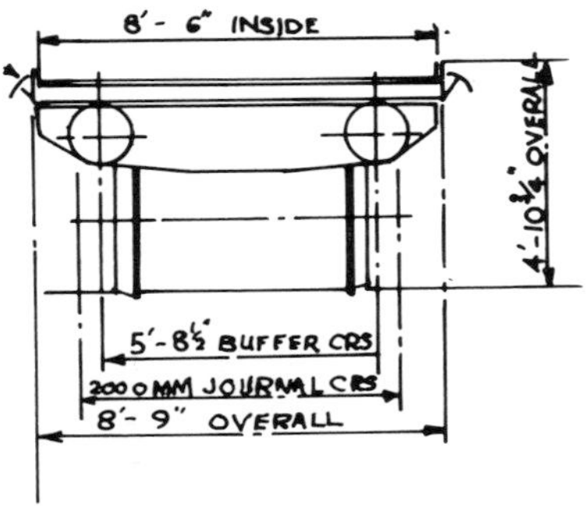

Figure 15. *10ton Carflat P — lettered Carflat P. Diagram 1/096. Another conversion utilising redundant carriage underframes but this time for palletised loads, hence the absence of a floor. See note in Appendix 4 for details.*

Plate 30. *10ton carriage truck — lettered Carflat. Diagram 1/097. There were numerous diagrams for Carflats since many different designs of carriage underframe were used. B748166 here was one of 144 such wagons which began life as Great Western Railway coaches. Most were converted to diagram 1/093 but twenty (including this one) were further modified to carry vehicles with wider wheel tracks than usual, and in consequence were classed as diagram 1/097. Millerhill, 5 April 1969.* (Author).

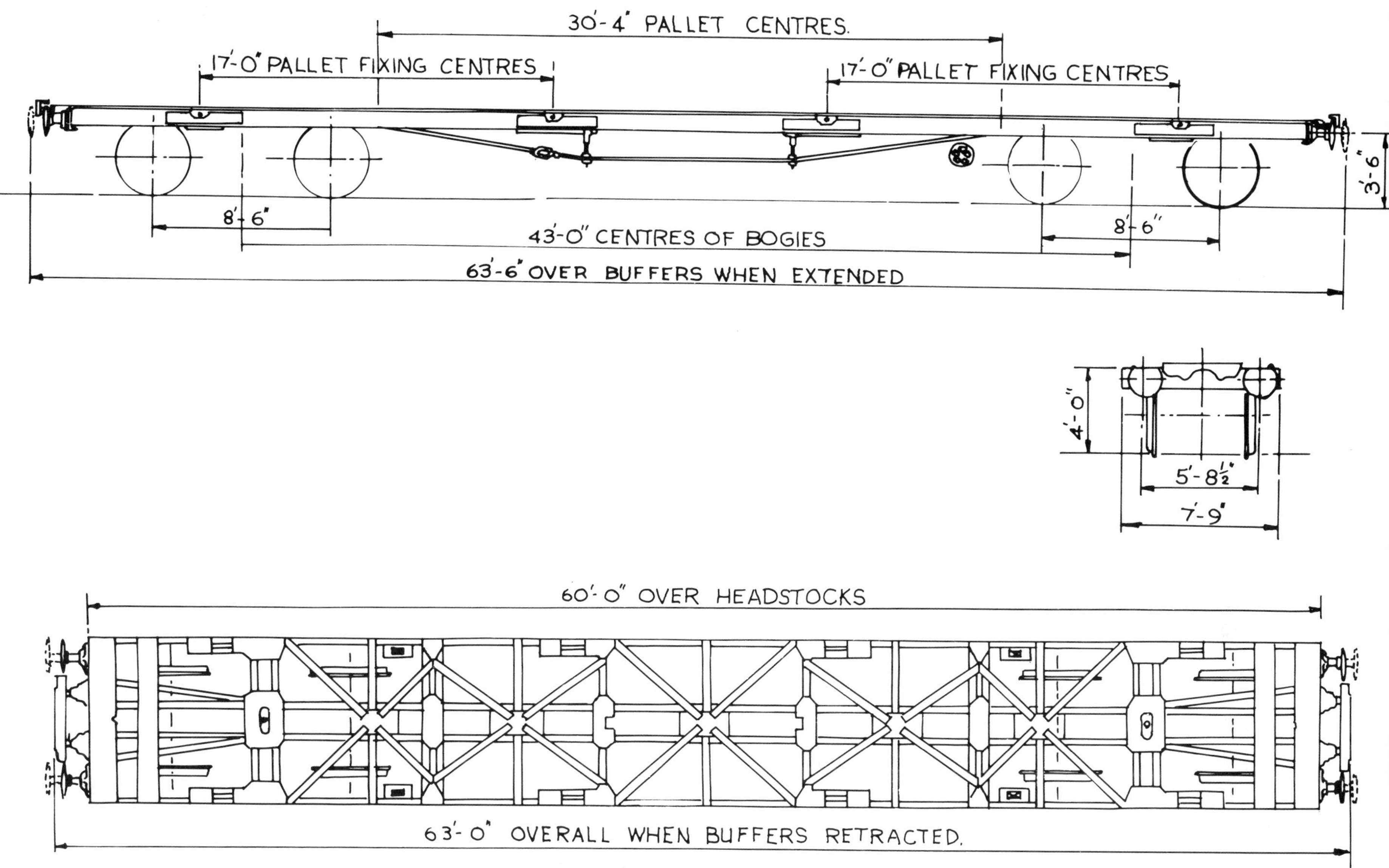

30'-4" PALLET CENTRES.
17'-0" PALLET FIXING CENTRES
17'-0" PALLET FIXING CENTRES
3'-6"
8'-6"
43'-0" CENTRES OF BOGIES
8'-6"
63'-6" OVER BUFFERS WHEN EXTENDED
4'-0"
5'-8½"
7'-9"
60'-0" OVER HEADSTOCKS
63'-0" OVERALL WHEN BUFFERS RETRACTED.

Plate 31. *Match wagon. Diagram 1/098. There were two diagrams for match wagons and this illustrates the later version with 10ft wheelbase, hydraulic buffers and no side angles on the wagon floor. Millerhill, 6 October 1962.* (Author).

Likewise, relatively few four-wheel carriage trucks have been built, the largest lot consisting of fifty vehicles to diagram 91. The lot and diagram books are not specific, but it would seem that the forty wagons built to diagram 92 were intended for continental traffic.

Although not carriage trucks, this chapter would not be complete without reference to the phantom match wagons of diagrams 98 and 99. First of all 200 were built to the latter followed by a further 150 to diagram 98. They had no means of carrying a load, purely being intended to protect overhanging loads on adjacent wagons. The first ones had an 8ft wheelbase, extended on the later design to 10ft, and both were a mere 15ft 6in over headstocks. Later diagram books make no reference to them, their places being taken instead by re-bodied 21ton and 16ton mineral wagons. Thus one can only assume they have all been scrapped, 350 wagons that never carried a single ton of payload.

Chapter 3

Mineral Wagons

British Railways has had a lot of mineral wagons. In this chapter alone there are over a quarter of a million to be dealt with, and that does not include the hopper wagons which are covered in Chapter 4. Here we are looking solely at the ordinary open mineral wagon with side doors and, in every case bar one, an end door, a prosaic animal if ever there was one.

Plate 32. *16ton end door wagon. Diagram 1/100. Although to a design originated by Charles Roberts & Co, B11816 was in fact built by P. W. McLellan & Co of Glasgow in 1945 for the Ministry of Transport. While the diagram as drawn shows pressed-steel side doors this example has rivetted ones, and other examples have one of welded construction. St Leonards (Edinburgh), 25 August 1962.* (Author).

16ton All-steel

Most of this chapter is about one type of wagon, the ubiquitous all-steel 16ton end door mineral wagon. Truly it was not the only type of mineral wagon built by British Railways; there were several designs and capacities of hopper wagon together with the 21ton and 24½ton side-door mineral wagons and substantial quantities of all these types have been built. Even so their numbers pale into insignificance when compared with the literally thousands upon thousands of 16tonners. As may be expected, the story is complex and intriguing. At times it is almost unbelievable. One could even venture the opinion that there is doubt over just how many 16tonners ever existed.

The story began before World War II when both the Butterley Company and Charles Roberts & Co produced steel 15ton mineral wagons as a more economic alternative to the wooden 12ton wagons then considered standard for coal class traffic. Some private owners took delivery, but the vast majority of private-owner mineral wagons requisitioned by the government at the start of the war were of wooden construction with capacities of between eight and twelve tons. As the war progressed the Ministry of War Transport began placing orders for all-steel wagons, apparently for two different purposes. Some were built for service in France after D-Day to get the French railway system back into commission after war damage. The others appear to have been intended solely for service in the UK, possibly to replace requisitioned wagons damaged beyond repair in collisions or air attacks. All the wagons of both groups were of 16tons capacity — wagon capacities in general having been uprated by one ton in the war — and of all-steel construction.

The wagons destined for home service were built by various contractors and were registered with the main line companies as privately-owned wagons. Although there were variations, especially in that those built by Charles Roberts & Co were of that firm's sloping-side design, basic features of 16ft 6in length over headstocks, 9ft wheelbase, one end door, two side doors and generally two bottom doors were common to all vehicles. Needless to say, braking was by hand lever brake only. After nationalisation these Ministry of War Transport wagons and the later examples built to the order of the Ministry of Transport were taken

Plate 33. *16ton end door wagon. Diagram 1/101. Apart from a desire to illustrate one of the former Ministry of Transport wagons in original livery, frankly this shot of a 16tonner with white tyres was hard to resist. The private-owner registration plate is clearly visible at the left-hand end of the solebar. Livery was a bauxite which memory suggests was redder than BR red bauxite. Lettering was white. Photographed at Renfrew in March 1947.* (A. G. Ellis).

into British Railways stock, but unlike other former private-owner wagons they were numbered into the British Railways series. This almost certainly consisted of adding a B prefix to the existing Ministry number. So far as is known lot numbers were never issued for these wagons. Details are given in Appendix 1. This information has been taken from official records and shows some apparent duplication of numbers.

Figure 16. *16ton end door wagon. Diagram 1/101. One of the earlier straight-sided end door designs of rivetted construction, this diagram shows a wagon without flap doors above the side doors and door stanchions extending below the solebars. What it does not show is that bottom doors and double brakes were fitted.*

From Appendix 1 it will be seen that these 60,000-odd wagons emanated from a whole variety of sources. All except one of the private wagon builders were destined to produce wagons for British Railways, the exception being D. G. Hall, which did not appear again as wagon or container builders — neither do the Royal Ordnance Factories. Amongst these ex-Ministry wagons there are inevitably design variations. The sloping-sided Roberts design has already been mentioned. Apart from these wagons there were numerous minor differences amongst the straight-sided designs. The principal ones were in the mode of construction, most manufacturers using rivetting, while a few preferred welding. To anticipate our story a little, welding was to become predominant but in the immediate pre-nationalisation years it was still regarded with suspicion in some quarters.

Since no lot numbers were issued for these wagons we are in the position of having to speculate over which diagrams relate to which wagons. The first sixteen-tonners built to a British Railways order were to diagram 104, which suggests that diagrams 100 to 103 had already been issued by then. Apart from lot 2287, which will be referred to later, no wagons were ever ordered to these diagrams so we can only assume that they were issued to cover the ex-Ministry wagons. Diagram 100 covers the Charles Roberts design, which is confirmed by a diagram note referring to lot 2287. Diagram 101 is for a design with rivetted body, pressed doors (two side and one end), bottom doors and double brakes. Similarly diagram 102 specifies a welded body with otherwise identical features, although a different design of doors is shown. To complete the picture, diagram 103 is again a rivetted body design very similar to diagram 101. It carries a note to the effect that some wagons have

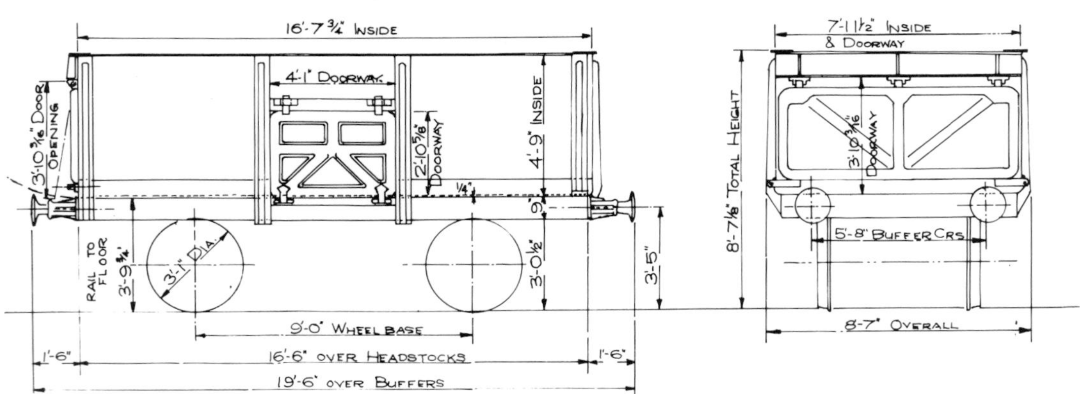

Plate 34. *16ton end door wagon. Diagram 1/102. B25312 represents in effect the welded body version of the previous diagram. By 30 June 1968, when the photograph was taken, the bottom doors may have been out of use as there are no chevron marks on the side doors. Note that the headstocks do not extend beyond the solebars. Millerhill.* (Author).

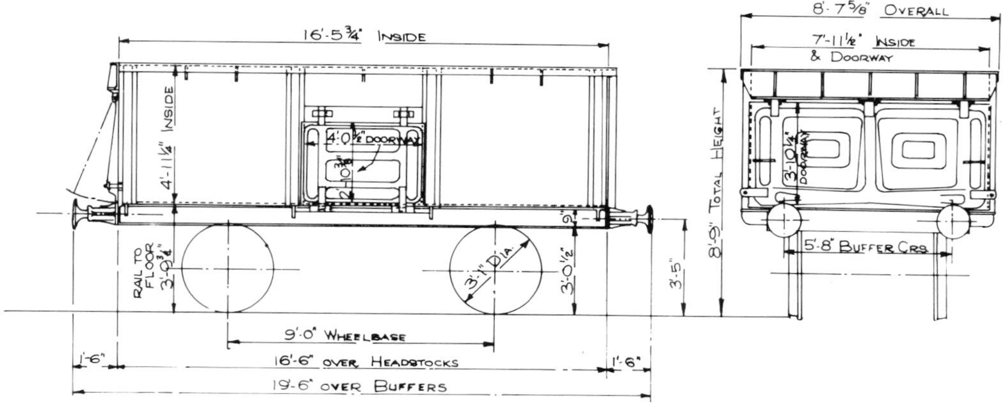

Figure 17. *16ton end door wagon. Diagram 1/102. The principal difference between this diagram and the wagon in the previous illustration is that of the pressed-steel door shown here. It is suggested that the fabricated door in the photograph is probably a replacement, possibly because the press tools were no longer available.*

Figure 18. *16ton end door wagon. Diagram 1/106. With this diagram (1/104 was similar except for lack of stiffening on the body corners) we see the introduction of flap doors above the side doors. Bottom doors, and consequently double brake, are still retained.*

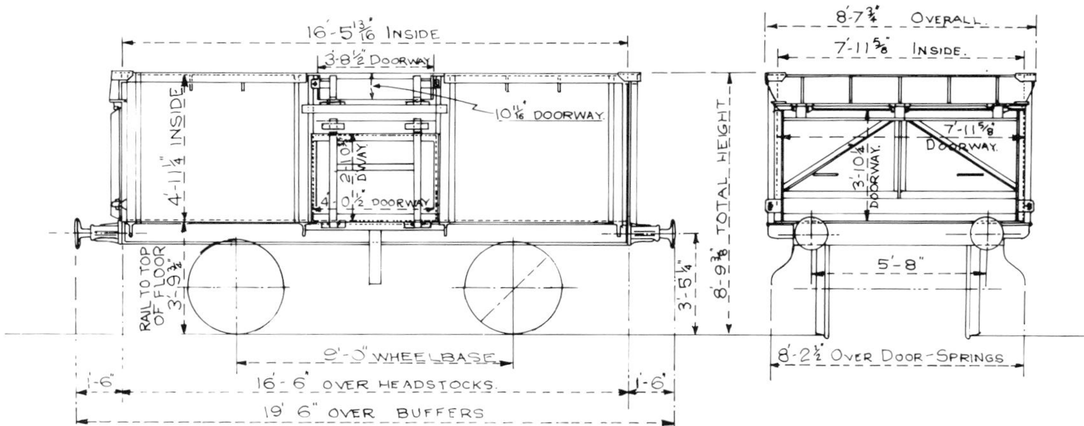

fabricated doors and some such wagons have been seen in traffic. It therefore seems highly likely that these four diagrams cover the ex-Ministry wagons, and observations tend to confirm this, but beyond that we cannot go.

The first 16ton wagons to be built for British Railways were probably an order for 100 placed with Fairfields Shipbuilding & Engineering, which completed delivery by 10 April 1950. The wagons were numbered B67000 to B67099 and were to diagram 104, lot 2160. The lot number was issued on 16 September 1949. Three lot numbers for other designs of 16ton wagon had been issued before this, but deliveries were not completed until later. It seems most likely that the order was a continuation of the one placed by the Ministry of Transport, especially since further orders for 1,250 wagons of this design were placed with Fairfields and other contractors which had built the Ministry wagons. It is also possible that some of the Ministry wagons, especially the later ones, were to this diagram 104. Construction was all-welded and there were now two doors each side, the main one now being surmounted by a smaller flap door. In place of the angle material along the top of the sides and ends there was now a heavier lipped angle which gave a channel effect and greater strength. Bottom doors (and consequently double brake since the doors would have fouled the cross-shaft of Morton brake) were still fitted, this being the main point of divergence with later designs.

The next diagram to be issued in the series, No 105 (one assumes they were issued in ascending numerical order), was in effect diagram 104 with rivetted body but retaining angle topping. Again no lot numbers were ever issued by British Railways for wagons to this design and one is therefore forced to the conclusion that like diagrams 100 to 103 it was issued to cover ex-Ministry wagons. If this is correct it is reasonable to assume that diagram 104 similarly covers wagons built for the Ministry of Transport, thus adding weight to the theory that those built against this diagram to British Railways lot numbers were in fact a continuation of Ministry orders.

The first British Railways *lot* number allocated for end-door mineral wagons was 2104 issued on 7 January 1949 for 1,500 16 tonners to be built at Derby. As B64000 to B65499 they were the lowest running numbers issued by the railways and more-or-less followed the ex-Ministry wagons.

Plate 35. *16ton end door wagon. Diagram 1/105. B40516 illustrates the rivetted version of diagram 1/106 above. Bottom doors here are still retained. Note that on this design the body stanchion at the fixed (left-hand) end is not secured to the solebar as are the others. Crewe, 21 September 1966.* (Author).

Apart from minor dimensional differences they were almost identical to diagram 104, the principal distinguishing feature being the reinforcement of the top corners of the body by substantial stiffening plates on the newer diagram. They differed only from the later British Railways design in having bottom doors and double brake. In the same way that diagram 104 probably originated in a Ministry design, it seems more than likely that these Derby wagons built to diagram 106 were a continuation of the LMS programme. After these first 1,500 the remaining 1,330 of the design were also built at Derby and all are remarkably similar to LMS diagram 2134.

Even as these first British Railways end-door wagons were being ordered the necessity of fitting bottom doors was in doubt because it was decided to follow lot 2104 with 1,000 wagons without them. There seems to be a slight hiccup in the diagram numbering sequence here because diagram 111 was issued; why, is not known. There is virtually no difference apart from thickness of body sheets between this and diagram 108 — which was to become the popular model — and yet construction of both types continued side by side for some years, by which time Derby and Shildon works between them had built 4,400 wagons to diagram 111.

On 22 March 1949 authority was given to build 500 all-steel mineral wagons using the Bulleid triangular frame., In a paper then recently pre-

Plate 36. *16ton end door wagon. Diagram 1/108. This was not only the most popular of all mineral wagon designs, but also the most popular of all BR wagon diagrams. With it, bottom doors were at last abandoned and the fitting of Morton brake was consequently made possible; on the first lots double brake, as the diagram states, was retained. B79047, seen here at Townhill wagon works on 5 July 1964, has been repaired. The lower parts of the body side sheets have been renewed and the wagon has been fully repainted in red bauxite.* (Author).

Plate 37. *16ton end door wagon. Diagram 1/109. Whether the welded body version (left) or the rivetted one seen here was built depended upon the production methods at the contractor's works. Cambrian Wagon works which built B145959 was one of the last to use rivetting. The body 'livery', with almost equal areas of rust and grey paint, illustrates the remarks made on page 21. Haymarket, 3 January 1967.* (Author).

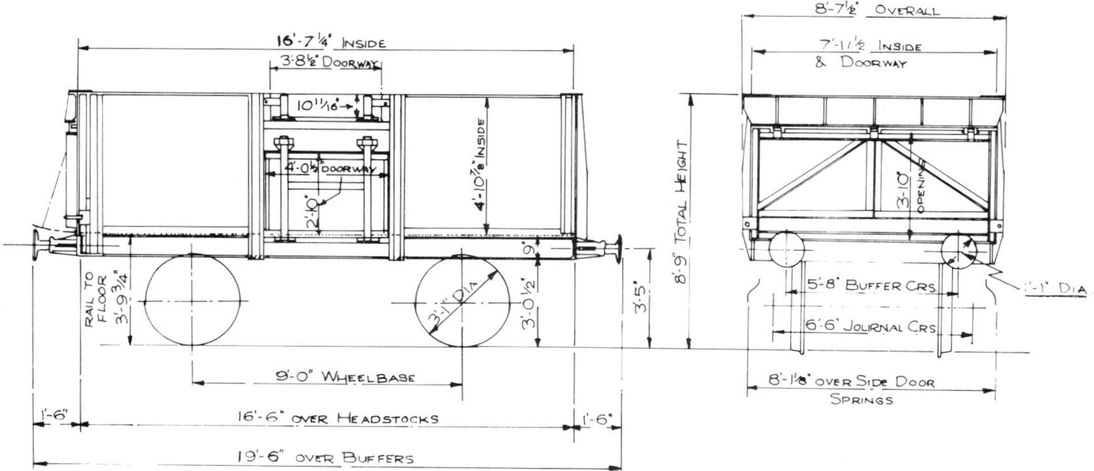

Figure 19. *16ton end door wagon. Diagram 1/109. As has happened before in this chapter we find when comparing diagram and photograph there are door differences. The end door here is shown to be rivetted whereas that in the previous illustration is clearly a steel pressing.*

sented to the British Association, Bulleid had described his concept of improved wagon design which gave significant savings in tare weight, and the paper was illustrated with examples of wagons incorporating these features which had recently been completed at Eastleigh. As noted in Chapter 1, the Ideal Stocks Committee had great hopes of what were described as 'Tension' brakes, and one assumes it was the brakes on these prototypes they had in mind. At last Bulleid was to get his chance.

But it was not to be. Bulleid left for Inchicore and CIE to develop his triangulated underframes there, and with his departure there was no one to press such new-fangled notions. A neat line was ruled through the entry in the lot book and a note was added: 'Amended 14/2/51 Coal — all steel 16Ton' and another 500 wagons to diagram 111 emerged from that bastion of tradition, Derby. The story does not quite end there because there is a little note added at the end of the amendment, just one word — 'Fitted'. Were these 500 actually fitted with real continuous brake? All the other lots say 'unfitted' and the diagram makes no mention.

By this time the Ideal Stocks Committee had produced its report. Chapter 1 gave an outline, but it is worthwhile considering the Committee's recommendations in detail so far as they refer to mineral wagons. The opening sentence of the section reads, 'Dealing first with the former privately owned mineral wagons, the most important first step towards increasing the efficiency of the wagon stock is the elimination of the 253,500 grease lubricated wagons in existence at December 31st 1949'. Over a quarter of a million vehicles! To make matters worse, even if all the life-expired wagons were broken up, by the end of 1953, 85,000 would still be left. After considering the pros and cons it was recommended that the condemnation of greasebox wagons be speeded up so that they be eliminated by the end of 1956 instead of 1967, which would have been the case if they had been allowed to go to the end of their life expectancy. This meant that after 1954 some 76,700 wagons would be broken up prematurely and replaced with 16ton wagons at a cost of £19.9 million.

This part of the report has been quoted in some detail because it set the stage for a truly fantastic wagon building programme. Replacing 253,500 wagons is a difficult enough task, even with slightly larger and therefore fewer vehicles, but to complete the task in six years makes it an even more formidable venture. Until the Committee's report appeared the costruction of mineral wagons had proceeded steadily. The report is dated March 1950 and it is surely no coincidence that on 17 March 1950 twelve lot numbers (2221 to 2232) were issued for no less than 5,600 16ton end-door wagons as part of a programme described as 1950 (Special). All were placed with the trade. The quantities in three lots were later reduced, but to compensate two further lots (2242 and 2243) for 750 wagons were issued on 4 April 1950. A little over one week later another ten lot numbers were issued (2250 to 2259) and this time each lot was for 2,500 wagons, all to diagram 108, and again the orders were contracted out to the trade. The remarkable thing was that all went to the same firm, Pressed Steel, and what is more, a firm new to the British Railways scene. In less than a month the railway had placed orders for over 30,000 mineral wagons of which 25,000 had gone to Pressed Steel. What an entry to the market place! In fact the first 2,500 were delivered by August 1951 and by May 1954 the last of the 25,000 had been completed. We shall come across Pressed Steel again in this book.

As if this were not enough to be going on with, British Railways seems to have gone shopping on the continent. The full story would probably be interesting, but one may surmise that in France SNCF was finding that those wagons sent over by the British (referred to at the beginning of this chapter) were just a little bit on the small side and agreed to send them back. The train ferries began unloading wagons which really looked rather familiar but had funny brake pipes and unreadable inscriptions. Into the workshops they went to appear as honest British wagons shorn of foreign *fol-de-rols*. Three lot numbers were issued. The first, 2286, was for 7,000 wagons of Metro-Cammell design ('ex French Govt.') for which diagram 112 was issued. The official records state that only 6,982 were put into traffic so perhaps some were not considered fit for re-conditioning. Lot 2287 covered similar wagons of Charles Roberts design. No new diagram was issued but they were classed as diagram 100, presumably along with ex-Ministry wagons. 1,892 numbers were allotted but only 1,867 wagons are recorded as having entered traffic. The final lot, 2288, was for 308 wagons of Hurst Nelson design. Diagram No 113 was issued but only 305 wagons entered service.

According to the lot books re-conditioning was done at Earlestown and New Cross Gate, but these works appear to have farmed out some of the task. The author has seen evidence that repair shops at Exmouth Junction, Bromsgrove and Barrow did some re-conditioning and probably other places took a share. There is also an interesting point about the builders' plates on these repatriates. Their British Railways plates did not show the builder but did show the correct building date so

Plate 38. *16ton open wagon — lettered Min. Diagram 1/112. Of the three designs of mineral wagon purchased from the French Government the 6,982 examples to this diagram were the only ones without end doors, also the only ones without an equivalent design already in use on British Railways. B196172 was photographed at Oakleigh Sidings on 26 March 1960 when it still had rings for securing wagon sheets, steps below the buffers and screw couplings as evidence of its former role.* (Author).

one could see, for example, a wagon of lot 2287 which was four years older than British Railways.

Even with these acquisitions the demand for 16tonners was not satisfied and on 28 July 1950 orders were placed for a further 14,161 wagons in thirteen different lots, 2290 to 2302. They were officially the 1951 programme and were all placed with outside contractors. In fact the railways were probably doing no more than placing orders well in advance to book workshop capacity, but nevertheless in 4½ months they had committed themselves to buying 54,000 mineral wagons. The LMS built or bought 62,500 of its most popular wagon, the 12ton open merchandise, but took twenty-five years to do it: here was British Railways well on the way to that figure in a few months.

For the next few years we get a mass of different orders for mineral wagons with private builders and railway workshops producing 16tonners, literally in their thousands. Shildon works even built a batch with aluminium bodies to diagram 116 but the experiment was not repeated. Slowly the number of firms using rivetting decreased, leaving only Hurst Nelson which was not employing welding techniques. Even the casual observer of the railway scene in the mid-1950s could not have failed to notice how the coal trains contained fewer wooden wagons and more and more new grey steel ones.

By the end of April 1955 no fewer than fifty-eight lot numbers had been issued for 16ton mineral wagons in that year alone, and out of these Pressed Steel had received orders for 27,500 wagons in four lots. Just how many were built in this part of the programme is very difficult to say. The figures given in Appendix 4 are taken from official records, but around this time they become very confusing, and in our opinion it would be a brave man who would swear that in the hectic days of 1957 when these wagons were actually being built all happenings were faithfully reported and recorded. Orders were amended, cancelled, re-instated and further amended again and again. What went un-recorded one shudders to think. The reason for all this confusion can be summed up in just two words — vacuum brakes.

As we have already seen, the Ideal Stocks Committee did not feel able to recommend adoption of continuous brakes for all wagons. Even so, as Table 1 shows (page 10) the number of wagons fitted with continuous brakes had increased steadily since 1948, and by 1955 the Modernisation Plan announced that henceforth all wagons would be so equipped. The big obstacle to such a policy was without doubt the mineral wagon. For all the increasingly large number of fitted wagons were

Plate 39. *16ton end door wagon. Diagram 1/117. A new vacuum-fitted mineral wagon in all its glory. The handle to the right of the door stop is the empty/loaded brake changeover device. The white stripe indicating the end door position has been spray painted against a template and has spread due to a ripple in the sheeting. Muirkirk, 9 May 1954.* (Author).

merchandise carriers; the minerals, to a wagon, remained staunchly unfitted. To get vacuum brakes fitted two steps had to be taken. First, for new construction, fitting of continuous brakes had to be standard. With orders in the pipeline arrangements could be made with manufacturers to fit the equipment from a certain point in the programme. Second, for wagons already in traffic, fitting had to be done as they went through the repair shops. Consequently, a massive component supply operation had to be arranged. The manufacturing problem was quite beyond the railways' own capacity and in the end supply contracts were placed with a number of firms including, surprisingly, the motor industry.

The organisation, ordering, tooling-up and kindred processes inevitably took time even though the railways were pressing for all speed. Seeing the way they had set about eliminating the greasebox wagon one can understand the enthusiasm with which this latest goal was pursued and within a comparatively short space of time the first vacuum-fitted 16tonners began to appear. One of them is featured in Plate 39 from which it can seen just how many additional fitments were involved. Ere long the first fitted mineral wagons began to appear in traffic, their fresh red bauxite paint making them stand out among their rusty grey brethren. Then reports began to come in of delays in making up trains while shunters coupled brake pipes. National Coal Board shunters just refused to do so. On top of all this there were the usual teething troubles, and drivers used to handling loose-braked trains inevitably had difficulties. To cap it all, brake gear was being wrenched off wagons at some power stations by drag shunting gear. Eventually the order went out: 'No more vacuum-braked mineral wagons'.

Plate 40. *16ton end door wagon. Diagram 1/117. Nine years on from the previous illustration sees a similar 16tonner now bereft of vacuum brake although still retaining fully-fitted brake gear and hydraulic buffers. According to the lot books vacuum brakes were never actually fitted to this wagon — they did not begin officially until B592200 — which serves to illustrate how rapidly things were changing in 1958. Millerhill, 27 July 1968.* (Author).

What had been difficult to start became equally difficult to stop, but eventually the flow of fitted wagons and components was halted. Some lots were completed as unfitted wagons but there were still a goodly number of the fitted sort around. When the automatic-braked mineral wagon did finally become established it was as an air-braked hopper wagon but that is a story belonging to another era. In effect the vacuum brake fiasco marked the beginning of the end for the 16tonner. Coal traffic began to decline and the last new 16tonner was delivered in November 1959, appropriately from the Butterley Company. Soon mineral wagons were an embarrassment to the railways and they were being scrapped almost as fast as they had been produced in their heyday.

Looked at in retrospect the all-steel mineral programme was a fantastic exercise in re-equipment at least equal to the dieselisation which was to follow it. It even had a phœnix-like element about it. After making heavy in-roads into the stocks of 16tonners the railways found coal carryings picking up. Scrapping ceased but the new financial climate meant they could no longer just go and order another 25,000 from Pressed Steel. Instead it was a case of make-do-and-mend with Derby and Horwich works re-bodying existing wagons to give the 16ton mineral wagons new leases of life. Even as we write some are still around, virtually the only unfitted, loose-coupled wagons in regular use.

24½ton All-steel

Although the Ideal Stocks Committee recognised that many 16ton mineral wagons would be built it really set sights on a larger vehicle. The ideal, in its eyes, was a wagon of 24½tons capacity, the largest that could then be carried on two axles. The Committee's report quoted annual charges as:

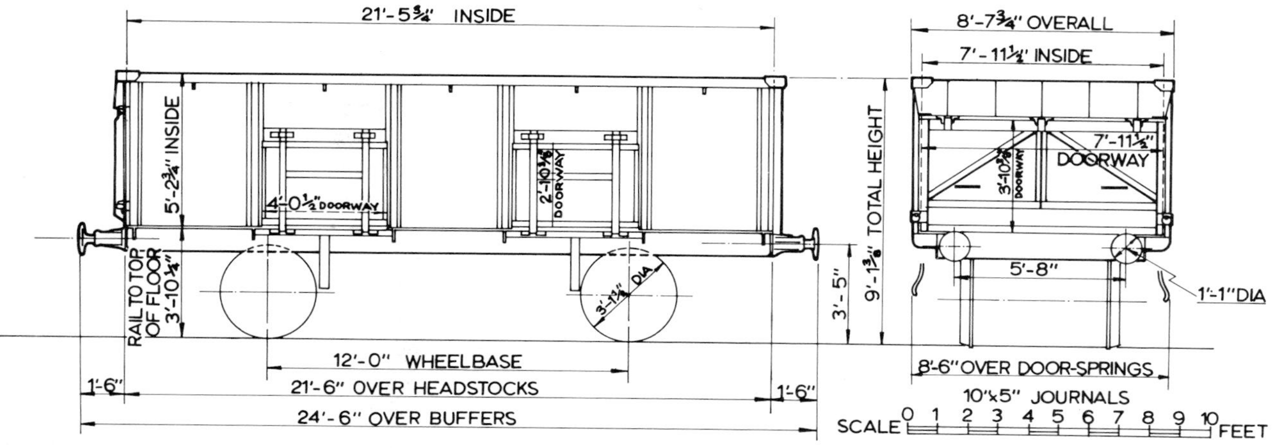

Figure 20. *21ton end door wagon. Diagram 1/107. A comparison with Figure 18 reveals that the 21ton end door wagon is in effect a longer and slightly taller version of the 16tonner. None of the 21tonners ever had bottom doors, and on this first design flap doors were not fitted.*

Description	*Annual charges per ton of capacity (£)*
13ton, two side, two bottom, one end door	1.9514
16ton, two side, two bottom, one end door	1.6700
21ton, four side, one end door	1.7189
21ton, hopper	1.7585
24½ton, four side, one end door	1.5697
24½ton, hopper	1.6047
42ton, hopper	2.4055
42.71ton, side discharge	2.2528
50ton, side discharge	2.3939

In spite of the cost advantage it was realised that the height of colliery screens and unloading facilities would restrict the use of such wagons, but there were sufficient opportunities for their use to allow the placing of the first order in June 1952. It was on Shildon works and covered 650 wagons to diagram 115. The lot number was 2460. This was followed by two further lots of 1,000 and 500 wagons respectively. Thereafter, construction was to an improved design, diagram 118, with roller-bearings and self-contained buffers. Only four lots, a total of 1,245, were built before construction ceased. The 24½tonner was really a beefed-up 16tonner, and like it was superseded by the air-braked hopper.

21ton End-door

One of the difficulties when considering the mineral wagon is that everything is so completely overshadowed by the 16tonner. Thus, although total production of the 21ton end-door type reached 7,450 wagons, a sizeable number by anyone's standards, it is small beer compared with the output of 16tonners.

As General Manager of the Great Western Railway, Sir Felix Pole was an enthusiastic advocate of the 21ton wagon as a great improvement over the wooden 10ton and 12ton mineral wagons then in general use for coal class traffic, but the type found little favour with the Ideal Stocks Committee

Plate 41. *21ton end door wagon — Diagram 1/119. B312940 is an example of the later design of 21tonner, complete with roller-bearings, vacuum brake and hydraulic buffers as well as flap doors over the side doors. Resolven, 23 July 1963.* (Author).

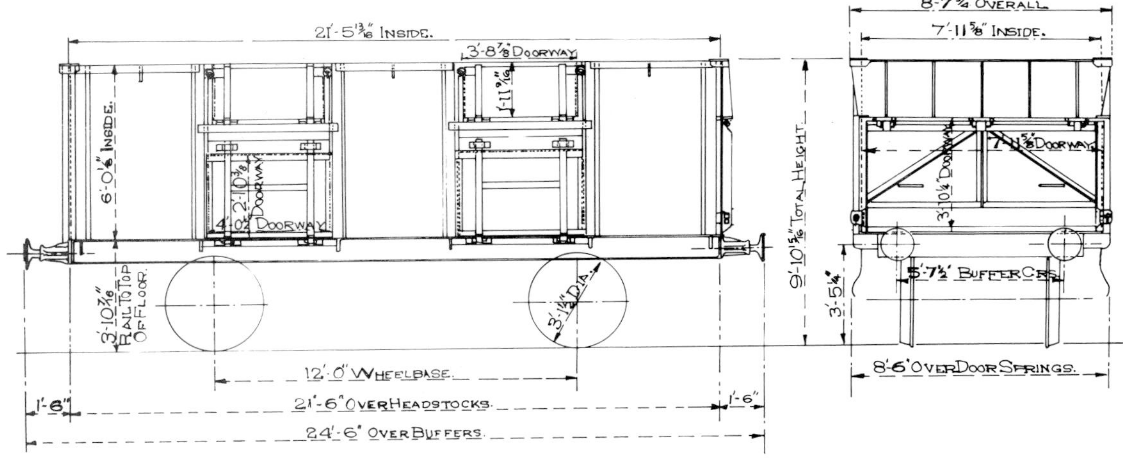

Figure 21. *24½ton end door wagon. Diagram 1/115. The 24½ton end door mineral wagon was a logical development of the 21tonner with higher sides and ends, yet retaining the same basic widths and door dimensions as the 16tonner.*

Plate 42. *24½ton end door wagon. Diagram 1/118. The height of the 24½tonner is clearly seen in this photograph of B283145 taken at Smeaton Junction (which, despite the branding, is nowhere near Bannockburn Colliery) on 21 September 1963. It is one of the later design with roller-bearings and hydraulic buffers.* (Author).

which preferred the larger 24½ton wagon. As a result, only four lots of 21ton wagons were produced up to the 1960s, to give a total of 2,500 wagons. Of these, 1,000 with rivetted bodies were built by Metropolitan-Cammell to diagram 110. The remainder had welded bodies and were to diagram 107. The last one appeared in March 1952. No more were even considered until December 1960, when construction of 1,000 was authorised to a new diagram 119. This new design had vacuum brake, roller-bearings and hydraulic buffers. It was followed by another design, diagram 120, which differed only in brake and buffer details. Four orders were placed for this latter design, producing some 2,450 wagons. Construction ceased in February 1964.

From evidence in the official records it appears that building of the 16tonner was phased out in favour of the 21ton version, since construction of the latter did not re-commence until after the last 16tonner had been delivered. Since 21ton wagons continued to be built after the last 24½tonner had been delivered there is perhaps a touch of irony in the fact that the last traditional-style mineral wagon to be built was the one type which did not find favour with the powers-that-were in 1950.

Chapter 4

Hopper Wagons

In this chapter we are dealing with a rather special group of mineral wagon designs, covering pages 140 to 185 of the diagram book. Most of them have the common feature that they have been specially constructed with hopper floors and bottom doors to allow complete discharge of the load by gravity. Having said that, there are the inevitable exceptions in that not all mineral wagons having bottom discharge facilities are included here, while some hopper wagon designs are excluded and some of the diagrams in this group cover mineral wagons with no discharge facilities whatsoever.

The early 16ton mineral wagon designs have always been set apart from hopper wagon types, even though they did have bottom doors, and indeed the first lots were clearly described as 'Coal — Not Hoppered'. We have already seen how other mineral wagons used for the carriage of china clay are included among the open merchandise wagons. They were later joined there by open wagons used for the carriage of soda ash although the lot book reveals that the original intention was to put them amongst the mineral hopper wagon types. In contrast, all covered hopper wagon designs are placed in a separate section of the diagram book. Finally, in this present series of diagrams and alongside hopper wagons designed for the carriage of iron ore we find a group of ironstone wagons built without doors or hoppers at all, and which have to be unloaded by rotary tippler.

Having set out our stall and dealt with the various exceptions the general features of the type merit some attention. By its design the hopper wagon requires special unloading facilities. Commonly, special loading facilities are also provided. These features, together with the speed at which such wagons can be loaded and unloaded, make them ideal for dealing with regular traffic flows such as the supply of raw materials to steelworks. In current railway operations hopper wagons are therefore specified wherever possible, hence the rise of the 26ton and 32ton air-braked hopper at the expense of the 16ton end-door wagon for coal traffic.

13ton Coal hopper

In the paragraph above we look ahead to the conditions of the early 1970s and outside the compass of

Figure 22. *13ton hopper coal wagon. Diagram 1/140. A time-honoured design, this 13ton wooden hopper could have come straight from the LNER or even the North Eastern Railway diagram books, yet 300 were built for British Railways under the 1949 wagon building programme.*

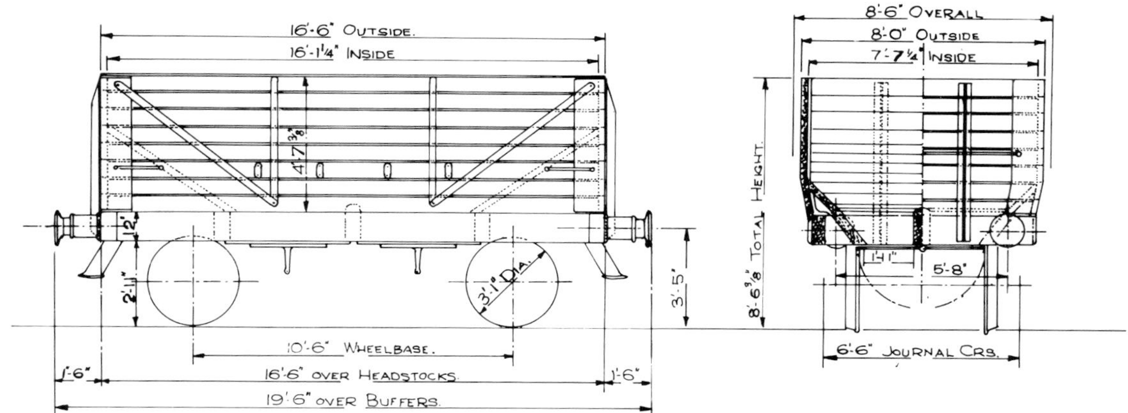

Plate 43. *13ton hopper coal wagon. Diagram 1/142. While Faverdale works was building the wooden hoppers shown in Figure 22, the steel version featured here was being built a few miles away at Shildon. In point of fact both designs were soon phased out in favour of 21ton vehicles. St Nicholas yard (Carlisle), 10 September 1960.* (Author).

this book. It is a measure of the progress made in wagon design that the first coal hopper wagons built by British Railways were a far cry from the merry-go-round hoppers being built 20 years later. They were in fact a single lot of 300 thirteen-tonners built at Faverdale Works, and were almost certainly the remnant of an LNER wagon building programme. As such they were the last of a long line of wooden hopper wagons to a basic design evolved nearly a century before. It is believed that these wagons, lot 2050, diagram 140, together with fifty ballast wagons to diagram 569, were the only British Railways wagons to have wooden solebars. Construction was completed on 5 November 1949.

It would seem that as they were being built Shildon works was producing the all-steel version of the same wagon with lot 2038 covering 200 wagons to diagram 142. A comparison of the two diagrams shows that while both designs had identical capacity and similar dimensions the all-steel 13tonner weighed 6tons 10cwt compared with the 6tons 18cwt of the wooden type. Altogether some 1,950 wagons were built to diagram 142, to be followed by a further 650 to diagram 144. The only significant difference appears to be that on the later diagram the wheels were the standard 3ft 1½in diameter rather than the 3ft 1in previously used. On both the 'all-steel' designs the bottom doors were specified as being made of wood. No more 13ton coal hopper wagons were built.

21ton Coal hopper

Like the smaller wooden hopper wagon the 21ton coal hopper was very much an LNER design. More than that, it was very much a North-East of England design as any observant rail traveller cannot have failed to notice. This fact, that the coal hopper wagon was so very much confined to one area, could well explain the approach of the Ideal Stocks Committee when dealing with mineral wagons, because although it dwelt at length on ideal capacities the Committee had virtually nothing to say about hopper discharge and its merits. In spite of this (or maybe because of it) 21ton hoppers continued to be built in substantial numbers.

The first design to appear under British Railways was to diagram 141. It is very similar to an LNER design and the diagram wording '*Right hand* lever brake both sides' is typically LNER. 1,250 wagons were supplied, all by outside contractors. Some wagons were built to a very similar design for the Ministry of Transport, but whether like the 16tonners they came direct into British Railways stock is not known. It is believed they may have been taken into LNER stock. These first 21tonners were followed by a further 2,750 to the almost identical diagram 143 and again contractors handled all construction. While the weight of the earlier design is given as 9tons 13cwt that of diagram 143 is

Plate 44. *21ton hopper coal wagon. Diagram 1/143. B412908 is an example of one of the earlier designs of 21ton hopper. The body is rivetted, brakes are of clasp pattern, and the brake lever is raised prominently when the brakes are off. Townhill, 5 July 1964.* (Author).

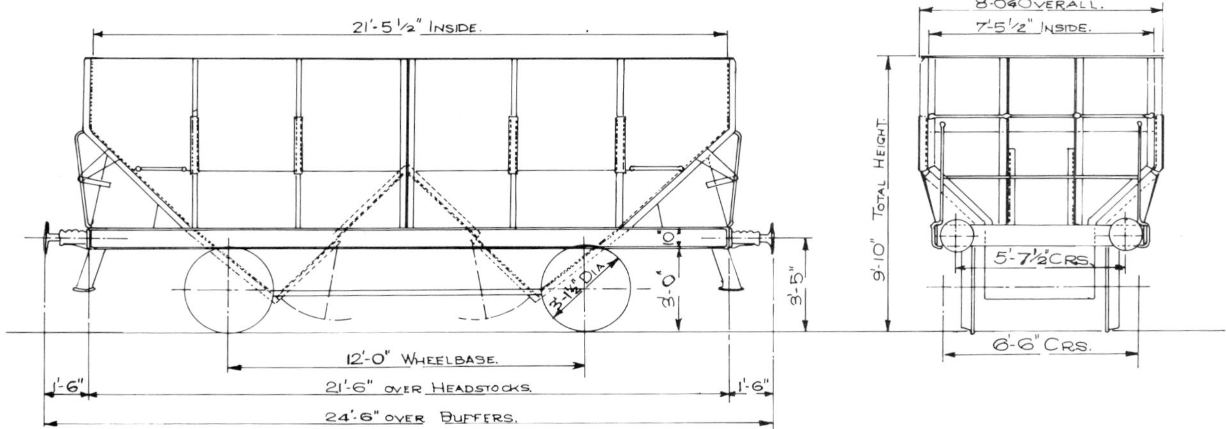

Figure 23. *21ton hopper coal wagon. Diagram 1/145. Apart from minor dimensional differences the principal change here compared with the previous design is that Morton brake is now fitted. The body still remains rivetted.*

stated to vary between 9tons 2cwt and 9tons 15cwt, perhaps suggesting differences between builders in sheet thicknesses.

The above lots were part of the 1949 and 1950 building programmes. None was called for in the 1951 programme, but from 1952 onwards we get a situation developing with the 21ton hopper very similar to that pertaining with the 16ton end-door wagon where two designs were beiong produced at the same time. Here the diagrams are 145 and 146. One suspects that the former is a rivetted design whereas the latter calls for welding. Relatively few wagons were built to diagram 145, all of them by Hurst Nelson and Metropolitan-Cammell. In later years both these firms switched to building diagram 146 alongside other contractors and Shildon Works. Again there are parallels with the 16ton programme. Construction continued until the 1958 programme when for the first time Pressed Steel took a hand. Appropriately this firm built the largest lot of any, totalling 2,950 wagons. The final order for this capacity showed the influence of the Modernisation Programme. It was for a single lot, No 3120, of 1,000 wagons to diagram 149. All were equipped with roller-bearings and one hundred were piped for automatic vacuum brake, although none appear to have been fitted. Continuous brakes were originally specified for the last lots built to diagram 146, but the requirement was later amended.

Plate 45. *21ton hopper coal wagon. Diagram 1/146. This diagram is the welded body version of the 21ton hopper coal. As happened with the 16ton mineral, this was to become the most popular version. As can be seen, the brakes are now the standard 20ton hand-lever pattern while this particular wagon has also been fitted with roller-bearings. Barrow, 2 September 1967.* (Author).

24½ton Coal hopper

Since the Ideal Stocks Committee had decided that a wagon of 24½tons capacity was ideal for coal traffic it is not surprising that a hopper design of

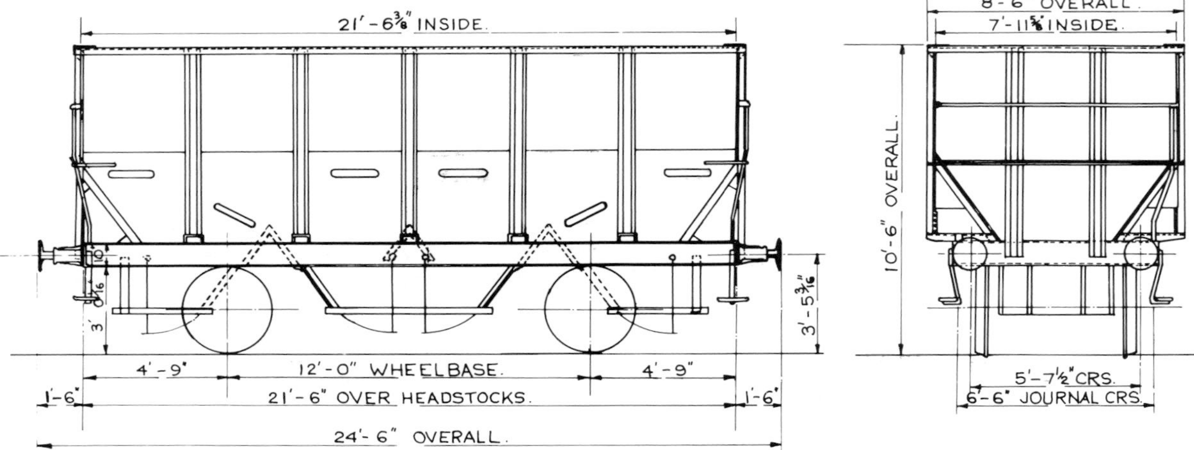

Figure 24. *24½ton hopper coal wagon. Diagram 1/148. As happened with the end door mineral wagon, the 24½ton hopper was developed from the 21ton version. Here the increased capacity was partly obtained by making the body six inches wider as well as increasing the height. The first two prototypes did not have the two end doors, but were later modified to bring them in line with this the production version.*

this capacity should have been introduced. The prototype wagon, the sole representative of lot 2504, appeared from Shildon Works at the very end of 1957. Diagram 147 showed it to be a taller, wider 21ton wagon with two bottom doors. Subsequent lots had two extra bottom doors, and to cover this diagram 148 was issued. There is evidence that the prototype was rebuilt to the improved design. Ashford Works also built a prototype eighteen months after Shildon's essay. The Ashford one, which was also to diagram 148, was described as 'Low Hopper Coal (Prototype)' but beyond that nothing further is known. Thereafter a further 3,376 wagons were built to diagram 148, all, apart from Ashford's prototype, at Shildon.

Like the smaller 21ton design the 24½ tonners do not appear to have been fitted with automatic vacuum brakes. Two later diagrams, pages 154 and 155, were issued but no prints have been seen. A scheme for fitting vacuum brakes was prepared but according to lot book evidence it was not put into practice, and all 24½tonners were built unfitted. It could be that wagon B338162 which entered traffic in February 1965 was the last unfitted three-link wagon to be built for British Railways.

Having said that all 24½tonners were unfitted there was also a 24ton design, quoted in the diagram book index as a 20ton design, which was equipped with automatic vacuum brake and disc brakes. We have never seen a print of the diagram (153) but luckily it has been possible to confirm details from an official photograph. 250 wagons of this type were built at Shildon.

20ton Hopper coke wagon

Despite its smaller capacity, the 20ton hopper coke wagon is much larger than either the 21ton or

Plate 46. *24½ton hopper coal wagon. Diagram 1/155. While most 24½ton hoppers were built to diagram 1/148, there was a later version with roller-bearings and hydraulic buffers, as seen here. From lot records the date of the photograph is assumed to be around December 1964.* (British Railways).

24½ton coal hoppers. This is due to the bulk of the load. The type is a direct descendent of an LMS design which first appeared in 1930. The first diagram, page 150, differed only from the LMS counterpart in that steel top rails were specified for BR construction, whereas the LMS had used wood. Lots 2039 and 2160, giving a total of 250 wagons, were built to this diagram. They were followed by seven lots to diagram 151, a slightly modified design which dispensed with coke rails at the ends by carrying the end sheeting up to the full height. Some 1,150 wagons were built to this diagram.

The final design variant, because basic dimensions remained the same throughout, carried this process one stage further by replacing the side rails with sheeting. At the same time roller-bearings were also fitted. There was one order, lot 3122, for 550 wagons of which 300 were welded and the balance rivetted. Some 279 (whether all-welded or a mixture is not known) were fitted with vacuum brake pipe. To add a little more variety twenty-one of the rivetted wagons were equipped with sheet support bars. Apart from one lot of one hundred wagons, Shildon Works has been responsible for all coke hopper construction.

Plate 47. *20ton hopper coke wagon. Diagram 1/151. After the first 500 coke wagons had been built a new design appeared — illustrated here — where the end raves were replaced by sheeting. The photograph was taken at Shildon works on or about 21 June 1955.* (British Railways).

Ironstone hopper

Whereas the coal hopper wagons, despite the numerous diagrams, could be classed into three groups according to capacity, ironstone hoppers do not lend themselves to such treatment. There are some eight diagrams covering 5,270 wagons in twelve lots yet with capacities of 22, 24, 25, 25½, 33 or 33½tons. Compared with their coal and coke brethren the ironstone hoppers are all rather small designs, only one exceeding 17ft 6in over headstocks. The following table compares typical designs of each type of wagon.

Wagon type	*Diagram*	*Capacity (tons)*	*Capacity (cu ft)*	*Length* ft in*	*Total height ft in*
Coal hopper	146	21	845	21 6	9 9 5/16
Coke hopper	150	20	1,380	25 0	11 0
Ironstone hopper	161	22	516	16 6	9 7¾

*over headstocks

The salient feature is the relatively small size of the iron ore wagon, a testimony to the high density of the load. Within the eight diagrams there are some quite wide variations, especially with regard to capacity, so it may be useful to compare them all in tabular form before dealing with history and construction.

Ironstone hopper wagons
Comparison of Designs

Capacity (tons)	*Diagram*	*Length over headstocks ft in*	*Body height ft in*	*Capacity (cu ft)*
22	161	16 6	9 7¾	516
24	162	16 6	9 7½	516
24	165	17 6	10 3½	663
25	160	17 6	9 6	594*
25½	163	17 6	10 3½	663
25½	166	17 6	10 3½	663
33	164	19 0	10 8	?
33½	167	17 6	10 3½	663

*also quoted as 699cu ft with 9in top load.

It is possible to generalise and say that there appear to be four main designs. The first is the smaller 16ft 6in vehicle which began as a 22tonner and later became a 24tonner. Then there was the 17ft 6in design with a body height of 10ft 3½in which was slowly uprated from 24tons to 33½tons. Diagrams 160 and 164 seem to be the odd ones.

Beginning in numerical order with diagram 160, one of the oddities, we find is that only 150 wagons were built to this design, all at Shildon Works. The first hundred, lot 2040, were part of

Plate 48. *25ton ironstone wagon. Diagram 1/160. Rather strangely the word 'hopper' is not used in the official description, yet this is obviously a hopper wagon. The principal point of interest is the braking system, with levers parallel to the headstocks working brakes on the far side of the wagon, a time-honoured arrangement dating back well into North Eastern Railway days. Photographed at Shildon works, probably in September 1949.* (Author's collection).

Plate 49. *24ton hopper ironstone wagon. Diagram 1/162. This is a very traditional shape for an iron ore wagon. Similar designs saw service not only with the LMS and LNER but also with various private owners. All 1,500 British Railways examples were built by outside contractors. Millerhill, 5 April 1969.* (Author).

the 1949 programme while the balance, lot 2130, were scheduled for the next year. The design seems to have been LNER-based; in fact the brake handles across the headstocks are strongly reminiscent not only of that company's practice but of that of a predecessor, the North Eastern Railway. Also included in the 1949 programme was one lot of 1,000 22ton ironstone hoppers to diagram 161. They were built by Charles Roberts & Co and were the only examples of this design.

Along with the fifty wagons of lot 2130 the 1950 programme also called for 1,500 24ton hoppers. Three consecutive lot numbers were issued, 2148, 2149 and 2150, each for 500 wagons and all were sub-contracted. There is evidence from the lot list that this design actually started life as a 22tonner but was later uprated. The only difference between it and the preceding diagram 161 is the 3ft 2in wheel diameter of the earlier design, later reduced

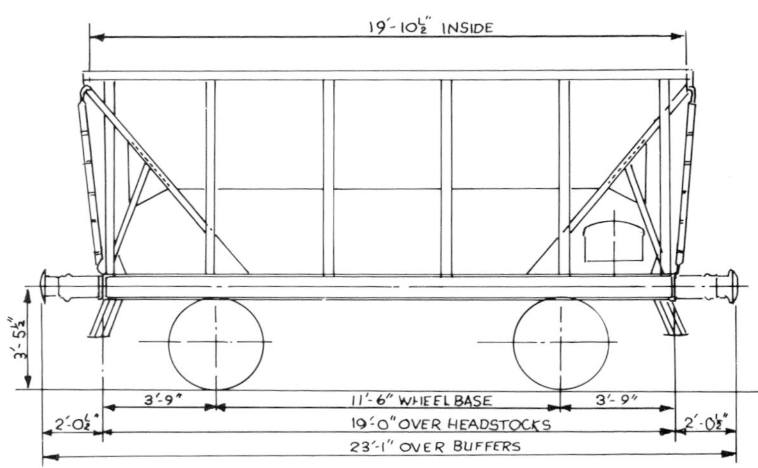

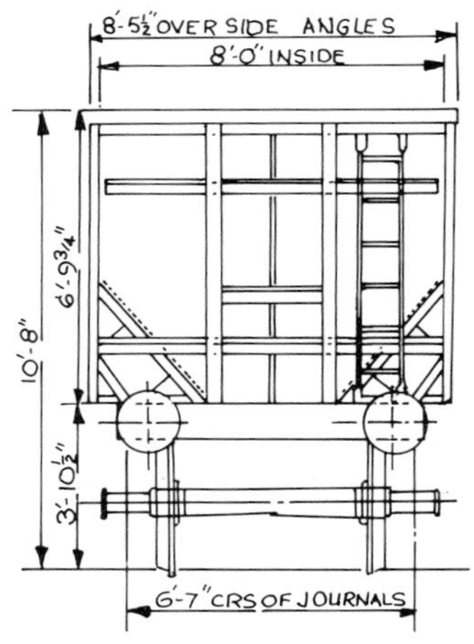

Figure 25. *33ton hopper ironstone wagon. Diagram 1/164 covered a later design of ironstone hopper with length and height increased, and payload some nine tons greater as a result. Vacuum brakes were fitted by putting the cylinders above the solebar out of the way of the bottom doors, a scheme frequently adopted with ballast hoppers.*

to the standard 3ft 1½in. Diagram 162 also states as do the others that the wagons were lettered 'Iron Ore', despite the official description.

At this point it is convenient to jump a few pages in the diagram book to page 182, a bogie iron ore wagon fitted for side discharge. Although not strictly a hopper wagon then it would have seemed more logical to have put it among the ironstone hoppers being dealt with above than among the tippler designs where it did appear. Some thirty wagons were built at Shildon as part of the 1951 programme and were given lot 2312. An impressive bogie design, they were fitted with automatic vacuum brakes and compressed-air door controls. Designed for the conveyance of iron ore from Tyne Dock to Consett Iron Works, a train of these wagons with attendant 2-10-0s in full cry was one of *the* sights of the steam age.

After their appearance no more ironstone hoppers were called for for several years and then, beginning with the 1955 programme, all future construction was at Shildon Works. The 1955 programme specified nine hundred 25½ton hoppers to diagram 163, all built as lot 2733. Next year's programme asked only for 270, but this time to diagram 164. This was one of the 'odd men out' and the wagons were unusual in being fitted with vacuum brake. Subsequent construction consisted of a further four lots, each to a different diagram; since only 1,550 wagons were involved and three of the diagrams appeared for the first and last time, one cannot help but wonder why so much design effort was called for. There was one further diagram, page 175, covering an unknown number of ironstone wagons converted to 30ton clinker wagons, but this is one of those diagrams of which no prints have been seen, so we have no more information.

Plate 50. *25ton anhydrite wagon. Diagram 1/179. The remaining hopper wagon design in this group covered one lot of 150 wagons built specifically for anhydrite traffic from Lazonby on the Settle & Carlisle line. Here the position of the vacuum cylinder and the connecting pipe can be clearly seen. Photographed at Shildon works, probably in December 1954.* (British Railways).

Plate 51. *56ton iron ore wagon. Diagram 1/182. The thirty side-discharge bogie wagons to this diagram worked solely between Tyne Dock and Consett. Discharge doors were operated by compressed air and wagon brakes were automatic vacuum. The mounds visible above the wagon are the load of iron ore, and the Class 9F 2–10–0 locomotive is actually assisting in rear. Annfield Plain, 23 July 1964.* (Author).

25ton Anyhydrite wagons

It is believed that these wagons were designed for traffic from Long Meg Quarry on the Settle & Carlisle line. There was but a single diagram, page 179, covering 150 wagons of lot 2597. All were fitted with automatic vacuum brake.

Ironstone wagons

Before nationalisation the LMS had developed the idea of using what was basically an all-steel mineral wagon without doors but with heavier journals for carrying iron ore. At receiving steelworks such wagons could be turned over bodily for unloading, hence the rather delightful code name of Iron Ore Tippler, by which the type became known. The Ideal Stocks Committee had noted

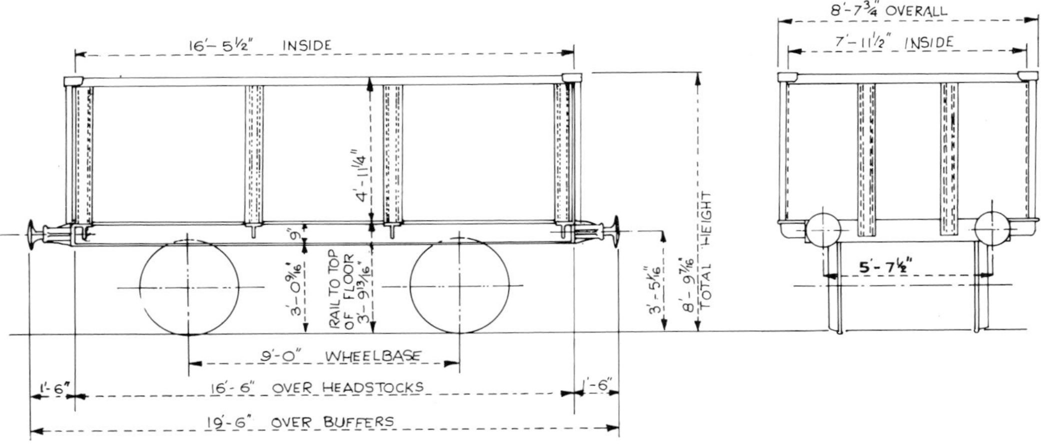

Figure 26. *27ton ironstone wagon — lettered Iron Ore Tippler. Diagram 1/180. At first sight this and the wagons in the next two illustrations could easily be mistaken for 16ton mineral wagons as basic body dimensions are the same, but on closer examination it becomes apparent that no doors are fitted. On all three diagrams bigger journals are provided to cope with the heavier loads.*

Plate 52. *27ton iron ore wagon — lettered Iron Ore Tippler. Diagram 1/183. For this and later designs the bodies were four inches shallower, presumably to prevent overloading. On this particular wagon the original 10in x 5in journals have been replaced by roller-bearings. Millerhill, 12 April 1964.* (Author).

how the British Iron & Steel Federation expected that increasing use would be made of such a type of wagon. The committee also anticipated that by 1952 there would be a 27% reduction in the demand for iron ore hopper wagons compared with 1949, which explains why relatively few hoppers were built. It therefore proposed the introduction of a 27ton tippler wagon, backing its choice with extensive tabular details.

In spite of the much larger quantities involved compared with the ironstone hopper wagon the tippler saw virtually no design change. Admittedly, five different diagrams were issued, but apart from the final one the differences are mainly minor dimensional changes together with the fitting of self-contained buffers. For the last order, lot 3363, roller-bearings and automatic vacuum brake were specified, giving rise to diagram 185. For this diagram capacity was reduced to 26tons, presumably to keep axle loading within limits. A number of Iron Ore Tippler wagons were actually built for chalk traffic, but how many is not known. There is also some doubt over lot 2988 which was originally for 500 wagons, all to diagram 183. The lot book shows numerous amendments, but it is believed that the final position was as shown in Appendix 4 with the lot being amended to cover 476 vehicles. The remaining twenty-four were fitted with Hoffman axleboxes and transferred to a new lot, No 3075.

Plate 53. *27ton iron ore wagon — lettered Iron Ore Tippler. Diagram 1/184. The 1,450 wagons of lot 3091 were built to this diagram, in which the wheelbase was increased to 10ft, while 9in x 5in diameter journals were fitted. Officially only two of these wagons had vacuum brake fitted, but it appears that B386358 also had it at one time. Basford Hall Sidings (Crewe), 11 October 1969.* (Author).

Plate 54. *Adaptor wagon for Ro-Railer. Diagram 1/190. The Ro-Railer concept will be discussed in the next chapter but to adhere to diagram sequence the adaptor wagon is illustrated here. Whether this is the prototype built by Pressed Steel or one of the six built by British Railways at York is not known, but it carries the paint date 5 July 1962.* (British Railways).

Chapter 5

Covered Vans

When dealing with vans we are considering a basic type of merchandise vehicle similar to the open merchandise wagon. Compared with the open wagon the van has become increasingly popular for merchandise on account of the protection given to its load. The high labour costs involved in sheeting loads in open wagons also tipped the scales in favour of the van. Indeed, since the early part of this century there had been a steady rise in the proportion of covered vans making up the merchandise wagon fleet to the point where in 1971 the number of vans on British Railways exceeded the stock of open wagons.

All general purpose vans built by British Railways have used a 17ft 6in underframe on a 10ft 0in wheelbase and apart from some early examples all have been fitted with automatic vacuum brake. Another almost universal feature has been the employment of pressed-steel ends, generally combined with wooden bodysides and hinged doors. On later designs improved buffers and brake gear appeared, and as with open wagons shorter-bodied shock-absorbing versions have been produced. Continuing the comparison with open merchandise wagons one finds that special body styles have been developed for particular traffics. Throughout the history of goods wagon development this has always been particularly true of vans, but if anything from the mid-1950s onwards the importance of these special vans has tended to diminish. In this chapter all types of covered merchandise wagon (to quote the official description) are considered. This excludes cattle wagons, which are treated specially as livestock vehicles, while horse boxes and fish vans are also omitted as they have always been looked on as passenger stock by British Railways. Even so, the list of types and diagrams remains a formidable one.

Figure 27. *12ton goods van, shock-absorbing. Diagram 1/201. Although the LNER was the last of the Big Four companies to take up the idea of shock-absorbing wagons, this British Railways design is of obvious LNER parentage, but the design was not perpetuated after the fifty examples of lot 2045.*

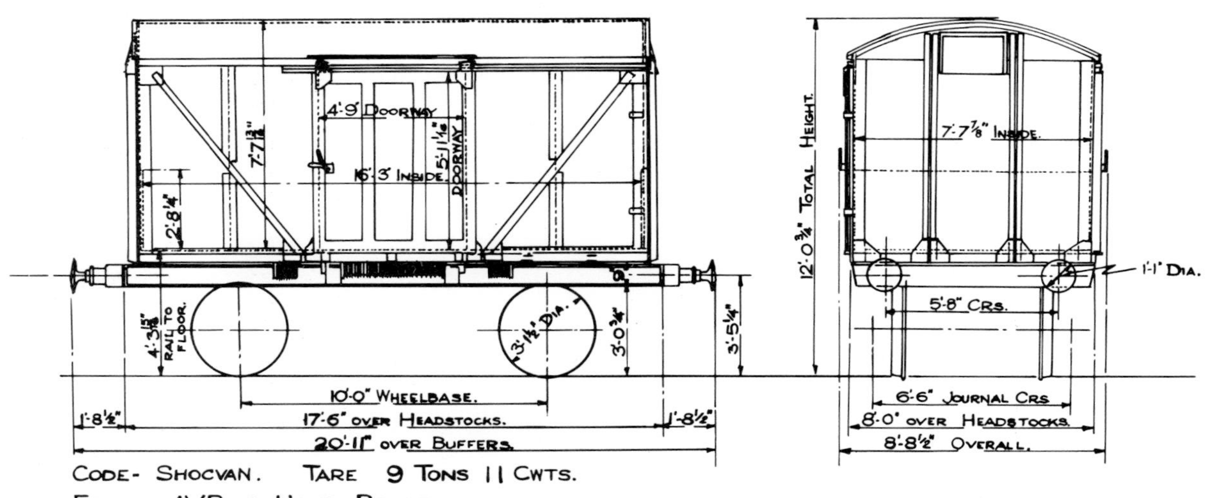

Ventilated goods vans

The development of the goods van, so far as it falls within the compass of this book, goes through three quite distinct phases. The first two coincide with the phases outlined in the Introduction with the initial construction of pre-nationalisation designs followed by extensive construction of the BR standard type. But as virtually all BR-built vans had vacuum braking from new, the only effect of modernisation was the appearance of designs with improved braking and buffers which marked the third phase of van development.

During the first phase some 5,030 vans were built, of which 600 were fitted with shock-absorbing apparatus. We have already shown how the first British Railways lot, No 2001, was an LMS van to that company's order taken over by the new regime. The 1,300 vans ordered were to diagram 200 and had plywood panel bodies with pressed-steel ends. They were built at Wolverton Works and were followed by 2,050 vans with the plywood panels replaced by planking. There were three lots, 2003, 2013 and, later, 2109, for which diagram 204 was issued. As part of the 1949 programme, Wolverton also produced one lot of shock-absorbing vans. They were the only examples of diagram 206. In spite of the necessarily shorter body their parentage was obviously LMS, and they were the last of that company's van designs to be produced.

In contrast to the vans described above, the only LNER contribution appears to have been some fifty shock-absorbing vans built at Faverdale as part of the 1948 programme, which makes one

Plate 55. *12ton goods van. Diagram 1/203. B753100 was the first of one hundred vans, the only lot built to this diagram. In spite of the letters LNE on axlebox covers the design is obviously GWR-inspired. Construction was carried out at Swindon. Currie, 8 October 1960.* (Author).

Figure 28. *12ton goods van. Diagram 1/205. In the early years British Railways carefully issued separate diagrams for fitted and unfitted versions of the same design, although as we have seen with mineral wagons, the idea tended to fall into disuse. This diagram covered the unfitted version of the van featured in Plate 55.*

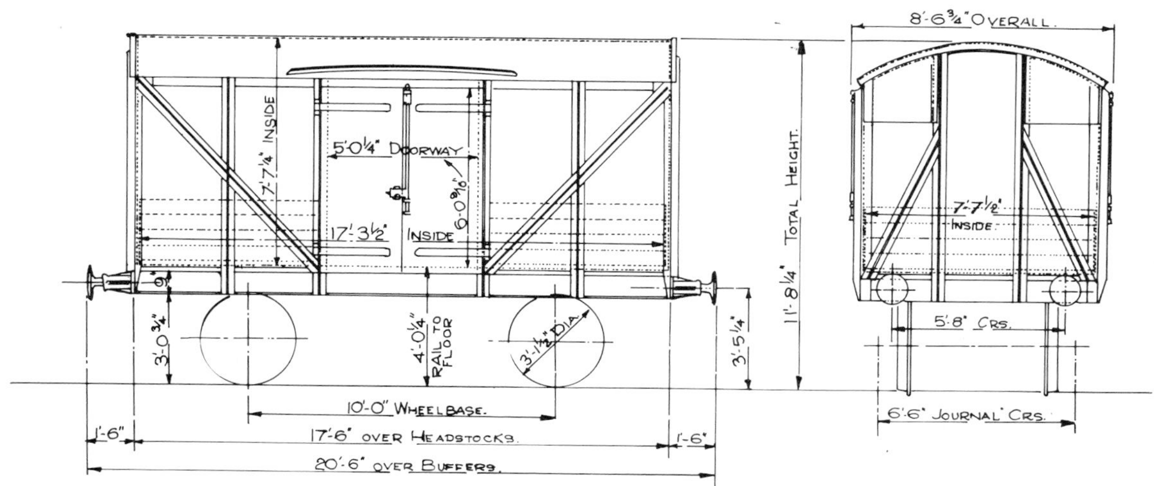

Plate 56. *Goods van. Diagram 1/204. Strangely, the official description makes no mention of capacity, but B752153 is obviously a 12ton van of LMS origin. The J-hangers to the springs and the fully fitted brake gear were standard on that company's vans intended for express freight working. Currie, 8 October 1960.* (Author).

Plate 57. *12ton ventilated goods van. Diagram 1/208. This was the basic design of British Railways van, but in the end the diagram covered many minor variants. This particular example has hydraulic buffers, plywood doors rather than ones of planked wood, and fully-fitted brake gear. It also has an experimental auto-uncoupler which was undergoing trials on 12 April 1964 when the photograph was taken at Millerhill.* (Author).

think they were also a company order taken over. Diagram 201 was allotted and plywood panels were used for the body, but unlike the LMS design plywood was also used for the ends. The same material was used for the 750 vans built at Ashford to diagram 202. They were to a Southern Railway design and probably represented an existing order taken over by British Railways. We cannot be certain because during the war all companies had taken delivery of vans to this self-same design. Despite the use of the same diagram for all 750 vehicles the 410 vans of lot 2062 were unfitted while the rest, lot 2063, were equipped with automatic vacuum brake. Whilst these vehicles were obviously of Southern inspiration Ashford Works also built 500 shock-absorbing vans to a design which from appearances, especially roof profile, could have been pure Swindon even though the drawings were done at Eastleigh. Diagram 207 was issued to cover them.

Though larger than the LNER share the Swindon contribution to this phase of van building was modest compared with those of Ashford and Wolverton, for it amounted to no more than 300 vehicles. There were two lots and two diagrams. First came lot 2079, one hundred vans to diagram 203 with plywood bodies and ends and characteristic Great Western twin end-vents. They were followed by 230 vans of lot 2083 to diagram 205 which was in effect the unfitted version. All these vans to Big Four designs were of 12tons capacity. Here ends phase one.

When considering merchandise wagons the Ideal Stocks Committe had recommended that the 12ton capacity be retained as standard and that all covered vans should in future be built with hinged doors. These two recommendations paved the way for the introduction of diagram 208, the British Railways standard 12ton van design. Swindon-style planked body sides and doors with angle bracing were combined with Wolverton-type pressed-steel ends to produce quite a pleasing body design mounted on a standard underframe. Morton brake with automatic vacuum, and Instanter couplings were fitted. Construction began with 1,000 vans built at Wolverton to lot 2181 and continued steadily, although on nothing like the scale of the mineral wagon programme. Except for one lot of 1,200 vans built by Charles Roberts & Co in 1959 Wolverton and Faverdale share all construction of the type which amounted in the end to 19,063 examples in twenty-two lots. In theory at least all were to the same design, but in practice there were numerous variation despite the use of the same diagram number. The early lots in line with official policy at the time had Morton brake, but later batches had fully-fitted brake gear with eight shoes. On some later examples also hydraulic buffers were fitted.

The original design allowed for the use of plywood panels in place of planking for body sides and doors. Some batches were later given doors of plywood while retaining planking for the sides of the body, but beginning with the 920 vans of lot 2422 there appeared diagram 213 covering the use of ply for both sides and doors. Seven lots, comprising some 3,699 vans were built to this diagram. To assuage the reader's curiosity, the odd van making up the 3,700 was one of lot 2735, originally B769635, which was actually built as a banana van to diagram 246 and given lot 3286 all to itself.

Before considering the shock-absorbing variants it is convenient to look at two derivatives. One hardly merits the word, let alone its own diagram. The 150 vans of lot 2585 were described as '12ton Ventilated Goods Van — Lettered Margarine' and given their own diagram on page 212. So far as is known, no constructional changes were involved, the lettering being an attempt to avoid contamination. In contrast, the one hundred vans of the other variant, lot 2961 and diagram 214, were quite apart. One end was of standard pressed-steel design with its single hooded vent, while the sides were planked without any doors or openings whatsoever. All entry had to be via the double

Plate 58. *12ton goods van — lettered Shocvan. Diagram 1/209 was the shock-absorbing variant of the standard van above, with the body being 12in shorter to allow for movement. B851692 was allocated to Carlisle when photographed at Portobello on 5 March 1960. The colourful traders' labels (Carrs of Carlisle in this case) were often applied to vans and containers, yet they are rarely seen on model railways.* (Author).

Figure 29. *24ton covered hopper van — lettered Covhop. Diagram 1/210. The first twelve lots to this diagram had hand brakes only, the next four lots had through pipes as well, while for the last lot (notwithstanding four hoppers) it proved possible to fit vacuum bakes.*

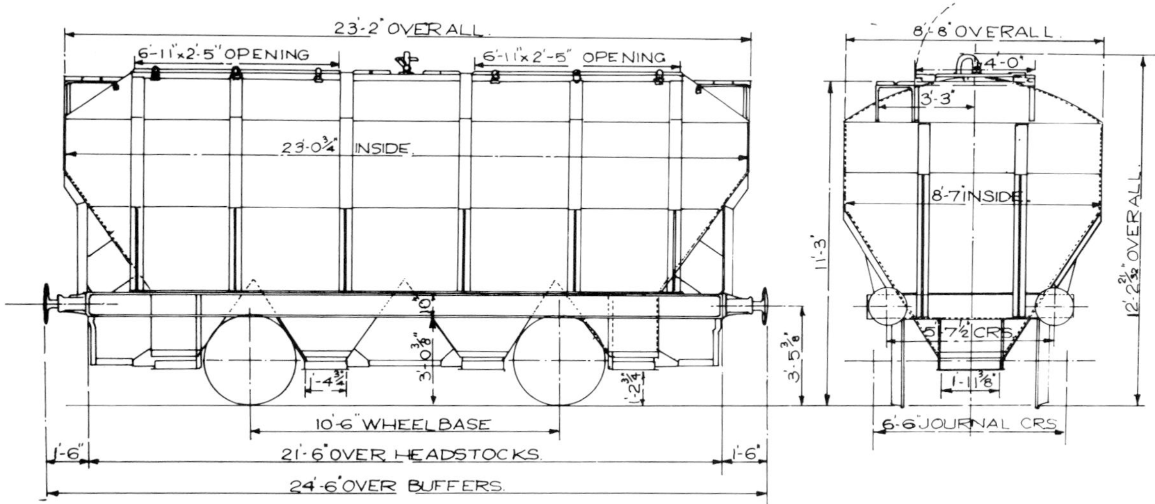

doors at the other end of the van. Unusually for a British Railways design, four roof vents were fitted.

In the same way that shock-absorbing variants of the open merchandise wagon had appeared alongside the ordinary design, so a shock-absorbing van was introduced after the first batches of the British Railways standard van had arrived on the scene. Not surprisingly, diagram 209 (the one allocated) bore a strong resemblance to 208 and as with all shock-absorbing wagons the body was shorter. The first lot, 2202, was for 400 vans and in succeeding years was followed by orders for a further 2,600 in six lots.

Pallet vans

When considering the development of the open merchandise wagon we recorded how the practice of packing bricks on pallets had given rise to the Palbrick wagon, where sides were removable to allow loading by fork lift truck. It was obviously only a matter of time before such methods had their effect on van design, and three LMS vans had been modified with double sliding doors to allow entry by fork lift trucks. Even so it was 10 March 1953 before the first British Railways pallet vans were authorised. Diagram 211 was issued to cover the type, which had some quite unusual features.

Plate 60. *12ton ventilated goods van — lettered Margarine. Diagram 1/212. A special diagram was issued to cover the 150 vans of lot 2585, branded for margarine traffic. Shortly before construction began the decision was taken to fit oleo-pneumatic buffers as seen here, but it is not known what other modifications, if any, were made to merit a special diagram for what was an otherwise standard design. Photographed about August 1954.* (British Railways).

Plate 59. *12ton ventilated goods van — lettered Palvan. Diagram 1/211. The rise and fall of the Palvan has been chronicled in the text, but when this photograph was taken at Basford Hall Junction (Crewe) on 5 September 1959 such vehicles were running in express freight trains without restriction.* (Author).

Body sides *and* ends were of plywood panels, suitably strengthened with steel angles and tee sections. Most unusual were the double hinged doors located at the extreme left-hand end of each side to give a doorway 8ft 5in wide compared with the 5ft opening of the normal van. Construction continued steadily until some 2,388 Palvans, to use the code name, had been produced in nine lots. Unfortunately, continued loading caused wear which made them unstable at speed and they were destined to have a very short life. Not surprisingly a shock-absorbing pallet van was also produced although only three lots were ordered, all to diagram 219. As with the Palvan the last order was curtailed and in the event only 200 saw service. Strictly speaking there was another shock-absorbing pallet van (actually called a Pallet *Wagon*) but only one example was built to lot 3292. The same was true to diagram 216, a goods van with roller shutters for pallet traffic where the only lot, No 3218, covered but a single wagon.

Just because the Palvan had not been a success the palletised load and the fork lift truck were not going to go away, and if it wanted to retain palletised traffic the railway obviously had to think again. This it did and the result was diagram 217,

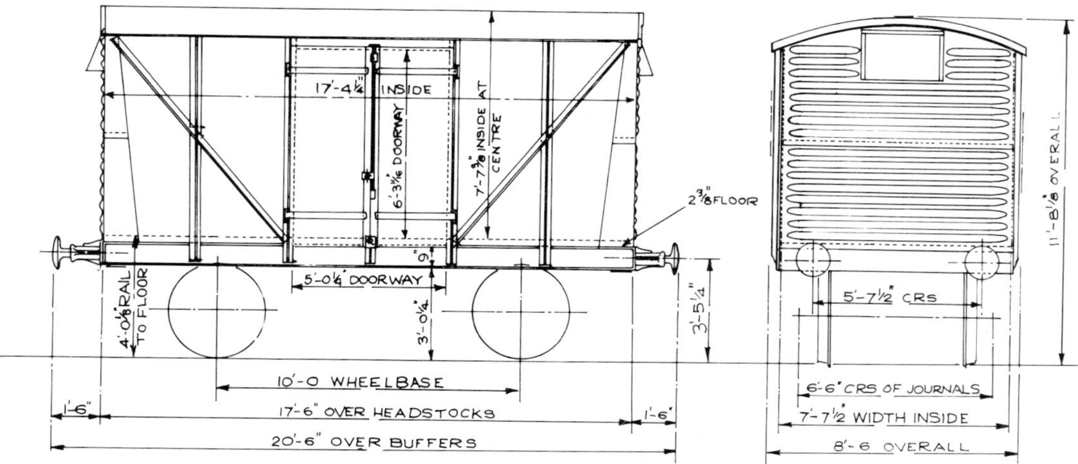

Figure 30. *12ton ventilated goods van. Diagram 1/213. Although a choice of either planking or plywood sheeting was envisaged right from the start for the body sides and doors of the standard van, this diagram was issued to cover the version with plywood sides.*

a type later given the code name Vanwide. Double doors were fitted centrally on each side, arranged to move out before sliding back to give a 9ft doorway. For a body length of 17ft 6in this was a definite achievement and the door design has been perpetuated on the current air-braked vans. In all 2,000 Vanwides were built, six of them to a modified design allocated diagram number 234. The final hundred were also equipped with translucent polyester roofs. No shock-absorbing variant appeared so we were at least spared 'Vanshocwide' or some similar code name. Instead there were a couple of new diagrams for vans which were in effect updated versions of diagram 209, namely 218 with planked body sides, and 220 using plywood.

As a variant of the Vanwide a new type of pallet van was produced, having a longer underframe and four opening doors each side. Five diagrams were issued of which three covered but a single lot. On all five the lack of side supports occasioned by the four doors per side was compensated by substantial end stanchions extending below the headstocks. The diagrams concerned were 221, 222, 223, 225 and 235 whilst length over headstocks gradually increased from 18ft 9in to the 35ft of diagram 235. This gradual extension of the overall length was the first indication that the traditional short wheelbase van was nearing the end of the line. Ashford Works and the Pressed Steel Company between them had built four hundred 20ton vans for train ferry traffic which were 41ft 11in over headstocks, harbingers of the 45ton GLW air-braked vans.

But the traditional van was not quite dead.

Plate 61. *12ton ventilated goods van. Diagram 1/214. End doors only were provided on the 100 vans to this diagram. Such a vehicle was obviously not practical for general service and this particular type was used to convey empty cans from the Metal Box Company factory at Carlisle to the Libby, McNeill & Libby creamery at Milnthorpe where it was photographed on 16 October 1965.* (Author).

Plate 62. *12ton ventilated goods van. Diagram 1/217. This design was an attempt to mate the double doors of the ill-fated Palvan with the standard ventilated van design on a 17ft 6in underframe. In so doing the designers actually reverted to the arrangement used on the very first pallet vans, which were three ex-LMS vans modified on these lines. By now fully fitted brake gear had become standard. Millerhill, 5 April 1969.* (Author).

Figure 31. *20ton ferry van. Diagram 1/227. While as yet the 17ft 6in underframe was still the norm for domestic use, British Railways built 400 of these much longer (41ft 11in) vans for continental working. Vacuum and Westinghouse brakes were fitted, the latter with loaded/empty changeover lever. (3mm — 1ft).*

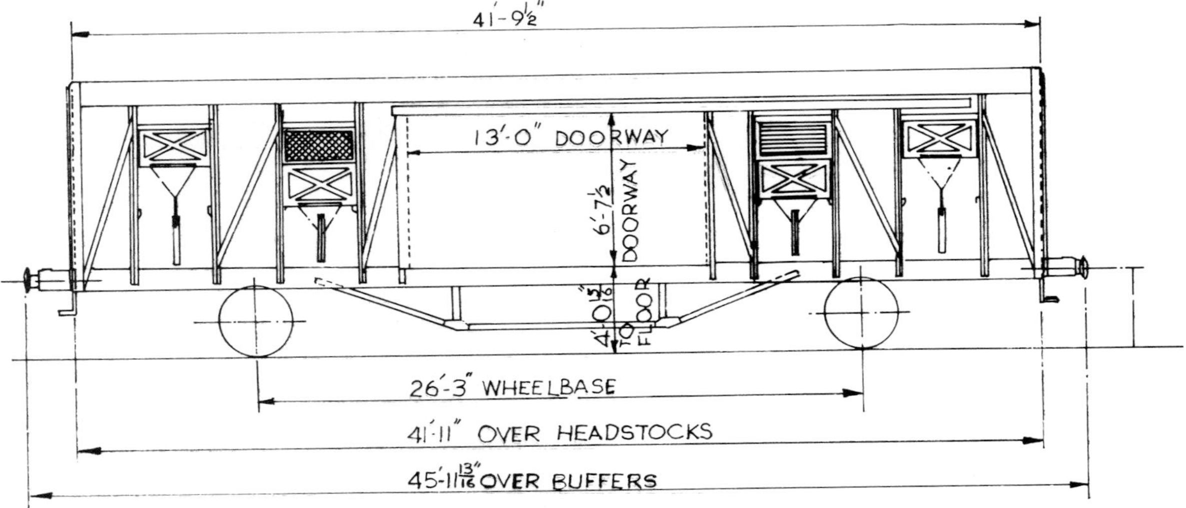

Aided and abetted by Pressed Steel it was to give one dying kick when the company was given an order for 2,000 vans to a design that was to all intents and purposes an updated version of diagram 208. As diagram 234 it was still rated at 12tons, but featured plywood sides and doors with oleo-pneumatic buffers. This same company was also responsible, in complete contrast with everything that had gone before, for a complete train of fifty-two two-wheeled vans which could run as a railway train or singly behind road tractors, using changeover wheels. The name Road-Railer was applied and the train was introduced amid much publicity, but after some trial runs and raising of eyebrows the idea just seemed to die quietly. The road was then clear for the introduction of the long wheelbase air-braked van.

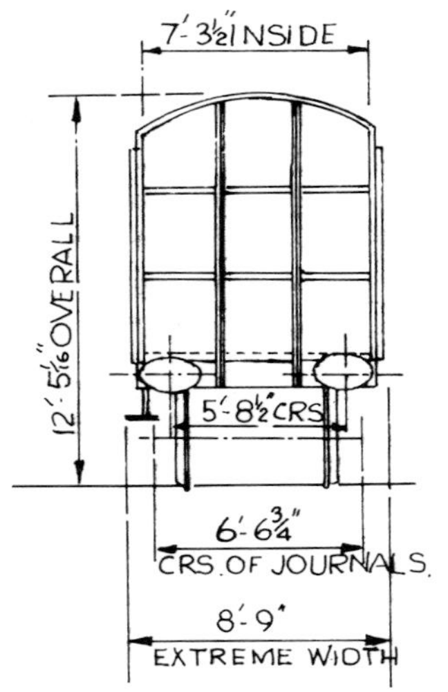

Plate 63. *22ton pallet van. Diagram 1/235. At this point it is convenient to break the numerical sequence of diagrams to consider the final development of the vacuum-braked van with the 123 pallet vans to this design. The underframe was now 35ft over headstocks, wheelbase was 20ft 9in, and the first signs of improved suspension are apparent. Lichfield (Trent Valley), 5 March 1966.* (Author).

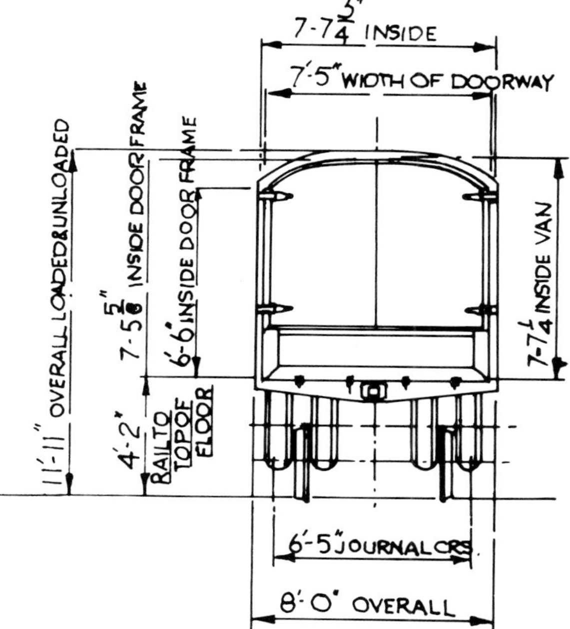

Figure 32. *Road-Railer van. Diagram 1/228. Even though it was not continued, the Road-Railer was a brave attempt to retain general merchandise traffic for rail. The idea was to have vans which could be hauled by road tractors or formed into trains which were hauled by locomotives. The diagram illustrates one of the vans; the adaptor wagon was illustrated in Plate 54.*

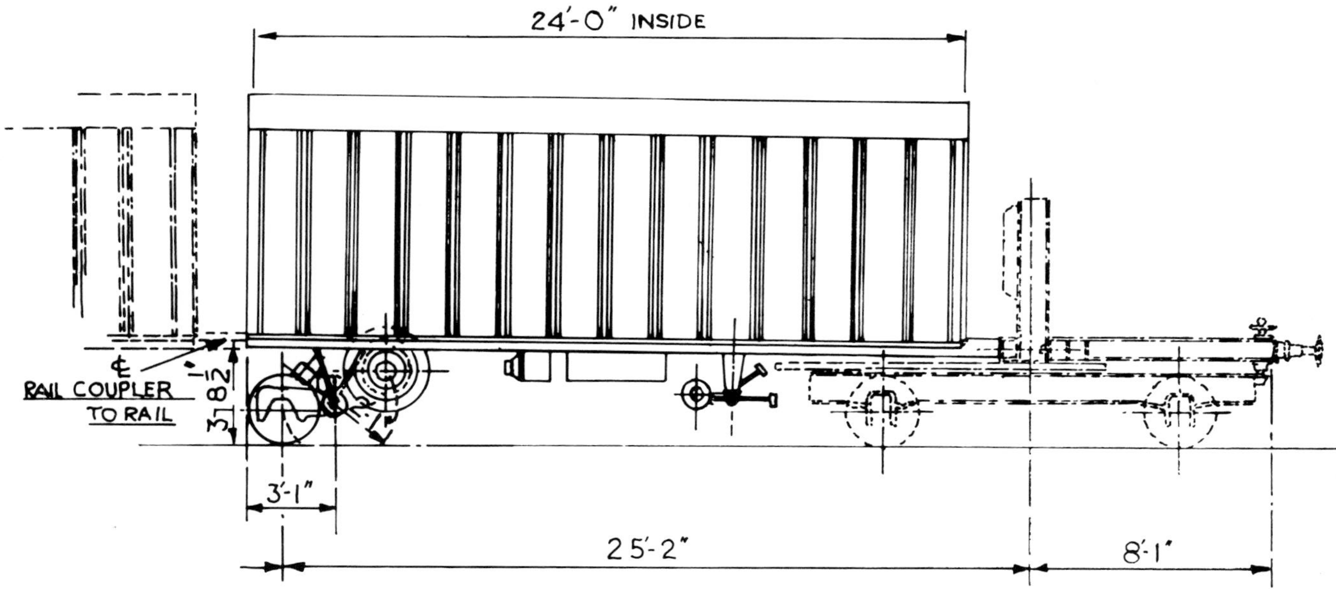

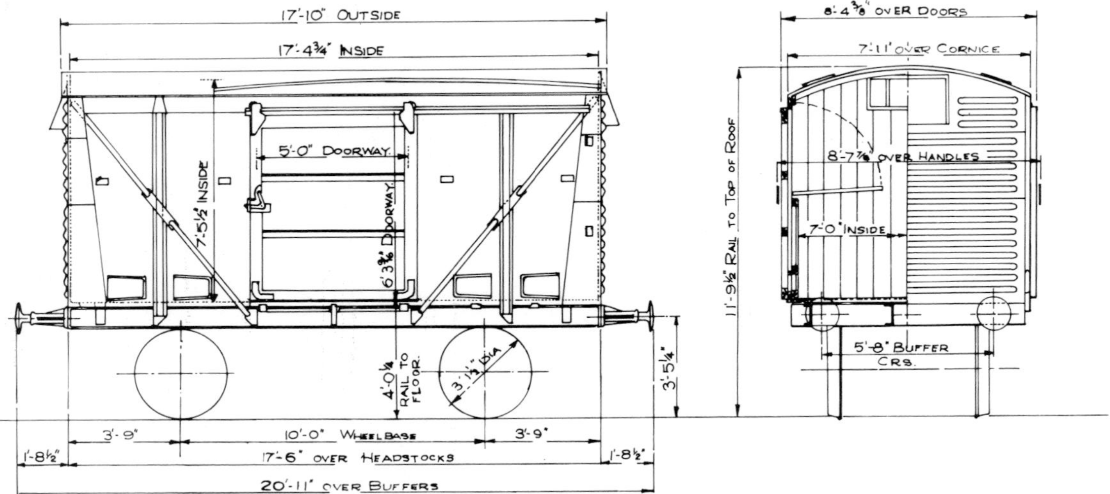

Fig 33. *Goods van — lettered Fruit. Diagram 1/230. In the early years British Railways developed numerous van designs to handle special traffics. This fruit van — an LMS inspiration — had air ducts to increase ventilation, and shelves for extra fruit baskets, which could be folded up when not required.*

Special vans

Fruit vans

The original layout of the diagram book allocated ten pages to fruit van diagrams, but in the event only four of them were used. The first three were pre-nationalisation designs built by British Railways which superseded them with its own design. In the event fruit traffic dropped off to such an extent that production of special vans for this purpose ceased altogether. A similar situation will appear several times more in later parts of this book.

Diagram 230 was basically an LMS design perpetuated by British Railways. The roof was insulated, hinged shelves were fitted inside the body, and air scoops were added to the body sides to increase ventilation. Two lots were produced, one by Wolverton and the other by Faverdale. Rather surprisingly the second lot followed an order for some 750 fruit vans to what was basically an LNER design, produced by the same works. This latter, diagram 232, featured louvred vents in the lower part of the body ends in place of the side scoops of the LMS design. The pre-nationalisation contribution was completed by one hundred vans, lot 2084, to diagram 231. Both their appearance, with twin end-vents and louvred sides, and their being built at Swindon, indicated Great Western ancestry.

The Railway Executive Ideal Stocks Committee had recommended that the LMS fruit van should form the basis for future construction of the type. Thus when it appeared the British Railways fruit van was in effect the standard ventilated van complete with scoops, shelves and insulated roof. Diagram 233 was issued and three lots of 100 vans each were produced before construction ceased with lot 3009.

Plate 64. *12ton ventilated fruit van. Diagram 1/233. B875649 is a fruit van of later design. Air scoops and hinged shelves are retained, but the body is now based on the standard ventilated van of diagram 1/208. Millerhill, 30 June 1968.* (Author).

Banana vans

The history of the development of the banana van under British Railways is similar to that of the fruit van, although the demise of rail use is complicated somewhat by a change in transport methods. Up until a few years ago it was considered necessary to heat the fruit on the last stage of its journey and the railways' ability to provide steam-heated vans ensured its share of the traffic. Present methods of handling do not call for heating, which has meant that no banana traffic now passes by rail.

Banana van development on British Railways has tended to follow LMS practice, even to the point of perpetuating its 9ft wheelbase on the first two designs. Construction began with two lots to diagram 240, rated at 10tons capacity. They were followed by 150 vans to diagram 241 which was nigh-on identical except for small journals and its being rated at 8tons. Beginning with lot 2346 construction was to yet another diagram, 242. Capacity was still 8tons but Derby's hallowed 9ft wheelbase had at last given way to 10ft. Eventually 700 vans were produced to this design.

Beginning with lot 3010, produced as part of the 1957 programme, steam heating was abandoned and vans to this design, diagram 243, were merely insulated and fitted with a steam pipe. Lot 3119, diagram 244, was a development of the design with improved buffing and brake gear while the final BR design, diagram 246, finally abandoned the LMS body style in favour of one closely akin to that of the standard ventilated van.

Plate 65. *Banana van. Diagram 1/242 (third diagram). No fewer than six different banana van diagrams were issued. B880876 was one of the first to feature a 10ft wheelbase, the previous ones being 9ft only. The trader's label was regularly used on banana vans, as seen here at Millerhill on 30 March 1963.* (Author).

Figure 34. *Banana van. Diagram 1/244. This was the fifth banana van diagram, the principal changes from 1/242 being the addition of body bracing and the provision of 2ft 0½in buffers in place of the usual 1ft 8½in ones.*

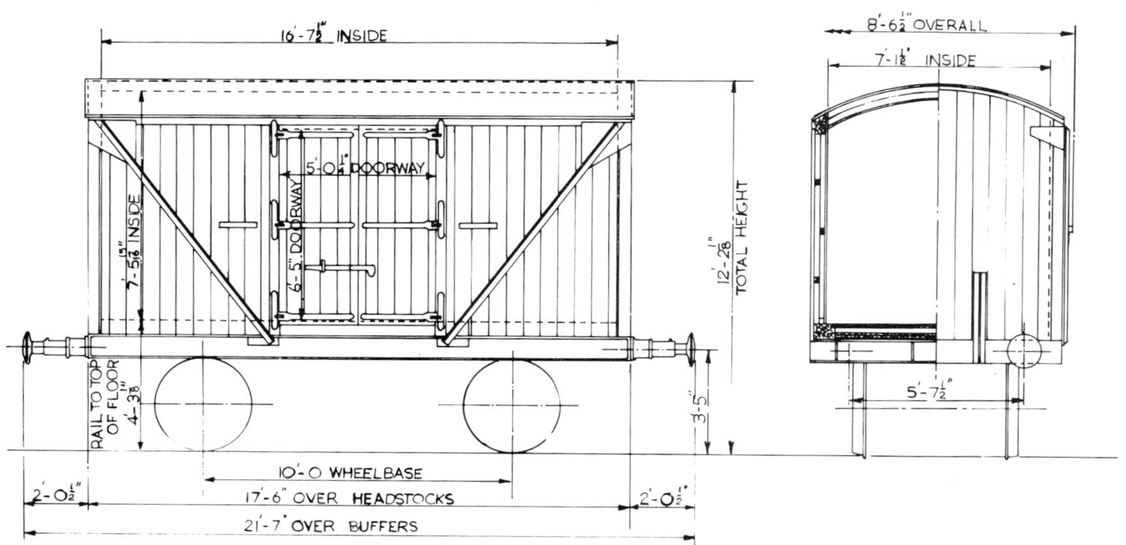

Meat vans

The Ideal Stocks Committee came to no firm conclusion over future meat-van requirements. In the event most rail movement of meat was to be by container, but not before two designs of meat van had been produced and two lots built to each design. Diagram 250 covered the ventilated version, which was to all intents the standard ventilated van equipped with meat bars and hooks and provided with side louvres and four hooded vents at each end. The most remarkable thing about these vans (there were 150 of them) was that at first they received passenger livery. The insulated version had no vents and reduced internal dimensions. 250 were built and received the white livery, later changed to light blue. All examples of both designs were built at Wolverton and were rated at 10tons.

Gunpowder vans

In appearance gunpowder vans built by British Railways were little different from those built before nationalisation and even some built before the grouping. Unlike the pre-group examples their livery has always been unexceptional, with only the word 'Gunpowder' to distinguish them.

Although some five lots were built to the first diagram, 260, they amounted to no more than 120 examples in total, of which Swindon built ninety-five. Apart from body lining they were all-steel and they closely resembled the GWR type. As part of the 1958 and 1959 programmes Swindon built a further 40 gunpowder vans, this time to the newer diagram 261. The body style was the same and length over headstocks remained at 16ft 6in, but wheelbase was now 10ft with vacuum brake and hydraulic buffers provided. Capacity remained at 11tons and no more gunpowder vans were built.

Miscellaneous

Before dealing with the covered hoppers there remains a group of vans best described as miscellaneous. British Railways seems to have allotted the last ten diagrams in the van series on this basis also.

Diagram 290 covered the 5ton Bocar, code name for a carflat with roof and ends and, like the carflat, probably derived from redundant carriages. It is believed that tarpaulin side sheets were provided. Thirty-six vehicles were built at Wolverton to lot 3090. A further eight vehicles, coded Bocar P, were built at Derby to diagram 293 as lot 3547.

Plate 66. *10ton ventilated meat van. Diagram 1/250. Although using the standard ventilated van body, these meat vans were recognisable by the four vents at each end, and originally by their crimson lake* (sic) *passenger livery. By 18 April 1965 this example had been converted for ale traffic, and like all the others was in red bauxite livery. Photograph taken at Millerhill.* (Author).

Plate 67. *10ton insulated meat van. Diagram 1/251. Again it is obvious that the standard 12ton van was the basis for the insulated meat van, the absence of any end vents being noticeable. The insulated sides and ends made for a reduced floor area, and as with the previous diagram meat bars and hooks were provided. When photographed at Millerhill on 23 February 1963 B872112's body was white with black lettering. It would later be changed to pale blue with white letters.* (Author).

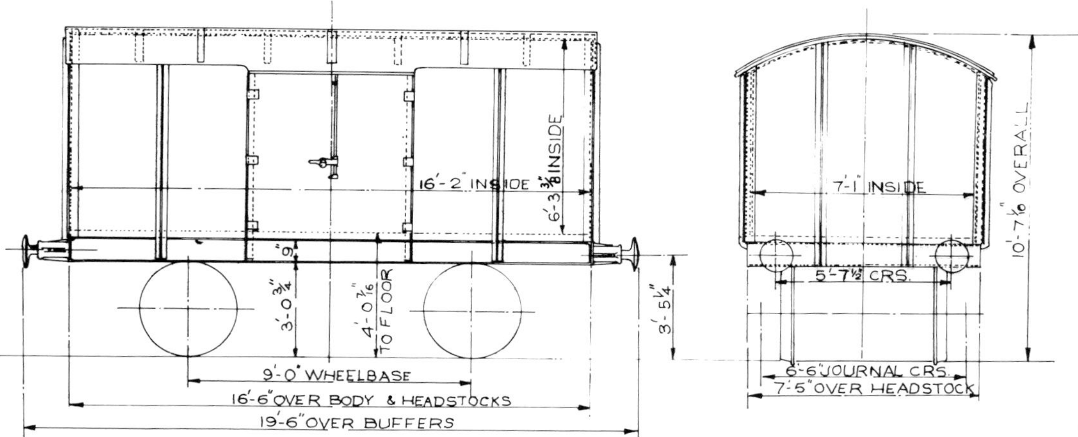

Figure 35. *11ton gunpowder van — lettered Gunpowder. Diagram 1/260. The basic design of gunpowder van on British Railways was established long before 1948, and BR produced no surprises. The second diagram (1/261) had vacuum brake, hydraulic buffers and a wheelbase increased to 10ft.*

Diagrams 291 and 292 covered vans for continental ferry services and appropriately construction was handled by former Southern Railway workshops. The first was a 14ton motor car van, a four-wheeled design 30ft 6in over headstocks, with side and end doors. In contrast the second, although still rated at 14tons and of similar profile, was a scenery van 56ft 11in over headstocks and carried on two four-wheeled bogies. Had it not been for their continental role both diagrams would have appeared in the carriage diagram book.

Apart from these diagrams two further ones, 255 and 256, were allocated for fish vans transferred from coaching stock. These were almost certainly ex-'Blue Spot' fish vans made redundant by the cessation of fish traffic.

Covered hoppers

At first sight it is rather surprising to find covered hoppers among the vans, yet there is a certain logic in such a placing since they carry merchandise (in commercial terms) rather than minerals and what is more they are, quite literally, covered merchandise wagons. Nevertheless, it must be conceded that the distinction is a rather subtle one, and what is more it is one which eluded British Railways. The first covered hopper design appeared in 1952 and in early diagram books it was allocated to page 192 amongst the mineral wagons. Later it was re-allocated to page 210 but with capacity shown as 24tons in place of the original 25tons. Construction of the first 1,337 vehicles to this design was in seventeen lots built at Derby, and all examples had hand brakes only. For the last two lots construction shifted to Ashford, and of these the penultimate one received through vacuum brake pipes, while the last lot was provided with vacuum-operated disc brakes. Some covered hoppers were converted to carry sugar.

Both the Great Western and LNER companies favoured wooden bodies for bulk grain hoppers while the LMS went in for all-steel vehicles. It is believed the grain trade favoured the wooden body, but nevertheless the LMS design was perpetuated. The first 20ton Hopper Grain van, diagram 270, was virtually the LMS design but only ran to one lot of 40 wagons. The following design, diagram 271, showed only minor changes to the body. After 570 wagons had been built to this second style, that in its turn was superseded by diagram 275 showing further slight dimensional differences but also having Dowty buffers. One hundred examples were produced before construction ceased in favour of larger wagons, owned by or leased to private operators.

In contrast to the hopper grain wagon the 20ton hopper cement wagon, code name Presflo, owed little if anything to the pre-nationalisation companies. As the name suggests, the wagon works on the principle that while loading is by gravity the contents are discharged with the help of compressed air. A prototype was ordered on 13 January 1954; lot number 2679 was allocated and diagram

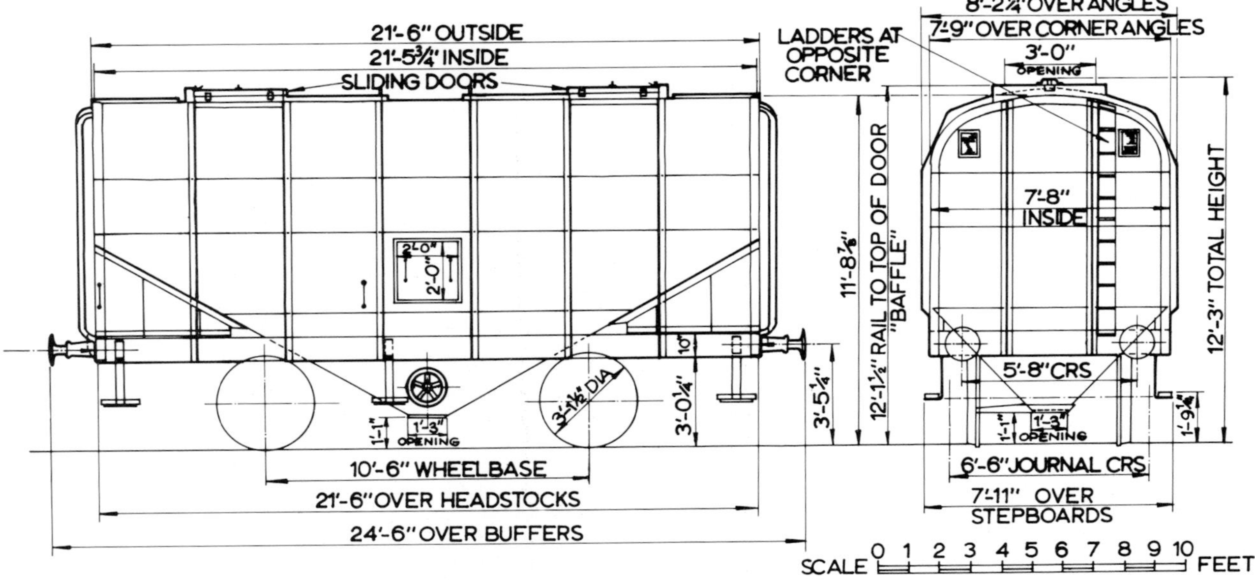

Figure 36. *20ton hopper grain van. Diagram 1/270. The first grain hoppers were built to this diagram which was basically an LMS design, even to the extent of repeating the observation windows at each end. These windows were omitted on the later diagram, 1/271, to which the majority of the type were produced.*

273 prepared. Shildon works had completed building by 19 June 1954. The lot book contains a note that the diagram was 'not issued'. Subsequent construction was all to the (apparently earlier) diagram 272 although, as this shows, it covered numerous variations. Including the prototype, some 1,891 cement-carrying Presflos were built plus a further thirty wagons of lot 3029, which were designated for salt traffic. These latter were followed by a lot of fifteen 20ton salt wagons built as side discharge wagons to lot 3134. Again there seems to have been confusion with digrams, because they were at first allocated to page 274 before being finally placed amongst the merchandise wagons as diagram 85.

Once released, diagram 274 was soon reallocated to a new design of air discharge wagon, the 20ton Prestwin. With its distinctive appearance it could almost be described as carrying two inverted whisky stills. Some thirty-one wagons were built to this diagram followed by one hundred to an improved design, diagram 277. These Prestwin wagons were followed by a series of pressurised dry fly ash wagons for the conveyance of

Plate 68. *20ton hopper grain van. Diagram 1/271. With roller-bearings, hydraulic buffers and fully-fitted brake gear B885689 — one of the last batch — has been updated and has also been fitted with air discharge apparatus. The author wishes to point out that the 'Sodd old Eddie' is entirely unofficial! Millerhill, 15 November 1964.* (Author).

power station ash. They were in effect a development of the cement Presflo — in fact the first was actually B873082, a Presflo from lot 3323, for which diagram 281 was allocated. It was rated at 17tons. A further twenty-two wagons were built new as lot 3483. They had a slightly increased capacity and were given a new diagram, No 278. In its turn this design was followed by a larger 21ton version, diagram 279. There was a similar story of a prototype, lot 3491, followed by 84 vehicles in two lots, 3515 and 3516. The remaining covered hopper design is the 23ton calcium carbide wagon. Like the Prestwin it consists of twin cylindrical hoppers but discharge is solely by gravity. The single order for forty wagons, lot 3371, was placed with Powell Duffryn, formerly the Cambrian Wagon Company.

Plate 69. *20ton hopper cement wagon. 1/273. The principle of using compressed air to assist the unloading of powders which compact in transit was first applied to cement traffic. This picture taken at Brentford on 11 August 1954 shows B888000, the prototype, lettered with the code name 'Presflo', being unloaded with the aid of a portable compressor.* (British Railways).

Plate 70. *20ton Prestwin wagon. Diagram 1/277. The Prestwin was a development of the Presflo idea, but with twin conical silos in preference to the single one. The first design used the standard 17ft 6in underframe but for this, the second one, an increase of 2ft in frame length allowed overall height to be reduced with capacity increased at the same time. Millerhill, 30 March 1963.* (Author).

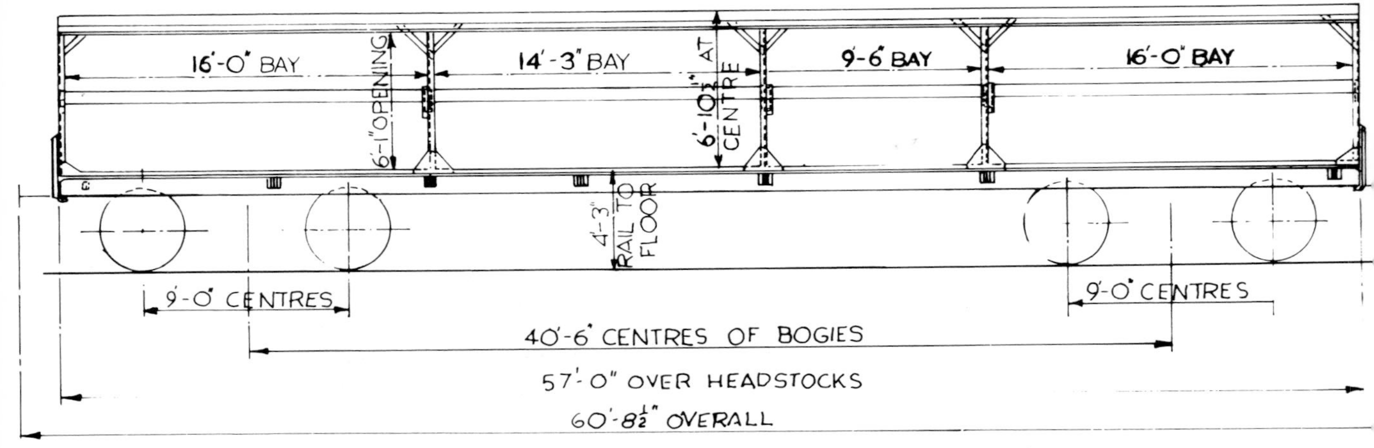

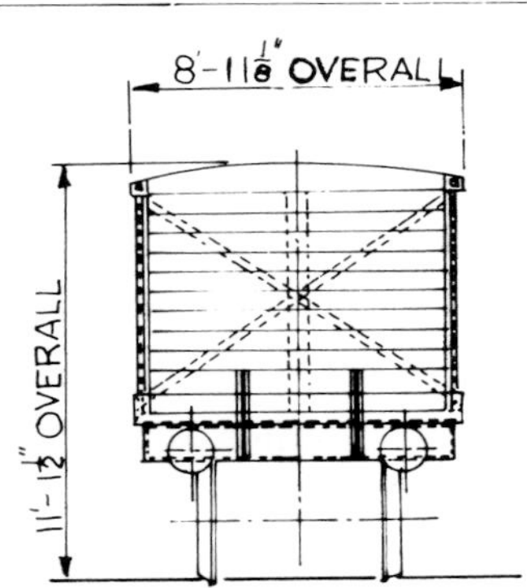

Figure 37. *Bocar. Diagram 1/290. At one time virtually every Rolls Royce motor car made its first journey in one of these wagons (or in one of the similar ones built by the Great Western) because they were used to transport the car bodies from the Pressed Steel plant at Oxford. Redundant passenger carriage underframes have been used, and although the diagram does not say so it is believed that tarpaulin side sheets, suspended from the roof, gave added weather protection. (3mm — 1ft).*

Chapter 6

Tank wagons

This chapter covers those railway-owned tank wagons classed as goods vehicles which are or were built as traffic stock. It excludes service vehicles (creosote tanks for example), privately-owned tanks (such as oil tanks) and passenger-rated milk tanks. Faced with such a formidable list of exclusions the reader may well wonder just what is covered. If he is thinking that, like some insurance policies, the answer is very little, then that is so. We shall consider twenty-seven separate diagrams covering some 184 wagons in total.

The reason for this state of affairs is that traditionally the tank wagon has been a privately-owned vehicle, the nature of its load not making for a common-user approach. Thus in the relatively few instances where the railway has built tank wagons it has almost always been as part of an agreement with a specific customer. Frequently, especially with demountable tanks, the railway has provided the underframe while the actual tank has remained the property of the customer.

Before considering the various designs it may be mentioned that there has been something of a mystery in the past over just how many tank wagons were in use. The British Transport Commission Report for 1962 (p126) can be no more specific than saying,

'In addition . . . the following were authorised for working over British Railways lines at the end of 1962:

(a) . . .

(b) 4,376 privately owned wagons (excluding tank wagons) for the conveyance of special traffics . . .'

It is believed that a special survey had to be undertaken before the inauguration of the TOPS wagon control system to find out how many had to be put on the rolling stock file. In the diagram book fifty pages were allocated for tank wagons, pp300 to 324 for designs with fixed tanks and pp325 to 349 for those with demountable tanks. As things turned out some eight and nineteen diagrams respectively have been issued.

Fixed tanks

The 40ton rubber latex tanks built to diagram 300 are a good example of the division of ownership referred to above. When the first six examples were built as lot 2076 they were unusual for this country as being bogie wagons — for this was 1949, not 1979 — and, apparently, in being railway-owned. But the three later tanks built as lot 2621 and the subsequent six of lot 3404 are all recorded as 'Underframes for Latex Tank — tanks privately owned H. Diaper & Co' and we assume this applies to the first six as well. The latex tanks were the only bogie tankers to appear, and with one exception all the other fixed tank vehicles were simple four-wheelers. The exception was lot 2306, a single six-wheeled tank for cable compound to diagram 303. The underframe was built at Derby and the tank by Andrew Barclay & Co for Scottish Cables of Renfrew.

Diagram 301 covered ten tanks for ethylene oxide built by M. & W. Grazebrook, but details of customer and ownership are not known. With diagram 302 we have details of the two fixed-tank beer wagons to this design. They were built and owned by British Railways and hired to William McEwan & Co (now part of Scottish & Newcastle Breweries) for the carriage of beer from Edinburgh to Glasgow for bottling. Diagrams 304 and 305 were both for wagons described as '20ton tank wagon for Class A liquids.' Hurst Nelson built the only ten examples of the first diagram. Diagram 305 covered the version for continental traffic and here twenty were produced, Hurst Nelson being responsible purely for the tanks (which were almost identical to those of diagram 304) while Ashford works built the underframes.

Plate 71. *40ton bogie tank wagon (rubber latex). Diagram 1/300. To the reader accustomed to the large bogie tank wagons which became popular on BR in the 1970s, it may come as a surprise to discover that the first six of these tanks were ordered on 22 December 1948, and they were vacuum-fitted from the start. As was often the case with tank wagons, the actual tanks (as opposed to the underframe) were owned by the customer.* (British Railways).

Plate 72. *Cable compound tank. Diagram 1/303. This wagon, B749350, was very similar to the other two tanks for the same traffic supplied by the LMS in 1939 and 1947 respectively. The tank for this vehicle was built by Andrew Barclay Ltd and may have had provision for steam heating the load.* (Scottish Cables Ltd).

Charles Roberts & Co built the corresponding design for Class B liquids, designated diagram 307. Two examples were built to carry unrefined oils for Townson Tankers of Oldham. The remaining fixed-tank wagons were a group of ten to diag-

Plate 73. *20ton tank wagon for Class A liquids (for continental traffic). Diagram 1/305. The twenty wagons of the single lot (2429) to this diagram were originally numbered B749660-679, but were later transferred to Traffic Services Ltd and renumbered, almost certainly as B500800-819 in the same order. Millerhill, 25 January 1970.* (Author).

Figure 38. *Tank wagon for conveyance of propane and butane. Diagram 1/306. Other than a capacity expressed as 4,921 gallons the diagram gave no indication of the loaded weight of these wagons, but the tare was a surprisingly high 19tons 8cwt. It is understood the design was developed for traffic from the Fawley refinery.*

ram 306, built at Lancing with tanks by M. & W. Grazebrook. They were rated at 20tons and carried butane/propane for an unknown customer.

Demountable tanks

In the years immediately before and after World War II the railways made strenuous efforts to popularise the virtues of the demountable tank wagon, where a tank was loaded to a rail chassis for the trunk part of the journey with the collection and delivery being undertaken by road. The tank component could be either a tank with securing gear or alternatively a road trailer complete with wheels. This latter arrangement was less common.

The rail chassis was normally a standard 17ft 6in underframe with securing fittings designed for the particular tanks carried. One suspects that in many cases redundant underframes were utilised

Figure 39. *20ton Class B tank wagon. Diagram 1/307. The lot book indicates that the two examples built to this diagram were originally ordered for traffic in unrefined oils for Messrs Townson Tankers of Oldham, but no other information is known.*

Figure 40. *Demountable tanks for beer. Diagram 1/326. In the early years of British Railways there were numerous diagrams for demountable tanks, generally for beer, with the main differences lying in the construction of the tanks and their means of securing. It is thought that the two wagons to this diagram conveyed McEwan's beer from Edinburgh to Glasgow.*

Figure 41. *Demountable tanks for paint and varnish. Diagram 1/328. There was a single vehicle to this diagram and it was probably derived from an old GWR six-wheel carriage underframe. The four tanks it carried were owned by ICI Ltd, Slough.*

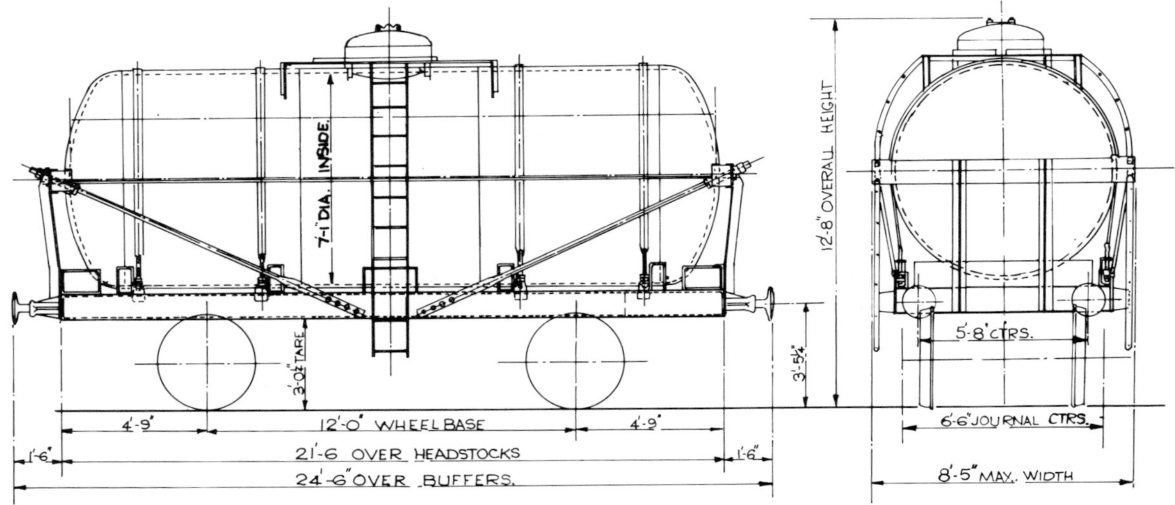

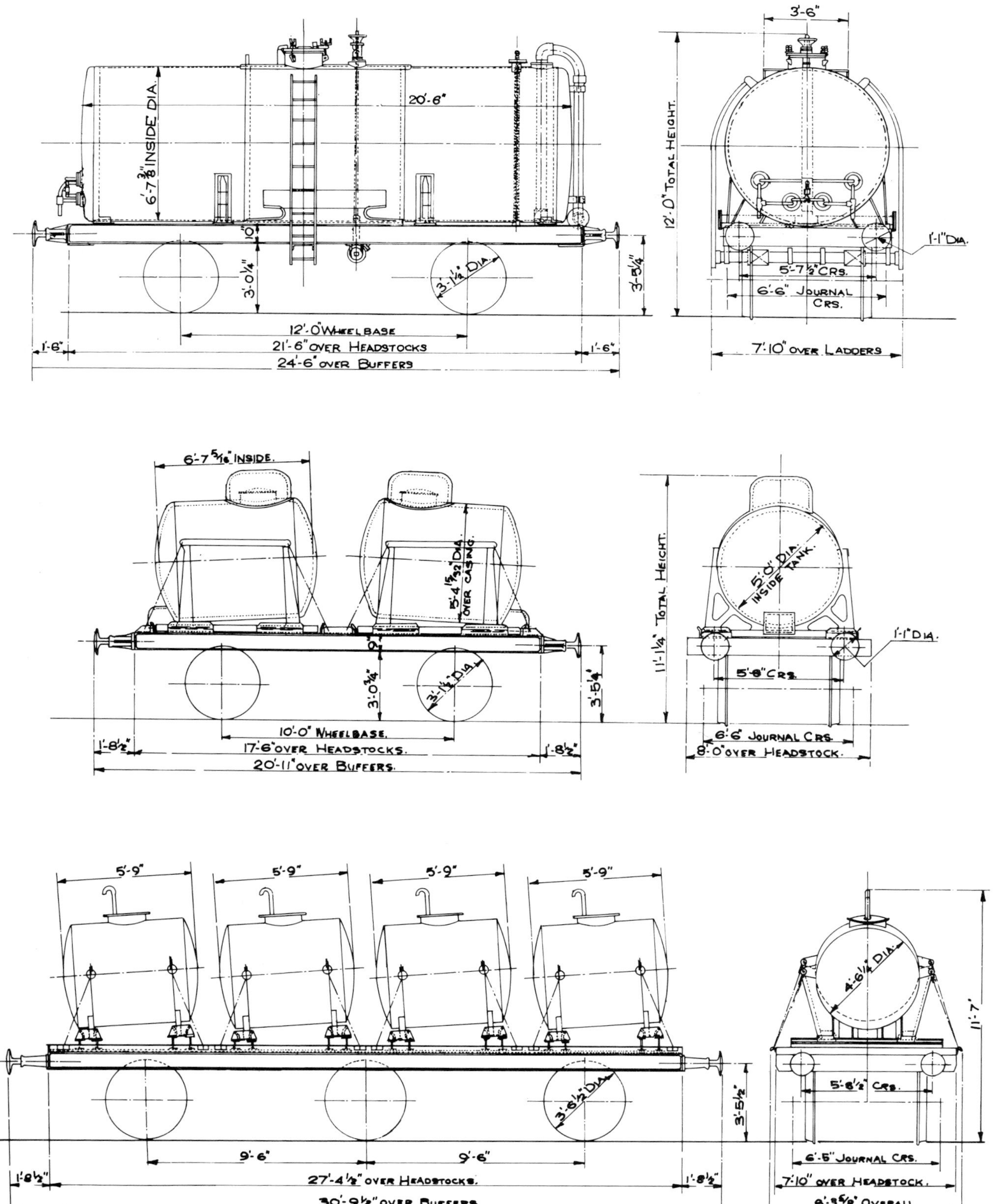

3'-6"
20'-6"
6'-7 3/8" INSIDE DIA.
12'-0" TOTAL HEIGHT.
10"
3'-0 1/4"
3'-1 1/2" DIA.
3'-5 1/4"
1'-1" DIA.
5'-7 1/2" CRS.
6'-6" JOURNAL CRS.
12'-0" WHEELBASE
21'-6" OVER HEADSTOCKS
1'-6"
1'-6"
24'-6" OVER BUFFERS
7'-10" OVER LADDERS
6'-7 5/16" INSIDE.
5'-4 15/32" DIA. OVER CASING.
5'-0" DIA. INSIDE TANK.
11'-1 1/4" TOTAL HEIGHT.
1'-1" DIA.
9"
3'-0 3/4"
3'-1 1/2" DIA.
3'-5 1/4"
5'-8" CRS.
10'-0" WHEELBASE.
1'-8 1/2"
17'-6" OVER HEADSTOCKS.
1'-8 1/2"
20'-11" OVER BUFFERS.
6'-6" JOURNAL CRS.
8'-0" OVER HEADSTOCK.
5'-9"
5'-9"
5'-9"
5'-9"
4'-6 1/4" DIA.
11'-7"
3'-6 1/2" DIA.
3'-5 1/2"
5'-8 1/2" CRS.
9'-6"
9'-6"
1'-8 1/2"
27'-4 1/2" OVER HEADSTOCKS.
1'-8 1/2"
30'-9 1/2" OVER BUFFERS.
6'-5" JOURNAL CRS.
7'-10" OVER HEADSTOCK.
8'-3 5/8" OVERALL.

for the chassis. The lot book in fact specifies that 'S/h underframes to be used' in an amendment for lot 2427 while for diagrams 339, 340 and 342 there are notes that the chassis have been converted from conflats. Diagram 341 was an LMS vehicle converted. In this connection it is interesting that when some plate wagons were converted to carry bulk malt tanks they were classified not as demountable tank wagons but as container flats to diagram 78.

There were numerous variations of size, shape and fixing arrangements among the tanks used with these underframes. On some of the later batches shock-absorbing apparatus was fitted. On top of all this the tanks carried the livery of their owners, with the result that the demountable tank wagons are a small but very mixed bag. (See table).

Plate 74. *Demountable tank for beer. Diagram 1/331. That is how the three wagons to this diagram began their careers but at least one of them, B749039, seen here, was later converted to carry adhesives from Cambridge to Inverness for use in chipboard manufacture. After this photograph was taken at Millerhill on 6 October 1962 it became redundant with the closure of the Inverness factory and was again converted, now as DB749039, to carry the water supply for the steam crane at British Railways' Haymarket depot.* (Author).

Diagram	*Chassis*				*Tank*	
	Wheels	*Wheelbase* *ft*	*Length over headstocks* *ft in*	*No of tanks*	*Wheeled*	*Tank capacity (gal/tank)*
325	4	10	17 6	1	No	1080
326	4	10	17 6	2	No	720
327	4	10	17 6	1	No	1080
328	6	19	27 4½	4	No	500
329	4	9 & 10	17 6	1	No	803
330	4	10	17 6	1	No	720
331	4	10	17 6	1	No	1080
332	6	16	24 6	1	Yes	?
333	4	10	17 6	2	No	724
334	4	10	17 6	1	No	1080
335	6	13	20 6	1	Yes	?
336	4	10	17 6	1	No	?
337	4	9	17 6	1	No	875
338	4	10	17 6	1 or 2	No	720
339	4	10	17 6	1	No	?
340	4	10	17 6	1	No	1981 or 2619
341	6	19	30 0	1	Yes	2000
342	4	10	17 6	1	No	?
343	4	10	17 6	1	No	2985

Plate 75. *Demountable tank for sodium silicate. Diagram 1/337. Apart from showing another type of demountable tank this picture illustrates such a vehicle in service. The livery should be compared with that of the same vehicles when new, in Plate 6.* (British Railways).

With changing methods in the brewing industry and the railways' decision to concentrate on block traffics, the demountable tank never really caught on. Many of the railway-owned chassis were scrapped, or in some cases converted. As an example of the latter, two examples may be cited. Wagons B749030 and B749039 were originally built for carrying beer, and put into service in 1951. By 1962 they had been converted to carry adhesives between Cambridge and Inverness. The fate of B749030 is not known, but sometime after 1962 (presumably after the closure of the chipboard factory at Inverness) B749039 was transferred to departmental stock to carry water for the breakdown steam crane at Haymarket locomotive depot.

Chapter 7

Cattle wagons

How are the mighty fallen! In all previous chapters we have recorded a steady decline in the number of wagons employed but when we come to consider the cattle wagon the description 'steady decline' is no longer appropriate — demise is the word which comes to mind. Open wagons, minerals, vans and hopper wagons can still be seen, but cattle and sheep traffic and the wagons which used to handle it are now things of the past on British Rail. From some 16,150 cattle wagons in 1938 stocks had dropped to 11,089 at the end of 1948. As 1963 dawned numbers had further dwindled to 4,409 and stocks continued to fall to the point where the National Railway Museum in 1975 just managed to claim the last two examples still in traffic to add to the National Collection. Gone then are the days when a through freight might well have a couple of cattle wagons marshalled right behind the locomotive, a sign that some yard foreman had done his bit to ensure a faster transit.

Coupled with the general decline in freight traffic the railways made a conscious decision in the 1950s to opt out of the general livestock business. As they had never been common carriers of livestock no special Parliamentary powers were required, and British Railways decided to ignore all except recognised flows of cattle and sheep traffic. The abandonment of cattle and sheep loading capacity was therefore the first reduction in facilities experienced at many smaller stations. A sign of this changed approach to livestock traffic can be seen from the fact that originally some fifty pages were allocated in the diagram book for cattle wagons. In the event only four diagrams were issued, and the last new cattle wagon entered service as long ago as 9 October 1954.

In the early years of nationalisation the picture was quite different. As part of the 1949 wagon building programme no fewer than six different lots were issued for cattle wagons, involving three separate diagrams. It seems almost certain that these were in fact the remnants of the LMS, Southern and GWR wagon building programmes. Certainly the wagons built to the first diagram, No 350, bore a strong resemblance to the last design of cattle wagon built by the LMS. What is more, of the 2,350 wagons produced all except one hundred came from Derby works and that hundred were built by a contractor. Likewise, the 150 cattle wagons of lot 2064 were all built at Ashford and the design itself (diagram 351) with the circular observation holes in the doors all suggest Southern Railway origin. Both designs were of 12tons capacity with movable internal partitions to give small, medium and large van sizes as the customer required.

Although the Great Western traditionally employed only 8ton cattle wagons, the first such wagons produced by Swindon works under the authority of British Railways were in fact rated at

Plate 76. *12ton cattle wagon. Diagram 1/350. The first three cattle wagon diagrams covered Big Four designs. Here the body is an LMS inspiration and while most wagons to this diagram employed that company's type of fully fitted brake gear some of the second batch, of which this is one, used LNER style. Millerhill, 3 February 1963.* (Author).

Plate 77. *12ton cattle wagon. Diagram 1/352. British Railways finally settled on an 8ton wagon as the standard cattle wagon, but in appearance it was very similar to the 12ton version seen here. Millerhill, 10 May 1963.* (Author).

12tons. Capacity and colour apart, the 400 wagons produced to diagram 352 as Swindon's part of the 1949 programme were much the same as those they had been turning out for some years. A further 600 were built under lot 2126 in the 1950 programme. This concentration on 12ton vehicles is rather interesting because when considering cattle wagons the Ideal Stocks Committee found that in effect only the LMS used that size. In its report the Committee came up with the following figures:

*Region**	*Number and type*			*Total*
	8ton	*10ton*	*12ton*	
Western	2,260			2,260
Eastern/North Eastern	69	1,797		1,866
Southern	51	708		759
London Midland	161	680	4,906	5,747
Total	2,541	3,185	4,906	10,632

*Despite the regional titles these may well be the totals for the 'Big Four' companies at the end of 1947 as there is no reference to Scottish Region.

The Committee recommended that in future only 8ton cattle wagons should be built, and that no steam heating pipes be fitted. The result of these recommendations in lot book terms was that all future construction was to diagram 353, which was in effect an 8ton version of the previous diagram with slightly different roof profile. In the event this amounted only to some 1,300 wagons before construction ceased.

Forty vehicles from diagrams 352 and 353 were later modified for use on the Dover–Dunkerque ferry service. Modifications involved re-sheeting of the lower sides to eliminate openings, together with fitting drains in the floor which led to a urine tank. A new diagram, 354, was issued which lists the vehicles involved in the conversion but no lot number was ever issued to cover the work.

Figure 42. *8ton and 12ton cattle wagons converted for use on the Dover-Dunkerque ferry service, from pages 352 and 353. Diagram 1/354. The title says it all, but the diagram does show the differences between the 8tonners and 12tonners. The running numbers are as written out on the diagram.*

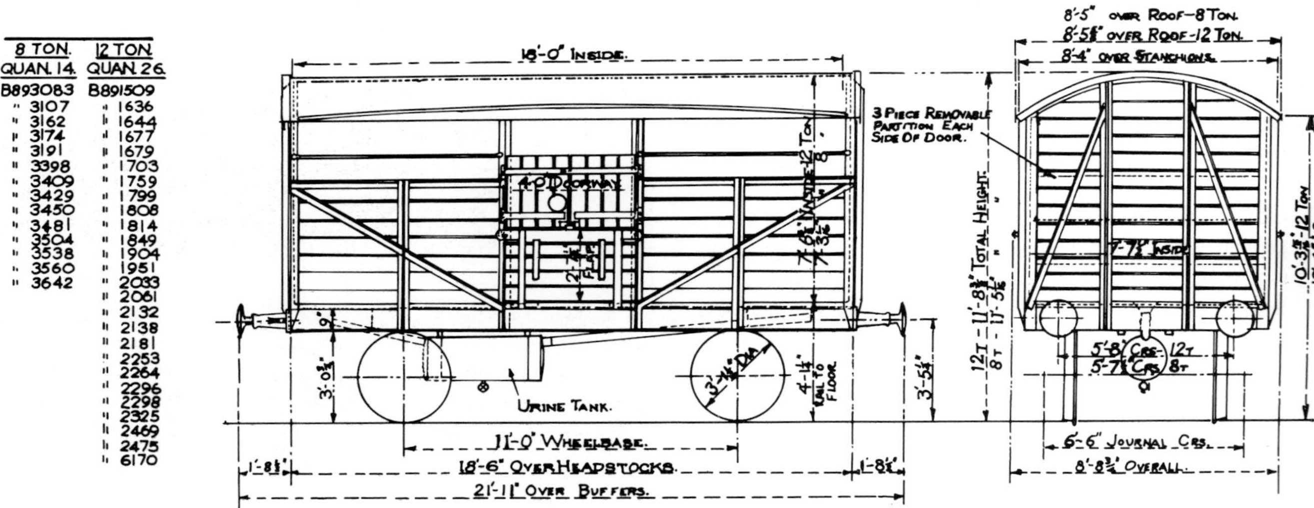

Chapter 8

Rail and timber wagons

In using the above description we are following official practice, since the statistics issued by British Railways always quote these wagons as a single group. It is believed that the practice stems from a legal requirement, possibly in the Railway Accounts Act of 1911. Certainly it is a misleading title since most of the steel carried by these wagons is in sheet, strip, plate, billet or tube forms, indeed almost anything but rail. This in itself suggests the title is archaic. In fact, most rail is carried in service vehicles which are in a separate class.

The transport of steel, for that is what this chapter is really about, has always formed a substantial part of railway freight business and one hundred pages were set aside in the diagram book (pages 400-499) for rail and timber wagons. We shall see when dealing with special types of wagon that many of them are designed to carry special loads of steel, but at this stage they will be omitted. As first set out the book allowed for single bolster wagons (15 pages), double bolsters (15 pages), plate wagons (15 pages), tube wagons (15 pages), pipe wagons (10 pages), bogie bolster wagons (20 pages) and bogie plate wagons (10 pages). In spite of the heading, timber wagons were not allowed for and the two types which did appear had to be slipped in at odd places. The fine orderly layout was then completely upset by the introduction of numerous designs of strip coil wagons, a type unforeseen when the book was first set out.

One of the main points made by the Ideal Stocks Committee was the tendency of the steel industry to change its requirements. How right it was. The Committee pointed to the steady increase in the length of tubes and pipes produced, as one example, but it is doubtful if even the members foresaw the increasing requirement for the carriage of large coils of steel strip. The Committee recommended continued co-operation with the British Iron & Steel Federation to anticipate any change in wagon requirements.

Single bolster wagons

The Committee's other recommendation was that no more single bolster wagons be built, bogie bolsters being considered more suitable. It was pointed out that only the LNER, for the North Eastern Area, was still building single bolsters at the beginning of World War II and it rather looked as if pages 400 to 414 would never be used. However, by the time the report appeared, Shildon works had already built its first 500 single bolster wagons for BR (lot 2034) and followed them with a further 500 to lot 2131. Their size (8ft wheelbase, 15ft 6in over headstocks) and their appearance all suggest they were to an LNER order taken over by British Railways, so diagram 400 was issued.

Then there was a break in single bolster production for several years, presumably in accordance with the official recommendation, but by the end of 1954 things had changed sufficiently for the North Eastern Region to get 3,000 into the 1956 programme. They were in three lots, two of them (2783 and 2860) each of 1,000 wagons to diagram 400, plus a further lot (2861) also of 1,000 wagons to a

Plate 78. *13ton single bolster wagon, steel body, wood floor. Diagram 1/400. This was very much an LNER design, even employing that company's axlebox covers. Probably the most noteworthy point is the absence of a patch for the tare weight. Photographed at Shildon Works, probably March 1949.* (British Railways).

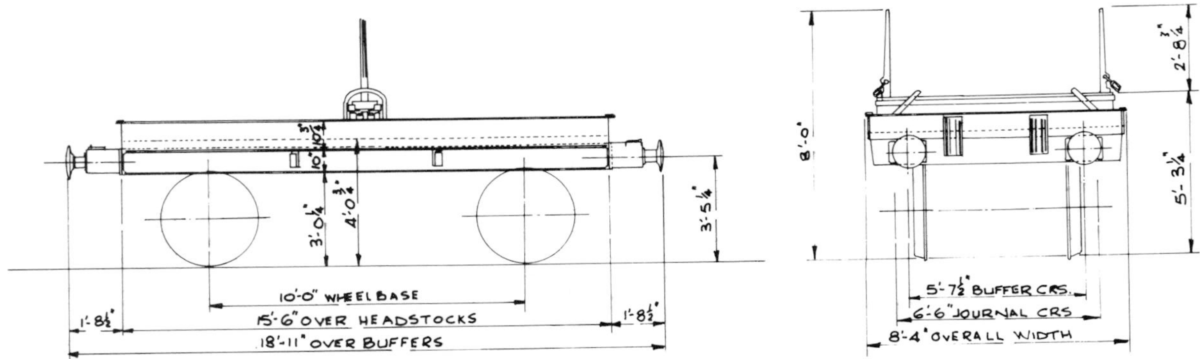

Figure 43. *13ton single bolster wagon. Diagram 1/402. Body length remains at 15ft 6in as it was in the two previous diagrams, but wheelbase has increased from 8ft to 10ft, and hydraulic buffers are fitted.*

new diagram 401. At least in one way it was a new diagram but in another it was not, because in 1951 Swindon works had built thirty-five 42ton strip coil wagons. They were a new type that no-one had foreseen and they were originally allocated to page 80 until someone twigged, when they were given instead the next available page among the steel carriers, which happened to be 401. By the time Shildon's new single bolsters appeared on the scene the Swindon wagons had all been converted and given a new diagram 407, so the bolsters were able to take their rightful place.

The next single bolster wagons to be built were two lots each of 2,000, part of the 1957 programme. They were still 15ft 6in over headstocks but the wheelbase had increased to 10ft and hydraulic buffers were provided. Diagram 402 was issued. The 1958 programme allowed for another 1,000 to be built, this time with oleo-pneumatic buffers and automatic vacuum brake to diagram 405. In the event the order was halted when only 496 had been built, and they were the last single bolster wagons to appear.

Plate 79. *13ton single bolster wagon. Diagram 1/405. This was the final development of the single bolster with fully-fitted brake gear and oleo-pneumatic buffers. It is believed that most of the wagons built to this diagram were quickly converted to twin bolster wagons. Millerhill, 3 February 1963.* (Author).

Double bolster wagons

Although the Ideal Stocks Committee did not inveigh against the double bolster wagon in the way it did against the single, very few double bolster wagons were actually built, some 400 to be precise. This was probably because a lot had been built for the carriage of 25ft-long steel billets during the war, and the traffic had tailed off once hostilities were over. Pages 415 and 416 both cover 21ton double bolster wagons and the differences between them are minor. As part of the 1949 programme Shildon works built 200 to diagram 415 and Wolverton works produced a further 200 to diagram 416.

While no more double bolster wagons were built this is probably the most appropriate point to deal with two groups of twin bolster wagons. All were conversions of existing wagons and in three of the cases very little is known. Diagrams 410, 437 and 438 all cover 26ton twin sets created by permanently coupling together two suitable wagons and, if required, fitting a bolster to each. Modified Lowfits were used in the first-mentioned, while Conflat As and single bolster wagons were used in the other two. Numbers involved are not known and no copies of the diagrams have been seen.

The fourth group involved forty-four 11ton ex-War Department ramp wagons which became

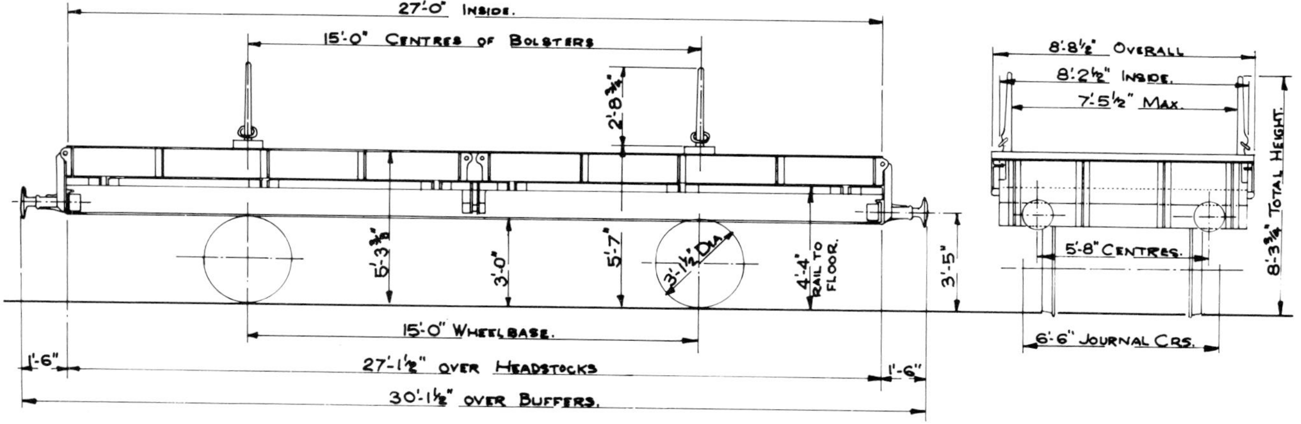

Figure 44. *21ton double bolster wagon. Diagram 1/415. The double bolster was in effect the plate wagon (*qv post*) with two bolsters. In fact on all the wagons to this particular diagram the bolsters were removable. The double bolster type was not perpetuated beyond two early lots of which some were converted to rod coil wagons and others to trestle wagons.*

Plate 80. *26ton twin sets. Diagram 1/410. The requirement for double bolster wagons was met by permanently joining pairs of redundant wagons, each of which had been fitted with a bolster. This diagram covered the conversion of an unknown number of Lowfits, two of which are seen here at Millerhill on 3 February 1963.* (Author).

Plate 81. *26ton twin sets. Diagram 1/437. Another conversion involved redundant Conflat A wagons, but again numbers involved are not known. On the two seen here the chain pockets have been removed, which alters their appearance significantly. The date of the photograph is probably March 1961.* (Author's collection).

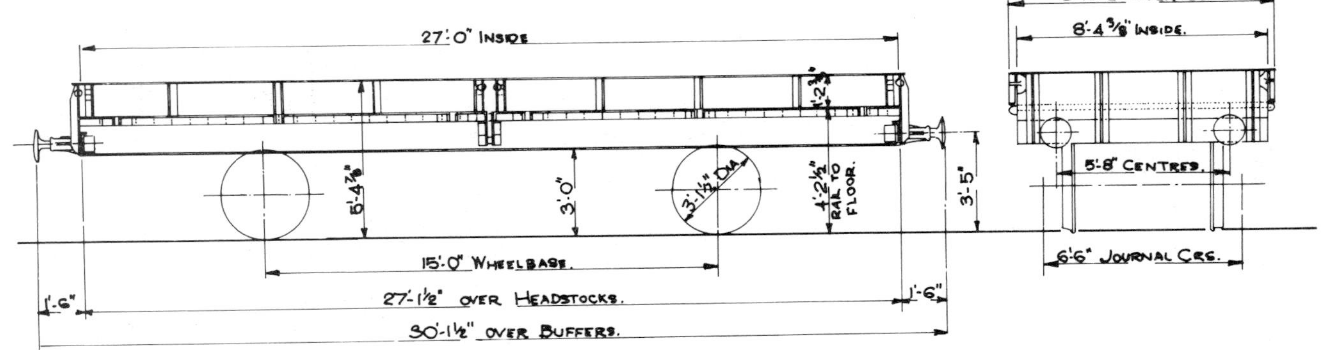

Figure 45. *12ton plate wagon. Diagram 1/430. The various plate wagon designs all shared a common body design, such variations as there were being confined to brakes, buffers and running gear. In this, the first design, the wagons were unfitted and plain 10in x 5in journals were provided.*

twenty-two sets of twin bolster wagons as lot 3419 under diagram 418. Lots 3414 to 3418 were issued at this time. We only know how many sets were covered by diagram 418 because the actual page reveals all. Indeed the whole story of these wagons and the others associated with them has some quite unusual features. As it happened, some War Department vehicles were taken into British Railways stock in 1961 and given running numbers in the former GWR series. It may well have been that the wagons had been on loan for some time and it was decided to do the honourable thing and buy them, but on paper it almost looks as if the men from Paddington had been to some mammoth Government Surplus sale to return home the proud possessors of 439 assorted Warwell, Warflat, Rectank and Ramp wagons. Certainly a study of the lot books gives the impression of some such goings-on. All the wagons were in stock by 25 March 1961, but it was not until 24 April 1961 that lot numbers were authorised and diagrams created. Just why, thirteen years after nationalisation they should have been given W-prefixed numbers is not known. To complete the story at least one wagon has been seen in traffic with a B prefix to its running number (apparently duplicating a 16ton mineral wagon) while ex-Warflat 161042 in the National Collection is recorded as carrying no prefix at all.

Plate wagons

Four diagrams were issued for plate wagons, together with one in the same range for plate wagons converted to carry BD and A containers. Between them they show a steady development of the basic design from the original version which was unfitted and had plain bearings and buffers to vacuum brakes, Isothermos or roller-bearing boxes and oleo buffers. All versions were 27ft 1½in over headstocks, with wheelbase of 15ft and capacity was constant at 22tons.

The LMS and LNER plate wagons were nigh-on identical, but it seems that the first British Railways plate wagons were in fact an ex-LNER order re-designated and given BR diagram and lot numbers 430 and 2073 respectively. In point of fact Wolverton works produced eighty-one double bolster wagons from lot 2020 without bolsters which were officially described as plate wagons, but all of lot 2020 was considered to be to diagram 416, so lot 2073 was the first plate wagons. Two more batches, a total of 800 wagons, were built to diagram 430 before it was superseded by diagram 431.

The only difference appears to be that the body was now set ¼in higher, presumably caused by improved springing. In all seven lots totalling 1,818 wagons were built to this diagram, and of these some forty-three were built for use by the Signal & Telegraph engineers. They were allocated numbers in the range reserved for service vehicles, while the last ones are recorded as having received the code name 'Winkle'. Commencing with lot 2734 a vacuum-fitted version was produced, for which diagram 432 was allocated. Instanter couplings were provided but axleboxes continued to have plain bearings. Unusually, if the diagram is to be believed, 1ft 6in buffers were fitted instead of the 1ft 8½in normally applied to vacuum-fitted stock. Beginning

Plate 82. *22ton plate wagon. Diagram 1/431. DB997539 was one of forty-three wagons to this diagram which were designated for Signal & Telegraph department use but which were otherwise identical to the remainder which were traffic stock. Ladybank, 15 March 1970.* (Author).

Plate 83. *22ton plate wagon. Diagram 1/434. The last plate wagons to be built had either roller-bearings, or as seen here Isothermos boxes, and fully-fitted brake gear. Townhill, 5 July 1964.* (Author).

with lot 3223 a further diagram (434) appeared showing hydraulic buffers in use with either Isothermos or roller-bearing axleboxes. All the final 1,000 plate wagons to this diagram, lot 3338, had roller-bearings.

In the meantime some of the original plate wagons to diagram 430 had been modified to carry two containers, a BD type and a smaller A type per wagon. As well as securing gear they had also been given automatic vacuum brakes and hydraulic buffers. As such they were re-classified diagram 433 and as a change from trundling around the country they were henceforth subjected to a nightly 400 mile run on the 'Condor' express container freight train. We shall come across these wagons again later in this chapter.

Tube wagons

Whereas all designs of plate wagon had the same basic dimensions, this is not so of the tube wagon. Length over headstocks and wheelbase both varied between designs, generally by nothing more than a few inches, and the reason for such variations is not apparent. Five diagrams were issued, and except in the case of the last one which was a design for continental traffic, each was a development of the previous version. The first tube wagons built for British Railways were of 20ton

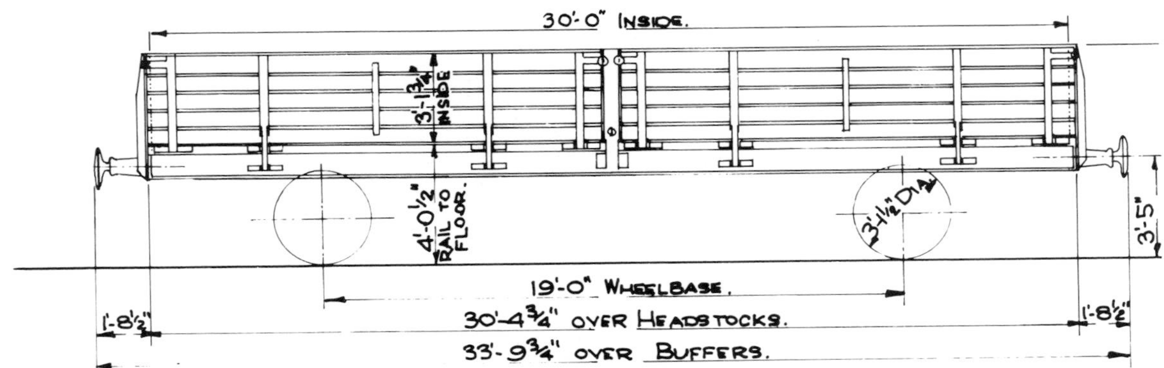

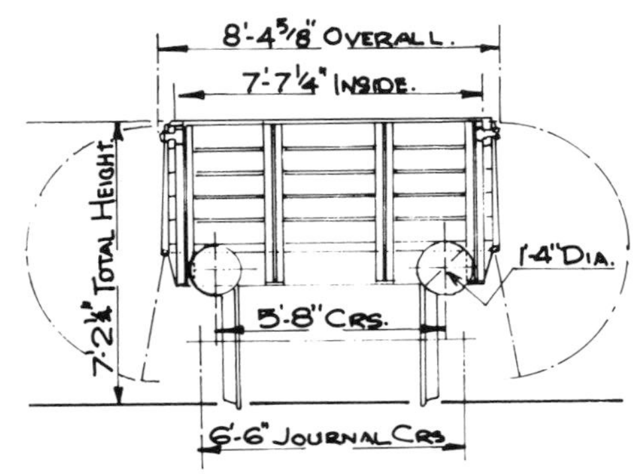

Figure 46. *20ton tube wagon — lettered Tube. Diagram 1/445. The LNER tube wagons on which this design was based had twin doors on either side. Along with a removable centre stanchion this meant that the whole side was clear for loading.*

capacity, unlike all subsequent examples which were rated at 22tons. These first 500 were built in two lots at Faverdale works; unusually for 1950 they were equipped with vacuum brakes. They were 30ft 4¾in over headstocks, giving 30ft exactly inside the body, had a wheelbase of 19ft and were allocated diagram 445. Next followed one hundred slightly smaller tube wagons to diagram 446. These were 30ft long over headstocks, had a wheelbase of 19ft 6in, no vacuum brake and had all the hallmarks of a Swindon design. They were probably an inherited Great Western order.

The next tube wagons to appear were to another diagram (447) and, with a 17ft 6in wheelbase and length over headstocks of 30ft 6in, yet another set

Plate 84. *22ton tube wagon — lettered Tube. Diagram 1/446. Like the LMS design, the Great Western tube wagons had a single small door at the centre of each side. This diagram covered a single lot of such wagons. The trussed underframe is typically Great Western. Millerhill, 27 April 1968.* (Author).

of dimensions. Although Swindon, Faverdale and Wolverton works each built a batch the design seems to have been LMS-inspired. Not until the appearance of lot 2554 in late 1953/early 1954 do we seem to have got down to a British Railways standard. Length was now 32ft and wheelbase 18ft 6in. Although the diagram on page 448 makes no mention, later examples were equipped with automatic vacuum brake. Altogether 2,350 wagons were produced to this design. Diagram 449 was essentially a variation covering twenty wagons equipped for continental working, and which as a result were 3tons 1cwt heavier.

Pipe wagons

In contrast to the tube wagons, with pipe wagons we have all four diagrams showing the same basic dimensions as we encountered with the plate wagons. Like the plate wagon the pipe wagon has been found useful for conversion, something that has rarely happened with the tube wagon. The first 300 pipe wagons were built at Derby works to diagram 460, and to what appears to have been an LMS drawing. They were followed by a further 300 from Faverdale works to diagram 461, virtually the same but to an LNER drawing and fitted with automatic vacuum brake. But fitting vacuum brakes to humble pipe wagons was really rather *avant garde* in 1949, so for the next four lots it was back to diagram 460. It remained that way until 1956 when Wolverton works began fitting vacuum

Plate 85. *22ton tube wagon — lettered Tube. Diagram 1/448. Numerically this was the most important tube wagon design, and all except the first lot were equipped with vacuum brakes from new. Later examples had Isothermos axleboxes. B733040 was photographed at Stooperdale (Darlington) works about April 1959.* (British Railways).

Plate 86. *13ton pipe wagon. Diagram 1/460. B740000 was the first pipe wagon to be built and was then rated at 12tons, later to be increased to 13tons. Also of interest is the livery with the unpainted body planking. Photographed at Derby about May 1949.* (British Railways).

Figure 47. *12ton pipe wagon — lettered Pipefit. Diagram 1/463. After the capacity had been increased from 12tons to 13tons it was later reduced to the original figure when the vacuum-fitted versions of the pipe wagon emerged. The twenty wagons to this diagram were fitted with hydraulic buffers from new.*

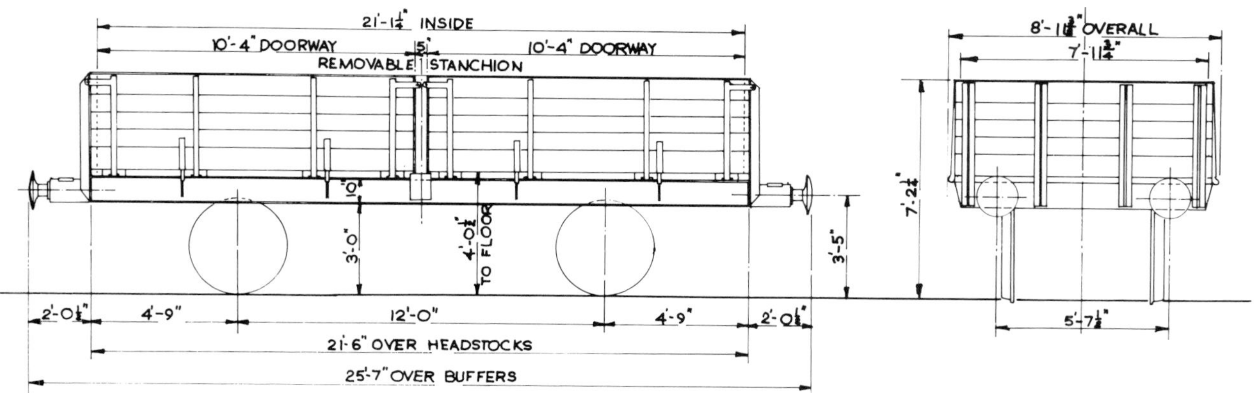

brakes to its pipe wagons for which a new diagram, No 462, had been issued. A further diagram, No 463, was issued to cover twenty wagons fitted with hydraulic buffers in 1957, but for lot 3335 construction reverted to spindle buffers and diagram 462.

Bogie bolster wagons

One result of the Ideal Stocks Committee's forecast of changes in the steel industry was the acceptance of an increased requirement for bogie vehicles. Consequently, right from the start, bogie steel carriers were not treated solely as special vehicles by British Railways and thirty pages were set aside for general service bogie steel-carrying wagons.

Bogie bolsters were far and away the most numerous of all traditional bogie freight vehicles. They were divided into a number of sub-groups according to overall length. As capacity is generally (although not always) related to length, then as a general rule the longer the wagon the greater its capacity. Going in alphabetical order the smallest are the Bogie Bolster As. There has only been one lot of five wagons and they were part of Swindon's bargain sale referred to above. They were in fact converted Rectank wagons 34ft over headstocks and were allocated diagram 487. Likewise all the Bogie Bolster Bs were from the same source, only this time there were two different types. Diagram 485 covered 255 converted Warflats of 50tons capacity and 40ft long over headstocks. Some are recorded as having been vacuum fitted. The other examples were one lot of forty converted Warwell As, some of which again were vacuum fitted. Diagram 486 was allotted to them and capacity was 30tons.

Coming to the larger Bogie Bolster Cs, we are dealing for the first time with a British Railways design. Five diagrams cover the type and all examples are 45ft over headstocks with a 30ton capacity. No fewer than 1,398 examples were built to diagram 471, which was the earliest of the five. Of these, forty-eight were service vehicles earmarked for use by the Signal & Telegraph department. Beginning with lot 2496 the journal size was increased from 8in x 4½in to 9in x 4½in and a new diagram, No 473, was issued to which 891 wagons, including twenty-one for the S & T department, were built.

There seems little obvious difference between diagrams 473 and 474 and, except for a further increase in journal size to 10in x 5in, between these two and diagram 475. The vehicles of lot 2583 built by Metropolitan-Cammell Carriage & Wagon Co were split between diagrams 473 and 475, those of lot 2818 by the same builder were split between diagrams 474 and 475 while lot 2616 from the Birmingham Railway Carriage & Wagon Co had representatives of all three diagrams. The final 2,000 Bogie Bolster Cs were even more of a mixed bag. Although they were all to diagram 477 there was a mixture of plain and roller bearings, hydraulic and self-contained buffers, Instanter, three-link and international screw couplings, while all bar the first 600 had vacuum, brakes.

The story with the Bogie Bolster Ds is very simi-

Plate 87. *42ton bogie bolster truck — code Bogie Bolster D. Diagram 1/470. Prior to 1948 bogie wagons had always been considered as special vehicles, but British Railways decided that bogie bolsters should be treated as ordinary stock. These were the first Bogie Bolster Ds to appear and had bar-frame bogies. Drem, 18 May 1963.* (Author).

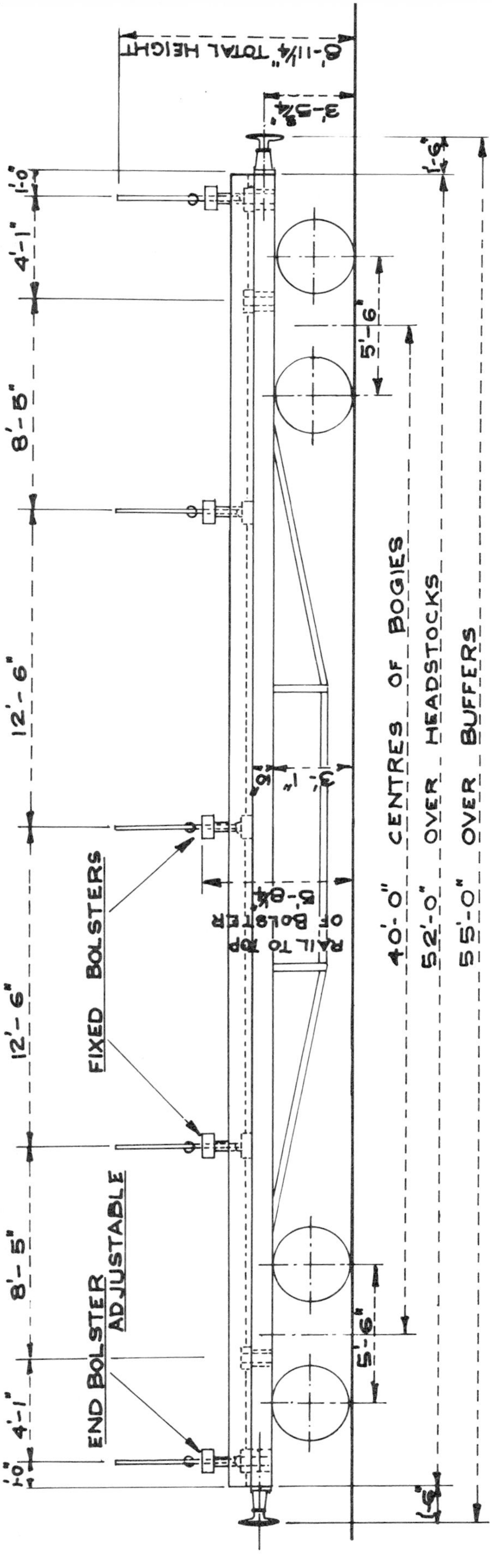

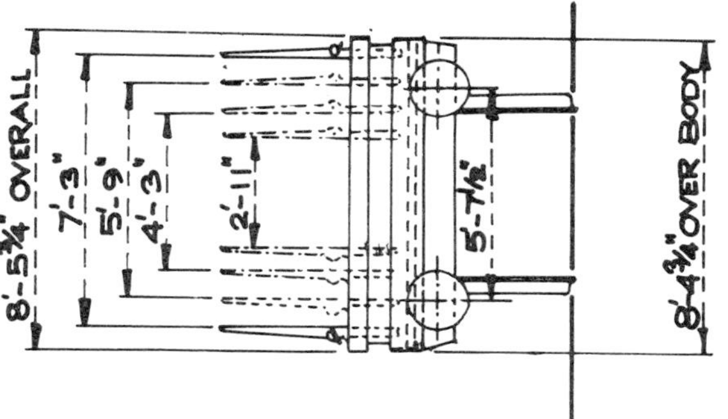

Figure 48. *42ton bogie bolster — lettered Bogie Bolster D. Diagram 1/472. After the 150 wagons to diagram 1/470 a further 2,094 were built to this diagram, the principal differences being that bolster stanchions were now 1ft taller and plate bogies were used.*

Plate 88. *30ton bogie bolster truck — lettered Bogie Bolster C. Diagram 1/473. The Bogie Bolster C was shorter than the D (45ft compared with 52ft) but like it was built in substantial numbers. This, the second diagram, called for heavier journals. The photograph was probably taken at Swindon in late 1953.* (British Railways).

lar. Again there are five diagrams, this time with a common length of 52ft and a capacity of 42tons. Construction began with a single lot of 150 wagons to diagram 470. These were followed by no fewer than eighteen lots to a new diagram, No 472, covering some 2,086 vehicles. With diagram 472 bogie wheelbase had been reduced from 6ft to 5ft 6in and braking was modified. Construction would have reached 2,272 had not 186 wagons of lot 3028 been built with shorter stanchions and designated diagram 476. Lot 3246 heralded the introduction of both vacuum brake and diagram 478. The 200 wagons to this diagram were followed by a further 400 with cast-steel bogies and designated diagram 484.

The above 400 wagons were the last Bogie Bolster Ds and were almost the last Bogie Bolsters built, until in 1961 Ashford works upset the

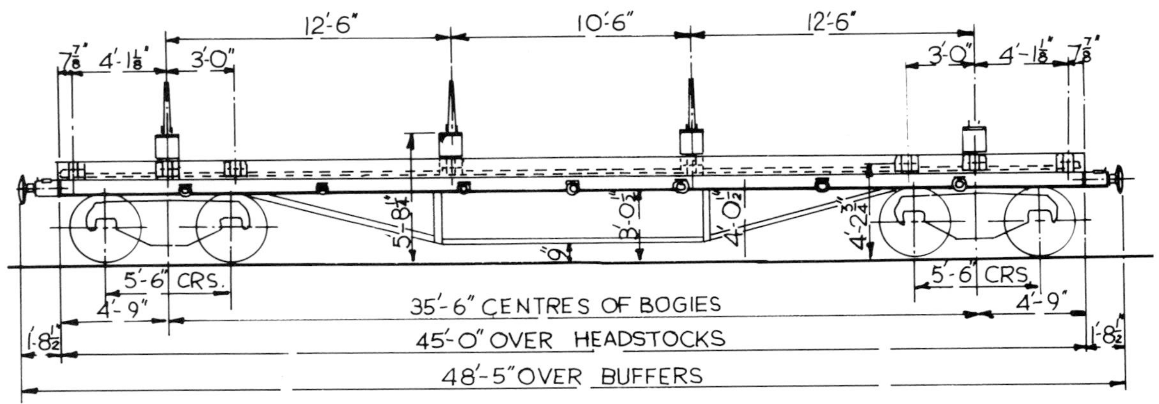

Figure 49. *30ton bogie bolster. Diagram 1/477. For a drawing we have selected a later Bogie Bolster C diagram, although strangely the code is not stated. These wagons had bogies of cast steel and some lots had vacuum brake from new. (3mm — 1ft).*

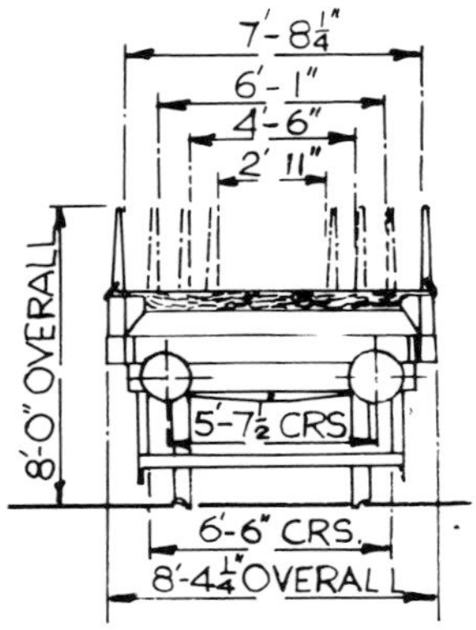

Plate 89. *30ton Bogie Bolster E. Diagram 1/479. At 32ft over headstocks the Bogie Bolster E was only 5ft longer than the four-wheeled Double Bolster. In fact it may have been considered as a direct replacement as the type was not introduced until the 1961 programme. All examples had cast-steel bogies and vacuum brake. Millerhill, 6 October 1962.* (Author).

smooth alphabetical progression by introducing the Bogie Bolster E, a 30ton vehicle which at 32ft over headstocks was shorter than the previous smallest, the Bogie Bolster A. All were vacuum-fitted from the start and all had cast-steel bogies. To complete the coverage of bogie bolster designs we must refer to two further diagrams, pages 489 and 493 respectively. Both cover the conversion of an unknown number of wagons from diagram 477. Those to diagram 489 were called Bogie Bolster Q and described as being for the conveyance of steel pipes, while those to diagram 493 were described as Bogie Bolster H without any note of intended load. Beyond that no further details are known.

Bogie rail wagons

The position with bogie rail wagons is not entirely straightforward because the diagrams describe

Plate 90. *30ton Bogie Bolster B converted from Warwell A. Diagram 1/486. This picture was taken at Ribblehead on 23 July 1960, before the wagons of this type were taken into BR stock. The words 'On loan to British Railways' are on the solebar.* (Author).

them 'Bogie Bolster Truck', the only difference being the use of the code name Borail, suitably suffixed, as opposed to Bobol for the straight bogie bolster wagons. The first diagram, 480, was for the 45ft Borail WE, which it shows to be little different from the Bogie Bolster C of diagram 473 except that capacity is now 40tons and journals are larger to cope with the heavier load. One lot of fifty wagons was built by Swindon Works as part of the 1949 programme and it may well have been an ex-Great Western order carried over. A note in the lot book claims they are 'Now described as Bogie Bolster C'.

The remaining Borail diagrams all cover wagons 62ft long over headstocks, the first three having a capacity of 50tons, later reduced to 40tons for the final diagram. Between the building of the first Borails of lot 2098 referred to above and the emergence of the next ones, fifteen of lot 3263 to diagram 481, there was a gap of ten years. The new design had roller-bearings and was vacuum piped. All the bogie wagons dealt with up to now have had the usual trussed underframe. With the Borails EC of lot 3267 and EB or MB of lot 3268 this method of construction gave way to fishbelly girders, and bogie wheelbase was extended to 10ft. The principal difference between the two types was that with the Borail EC, designed for the carriage of pre-stressed concrete beams, the load was carried on the vehicle floor whereas with the EB or MB types it was carried on bolsters. This use of a two-letter suffix will be dealt with when considering special wagons in Chapter 11. These initial orders were followed by two more, one for each diagram, giving a total build of thirty wagons to diagram 482 and 105 to diagram 483.

The final bogie rail wagons, some nineteen to diagram 488, also merit some attention. The first ten, code name Borail WF, were to GWR lot 1305 and did not receive BR numbers. The remaining wagons, code name 'Borail SA', were the last nine of an order for seventy-nine (lot 2208) Engineer's Rail wagons to diagram 641. They were given

Plate 91. *50ton Borail for conveyance of pre-stressed concrete beams — lettered Borail EC. Diagram 1/482. Another omnibus title, after which all that remains really is to draw attention to the use of fishbelly girders for the frames rather than the more usual trussing. Slateford, 3 February 1962.* (Author).

numbers in the service vehicle range (B996795 — B996803) but without the D prefix and re-allocated to diagram 488. Constructionally they were straightforward with trussed underframes, 5ft 6in bogies and 10in x 5in journals.

Bogie plate wagons

In contrast with the story of the bogie bolster and bogie rail wagons, that of the bogie plate wagons is nice and straightforward. There are three diagrams, each covering a development of the previous one. All three types are 52ft long over headstocks with shallow two-plank sides and a capacity of 42tons. There is the usual progression from plain bearings to roller boxes, buffers become hydraulic and, although the diagram does not mention it, vacuum brakes are fitted to the later examples. As can be seen from Appendix 4 construction was substantial, especially for such a relatively specialist type of wagon. The majority of the bogie plate wagons built (1,037 out of 1,412) were to the original diagram (490) followed by fifteen to diagram 491 and a further 300 to the last diagram. Two vehicles, lot 2456, were considered to be service vehicles and were numbered in the service vehicle range.

Coil wagons

Up to now this chapter has considered the development of established types of wagon. Two trends have become apparent, namely the decreasing use of the smaller wagons such as the single and

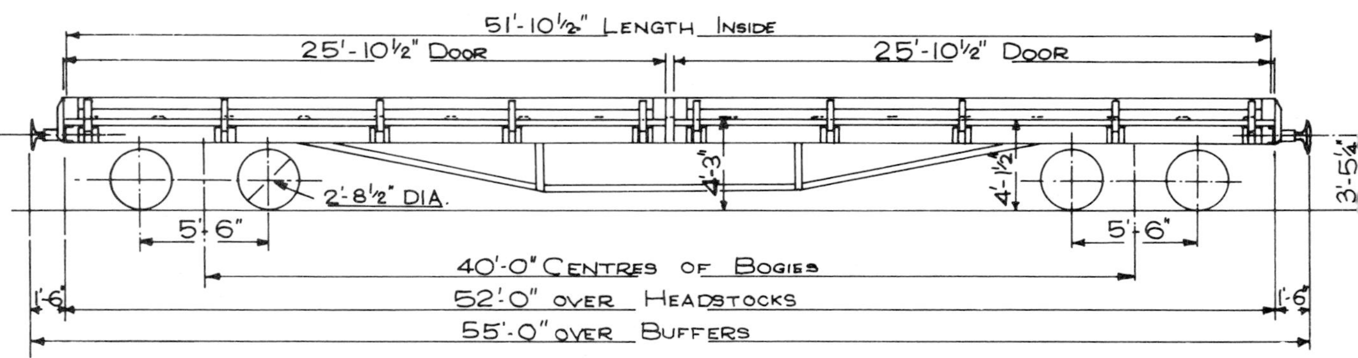

Figure 50. *42ton bogie plate wagon, code Boplate E. Diagram 1/490. There were over 1,000 of these wagons built to this diagram and they were followed by a further 300 with roller-bearings to diagram 1/492. These latter wagons had wheels 3ft 1½in diameter.* *(3mm — 1ft)*

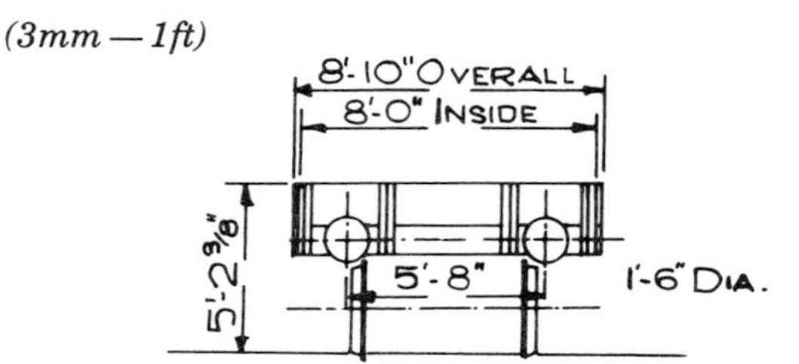

Plate 92. *42ton bogie plate wagon. Diagram 1/491. There was also a single lot of seventy-five bogie plate wagons built to this diagram at Shildon Works, but thereafter construction reverted to diagram 1/490. The photograph was taken in about February 1950.* (British Railways).

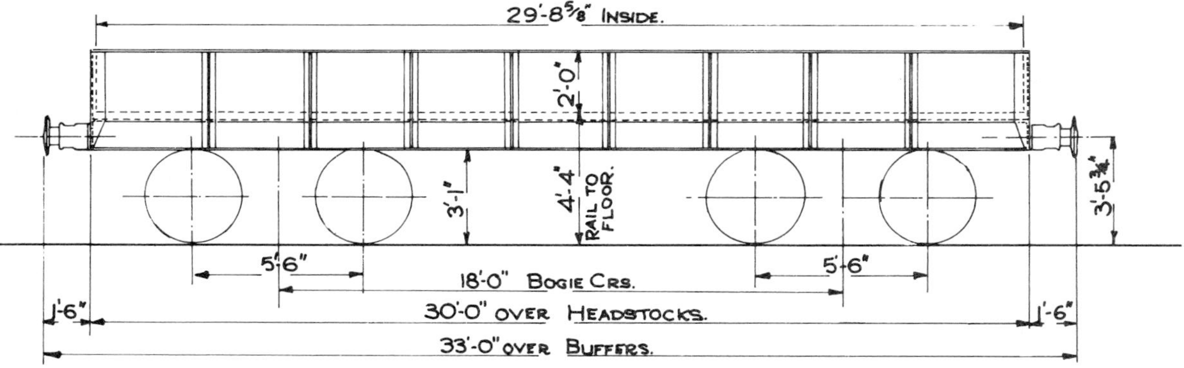

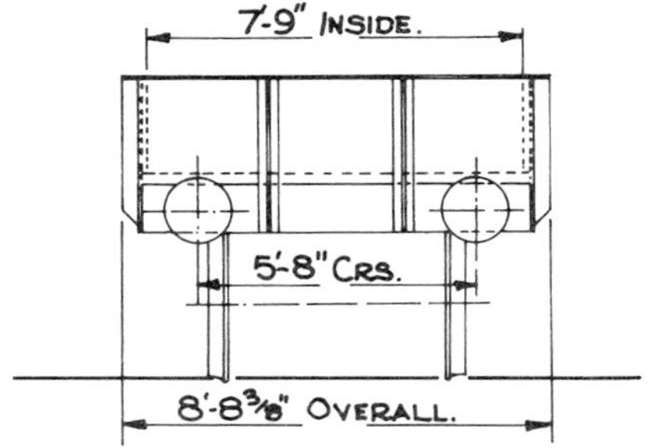

Figure 51. *42ton strip coil wagon — lettered Strip Coil. diagram 1/401. The thirty-five wagons of lot 2209 were originally considered to be to diagram 1/080 until the diagram was re-issued as shown here. This was the first issue of diagram 1/401. All the wagons were later converted to diagram 1/407, one wagon (B949004) going via diagram 1/406 in the process.*

double bolsters in favour of larger vehicles, together with the general movement towards improved brakes, bearings and buffers noted throughout the book. The Ideal Stocks Committee had allowed for changes in steel production affecting types of wagon required, but even so it is difficult to believe that the railways were not caught napping by the rapid increase in the production of rolled steel strip. They discovered that they had neither the required types nor quantities of wagons available to cope with the traffic on offer.

The reason for this suggestion lies in the fact that no less than thirty different diagrams were issued to cover a whole range of shapes and sizes of coil wagon with many different capacities. Many of the diagrams cover but a handful of wagons and in most cases they were conversions of existing types. One is tempted to wonder if there was any single wagon type that had not yielded some examples for conversion to coil wagons, but that would be rather overstating things. In fairness to the railways it should be pointed out that the upsurge in demand for coiled strip came when there was a surplus of wagons. Thus it was sound economic sense to convert existing wagons, which goes some way to explaining the plethora of diagrams. It is believed that diagrams were issued by the simple expedient of taking the next page available, but to try to make things a little simpler we shall deal with coil wagons in ascending order of capacity.

On this basis the first type is the 12ton strip coil wagon to diagram 452, covering an unknown number of converted Palbrick wagons from diagram 23. This is followed by the 13ton rod coil wagon to diagram 450, again a conversion, but in this case from high-sided open wagons to diagram 32. Once more we have no details of the number of wagons involved and in neither case have we seen a copy of the diagram.

Mention of vehicles of 16ton capacity makes one think of mineral wagons, and not surprisingly the first diagram for a strip coil wagon of this capacity, diagram 409, covers some converted mineral wagons. Two hundred vehicles from diagrams 108 and 117 were converted and the diagram even gives wagon numbers. Conversion involved securing end doors and fitting timber baulks to hold the coils. In contrast information on the other 16ton types is scarce. They were both classed as 'Coil P' with diagram 442 relating to an unknown number of wagons converted from Palbrick Bs originally built to diagram 25, while diagram 443 covers a similarly unknown number of Palbricks, this time originally built to diagrams 22 and 24.

Only one design of strip coil wagon had a capacity of 20tons, and this was diagram 423. This particular diagram was issued to cover an unknown number of pig-iron wagons from diagram 4 being

Plate 93. *20ton strip coil wagon converted from 20ton pig iron wagon to BR Diagram 4. Diagram 1/423. The drawing of the diagram shows three cradles with stanchions which should be visible over the sides but clearly are not in this view. Millerhill, 30 June 1968.* (Author).

Plate 94. *13ton coil wagon., Diagram 1/(?). We have not been able to discover what diagram (if any) was allocated to these former single bolster wagons, built in the first instance to diagram 1/402, after their conversion to sheet coil wagons. Basford Hall Sidings (Crewe), 11 October 1969.* (Author).

converted to their new role. It shows the conversion to have been similar to that carried out for diagram 409. Only slightly larger in terms of capacity were the two 21ton designs, the one code named Coil A, diagram 412, the other a rod coil wagon of diagram 429. The former covers fifty wagons built new to lot 3450 and featured a four-wheel wagon 21ft 6in long with roller-bearings and vacuum brake. Coils were carried transversly in a well 18ft long under a nylon hood supported by three movable bars. Of the rod coil wagons to diagram 429 we know little save that an unknown number were converted from double bolster wagons.

While dealing with the 21ton wagons it is a convenient point to mention that other vehicles have been converted to coil wagons over and above the types recorded. We have observed, for example, an ex-LMS 21ton locomotive coal wagon adapted for coil traffic as well as some single bolster wagons. So far as is known, details have not reached the diagram books.

Diagrams have however been prepared for four different types of 24ton coil wagon, covering a mixture of new construction and conversion. Diagram 414 is for some fifty-eight strip coil wagons built new at Derby works. Construction was spread over five separate lots and in appearance the wagons are similar to those of diagram 412. Diagram 422 was issued for an unknown number of wagons converted from pig-iron wagons which had themselves originally been built to diagram 7. The 24ton strip coil wagons of diagram 424 were code named 'Coil F' and were former plate wagons each adapted to carry four coils on cradles. Twenty-five vehicles were so treated.

Some seventy-one plate wagons were also converted to 'Coil D' wagons, this time carrying three coils each under a nylon hood. Page 435 was allocated to them in the diagram book. The next diagram, No 436, was issued to cover a single 25ton zinc ingot wagon converted from a 21ton coal wagon of lot 3390. The two remaining four-wheeled coil wagon designs were both derived from 30ton pig-iron wagons built in the first instance to diagram 5. Ten wagons were converted to diagram 428 while a further (unknown) number were converted to diagram 444.

Earlier in this chapter it was pointed out that the thirty-five 42ton bogie strip coil wagons of diagram 401 were all later converted to diagram 407. One vehicle, B949004, was first converted to diagram 406 but remained the sole example until it was further altered to conform with the remaining thirty-four wagons. In their converted form they all carried hot coils, for which purpose the steel floors were backed with asbestos. The only other 42ton strip coil wagons were fifteen wagons of diagram 403 built as lot 3014 and similar in appearance to those of diagram 407.

With the next size, the 44ton coil wagon, we are back among the Western Region's war surplus stock, for some of the 255 ex-Warflats of lot 3414 were converted to coil wagons. Thirty, designated 'Coil E', were rebuilt and classed as diagram 421. A further 20, also designated 'Coil E', were rebuilt slightly differently and classed as diagram 426,

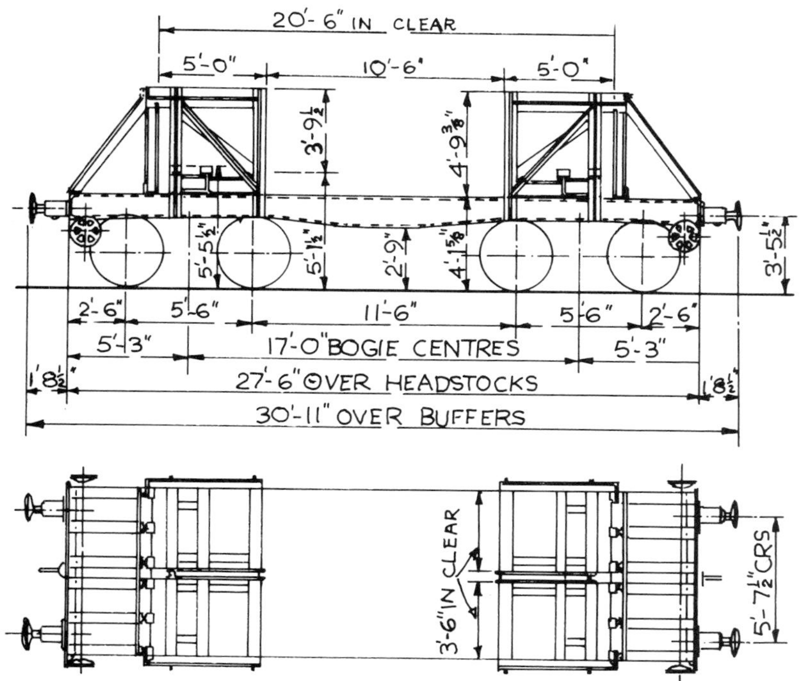

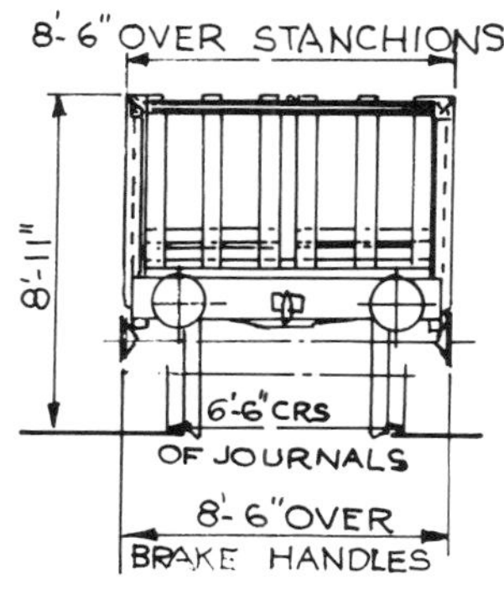

(3mm — 1ft).

Figure 52. *60ton slab wagon, double-tier loading. Diagram 1/408. The fifty wagons built as lot 3359 were all to the same basic dimensions, but there were minor variations to allow for different slab sizes, with the result that twenty were to this diagram with a further seventeen to diagram 1/417 and the rest to diagram 1/419. The latter two types had a capacity of 57tons.*

while some fifty more were also rebuilt; although similar in appearance they were considered to be to diagram 427 and were designated 'Coil G'. To complete this part of the story ten more wagons were adapted to carry coils with their axes vertical. They were uprated to 50tons and given diagram 425. Unlike the previous conversions from lot 3414, no hoods were fitted.

There was one design of coil wagon rated at 45tons and it was designed for the transport of slabs or coils if the official code name 'Slab/Coil' is

Plate 95. *45ton slab/coil wagon. Diagram 1/411. These wagons, unlike many of the smaller coil wagons which were conversions, were designed for steel slab or coil traffic from the beginning. The paint date on the wagon is 2/62.* (British Railways).

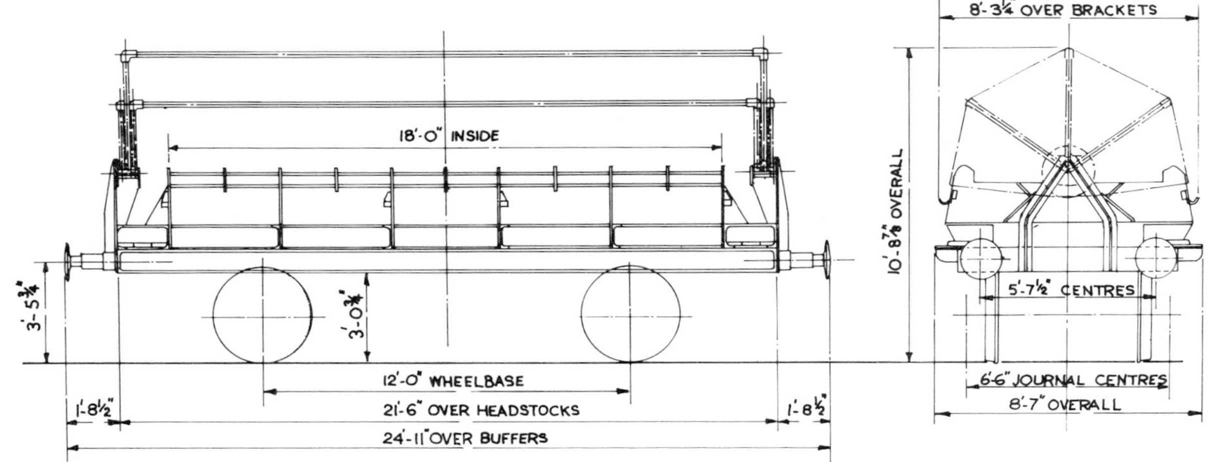

Figure 53. *24ton strip coil wagon, fitted with nylon hood. Diagram 1/414. Even though these wagons were smaller, they were built new for strip coil traffic and roller-bearings were fitted. The nylon hood was to protect the load from rain which would cause rust, and was much easier to manipulate than a wagon sheet.*

Plate 96. *56ton strip coil wagon. Diagram 1/404. A single lot of forty wagons built by Head Wrightson & Co, this design was later uprated to 60tons and a single nylon hood fitted to each wagon. The paint date is 21 February 1957. The small plate at the centre of the solebar is a 'Due for Paint 19xx' plate, the fitting of which was soon abandoned.* (British Railways).

anything to go by. Some fifty-eight wagons were built new as lot 3424 to diagram 411. They were basically well wagons with load supports. There was also a single 56ton design of coil wagon to diagram 404. Some forty wagons were built as lot 3015 but another copy of the same diagram, presumably a later revision, refers to these same vehicles as '60ton Coil Strip Wagons' and shows that nylon hoods were then fitted.

Something similar happened with lot 3359 which consisted originally of fifty 57ton Slab wagons. In fact only 20 were produced in this form (diagram 408). Of the remainder, seventeen were modified to a slightly different Slab B type, diagram 417, while the other thirteen were classed as Slab C for which diagram 419 was prepared. In the end all but one of these last thirty wagons were further modified to diagram 458 and classed as Coil T. It should be stated that for diagrams 417, 419 and 458 the capacity was quoted not as 57tons

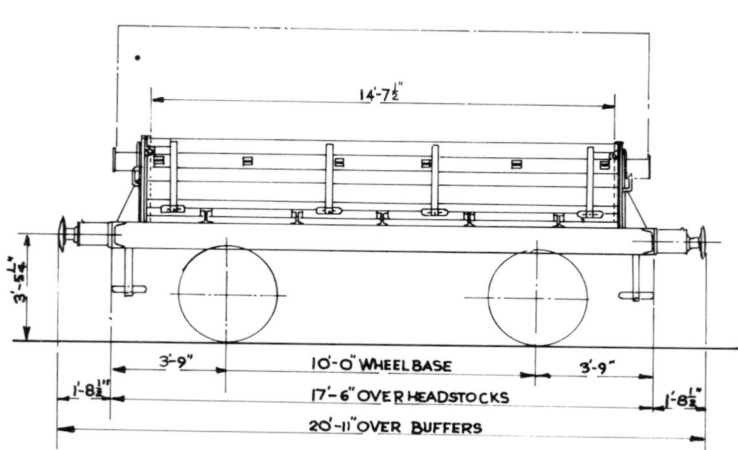

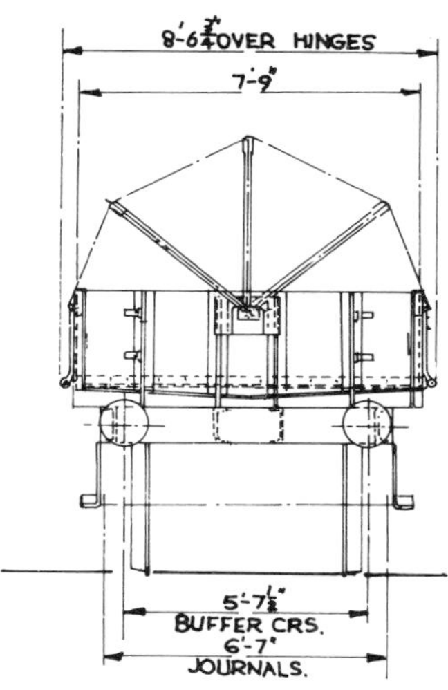

Figure 54. *30ton strip coil wagon for the conveyance of steel coil in stillages. Ex 30ton pig iron wagon. Diagram 1/428. The description is virtually a caption by itself. Ten wagons were involved. They were from lot 2857 and were originally to diagram 1/005.*

but as 60tons. The final entry in this catalogue of coil wagons is diagram 413 covering forty strip coil wagons of lot 3399, originally quoted as 56tons but later uprated to 60tons. The design itself was an uprated version of diagram 406/407, alias 401.

Timber trucks

If the reader, having become bemused by the seemingly endless catalogue of types of coil wagon, is now wondering how trucks for carrying timber can legitimately appear amongst steel-carrying vehicles we can only sympathise and offer the excuse that we are following official practice as explained at the beginning of this chapter. For among that host of plate, bolster and coil wagon designs there appear, almost at random it seems, just two timber truck diagrams.

The first, page 420, covered a group of eighty 15ton timber wagons built as a single lot at Ashford Works in 1962-3. They were all vacuum-fitted from the beginning and had a straightforward history, in contrast to the second group. The second diagram, page 439, is for the 22ton Timber P. It covers an unknown number of wagons converted from Conflat Ps which were themselves conversions from plate wagons to diagram 60. Diagram 60 claims that the original wagons were all from diagram 430 but examples from diagram 432 have also been seen. Be that as it may, they became Conflat Ps, a roller-bearing version of diagram 433. To handle traffic to the pulp mill at Corpach near Fort William some were later converted at Barassie works to become Timber P wagons, thus forming diagram 439. One rather quaint feature of the conversions was that in both instances the wagons retained their original plates, but for the second one the name of their birthplace was *chiselled* off each plate and, with a touch of local pride, 'Barassie' was neatly painted on.

Chapter 9

Brake vans

After that welter of steel wagon types, diagrams and conversions, it is both a pleasure and a relief to be able to say that British Railways produced virtually only one size of brake van and, once the official mind had been made up, virtually only one design. We have to use the word 'virtually' when talking about size, because although thousands of brake vans were built by BR and the vast majority were 20ton vehicles two, just two, 10ton examples were built for a special working. A few years back there were ominous threats of doing away with goods brakes altogether and running trains without them, something that just was not done in Hornby train-set days! However, at the time of writing, the 20ton brake van was fighting a magnificent rearguard action in every sense.

The idea of a standard brake van goes back many years. In 1934/5 unanimity was reached amongst the main line companies on all points except the provision of sanding gear. Nevertheless it was agreed that each company should be free to build either the standard van or its own design, and each built its own design! During the war the LMS built four standard vans, one for each company, but despite some prodding by the National Union of Railwaymen nothing more was done. The Ideal Stocks Committee in its report gave blessing to the idea of a standard design, and after two prototypes had been evaluated construction of the British Railways standard brake van began.

Even so, before this came to pass some 1,666 brake vans of Great Western, LMS and LNER parentage had taken to the rails under BR lot numbers. Of these, Swindon works was responsible for seventy-six, all but two of them to its standard 20ton design built as lot 2099 and allocated page 502 in the diagram book. The other two

Plate 97. *20ton goods brake van. Diagram 1/500. Although at first glance this may seem to be the British Railways standard goods brake, the stepboards stopping just beyond the axleboxes and the lack of handrails to the end platforms confirm that it is in fact an LNER design built by British Railways. Oakleigh Sidings, 26 March 1960.* (Author).

Plate 98. *20ton goods brake van. Diagram 1/502. One batch of Great Western design brake vans was built for British Railways. Together with their older brethren they were retained on ex-GWR lines for many years by the 'Not in Common Use' branding seen here. Even so, some did escape from time to time, like this one photographed at Chelford (ex-LNWR) on 16 February 1963.* (Author).

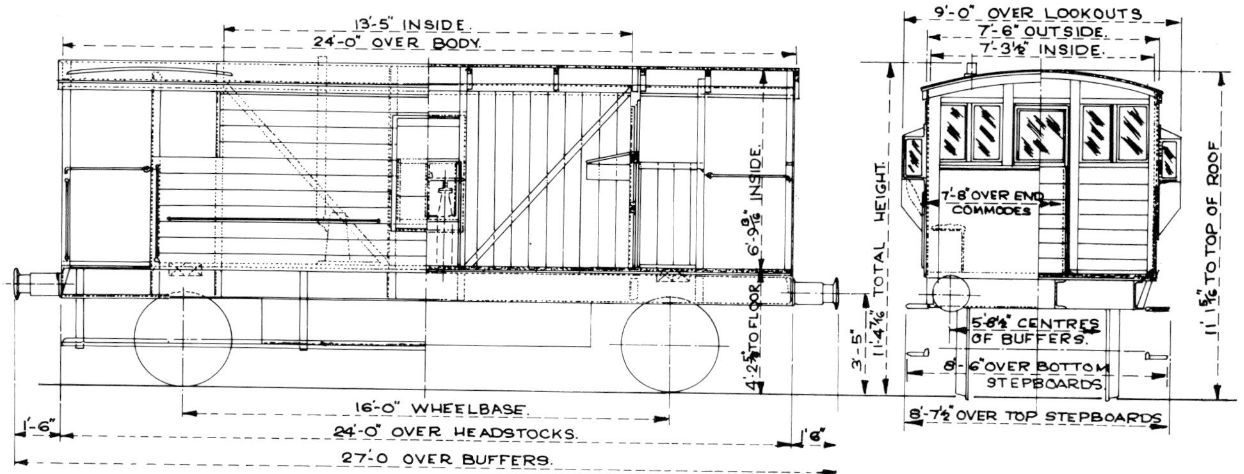

Figure 55. *20ton goods brake van. Diagram 1/503. This is the diagram for the unfitted version of the ex-LMS design brake van pictured in Plate 2. In spite of the great amount of detail the drawing is inaccurate (and the LMS version was the same) in that the lower horizontal handrail is omitted.*

Figure 56. *20ton goods brake van. Diagram 1/506. This is the British Railways standard design of goods brake which was developed from the ex-LNER type. Note that here the stepboards run the full length of the solebars and there are handrails to the end platforms. The diagram covered both fitted and unfitted versions.*

20 TON GOODS BRAKE

506

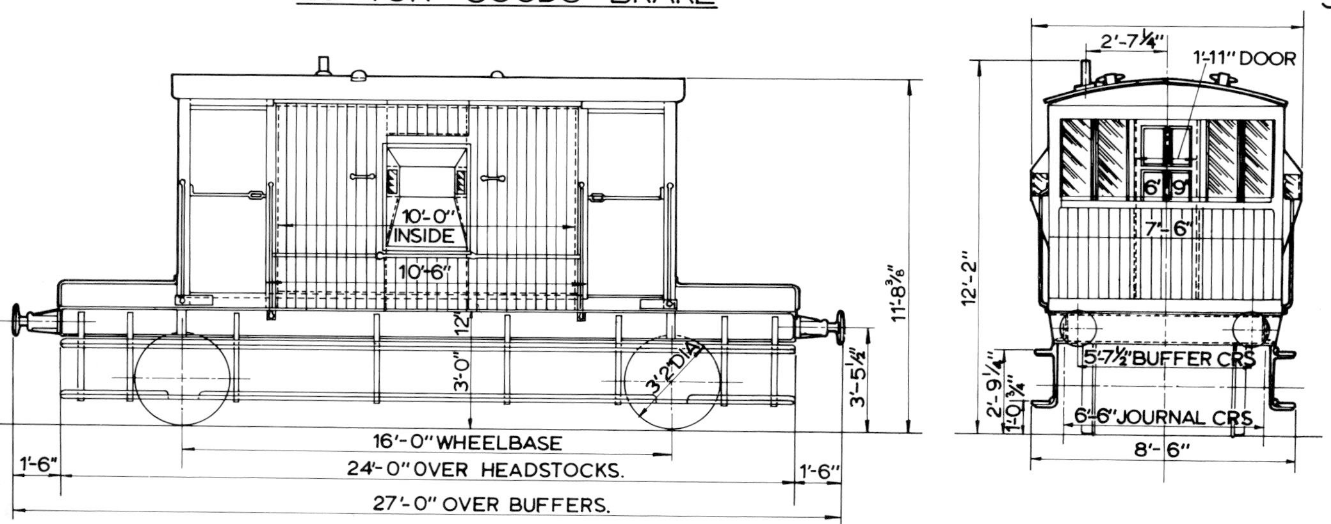

TEL.CODE – TOAD. TARE 20 TONS.
SCREW HAND BRAKE
MINIMUM CURVE 1½ CHAINS.

were the exceptions noted at the beginning, a pair of very small 10ton vans for special duties in Wales. They were to diagram 501. The LMS provided 250 to its standard design. There were two diagrams and two lots, each of 125 vans. Diagram 503 and lot 2026 covered non-fitted vans while diagram 505 and lot 2025 were issued for the piped version illustrated in Plate 2. No brake vans of Southern Railway design were built to BR orders.

All the above were built as part of the 1949 programme together with some 290 brake vans of LNER design lot 2051. These latter were the only ones among the early orders to receive automatic vacuum brake. They were to diagram 500. The

1950 and 1951 programmes perpetuated the LNER design, except that in keeping with LMS policy only brake pipe, valve and gauge were fitted. Diagram 504 was allotted for this variant and 550 examples were built together with a later 400 as part of the 1955 programme.

The British Railways standard brake van when it did appear was very like the LNER design. The principal change was that stepboards were extended to the full length of the underframe and handrails were provided along the end platforms to suit. The diagram, page 506, records that these brake vans were unfitted, as the first examples undoubtedly were, but the lot book records that the final four lots were vacuum-fitted. Beginning with lot 3227 improvements were incorporated in the form of roller-bearings and hydraulic buffers. Diagram 507 was issued to cover this variant. Faverdale shops, which had produced all previous BR design brake vans, built the first lot to this new design but the next batch, lot 3394, was entrusted to Ashford Works. They were followed by a further lot of six vans to the same design but destined for London Transport and numbered 580 to 585 inclusive. Since then no more goods brake vans have been built.

Plate 99. *The guard's domain. Somehow it did not seem right to produce a book on goods wagons without a single reference to the sometimes snug, often (to use a good Scots word) shoogly, but invariably lonely, interior of the guard's van. B951292 was actually an LNER design brake to diagram 1/504, built 1951.* (British Railways).

Plate 100. *20ton goods brake van. Diagram 1/507. A later version of the standard van with roller-bearings and hydraulic buffers. These vans had brake valve and through pipe but no vacuum brakes. British Railways also built six vans to this design for the former London Transport Executive.* (British Railways).

Chapter 10

Service vehicles

The simplest way to define the contents of this chapter is to say that it covers pages 550 to 653 of the freight stock diagram book. Allowing for gaps this involves the formidable total of sixty-three diagrams and reference to Appendix 4 will show that they cover a large number of vehicles. Even so, this is only part of the story, since for a variety of reasons many service vehicles are omitted from the chapter.

First and foremost, no account is taken of wagons built originally as traffic stock and subsequently transferred to departmental use. In recent years especially many hundreds of wagons have passed this way. Many of them were open goods wagons and at the beginning of Chapter 2 reference was made to such transfers. Secondly, there is no consideration of pre-nationalisation wagons inherited by British Railways. This is also true of all the other chapters, but wagons in service stock seem to linger much longer than their brethren in revenue-earning service.

Unlike the figures for freight vehicles and containers given in Tables 1 and 3 in Chapter 1 which coincide with the diagram books, those for rail service vehicles do not tie up completely. This is because the statistics also refer to such groups of vehicles as power-driven trolleys and trailers which the diagram book does not regard as wagons, thus forming the third main reason for omissions. If 1960 is taken as an example, the opening stock of 26,749 vehicles may be further broken-down as shown in the table below.

Wagons, cranes etc,

Type of vehicle	*Opening stock*	*In diagram book?*
Ballast wagons	13,989	Yes
Ballast brake vans	640	Yes
Timber, rail and sleeper trucks	3,428	Yes
Maintenance, inspection and construction	3,030	Yes
Breakdown and travelling cranes	769	No
Runner and shunt wagons	1,242	Yes
Power-driven trolleys and trailers	645	No
Mobile plant and machinery	406	No
Stores and material vehicles	2,600	Yes
Total	26,749	

Even for those categories stated as being in the diagram book coverage is not always complete by any means. In the above table, against the figure of 1,242 runner and shunt wagons, it is correctly stated that the diagram book covers the type but in fact only one shunting truck (and no runners at all) was ever built new to a British Railways diagram, so the remaining 1,241 examples must have been inherited or converted from other wagons. This is an extreme case, to be sure, but it does illustrate the main points made so far.

Increasing labour costs have added impetus to the mechanisation of many civil engineering jobs on British Railways, hence the widespread introduction of track-laying machines, tamping machines and the like. Alongside this development has been the introduction of many specialist wagons. Although the engineers may have a seemingly insatiable appetite for old wagons, the mainstay of their fleet can be seen to consist of a good stock of relatively modern custom-built wagons. The majority of these are rail, ballast and sleeper wagons of varied capacities, and to aid recognition code names have been allocated to each type. The names have been painted on the wagons concerned and will be used throughout this chapter. Another practice peculiar to service vehicles has been their allocation to regions and within each region to districts with details painted on.

Two other points deserve attention before we wade in among the diagrams. First is the fitting of automatic brakes, and here service vehicles as a whole are almost universally fitted and have been for some time. The days when a ballast train consisted of a collection of quite antiquated wagons are past, and most such trains today are composed of vacuum- (or air-) braked stock. Secondly, service vehicles have their own number range beginning at 964000 and ending (less gaps) at 999999.

Plate 101. *Staff & Tool van. Diagram not known. DB975535 has been chosen to illustrate a typical vehicle transferred from capital to service stock and converted for service use in the process. It began life as a corridor brake second coach built in 1951 to lot 30021, and was converted at Stewarts Lane in 1970 under lot 3719. Photographed at Folkestone Warren on 14 July 1971 when allocated to the Soil Mechanics Section.* (Author).

Within this range all numbers are prefixed DB as opposed to the normal B of revenue-earning stock although the introduction of the TOPS system has seen the adding of extra prefixes.

Inspection saloons

The first three pages of diagrams relating to service vehicles, namely 550, 551 and 552, cover inspection saloons. It is solely that the vehicles are never employed in revenue-earning service which prevents them appearing in the carriage diagram book because all eight vehicles are very much coaching stock.

Three lot numbers were issued on 30 August 1957 covering six saloons. Lot 3094 was for four vehicles to diagram 550, while lot 3095 was for one to diagram 551. All five were built at Wolverton, and not only were they very much of LMS design in appearance, but the lot book shows they were in fact LMS lot 1432 built under BR aegis. The remaining lot, No 3095, was for one saloon to be built at Swindon to diagram 552, and was later followed by lot 3379 covering two further examples.

Diesel brake tenders

As the number of diesel locomotives increased and their use on unbraked freight trains became more widespread it was found that they were deficient in brake power. The remedy was considered to lie in the provision of diesel brake tenders. The use of the word 'tender' is a little misleading because they are in effect brake vans without guards' accommodation. All are bogie vehicles and consist of a minimum length underframe with automatic vacuum-brake equipment, the whole being weighted with concrete or scrap to give a tare weight of 35tons to 37½tons. They were built from redundant material which accounts for the existence of four separate diagrams, 555 to 558 inclusive.

Altogether 122 tenders were put into traffic, seventy-eight of them being built at York carriage works. Their provision seems to have been a crash programme, and York is by no means the only unusual name among the builders, as Appendix 4 shows.

Ballast wagons

Coming to ballast wagons we are among the service vehicles pure and simple. In fact ballast wagons are far and away the most common type. Not surprisingly there is a profusion of both types and code names, with some ten different capacities and twenty-two different diagrams in all. One cannot help but wonder if there is really *all* that much difference between, say, a 19ton wagon and a 20tonner.

The smallest is the little 10ton wagon called the Starfish — the temptation to code name it 'Tiddler'

Plate 102. *Diesel brake tender. Diagram 1/556. It seems likely that the first fifteen diagrams in the service vehicle section were originally set aside for locomotive coal wagons but never used. In the event they were given over to inspection saloons and diesel brake tenders. B964003 is typical of this latter group of vehicles. It was one of five such tenders built by the Derbyshire Wagon Company.* (British Railways).

must have been great — of which eighty were built at Swindon works to diagram 566. They were no doubt a carry-over from the Great Western, since the company used the same type of wagon.

Likewise the only slightly larger 12ton Sole (diagram 565) was an LMS inspiration, basically an extended version of that company's standard three-plank open wagon but having drop doors at

Plate 103. *12ton ballast wagon. Diagram 1/565. With this diagram we begin the service vehicles proper with an ex-LMS design three-plank dropside wagon that also has drop ends. These vehicles were actually 20ft 8in long over headstocks rather than the more usual 17ft 6in. They were code named Sole. Note that only body ironwork and patches of planking are painted. The body colour is not known but memory suggests it may have been red oxide. Photograph taken in 1949, probably at Wolverton.* (British Railways).

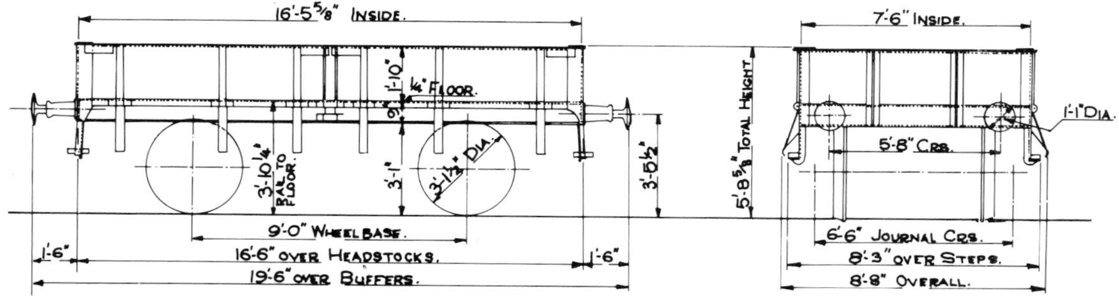

Figure 57. *10ton ballast wagon — lettered Starfish. Diagram 1/566. This diagram and the two which followed it all covered ex-GWR all-steel ballast wagon designs of 10tons, 14tons and 20tons capacity respectively. Swindon works built a single lot of each.*

Figure 58. *20ton ballast wagon — lettered Tunney. Diagram 1/568. The family likeness between this wagon and the one in Figure 57 is obvious in spite of the increased dimensions and the fact that here there are three doors per side in place of the two on the Starfish.*

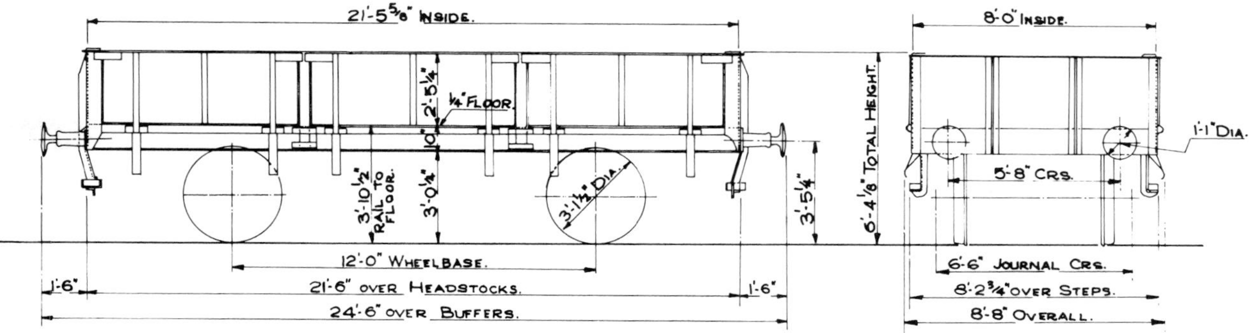

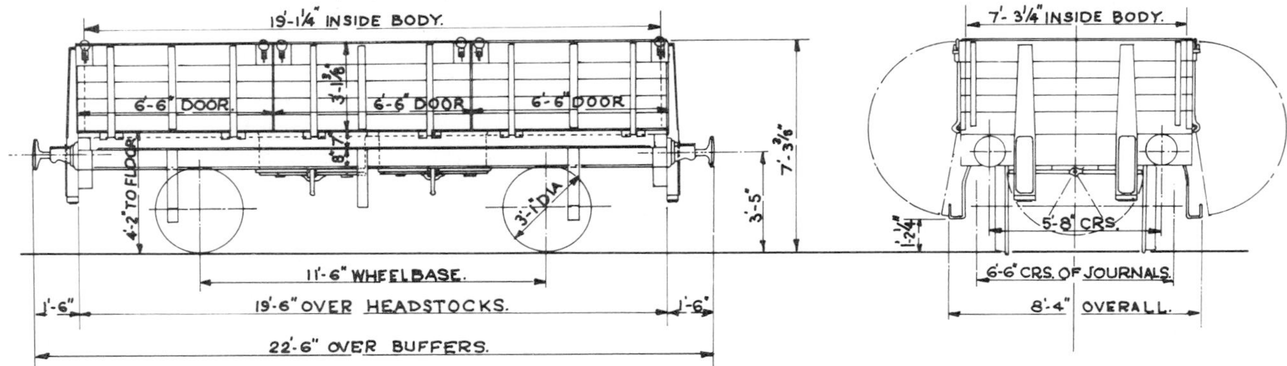

Figure 59. *20ton ballast and sleeper wagon. Diagram 1/569. We have already commented (page 52) on the fact that the 13ton hopper wagons of lot 2050 still featured wooden solebars and headstocks. The fifty wagons to this diagram — code name Gudgeon — also incorporated extended wooden end stanchions, which could buffer with chaldron wagons.*

the ends as well as at the sides. Here some two lots were built, giving a total of 350 wagons.

The next largest ballast wagon, the 14ton Ling of diagram 567, is again a Swindon design and is virtually an enlargement of the Starfish with three doors per side as against the former's two. Swindon works built the only lot, 200 wagons, as part of the 1949 programme. The remaining 14ton ballast wagon designs are both side-tipping types with the second diagram, No 575, being an updated version of the earlier diagram 573. The first Mermaids (the code name for both diagrams) were not ordered until the 1952 prorgramme but the design closely follows that of some wagons purchased by the Great Western Railway from the Metropolitan-Cammell Carriage & Wagon Co. 239 Mermaids were built to the first diagram, followed by a further 400 with vacuum brake and improved buffers, all built by MCW.

This firm has been particularly prominent in building service vehicles for British Railways, and has handled all the orders for 17ton and 19ton hopper ballast wagons. After only one lot, production of the 17ton Mackerel ceased in favour of the 19ton Catfish, which was in effect a slightly longer Mackerel fitted with vacuum brake. Page 583 was

Plate 104. *20ton ballast and sleeper wagon — lettered Grampus. Diagram 1/572. After the various lots of pre-BR inspired ballast wagons had emerged British Railways opted for the 20ton Grampus as the standard design. Some 4,059 of them were built to this diagram followed by another 722, all vacuum-fitted, to diagram 1/574.* (British Railways).

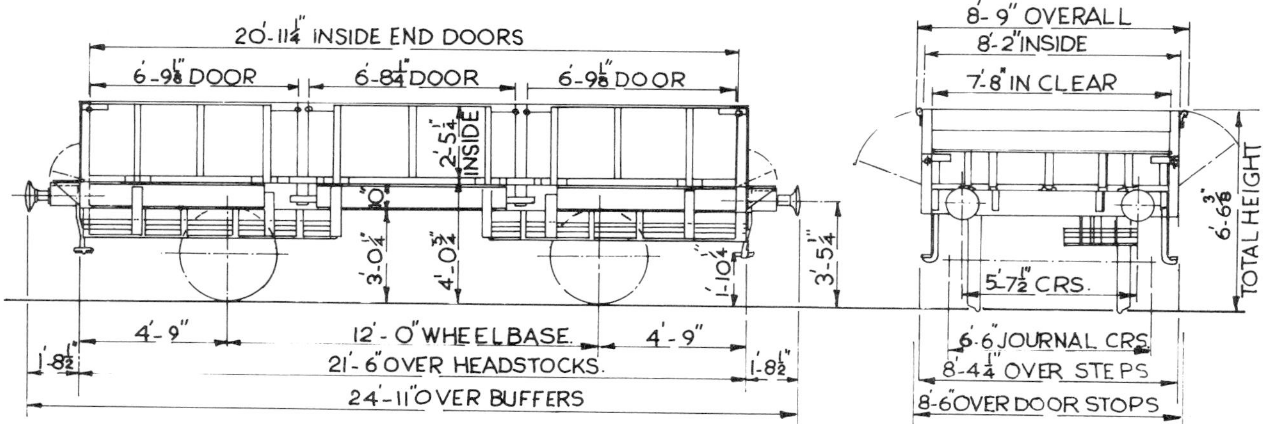

Figure 60. *20ton ballast and sleeper wagon — lettered Grampus. Diagram 1/574. The second Grampus diagram covered the vacuum-fitted version. The arrangement of bars below the solebars provided shelving for the stowage of side and end doors when these were not in use.*

allocated to the Mackerel and page 586 to the Catfish. Following on the 239 Mermaids and 134 Mackerels it is a convenient point to comment that whereas wagons for traffic were generally ordered in multiples of 50 or 100, one frequently comes across odd numbers of service vehicles being specified.

Whereas a capacity of 13tons was general for merchandise stock with 16tons normal for mineral wagons, the most popular capacity for ballast wagons was 20tons. Certainly there were other capacities of merchandise and mineral wagons, just as we have seen that there were other sizes of ballast wagon, but still there were no fewer than eight separate diagrams issued for 20ton ballast wagons. Furthermore, the numbers of wagons involved were large even if they were not quite on a par with those for 16ton minerals.

Two of the eight diagrams covered straight-side ballast wagons with side doors. The first of these, diagram 568 with code name Tunney, was in effect a larger Ling with the same fixed ends and three doors per side. Again Swindon works built the only lot, this time of 120 wagons. The 20ton Lamphrey (diagram 570) shared the same basic dimensions of 12ft wheelbase and 21ft 6in length over headstocks, but had drop-ends in addition to its side doors, and the design originated on the Southern Railway. Lancing and Ashford works each built a lot for British Railways. These seventy-one wagons were followed by an order for 160 more, which was fulfilled by the Butterley Company.

In addition to these two diagrams for drop-side ballast wagons a further two were issued for 20ton hopper ballast wagons. Both were given the code name Herring, but in appearance and basic dimensions they were quite different. All examples were built by Metropolitan-Cammell. The forty wagons built to diagram 582 appear to have been Swindon-inspired, but after this single lot the design was not repeated. The other wagons, again a single lot but this time one of 100 vehicles to diagram 584, were virtually a development of the Catfish but with body sheets six inches higher to give a further three tons payload.

The remaining four diagrams cover what are described as ballast and sleeper wagons, but in

Plate 105. *14ton ballast side-tipping wagon — lettered Mermaid. Diagram 1/575. The only other non-hopper ballast wagon to be ordered was the 14ton side-tipping design seen here. It was probably a Metro-Cammell patent, as the firm handled all construction which amounted to 639 wagons. Note the rail clamp hanging from the solebar. This prevents the wagon from tipping over when the load is being discharged. Rose Grove, 4 August 1968. (Author).*

Plate 106. *25 ton hopper ballast wagon. Diagram 1/580. While the civil engineer rapidly standardised on the Grampus and Mermaid, the selection of standard ballast hoppers seemed to take much longer; this illustration together with the six which follow it show the profusion of diagrams which appeared. This is the 25ton Trout, the GN2 marking denoting a wagon allocated to Glasgow North district, which was quite some way from Ladybank where the photograph was taken on 15 March 1970.* (Author).

Plate 107. *17ton hopper ballast — lettered Mackerel. Diagram 1/583. The only difference between the 134 wagons to this diagram and the one hundred 20ton examples to diagram 1/584* (qv post) *is that here the body lip was six inches shallower, giving three tons less capacity. The vacuum brake pipe can be seen atop the solebar. Ladybank, 15 March 1970.* (Author).

appearance all the representatives are similar to dropside ballast wagons. Indeed the first two types, diagrams 569 and 571, are both code named Lamphrey (sometimes officially spelled Lamprey) like the 20ton ballast wagons to diagram 570. The fifty wagons of lot 2120 built by the Butterley Company were the only vehicles to diagram 569 and had several unusual features. Along with the 300 hopper wagons of lot 2050 (see page 52) they were unique in having wooden solebars. Furthermore the fixed ends were supported by massive wood end stanchions which extended below the headstocks to buffer up to chaldron wagons. In fact the design was not just pre-nationalisation but pre-grouping, having originated on the North Eastern Railway.

Diagram 571 also covered a design which originated in the north-east, even if a little later than the one above, although in appearance the two designs were quite different, for the 50 wagons to this second diagram were three-plank bogie wagons with the floor a mere 3ft 1½in above rail level. Headstocks had to be specially built up to give a standard buffer height.

One gets the impression that none of the designs dealt with up to this point gained universal acceptance, since in few cases was more than a single lot ordered. The arrival of the 20ton Grampus changed all that and it is assumed that it was one of the Ideal Stocks Committee's 'six main types' chosen as standard for civil engineering purposes. In the event 4,059 wagons were built to the original design, diagram 572, plus a further 722 with hydraulic buffers to diagram 574. All were 21ft 6in long over headstocks with a 12ft wheelbase, and had three flap doors per side as well as drop ends. Construction continued steadily from 1951 until mid-1961 with Shildon building the first and last batches. Apart from one other lot built at Ashford works the rest of the construction was handled by the trade.

The remaining ballast wagon designs are all hoppers with the smaller 24ton and 25ton types being four-wheeled and the larger 40ton and 50ton examples being bogie vehicles. The 24ton Dogfish would appear like the Grampus to be one of the types picked as standard, since ten lots were ordered giving a total of 1,249 wagons. Of these 221 were subsequently modified for the conveyance of slag. The exact nature of the modifications is not known. In contrast, the slightly larger 25ton ballast hopper was not built in anything like these quantities. There were two types, both code named Trout. The first diagram, 580, had hopper doors controlled from an end platform like the 24ton Dogfish while side control was incorporated in the wagons of diagram 581. Construction of the first type amounted to 113 wagons in three lots, while there were a further eighty-four examples, this

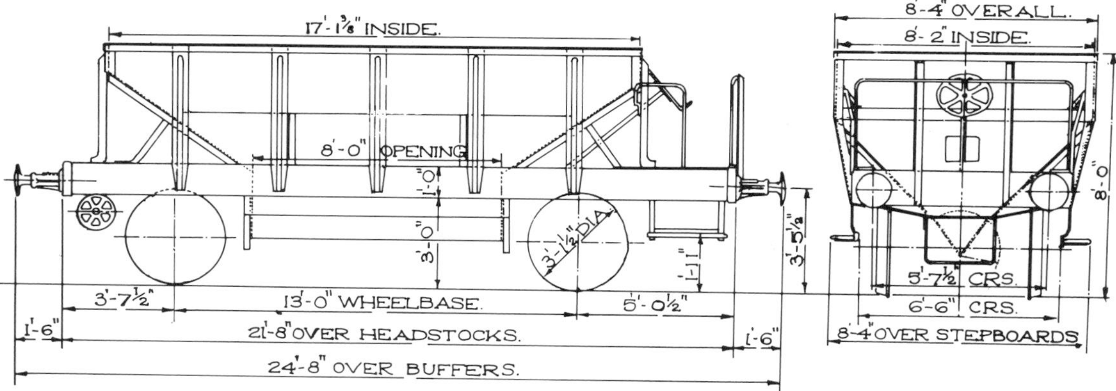

Figure 61. *20ton hopper ballast wagon — lettered Herring. Diagram 1/584. There were in fact two designs coded Herring and this is the second. The wagons to the earlier diagram (1/582) were quite different, being shorter, higher, and without the end platform. Both designs could discharge only into the four-foot way.*

Plate 108. *40ton hopper ballast — lettered Walrus. Diagram 1/585. The use of bogie ballast hoppers seemed to find particular favour with Southern Region. Appropriately, this example was photographed at Ashford on 6 July 1971. The type is versatile in that the load can be discharged between the rails, outside them, or in all positions as desired.* (Author).

time in two lots, of the second design.

Since 1965 new ballast wagon construction has been limited and confined to bogie hopper wagons of both 40ton and 50ton capacities. Most of them have been air-braked and therefore outside the compass of this book, but one batch of 40ton Sealions has had both air and vacuum brake.

Ballast plough brake vans

The idea behind the plough brake van is that a ballast train moves slowly over the section of track to be ballasted depositing its load whilst a plough

Plate 109. *19ton hopper ballast — lettered Catfish. Diagram 1/586. After acquiring single lots of a variety of designs, British Railways adopted the 19ton Catfish for quantity purchase, all 716 examples being built by Metro-Cammell. The design was a lower and longer development of the Herring to diagram 1/584. The photograph is dated 20 April 1960.* (British Railways).

Plate 110. *24ton hopper ballast wagon — lettered Dogfish. Diagram 1/587. The success of the Catfish design notwithstanding, the most popular ballast hopper in terms of numbers built was in fact the 24ton Dogfish, of which there were 1,249. All were vacuum-fitted from new. Not only could the design hold five tons more ballast than the Catfish, but with three bottom doors could discharge between or on either side of the rails. Ladybank, 15 March 1970.* (Author).

Figure 62. *24ton hopper ballast wagon — lettered Dogfish. Diagram 1/587. This drawing complements the picture above. The arrangement of the bottom doors and the handles on the control platform becomes apparent here. The handwheel at the left-hand end controls the handbrake.*

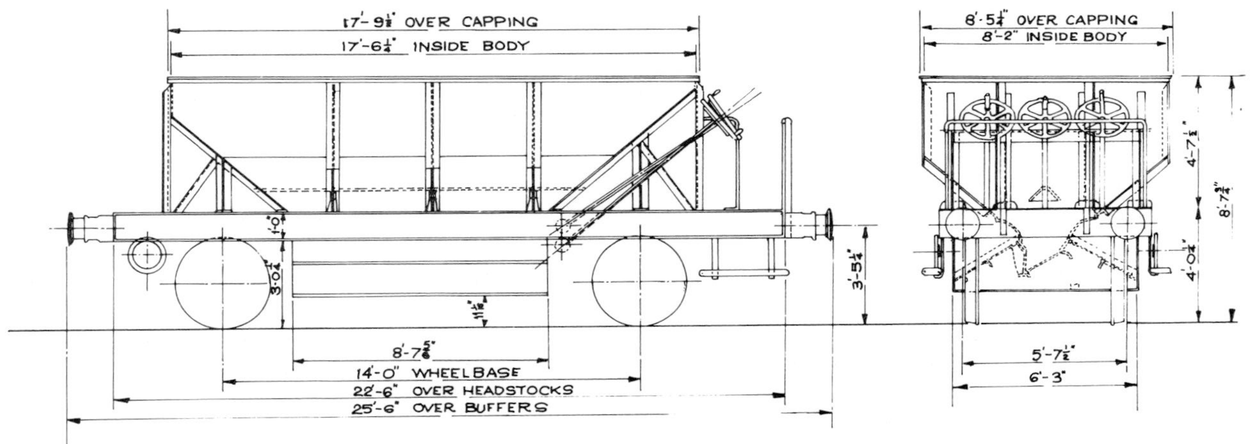

Figure 63. *12ton ballast plough brake van. Diagram 1/595. The idea of using a plough to spread ballast originated on the Caledonian Railway and gained widespread acceptance. The LNER used such vehicles with the ploughs (one facing either direction) mounted inside the wheelbase. One lot of six vans was built to this design for British Railways.*

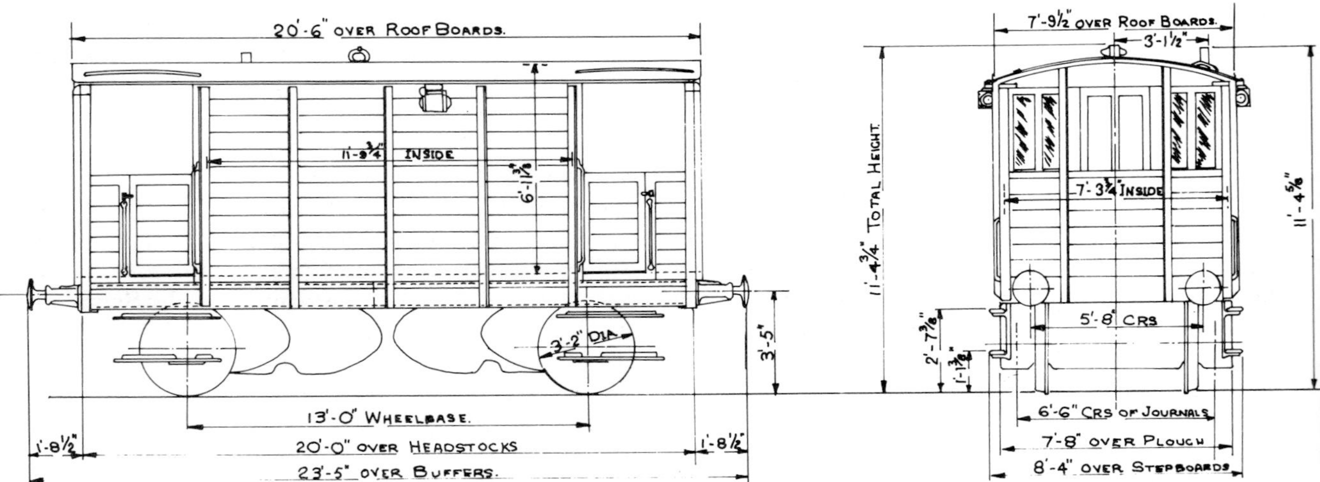

attached to the last wagon would spread the material where it was required. It was logical to attach a plough to a ballast brake van, so both the LMS and LNER companies made use of the idea. The former tended to use a short wheelbase van with ploughs (one for each direction of travel) mounted outside the wheelbase, while the LNER opted for the opposite arrangement. British Railways adopted the LMS arrangement, but not before one lot of vans to the LNER design had been delivered. These were six 12ton plough brakes to diagram 595 built by Metropolitan-Cammell in the 1948 programme.

The contemporary LMS design was a 16ton vehicle which British Railways perpetuated as page 596 of the diagram book. Nine were built, two at Derby works and the remaining seven by R. Y. Pickering Ltd. For the 1951 programme and subsequent construction the same design was uprated to 20tons and fitted with automatic vacuum brake. In this form 206 examples were built in eight separate lots, all to diagram 597. They were followed by twenty more vans with roller-bearings and hydraulic buffers, to diagram 598. Like all the other plough brakes they received the code name Shark.

Plate 111. *20ton ballast plough brake van. Diagram 1/597. The LMS on the other hand used a heavier 16ton van with ploughs at each end outside the wheelbase. From this the even heavier 20ton version was developed, as seen here, and became the standard type. Wick, 26 June 1968.* (Author).

Signal and Telegraph department wagons

When dealing with steel carrying wagons in Chapter 8 we noted instances where plate and bogie bolster wagons had been ordered specifically for signal and telegraph engineers' use although no special diagram was issued. For the six wagons of lot 2608 a special diagram, page 619, was issued because in this instance the wagons seem to have been purpose-built. They were in effect an elongated version of the LMS three-plank ballast wagon, but the design was not perpetuated beyond this single lot.

Rail and sleeper wagons

Under this sub-heading there appear wagons variously described as rail wagons, sleeper wagons and rail, ballast and sleeper wagons, which seemed best treated as a group. Up to this point we have been able to follow the sequence of diagram numbers more or less, but to continue to do so slavishly now would have been confusing.

The first two diagrams to claim attention are two described as sleeper wagons, the one a 12ton vehicle, the other rated at 14tons. The first, code name Haddock, is for a single lot of three-plank drop-side wagons of obvious LMS parentage, although all fifty were built by the Butterley Company. The 14ton design, code named Minnow, was a larger wagon with fixed four-plank sides and higher ends. Page 620 of the diagram book was allotted and Swindon built two lots, giving a total of 25 wagons.

The Whiting, a 14ton rail wagon, was merely a two-plank version of the Minnow. Both designs originated on the Great Western although one of the three lots was built not at Swindon but at Wolverton works. As diagram 622 shows, inside body length was 28ft 0¼in and from this one must assume they were used solely for point and crossing materials. For transport of plain track, whether prefabricated or not, a longer wagon was obviously required, and here we are in the realm of the bogie rail wagon. Two capacities have been used, the 40ton and the more popular 50ton. The 40ton was again a Great Western inspiration. Under British Railways the code name Oyster and diagram 641 were allotted. Two lots were built, one by Swindon Works and the second by Cravens Ltd, but some of the vehicles of the latter group (nine wagons) were delivered as traffic stock without the D prefix to the running numbers and allocated to diagram 488.

The first two diagrams for 50ton bogie rail

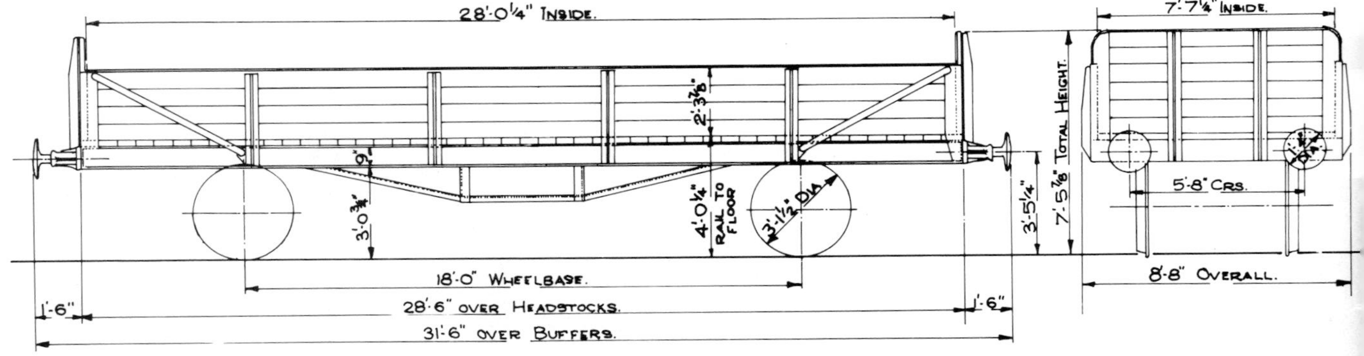

Figure 64. *14ton sleeper wagon. Diagram 1/620. At first sight the provision of a wagon 28ft 6in long to carry 8ft 6in sleepers seems unnecessary, but the design was almost certainly developed to convey timbers for point and crossing work. After two batches built as part of the 1949 programme the design was not perpetuated.*

wagons are almost identical, the main difference being that page 637, the earlier design, has side rails which were later dispensed with on diagram 628. All code named Salmon, 216 wagons were built to these diagrams in five different lots. The remaining four Salmon diagrams exhibit similar small variations but relate to what is basically the same design. They are respectively diagrams 640 (162 wagons in three lots), 642 with 147 wagons in two lots, a single lot to diagram 644, and finally the 315 wagons in four lots to diagram 646.

Plate 112. *12ton sleeper wagon for the Engineer's Department. Diagram 1/621. This was the LMS idea of a sleeper wagon (1/620 was GWR-inspired) of which British Railways built a single batch of fifty wagons. Note that capacity had become 13tons and that Ditton is a long way from Ladybank where the photograph was taken on 15 March 1970.* (Author).

All the above bogie rail wagons were in effect bogie bolster vehicles, but Lancing works also produced a single 30ton bogie bolster with removable three-plank sides. Diagram 643 was allotted to cover the prototype but no more examples were built. Alongside all these bogie rail wagons British Railways also ordered substantial numbers of 40ton and 50ton bogie rail sleeper and ballast wagons which were in effect low three-plank open wagons having removable sides and yet long enough to carry rail or track sections. The design stemmed from LNER practice.

A single lot was produced to the sole 40ton diagram, page 639. Ninety wagons were built, code named Dolphin, with an interior length of 63ft 5¼in. As with the 50ton version, sturdy raised ends were fitted. All the 50ton designs were 66ft 1in long over headstocks, giving an internal length of 64ft. The first wagons built to diagrams 638 and 645 had hand brake only whereas most of the ones built to diagram 647 had through vacuum pipe.

Independent snowplough

Together with the requirement for brake tenders dieselisation also brought the need for more independent snowploughs. Various redundant locomotive tenders to a total of forty-one were converted, and despite slight variations all were considered to be to diagram 623. Lot 3539 covered all work, which was shared between Cowlairs, Eastfield and Swindon works.

Crane match and flat wagons

Diagrams were also issued to cover various designs of match and flat wagons used with travelling cranes, although as noted the cranes themselves were not covered. To complicate things a

Plate 113. *Independent snowplough. Diagram 1/623. Apart from the necessity of providing brake tenders, another side effect of the dieselisation programme was the need for independent snowploughs. It was met by modifying surplus steam locomotive tenders, one of which is seen here at Etterby Road (Carlisle) on 16 May 1970.* (Author).

Plate 114. *Crane flat wagon. Diagram 1/?. Whilst the diagram book allots several pages to various designs of crane match or crane flat wagons no lot numbers appear to have been issued for such vehicles. It is assumed that cranes would probably have been purchased each with an attendant wagon. Certainly DB998536 here had no works plates or lot details when photographed at Etterby Road depot, Carlisle, on 16 May 1970.* (Author).

little more, lot numbers were not issued when the wagons were ordered, so that the only information available is taken from the diagrams themselves. Even this is not wholly correct, because one exception was made for the single crane match wagon built to diagram 630 for which a lot number was issued.

Shunting truck

Both diagram, page 631, and lot number were issued to cover the one and only British Railways-built shunters' truck, a rather charming little vehicle just 17ft long over buffers, for which Swindon works was responsible.

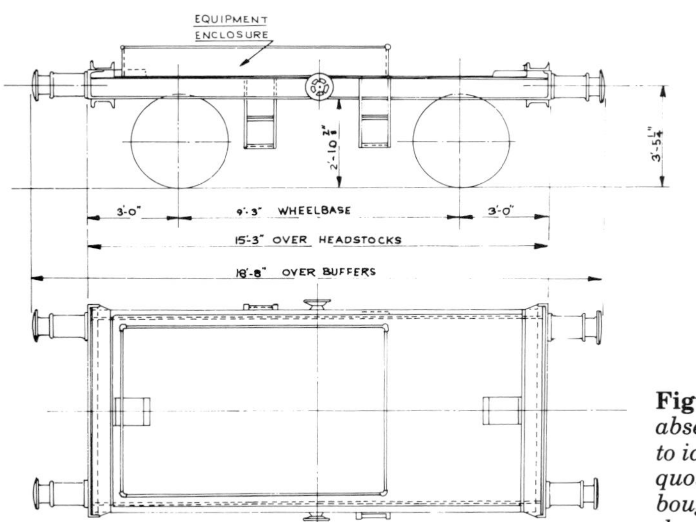

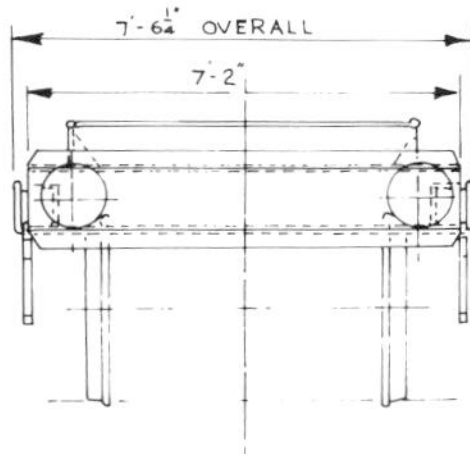

Figure 65. *Crane flat wagon. Diagram 1/624. In the absence of lot numbers the only way we have been able to identify these wagons is from the running numbers quoted on the diagram. Other wagons may have been bought or built since this issue of the diagram was drawn.*

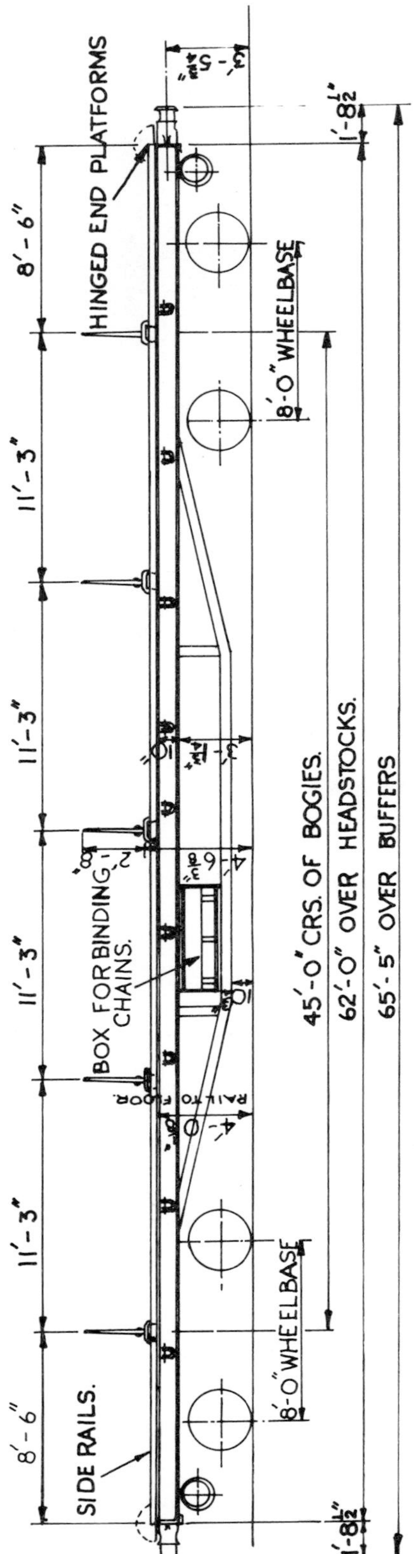

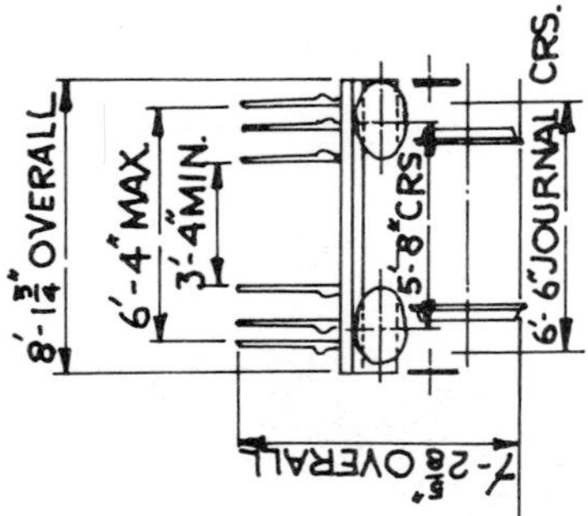

Figure 66. *50ton bogie rail wagon — lettered Salmon. Diagram 1/628. There were two very similar diagrams for these wagons. On both, the wheels were 2ft 8in diameter, but the wagons to this diagram had 1½in side rails fitted to the body, whereas they were absent from the wagons built to diagram 1/637. (3mm — 1ft).*

Plate 115. *50ton bogie rail wagon — lettered Salmon. Diagram 1/637. This is the version without the side rails referred to above. The paint date is December 1959 and the photograph was probably taken at Wolverton. The livery is almost certainly black with yellow lettering.* (British Railways).

Plate 116. *14ton refuse wagon — lettered Sludge. Diagram 1/632. We have never learned the precise nature of these wagons' traffic, but then we have never investigated all that thoroughly. Suffice to say there are four compartments with drop doors on each side fitted with rubber seals, the whole being mounted on a 16ft 6in underframe. Ashford, 6 July 1979.* (Author).

Plate 117. *14ton creosote wagon. Diagram 1/633. In Plate 5 we illustrated the larger 22ton creosote wagon. This is the smaller 14ton version of which twenty-two examples were built before construction switched to the larger design. Paint date is March 1953.* (Charles Roberts & Co).

Refuse wagon

Ashford Works' contribution to this collection of odd wagons was some twenty-three 14ton refuse wagons lettered, so diagram 632 assures us, simply 'Sludge'. The side doors had rubber seals to prevent seepage of the load, and the wagons were ordered in two lots as part of the 1954 and 1955 programmes.

Tank wagons

For the carriage of creosote to its sleeper preparation plants before the use of concrete sleepers became widespread, British Railways ordered five

Figure 67. *50ton bogie rail sleeper ballast and general utility wagon — lettered Sturgeon. Diagram 1/638. The LNER used this type of wagon extensively and it continued to find favour with British Railways, being particularly useful for carrying complete 60ft panels of track. The wheels were 2ft 6in diameter. (3mm — 1ft).*

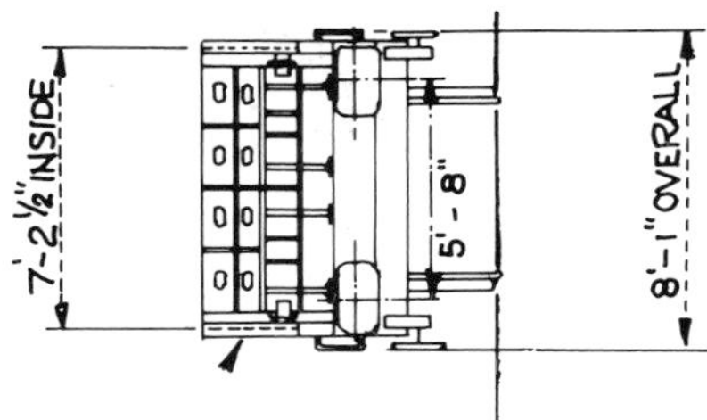

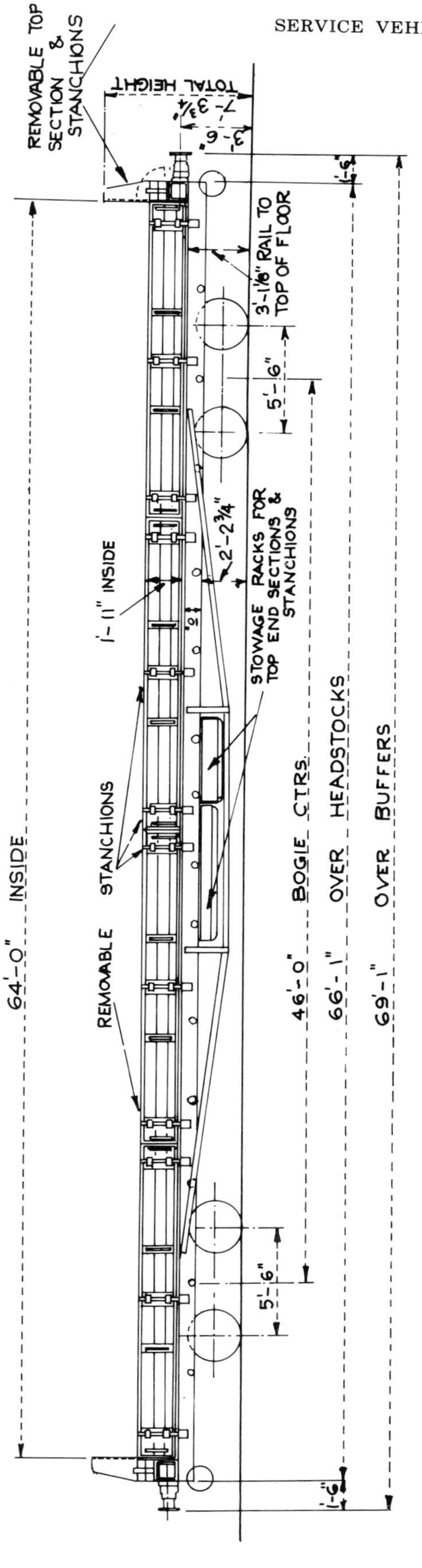

Plate 118. *40ton rail sleeper and ballast wagon — lettered Dolphin. Diagram 1/639. The Dolphin was six inches shorter than the Sturgeon and had smaller journals, hence the lower capacity, but wheel diameter remained at 2ft 6in. Fort William, 21 September 1970.* (Author).

Plate 119. *50ton bogie rail sleeper ballast wagon — lettered Sturgeon A. Diagram 1/645. The Sturgeon A had some detail improvements over the Sturgeon but the principal one, the provision of removable bolsters and stanchions, did not come until the later diagram 1/647. Paint date is 5 April 1955, at which time it will be noted that woodwork is unpainted.* (Author's collection).

separate lots of creosote tank wagons. All were built by Charles Roberts & Co. The first three lots, some twenty-two wagons in total, were of 14ton capacity, to diagram 633. They were followed by a further forty-two 22ton wagons of diagram 636. Automatic vacuum brake and roller bearings were fitted to later wagons.

R. Y. Pickering Ltd also supplied tank wagons to the service vehicle fleet, but in their case they were 20ton vehicles for the transport of marine fuel oil. There was a single order for fifteen as lot 2781 for which diagram 634 was issued. Then in 1969 and 1970 and possibly since, British Railways bought second-hand from Shell Mex and BP some tank wagons for traction oil. Lot numbers and diagrams were duly provided, the nine wagons of 14tons capacity becoming lot 3700 to diagram 617, while a further four larger vehicles, 33½tons gross loaded weight, were authorised as lot 3716 and diagram 618. All were hand braked only.

Miscellaneous vehicles

Flat wagons for diesel units

Another result of dieselisation was the ordering of four wagons designed to carry the engines for diesel locomotives to and from main workshops. Diagram 635 covers the four examples which were built in two lots at Ashford works.

Overhead line maintenance vehicles

Two such wagons were ordered from the firm of E. E. Baguley in March 1950 but the second is not recorded as having entered traffic until February 1958. They were in effect self-propelled diesel units with extendable inspection platforms. The information given on page 648 of the diagram book is most comprehensive, describing not only the vehicle but also the equipment carried.

Dynamometer car

Page 649 covers a single dynamometer car built at Doncaster in 1951 and numbered DE320041. It was originally ordered in 1938 and is very much an LNER main line coach suitably modified. It was re-numbered as DB999500.

Flat wagons

The last page in the wagon diagram book (our copy at least; others may have been added since) rather appropriately covers the last wagon lot issued for non air-braked vehicles. Lot 3752, issued 3 November 1970, was for twelve flats for the conveyance of reinforced concrete beams. They were converted from Bogie Bolster Ds at St Rollox works and diagram 653 was allocated.

Plate 120. *Dynamometer car. Diagram 1/649. This chapter began with a picture of a carriage and it finishes with one. We can only assume that custom and practice dictated a diagram be prepared for this vehicle, and that among the service vehicles seemed the best place for it to go. It was actually ordered in 1938 but was not built until 1951 and was later re-numbered DB999500.* (National Railway Museum).

Chapter 11

Special wagons . . .

. . . or, as the diagram book describes them, 'Specially Constructed Vehicles'. They are rather an elite bunch, the specials, with a diagram book all to themselves even though their numbers are few. Basically they owe their origin to the requirements of early legislation under which the railways were established as common carriers, and which as such had to be able to transport such exceptional traffic as was offered to them. In anticipating these demands they maintained a stock of sundry types and sizes of specially constructed wagons. British Railways inherited the common carrier obligations, and for many years was obliged to maintain (and replace with new wagons where required) its stock of such vehicles.

From the railway historian's point of view the main result of these obligations is a large number of different wagon types (and in consequence a lot of diagrams) with relatively few examples of each. Since special wagons, by definition, are unusual they have received more than their fair share of publicity in popular railway publications. One immediately thinks of the many official photographs of gun barrels, distillation columns, transformers and the like being carted up and down the country. In this chapter we shall not therefore deal with each particular diagram, which would often encompass no more than one or two wagons, but rather with groups of wagons. British Railways has made our task easier here by grouping all similar designs of each type together and referring to them by a generic code name. Thus all flat trolleys are called FLATROLs and their diagrams are grouped together. We shall use these code names throughout this chapter.

The names themselves are followed by a code, generally of two letters but on occasion three. Because of the nature of their movements all special wagons are controlled individually so that a station requiring a 40ton armour plate truck can ask for one and the special wagon controller will know there is one empty at Norwich for example. (With the computer-controlled TOPS system this is now true of all wagons but in the days of manual control only specials got such treatment.) As control was originally based on the old companies the first code letter indicates the controlling region, with A for Scottish Region, while the second covers the particular design of that type of wagon.

We have already stated that a separate diagram book exists for special wagons. Within it the various types appear in alphabetical order and we shall stick to this division. There are some seeming anomalies, but close inspection reveals that the reason is a strict alphabetic interpretation of purpose. Thus, though Flatrols follow Trestles this is because they are looked on as Trolleys (Flat) and consequently are themselves followed by Trolleys (Propellor).

British Railways adopted a fairly vigorous construction policy for special wagons in the mid-1950s, with Lancing and Swindon works undertaking much of the work. For some reason quite a number of special wagons seem to have been subject to undue delay and were eventually considered to be part of later programmes. As an example one may take lots 2878, 2879 and 2880 comprising in total some seven trolley wagons all to be built at Swindon works. The orders were issued on 18 March 1955 but construction was not complete until 21 May 1960. Eventually, these three lots, along with others, were deemed to have been part of the 1959 programme.

While falling freight traffic meant that British Railways was free to reduce its stocks of general merchandise wagons at will, it was the eventual removal of common carrier obligations which allowed BR to retain only such special wagons as was thought could be profitably employed. Thus it was that the late 1960s saw a sharp decline in the number of special wagons, caused by a halt in construction coupled with extensive withdrawals.

Even so British Railways would still build wagons when there was a demand. As late as 20 February 1970 orders were placed for two 199ton bogie girder wagon sets which happened to be some of the last unfitted wagons built. They were probably the last unfitted wagons built new.

Armour plate wagons

Three diagrams, pages 1, 2 and 3, have been issued to cover armour plate wagons. The first relates to a 40ton design while the others cover 55ton versions, with diagram 3 being an updated version of diagram 2. All examples are short bogie flat wagons used for the conveyance of slabs of armour plate, billets and similar heavy pieces of steel.

As an example of the code naming referred to in the introduction let us consider the vehicles, twenty-two in all, built to diagram 2. The table below shows the use of different suffixes.

Lot	*Quantity*	*Coded*	*Running Numbers*
2174	4	ARM ET	B908000 — B908003
2174	5	ARM MD	B908004 — B908008
2622	7	ARM ET	B908009 — B908015
2651	4	ARM ET	B908016 — B908019
2938	1	ARM WF	B908020
3057	1	ARM WF	B908021

Plate 121. *40ton armour plate truck — lettered Arm EL. Diagram 2/001. As is obvious from the photograph, the Arm was a simple but sturdy bogie platform wagon used for conveying heavy ingots and pieces of armour plate. It should be noted that although the code Arm applied to all wagons of the type the suffix — in this case EL — concerned the controlling region and varied from wagon to wagon, so throughout this chapter we shall not use suffixes. London Road Goods (Carlisle), 10 September 1960.* (Author).

It is believed that as with other special vehicles wagons of this type had been built for both the LMS and LNER.

Boiler wagons

It is convenient to subdivide these wagons into two groups, both code named Boiler. In the first group there are three different diagrams, pages 30, 31 and 32. Each is for a 35ton bogie flat wagon covering some five vehicles in total.

The other boiler wagon is by any standards a formidable assemblage. It consists of four sets of six-axle bogie units plus two four-wheel match trucks which can be assembled in a variety of ways to give a boiler wagon of 150tons or 290tons capacity, the whole taking three pages of the diagram book to describe. The full set, when close-coupled and without match trucks, measures 138ft 6½in overall; by disconnecting the units and allowing the load to act as a chassis it can be much longer. The wagon or wagons can truly be described as 'special'.

Flat wagons

Under the code name Flat there are six different diagrams covering 129 different wagons. Capacities range from 12tons to 60tons and there are four- eight- and twelve-wheeled wagons. The baby of the family is the 12ton Flat ED, diagram 72, a four-wheeled wagon very similar in appearance to the former LMS Deal truck. Thirty-two were built. There were but two examples of the Flat EL, a very low-slung bogie design to diagram 71, which was the next largest capacity. On the other hand the 45ton Flat ET was ordered in three separate lots giving a total thirty-seven examples, all built by

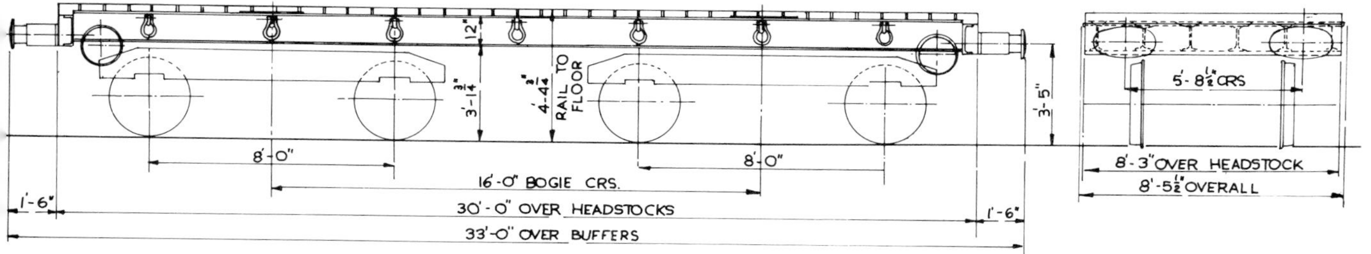

Figure 68. *55ton armour plate truck — lettered Arm. Diagram 2/003. The 55ton Arm was 6ft longer and had bogies of 8ft wheelbase instead of 6ft. The buffers now had oval heads but wheel diameter remained at 2ft 8½in, a figure which was quite common with special wagons.*

Plate 122. *35ton boiler wagon — lettered Boiler. Diagram 2/030. This is one of a pair of boiler wagons built by Hurst Nelson & Co. The most obvious feature is the use of inside bearings on the wheelsets. Paint date is May 1951.* (British Railways).

R. Y. Pickering & Co. The largest single group was the 50ton type which consisted of some 60 Warflats purchased by the Western Region in the manner previously described and for which diagram 73 was allocated. The first and last diagrams in this range, pages 70 and 75, both cover the 60ton Flat EQ. Both are twelve-wheeled bogie vehicles, the principal difference being that the later design had roller-bearings and through vacuum pipes.

Girder wagons

There are two diagrams, 150 and 151, allotted to girder wagons and both types are large and unusual, even amongst special vehicles. With the first diagram there is some conflict between diagram and lot books over how many wagons were actually built. The confusion seems to have arisen over just what constitutes a 40ton Girder wagon set. The diagram shows two four-wheeled trucks, each with a bolster and buffers at one end, and considers that to be two lots, giving a total of two sets and four wagons built. The lot book agrees that two lots were ordered, but from numerous amendments it would seem that ideas changed and it was eventually decided that eight separate wagons were built.

Presumably the lesson had been learned, because the lot book later describes diagram 151 as being four wagons 'Bogie Girder Set "Conger" — for use in pairs, 100tons a set'. As stated, they were the last unfitted wagons built new by British Railways.

Glass wagons

When doing the research for this chapter we were surprised to find just how few glass wagons were built for British Railways considering the scale of glass traffic, in the St Helens area especially. We were also surprised to find that apart from two all examples had been built at Swindon works.

The exceptions were two 30ton bogie glass wagons, coded Glass EO, built at Lancing works to

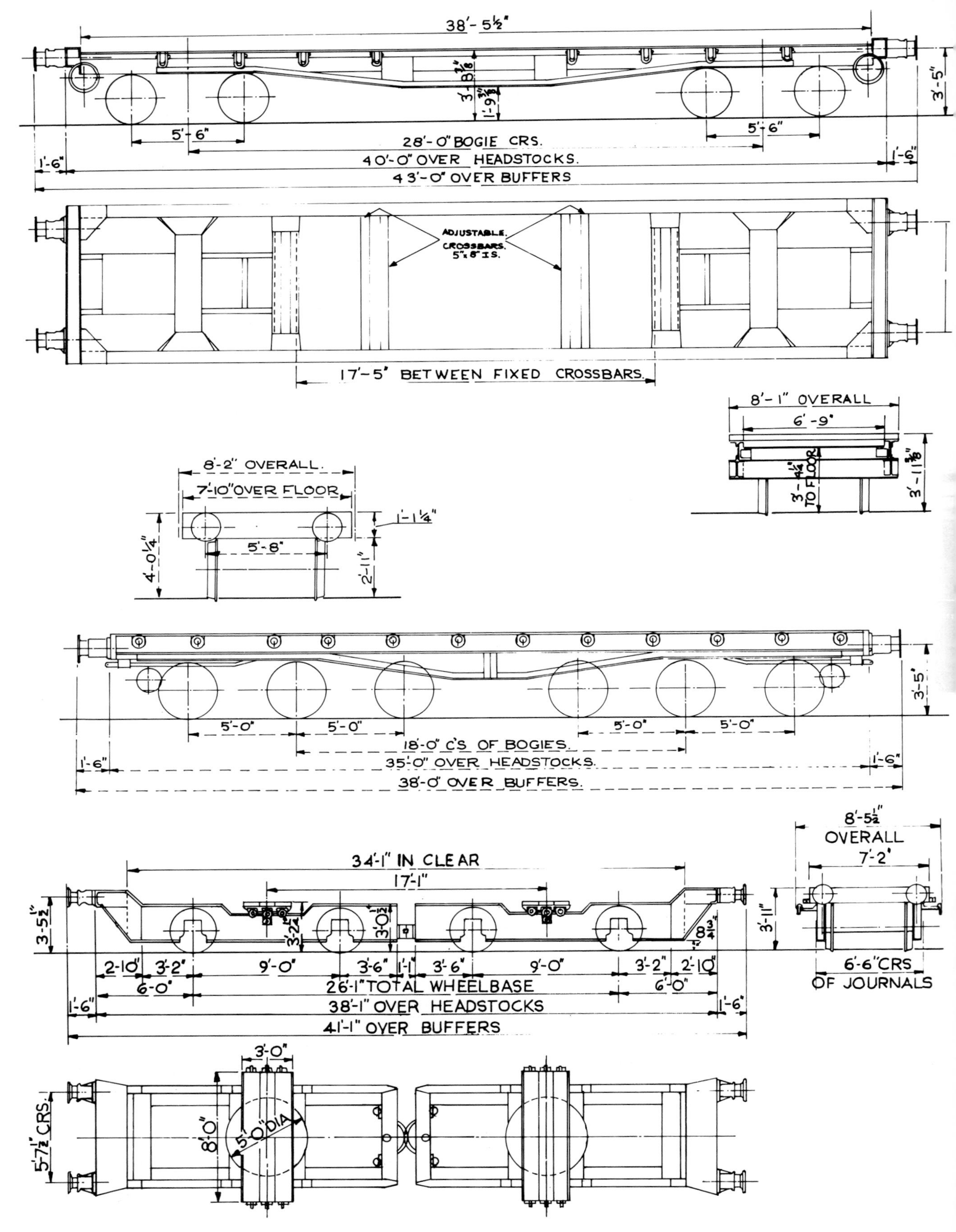
38'-5½"
3'-8⅛"
1'-9 3/16"
3'-5"
5'-6"
5'-6"
28'-0" BOGIE CRS.
40'-0" OVER HEADSTOCKS.
1'-6"
1'-6"
43'-0" OVER BUFFERS
ADJUSTABLE CROSSBARS. 5"x 8" I.S.
17'-5" BETWEEN FIXED CROSSBARS.
8'-1" OVERALL
6'-9"
3'-4¼" TO FLOOR
3'-11⅛"
8'-2" OVERALL.
7'-10" OVER FLOOR
1'-1¼"
4'-0¼"
5'-8"
2'-11"
3'-5'
5'-0"
5'-0"
5'-0"
5'-0"
18'-0" C'S OF BOGIES.
1'-6"
35'-0" OVER HEADSTOCKS.
1'-6"
38'-0" OVER BUFFERS.
8'-5½"
OVERALL
7'-2"
34'-1" IN CLEAR
17'-1"
3'-5½"
3'-2¼"
3'-0½"
8¾"
3'-11"
2-10"
3'-2"
9'-0"
3'-6"
1'-1"
3'-6"
9'-0"
3'-2"
2-10"
6'-0"
26'-1" TOTAL WHEELBASE
6'-0"
1'-6"
38'-1" OVER HEADSTOCKS
1'-6"
41'-1" OVER BUFFERS
6'-6" CRS OF JOURNALS
3'-0"
8'-0"
5'-0" DIA
5'-7½" CRS.

Figure 69. *35ton boiler wagon — lettered Boiler. Diagram 2/031. The trussed underframe of the wagons above was replaced by fishbelly girders on the two wagons to this diagram plus the single wagon to diagram 2/032, which was the updated version complete with through vacuum brake pipe.*

Figure 70. *60ton bogie flat wagon — lettered Flat. Diagram 2/070. To illustrate the flat wagon as a type we have selected the 35ft version with its six-wheel bogies and trussed underframe. Two wagons were built to this diagram, followed by three more with roller-bearings and through vacuum pipe, to the very similar Diagram 2/075.*

Figure 71. *40ton girder wagon set — lettered Girder. Diagram 2/150. A set comprised two individual wagons, each with its own number. Four sets were built. The 100ton bogie sets lettered Conger to diagram 2/151 were similar in conception but heavier, and each wagon had three axles. (3mm — 1ft).*

Plate 124. *12ton glass wagon — lettered Glass. Diagram 2/170. With special wagons it is often difficult to attribute designs, since the LMS and LNER in their later years shared these in common and built special wagons for each other. In this case there is no doubt, for this design is very much Great Western inspired. One lot of six wagons was built before construction ceased in favour of the ex-LMS type. Millerhill, 26 July 1964.* (Author).

Plate 123. *40ton girder wagon set — lettered Girder. Diagram 2/150. A stroke of sheer good fortune has to be thanked for being at Carstairs on 10 June 1966 just as this special freight train came through. The picture shows one end of a pair of girder wagons in use. The load itself is secured to the rotating bolster on each wagon, the wagons being otherwise unconnected. The vehicle is B907500.* (Author).

Figure 72. *12ton glass truck — lettered Glass. Diagram 2/171. This is the ex-LMS design referred to above which was chosen for future construction, possibly on account of its having a longer well. Even so, total build only amounted to forty-two wagons, all of which were constructed at Swindon works.*

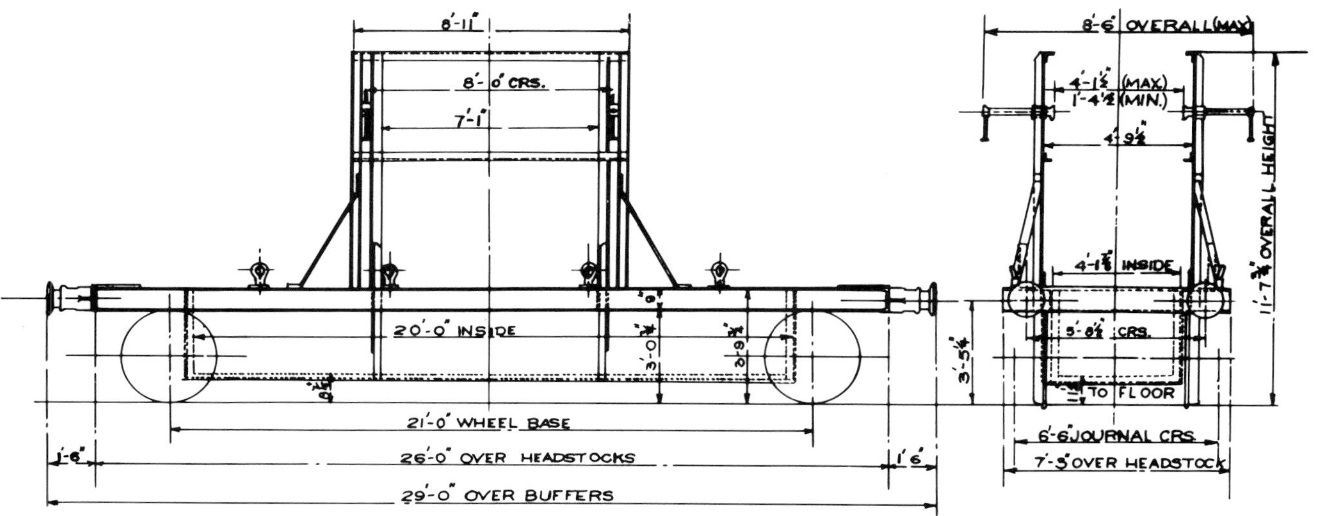

(3mm — 1ft).

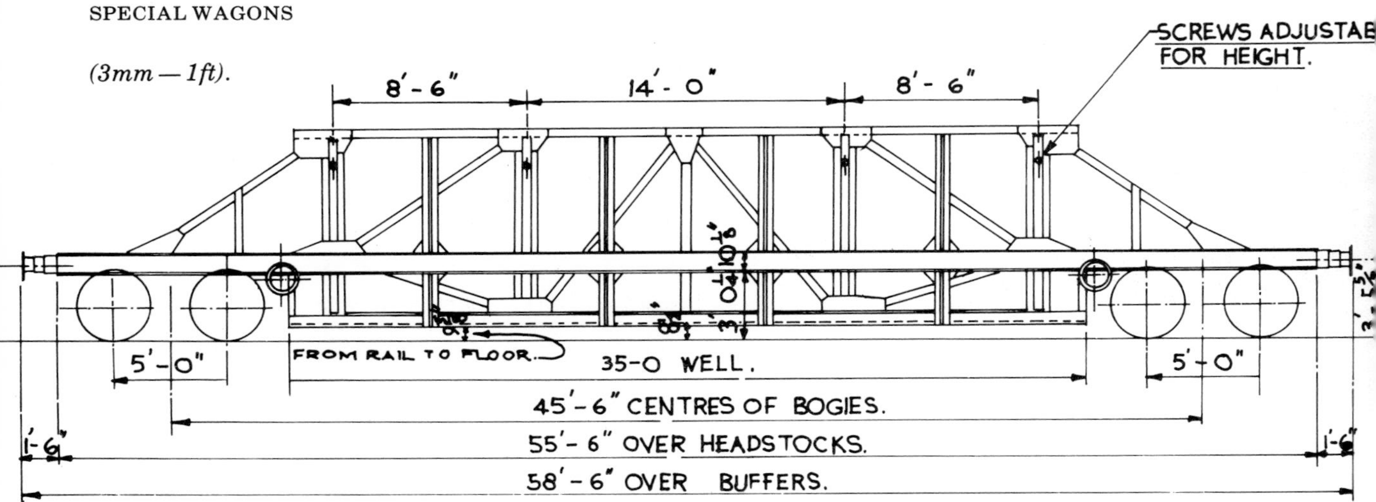

Figure 73. *30ton glass wagon — lettered Glass. Diagram 2/172. The largest glass wagons were the two examples built to this diagram. Wheels were the usual 3ft 1½in diameter and tare weight was 23tons 18cwt, which was high for a vehicle of only 30tons capacity.*

diagram 172. All the others were four-wheelers of 12tons capacity. The first six, to diagram 170, were in effect the GWR Coral C and were coded Glass WC by British Railways. They were followed by forty-two wagons to diagram 171 which was an LMS-inspired design, the wagons being coded variously Glass MD, EP and WE. The final pair of glass wagons, also coded Glass EP were to diagram 173, effectively an updated version of diagram 171.

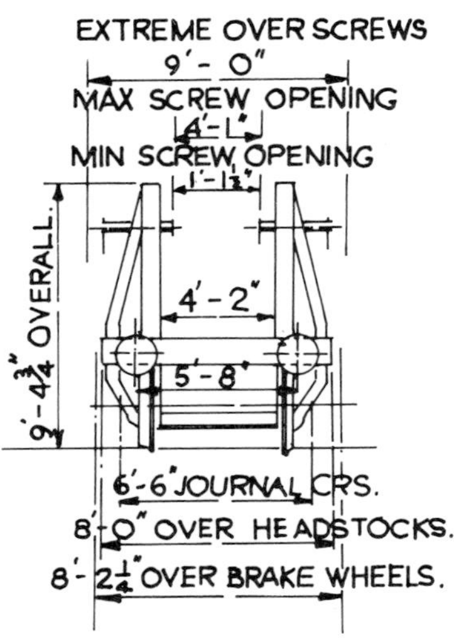

Machine wagons

Low machine wagons

The Lowmac, code name for the low machine wagon, is the most popular of all the special wagons. Having said this, total British Railways construction amounted to no more than 510 examples,

Plate 125. *12ton Glass truck — lettered Glass. Diagram 2/173. The two final glass wagons to be built were those to diagram 2/173, which was the updated version of diagram 2/171. They had roller-bearings, hydraulic buffers and through vacuum pipe. As can be seen, such wagons were sometimes used for loads other than crates of glass. Crewe, 23 September 1961.* (Author).

Plate 126. *21ton Lowmac — lettered Lowmac. Diagram 2/240. In the text we refer to a succession of Lowmac diagrams, all with slightly varying dimensions. They are all described on the diagrams not as Low machine wagons but by their code name, Lowmacs. B904147 was one of the last batch of wagons to this diagram and has roller-bearings as well as a through brake pipe. Thurso, 27 June 1968.* (Author).

Figure 74. *15ton Lowmac — lettered Lowmac. Diagram 2/241. The frame shape here, together with the relatively short wagon, betray a Lowmac design from the Swindon stable. All thirty examples were built at Swindon Works.*

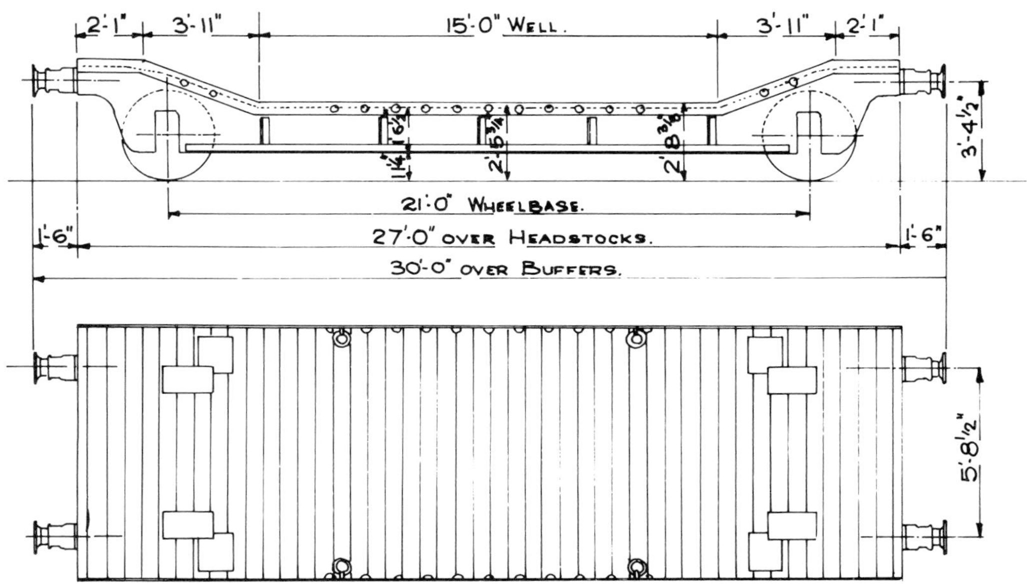

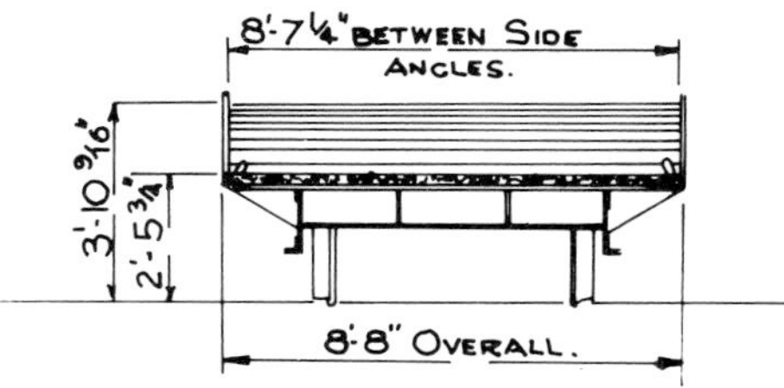

thus giving some idea of how relatively uncommon such wagons are. Even those 510 wagons were spread over fourteen separate diagrams (pages 240 to 254 with page 251 not used) and thirty different lots. All the Lowmacs were four-wheeled, with capacities ranging from 14tons to 25tons. In appearance they can best be described by imagining a strip cut through the centre of a saucer with an axle tucked under each end. As with a saucer the load is carried in the central flat portion.

The saucer analogy is particularly apt, because as anyone who has tried to match a broken one will know, there is an immense scope for variety in that same basic shape. So it is with Lowmacs. They all look the same so that one wonders just why so many diagrams were issued. It was therefore decided to draw up the table (page 123) which summarises the main features of each type.

Figure 75. *25ton Lowmac — lettered Lomac. Diagram 2/242. This was the first British Railways Lowmac design to be built with automatic vacuum brake. There were two brake cylinders, one at each end of the wagon between the headstocks and the axles.*

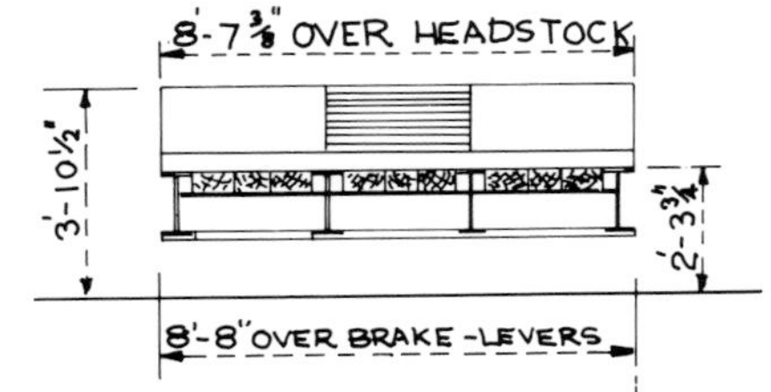

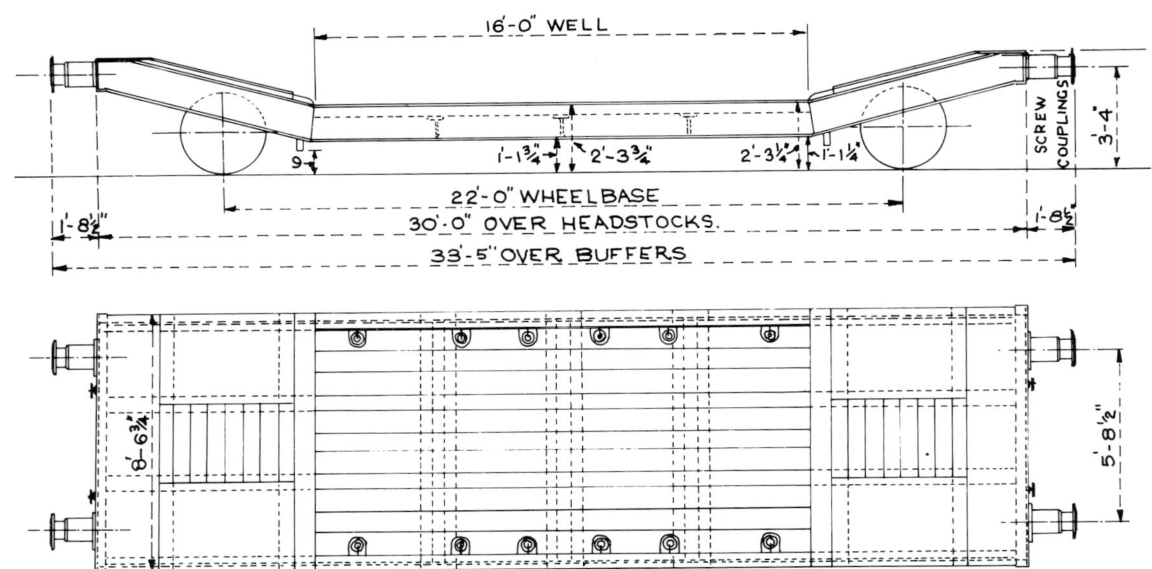

Plate 127. *25ton Lowmac — lettered Lowmac. Diagram 2/243. In terms of numbers built this was the most popular Lowmac design. There were 126 examples, built in four lots. Photographed at Millerhill, 27 July 1968.* (Author).

Plate 128. *20ton Lowmac — lettered Lowmac. Diagrams 2/250 and 2/245. Two for the price of one. The nearer wagon is B904126 with the vacuum cylinder clearly visible below the headstock at the right-hand end. The far Lowmac is B904107, another 20tonner but to diagram 2/245 which was the precursor of diagram 2/250, this latter being the vacuum-fitted version. However, as can be seen from the pipe running outside the solebar the earlier wagon has at least had a through pipe added and may well be vacuum-fitted as well. Millerhill, 5 April 1969.* (Author).

Low Machine Wagons — Summary of Types

Diagram	Capacity tons	Wheelbase ft	Wheelbase in	Length over headstocks ft	Length over headstocks in	Length over buffers ft	Length over buffers in	Length of well ft	Length of well in	Floor height above rail ft	Floor height above rail in	Numbers Lot	Numbers Qty	Code suffixes (all Lowmac)	Remarks
240	21	36	6	36	6	39	6	16	0	2	6½	4	92	MR,AB	ABs vacuum piped, others unfitted
241	15	21	0	27	0	30	0	15	0	2	5¾	2	30	WE	Unfitted
242	25	22	0	30	0	33	5	16	0	2	3¾	1	38	EP, SC	AVB
243	25	22	0	30	0	33	0	16	0	2	1¾	4	136	ER, WP, MS	Unfitted
244	14	20	0	25	6	28	6	15	1	2	5½	2	52	EK	Unfittede
245	20	25	6	33	6	36	7	15	0	1	3¼	3	38	WN, ET	Later ones vacuum piped
246	25	22	0	30	0	33	0	16	0	2	1¾	2	10	WBB, ES	AVB
247	25	22	0	30	4	34	5	16	0	2	5¾	1	13	EU	RIV, Westinghouse pipe
248	15	22	6	30	0	33	5	15	0	2	6½	4	37	WV	AVB
249	20	24	0	29	6	32	11	14	0	1	4½	1	3	EO	AVB
250	20	25	6	33	6	36	11	15	0	1	3¼	1	12	MU	AVB
251	?														See text for details
252	20	25	6	35	0	38	5	15	0	1	3¼	2	13	SG,MU	AVB
253	25	22	0	31	6	34	11	16	0	2	1¾	2	28	MS, SH, WP	AVB
254	25	22	0	30	4	34	5	16	0	2	5¾	1	8	SF	AVB & Westinghouse pipe RIV

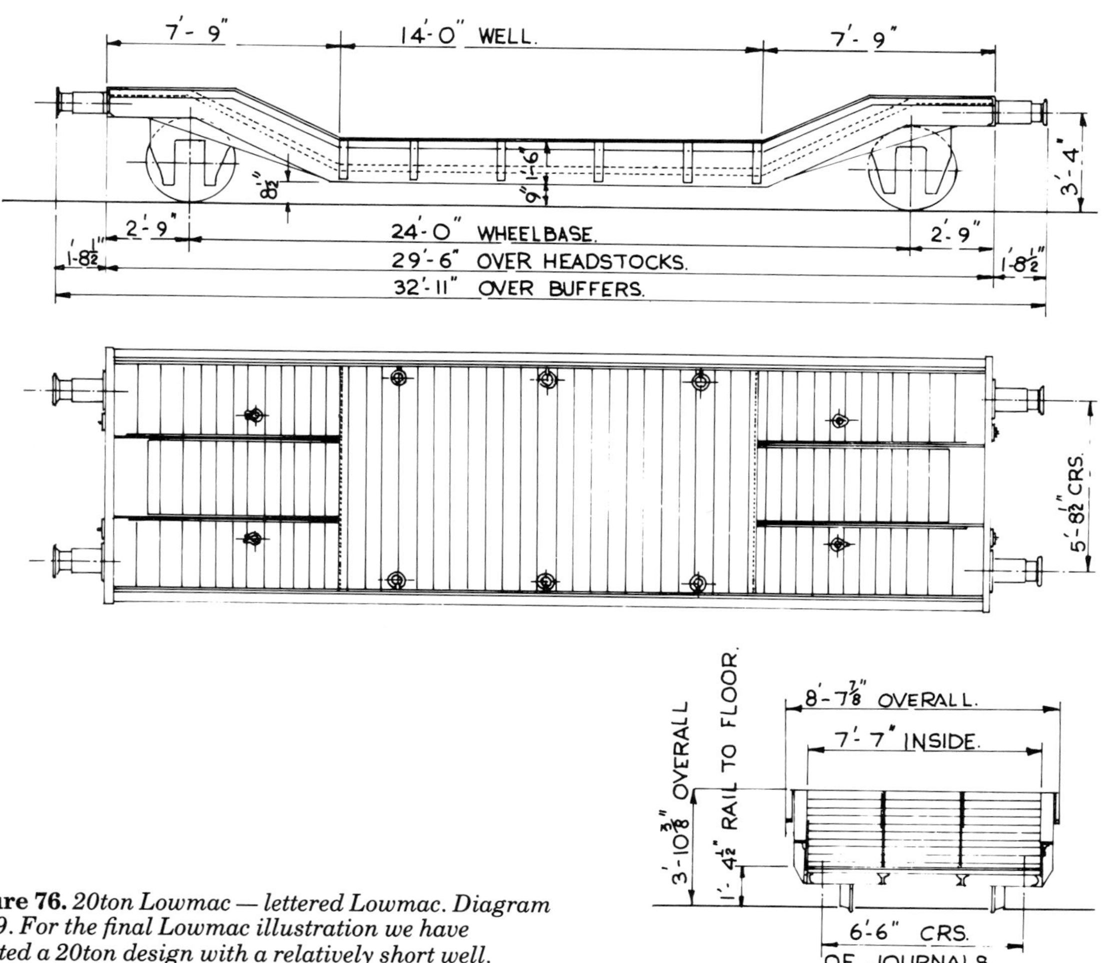

Figure 76. *20ton Lowmac — lettered Lowmac. Diagram 2/249. For the final Lowmac illustration we have selected a 20ton design with a relatively short well. Wheels are the usual Lowmac diameter of 2ft 9in.*

Diagram 251 was apparently never issued. The lot book indicates that lot 3100 was originally destined to be to this design, but before construction began it was changed to diagram 248. It will be noted that the two types used for train ferry traffic (RIV in remarks) also had Westinghouse through pipes.

Car transporters

On page 293 of the diagram book, sandwiched between the low machine wagons and the high machine wagons, is a single diagram for a 12½ton two-tier car transporter, code named Tierwag. One lot of six wagons was built as a first essay in Motorail train traffic. The design was not repeated

Plate 129. *12½ton two-tier car transporter — lettered Tierwag. Diagram 2/293. In between the Lowmacs and the Hymacs there appears this diagram for a single batch of six car transporter wagons. There* may *also have been at least one more batch of these wagons built for continental working and supplied to MAT Transport Ltd, but this cannot be confirmed.* (Newton Chambers & Co Ltd).

Figure 77. *21ton Hymac — lettered Hymac. Diagram 2/391. With the high machine wagon the full title was never used, just as happened with the Lowmac, but with just twenty-seven examples in all spread over four diagrams the Hymac was nothing like as popular. This diagram covers fifteen of those wagons, all built in a single lot by Hurst Nelson & Co.*

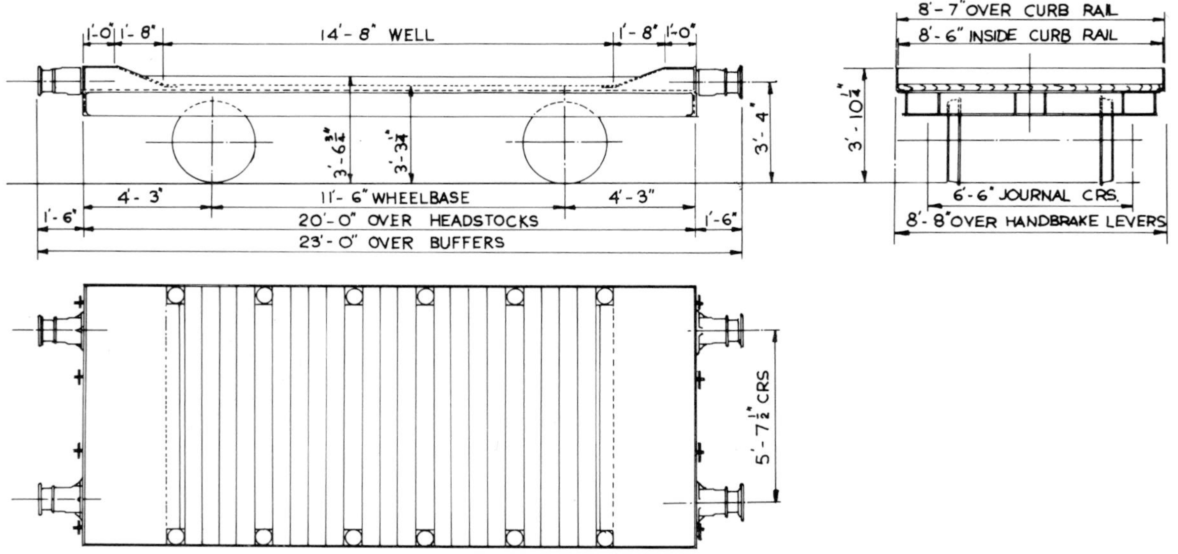

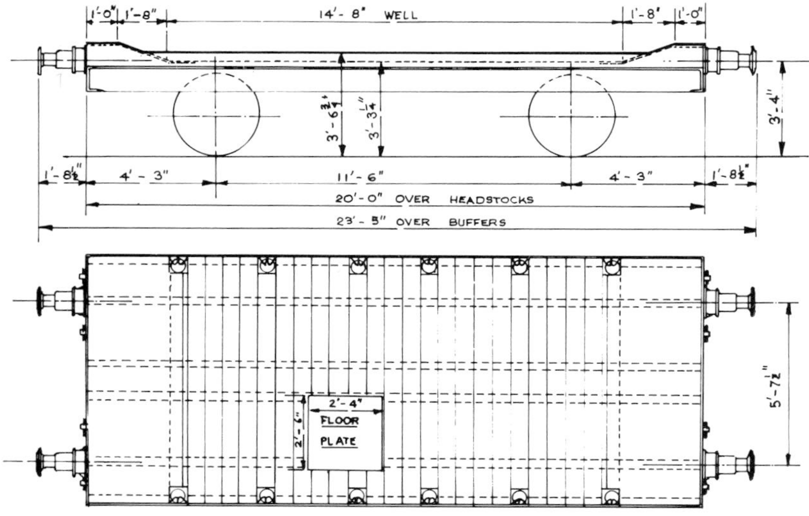

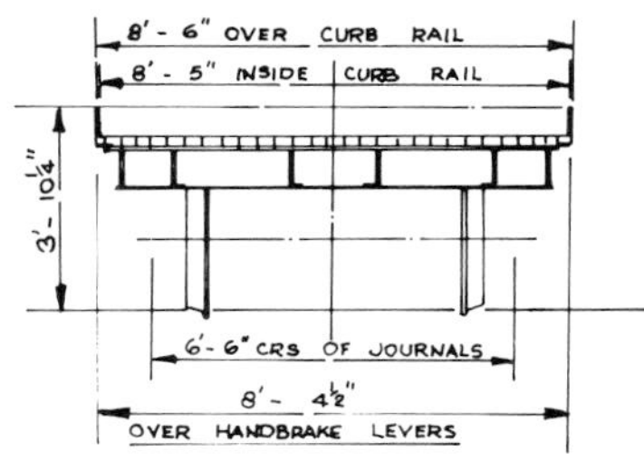

Figure 78. *21ton Hymac — lettered Hymac. Diagram 2/393. The final Hymacs, a batch of five to this diagram, were in effect the vacuum-braked version of the previous illustration, diagram 2/391. There were subtle differences between the two (for example, wheels were now 2ft 8in diameter compared with 2ft 9in on the earlier design) so this diagram has been chosen to give a comparison.*

and the vehicles spent a long time sitting in a siding outside Paisley (Gilmour Street) out of use prior to being hauled away for scrapping.

High machine wagons

Alphabetically the Highs should come before the Lows but that is not the way the diagram book treats them. In any case they are much less common than the Lowmacs, with a mere twenty-seven examples spread over four diagrams. In appearance there is a certain similarity with the Lowmac, although as the name implies the well floor is higher and this gives a shorter wagon.

In effect there are two basic designs. Diagram 390 covers the 20ton Hymac EP in its hand-braked form while diagram 392 was issued to cover the single wagon of lot 3019 which was modified with self-contained buffers. The other design is the 21ton Hymac EX, and here diagram 391 covers the hand-braked version while 393 covers the five subsequent vehicles fitted with automatic vacuum brake.

Rectank wagons

The history of the Rectank as a type goes back to World War I when it was developed on behalf of the Railway Executive Committee to transport the then new military tanks. British Railways built three lots, a total of seventy-eight wagons, all to diagram 440. In appearance they are very similar to the original design, but with such detail improvements as cast-steel bogies and roller-bear-

Plate 130. *38ton Rectank — lettered Rectank. Diagram 2/440. The Rectank as a type appeared for military use during World War I and again in World War II but this particular example was a British Railways design built in 1960, as evidenced by the cast-steel bogies and roller-bearings. It has been modified to convey nuclear waste. Millerhill, 12 April 1964.* (Author).

ings. Suffixes EC and WC are used with the code name.

Roll wagons

Although the provision of special types of wagon for the carriage of sheet steel in rolls was dealt with in Chapter 8, a special diagram was issued (page 450) to cover a group of ten wagons designed to carry solid steel rolls. The design is basically a one-plank open wagon, 17ft 6in over headstocks, fitted with movable blocks for securing the load. All wagons were coded Roll WC.

Transformer wagons

In direct contrast with the previous diagram we are once again among the giants of the wagon world. There is a single diagram, page 470, covering the two transformer wagons coded Transformer MC. The load is carried suspended between a pair of 65ft beams, the ends of which rest on two pairs of three-axle trolleys. A special feature of the design is that the load can be slewed twelve inches either side of the centre line if required to clear an obstruction. The diagram states that a load causes a ⅝in drop in buffer height and a 2in drop in the beams. In traffic these wagons have always been observed with an attendant 12ton van to store packing material, and the end of one such van can be seen in Plate 132.

Trestle wagons

To overcome the problem of conveying steel plates which are wider than the loading gauge allows it is usual to transport them at an angle mounted on a supporting trestle. The first British Railways wagons to be so equipped were a group of twenty-three double-bolster wagons converted to become 21ton trestle wagons, coded Trestle EA, and designated diagram 490. They were followed by two lots of 42ton bogie vehicles, Trestle ED, built in this style from new to diagram 491. Further new construction comprised updated versions of both types, with diagram 492 being a vacuum-braked version of the Trestle EA — some of the new ones

Plate 132. *135ton transformer trolley — lettered Transformer. Diagram 2/470. At the other end of the scale from the roll wagon this transformer trolley was 89ft 0in long over headstocks. Side beams were removable for loading, and when a transformer was being carried it could be traversed by a maximum of twelve inches on either side of the centre line to clear an obstruction. Millerhill, 25 January 1970.* (Author).

Plate 131. *12ton roll wagon — lettered Roll WC. Diagram 2/450. This design used the standard 17ft 6in underframe. The wooden blocks were movable to accomodate different roll sizes. Note that while almost all the lettering is standard BR sans-serif style the tare weight is genuine old-fashioned Swindon script. Paint date is August 1956.* (British Railways).

Plate 133. *21ton trestle wagon — lettered Trestle. Diagram 2/490. Unlike most special wagons which were built specifically for the job, the wagons to this diagram were in fact double bolster wagons modified from diagrams 1/415 and 1/416. In many cases the full-length side planks were retained, but obviously not with B920272 seen here at Stainforth (Doncaster). August 1969.* (Dave Larkin).

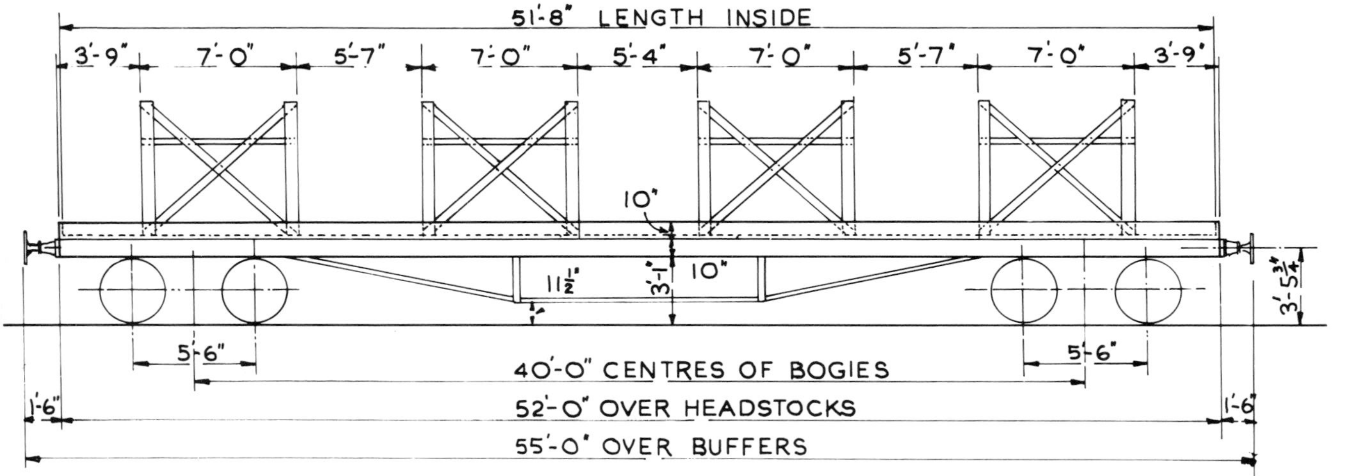

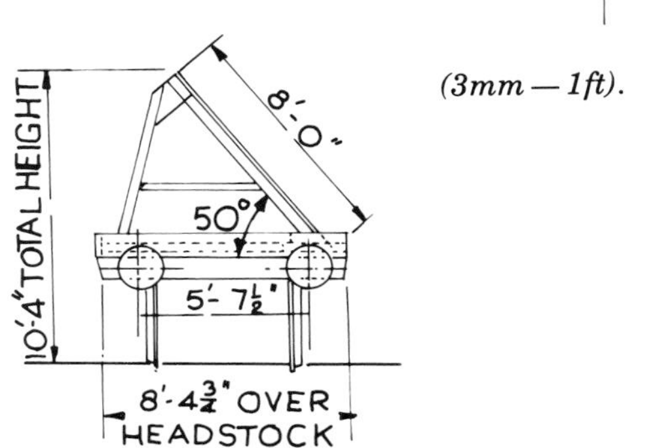

(3mm — 1ft).

Figure 79. *42ton trestle wagon — lettered Trestle. Diagram 2/494. These bogie trestle wagons were a conversion, this time from bogie bolster wagons to diagram 1/472. The diagram as drawn quotes ten vehicles as having been converted, but others may have been added on later issues of the diagram.*

Plate 134. *42ton trestle wagon — lettered Trestle. Diagram 2/495. At last we have a vehicle built as a trestle wagon from the start. Diagram 2/491, which had plain bearings and hand lever brake, gave way to the vacuum-braked version, diagram 2/493, which in turn led to this version with cast bogies and roller-bearings. Millerhill, 12 April 1964.* (Author).

were also coded Trestle AA — while both diagrams 493 and 495 were similarly updated Trestle EDs, the latter with roller-bearings as well. The other two diagrams in this group relate to conversions, the Trestle ABs on page 494 having started life as 42ton bogie bolsters and the 50ton Trestle EHs of page 496 being ex-Warflats, part of the Swindon bargain lot.

Trolleys

Flat trolleys

When reviewing the various types of flat trolleys there is a great similarity with low machine wagons in that we have a specialised vehicle type with a lot of designs but relatively few examples of each. In actual fact there are more Flatrol diagrams but fewer wagons in total. We have therefore

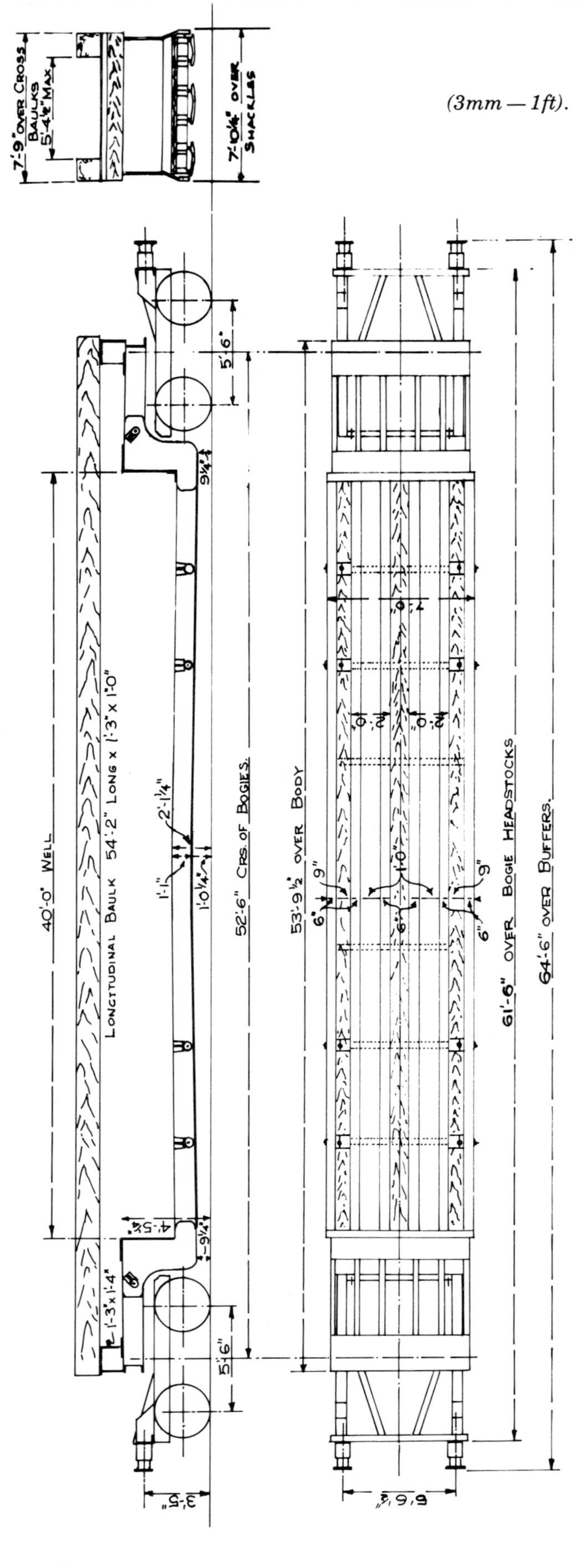

(3mm — 1ft).

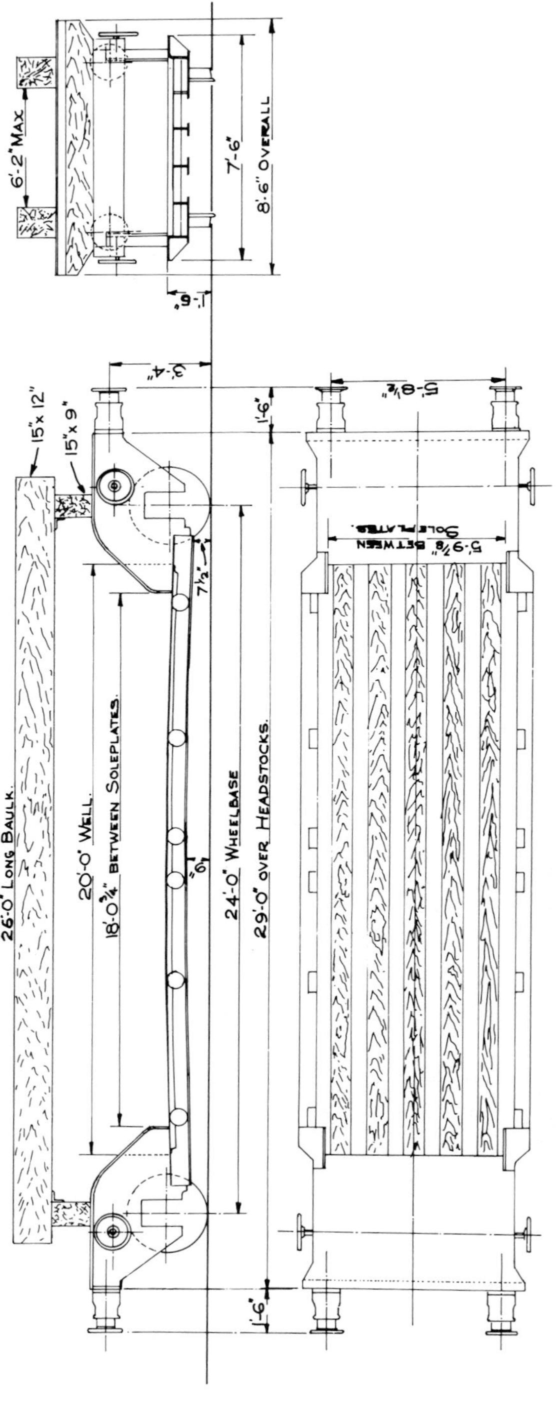

Figure 80. *20ton bogie trolley — lettered Flatrol. Diagram 2/510. The Flatrol family occupied a series of twenty-four diagrams, many of the later being updates of the earlier ones. This particular diagram was one of the first to be issued, and covered ten wagons built as part of the 1949 programme. With its tare weight of 26tons 8cwt without baulks the tare to load weight ratio was decidedly low.*

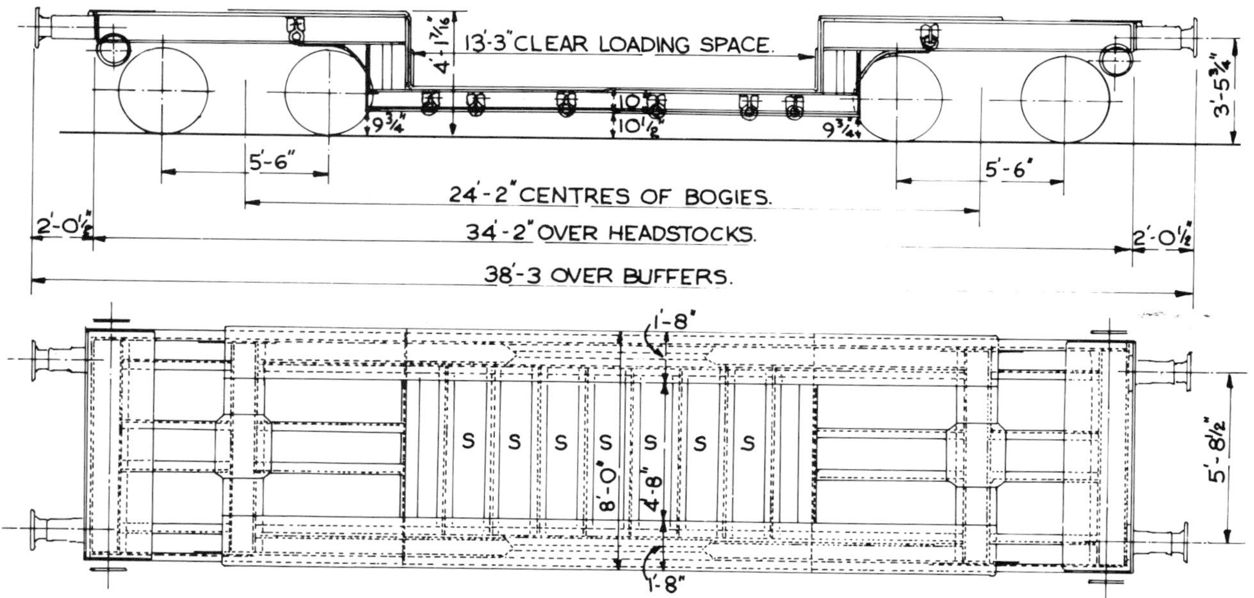

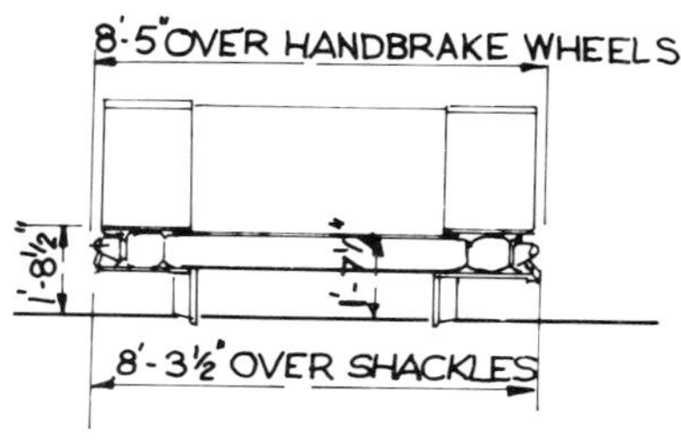

Figure 82. *35ton bogie trolley — lettered Flatrol. Diagram 2/518. For the third Flatrol illustration we have selected a bogie design with a short well, yet one obviously designed for heavier loads. Only one wagon was produced to this diagram. It was intended for continental working and fitted with through Westinghouse brake pipe. As can be seen, there was no provision for baulks to support the load.*

Left:
Figure 81. *20ton four-wheeled trolley — lettered Flatrol. Diagram 2/512. Another early Flatrol design with the same capacity as the previous one but a shorter well. Thirty-three wagons were built to this diagram, quite a respectable total for any special wagon.*

Plate 135. *20ton four-wheeled trolley (RIV) — lettered Flatrol. Diagram 2/527. The Flatrol section is completed with another wagon for continental working. but this time a four-wheeler. Note in particular the volute springs, Westinghouse pipe and the plate to prevent the coupling damaging the brakewheel spindle. Niddrie (Edinburgh), 6 April 1963.* (Author).

followed the same course and summarised the salient features of all flat trolley designs in the accompanying table.

Flat Trolleys — Summary of Types

Diagram	Capacity tons	Wheelbase ft	Wheelbase in	Length over headstocks ft	Length over headstocks in	Length over buffers ft	Length over buffers in	Length of well ft	Length of well in	Axles	Baulks	Numbers Lot	Numbers Qty	Code suffixes (all Flatrol)	Remarks
510	20	52	6	61	6	64	6	40	0	4	Yes	1	10	MSS	
511	40	48	0	58	0	61	0	35	6	4	Yes	3	18	MHH	
512	20	24	0	29	0	32	0	20	0	2	Yes	6	33	MVV	
513	40	42	0	52	6	55	7	30	0	4	No	1	6	WX	
514	50	45	6	55	6	58	7	32	0	4	Yes	2	6	EZ	
515	20	57	6	66	6	69	0	45	0	4	Yes	1	4	MUU	
516	21	22	6	28	6	31	6	18	4	2	Yes	4	9	EAB	
517	25	42	0	52	0	55	0	31	0	4	Yes	3	3	ED, EDC	
518	35	24	2	34	2	38	3	13	3	4	No	1	1	EN (EH?)	Westinghouse pipe
519	120	57	0	86	0	89	0	22	2	12	Yes	1	1	EA	Understructure and bogies ex LNER diagram 134.
520	50	38	6	48	8	51	8	25	0	4	No	1	2	EX	
521	30	49	6	59	6	62	7	36	0	4	Yes	1	2	EL	Westinghouse pipe
522	50	38	6	48	6	51	7	25	0	4	Yes	1	1	EY	
523	30	49	6	59	6	63	8	36	0	4	Yes	1	1	EL	Westinghouse pipe RIV
524	40	48	0	58	0	61	0	35	6	4	Yes	3	11	ET, MHH	
525	20	26	2	32	2	36	3	21	0	2	Yes	1	8	SB	Westinghouse pipe
526	25	57	6			70	7	45	0	4	Yes	2	3	EV	AVB, Westinghouse pipe*
527	20	25	0	29	8½	33	9½	20	6	4	Yes	1	1	EG	Westinghouse pipe RIV
528	20	25	0	31	0	34	5	20	0	4	No	2	5	WW	AVB pipe
529	40	42	0	52	6	55	11	30	0	4	No	1	2	MDD**	AVB pipe
530	21	24	0	33	9	37	10	18	4	2	Yes	1	20	EAC	AVB Westinghouse pipe RIV
531	40	38	0	48	0	51	5	25	6	4	Yes	2	10	MCC**	AVB pipe
532	50	31	0	49	0	52	5	9	0	6	No	1	24	MJ	AVB pipe
533	20	26	2	32	2	36	3	21	0	4	Yes	1	2	SB	Westinghouse pipe RIV

*Lot book states AVB pipe, Westinghouse pipe and RIV. **Originally bogie well wagons

From this table it can be seen that there is a wide range of designs with a very few basic dimensions (gauge and buffer height apart!) common to more than one diagram. There are exceptions; diagram 524 is an updated version of diagram 511 as page 533 is of 525. Likewise, the sole example of diagram 523 is to RIV standards whilst the otherwise similar wagons of diagram 521 are not.

Height above rail level has not been quoted because although basically the Flatrol is designed with the floor carrying the load, there are some examples with wells and some with sides raised above the floor. Furthermore, the wagons are built so that the floor is slightly arched when the wagon is empty but straightens under load. With many designs timber baulks are available if required to bear some of the load weight.

Propellor trolleys

The propellor trolley is a specialised version of the flat trolley for the carriage of ships' propellors. British Railways produced four different designs, all four-axle bogie wagons with timber baulks, similar in appearance to flat trolleys. Even though just seven were built one wonders how often all would be in use at once, even when shipbuilding was thriving in the UK.

Figure 83. *20ton propellor-trolley — lettered Protrol. Diagram 2/660. All four propeller troller designs were of the same basic shape, with the three 40ton diagrams showing only minor differences. This 20ton design was in effect similar, but 7ft shorter in the well.*

Figure 84. *40ton bogie trolley — lettered Trestrol. Diagram 2/680. There were five Trestrol diagrams with most of the wagons being 40ton capacity. This is the first 40ton design; there were ten of these wagons built by Head Wrightson & Co.*

(3mm—1ft).

(3mm—1ft).

Plate 136. *40ton bogie trolley — lettered Trestrol. Diagram 2/681. This second 40ton design differed only in detail from the previous diagram. The diagram states that the wagons had 10in x 5in journals whereas this example, B901531 of lot 3112, clearly has roller-bearings. The eleven wagons which comprised this lot were actually built at Ashford locomotive works. Millerhill, 3 February 1963.* (Author).

Diagram 660 covered the only 20ton design, the Protrol ED. Here length over buffers was 42ft with an 18ft well. The remaining three diagrams, 661, 662 and 663, covered successive updatings of the 40ton Protrol EG, a larger vehicle with a 25ft well.

Trestle trolleys

The trestle trolley may be looked upon as a special version of the trestle wagon where the well is used to accommodate plate sizes larger than those which can be handled by either the trestle wagon or the plate wagon. There are five diagrams, pages 680 to 684. The baby is diagram 683, the 20ton Trestrol EJ, of which one example was built. The next in size is the 30ton Trestrol EN to diagram 684. Two were built at Lancing as part of the 1954 programme. The diagram is particularly interesting, because from it we learn that 'This wagon will carry rectangular plates ranging from 40ft 0in by 12ft 9$\frac{1}{8}$in on NB area to 40ft 0in by 13ft 2$\frac{3}{8}$in on NE area'. And all this in 1954, too!

Diagrams 680 and 682 both refer to 40ton Trestrol MOs of very similar design, of which 147 examples were built. The later ones were coded Trestrol EO and some were built in Ashford locomotive works. The 'big daddy' Trestrol was the 55ton Trestrol EC, a six-axle bogie design, in contrast to all the other Trestrols which were four-axle bogie wagons. Diagram 681 was allocated, but despite its larger capacity it could only accommodate a plate length of 36ft, smaller than the 30ton wagon, although of course thicker plates could be dealt with.

Well trolleys

When we come to the well trolleys we are dealing with the last major group of special wagons. In fact, we are just about at the end of the special wagons *per se*. Again a tabular summary seems the most appropriate treatment, for we are dealing with even fewer wagons, 107 in all, spread over twenty-two different diagrams. The number of dif-

Well Trolleys — Summary of Types

Diagram	Capacity tons	Wheelbase ft	in	Length over headstocks ft	in	Length over buffers ft	in	Length of well ft	in	Axles	Baulks	Numbers Lot	Qty	Code suffixes (all Weltrol)	Remarks
730	20	32	6	42	0	45	0	20	0	4	Yes	1	10	MC	
731	40	26	0	35	6	38	6	15	0	4	Yes	2	9	MV	
732	30	44	6	54	6	57	6	35	0	4	Yes	1	1	EC	
733	20	25	6	30	6	33	6	20	0	4	Yes	1	10	MA	
734	35	51	6	62	0	65	1	41	0	4	No	2	4	WW	
735	25	31	0	40	6	43	6	20	0	4	Yes	2	6	WBB	
736	40	48	0	58	6	61	6	36	0	4	Yes	1	3	EB	
737	120	55	0	86	6	89	7	19	0	12	No	1	1	WL	Detachable girders
738	50	45	6	59	6	62	11	28	11	6	No	1	2	EP	Westingouse pipe
739	25	36	6	47	0	50	0	25	6	4	No	1	1	WZ	AVB pipe
740	25	45	6	55	6	58	6	35	0	4	Yes	1	2	EL	AVB pipe
741	25	42	6	53	0	56	0	32	0	4	No	2	25	WP	AVB pipe
742	50	43	6	54	0	57	0	32	7$\frac{1}{2}$	4	No	1	1	WJ	AVB pipe
743	25	42	6	53	0	56	0	32	0	4	No	1	2	WP	AVB pipe
744	65	32	0	42	6	45	6	21	1$\frac{1}{2}$	4	No	1	2	WH	AVB pipe
745	25	36	6	47	0	50	0	25	6	4	No	1	3	WZ	AVB pipe
746	20	32	6	42	0	45	5	20	0	4	Yes	2	4	MC	AVB pipe
747	35	51	6	62	0	65	5	41	0	4	No	2	4	WW	AVB pipe
748	40	36	6	47	0	50	5	26	1	4	No	2	8	WGG, MV	AVB pipe
749	120	58	6	87	6	90	11	22	2	12	No	1	1	ENN	
750	55	54	0	71	3	75	4	32	0	6	No	3	6	EJC	AVB pipe Westinghouse pipe
751	35	51	6	62	0	65	5	41	0	4	No	1	22	WW	AVB Pipe

Figure 85. *20ton four-wheeled trestle trolley — lettered Trestrol. Diagram 2/683. According to the diagram this wagon — the only one built — was designed for carrying circular plates, special chocks being provided for the purpose. There was no point in providing a longer wagon, since the height of such plates would foul the loading gauge.*

Plate 137. *20ton bogie well trolley — lettered Weltrol. Diagram 2/730. We complete the trolleys with the Weltrols, a group which is very similar in appearance to the Flatrols. In this instance the baulks are only being used to give side support to the load and are not taking any of the weight. This particular wagon, B901801, was built with plain bearings which by 10 May 1963 had been replaced by roller-bearings. Millerhill.* (Author).

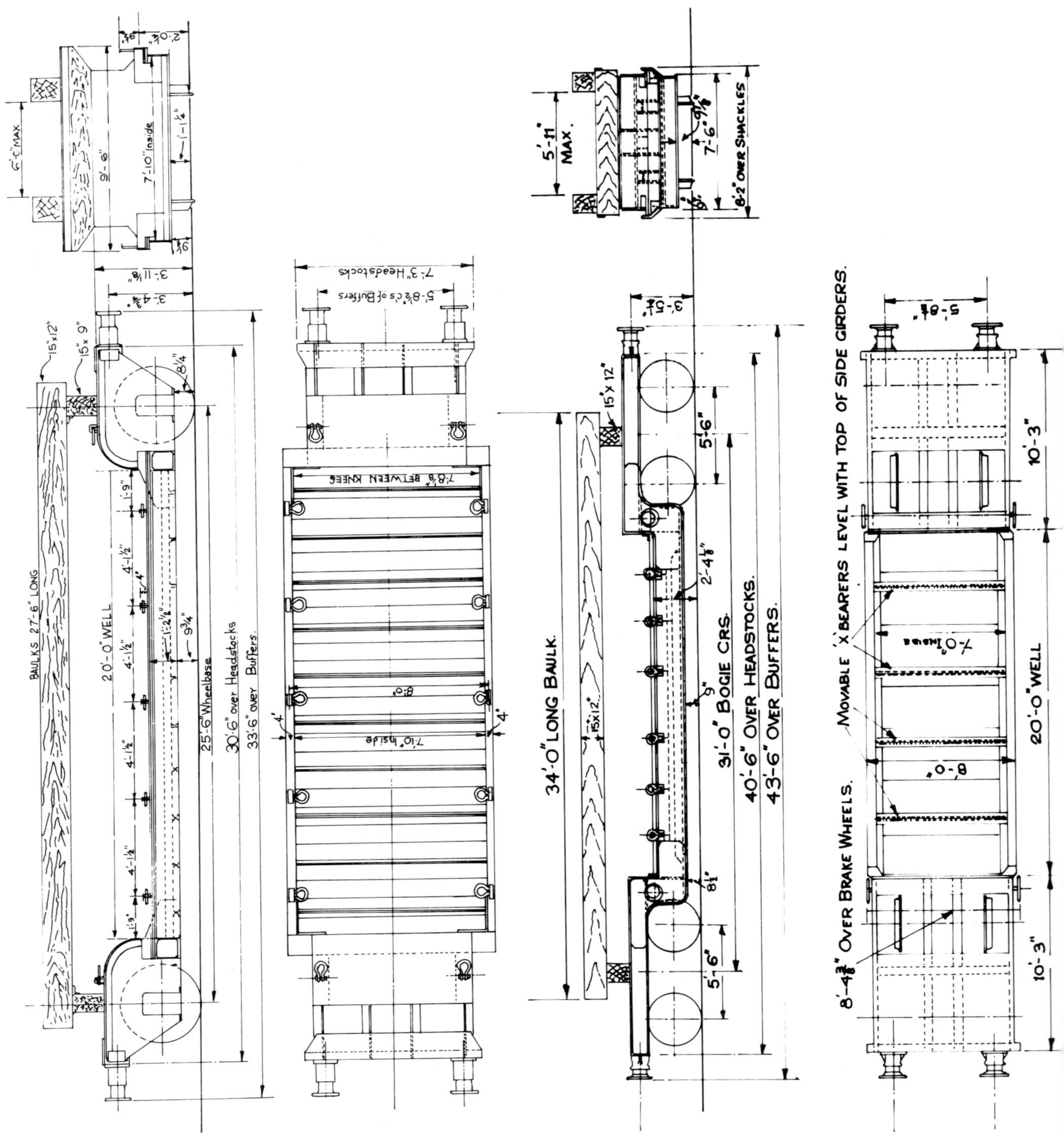

Figure 86. *20ton four-wheeled trolley — lettered Weltrol. Diagram 2/733. There was just this single four-wheeled Weltrol design to which one lot of ten wagons was built. The most significant feature is the unusual width (for a British wagon) of 9ft 6in.*

Figure 87. *25ton bogie well trolley — lettered Weltrol. Diagram 2/735. This review of the Weltrols is completed with two different kinds of 25ton bogie vehicle. First there is this relatively short well design with timber baulks to support the load. (3mm — 1ft).*

Plate 138. *25ton Weltrol WP, wood floor. Diagram 2/741. In contrast there is this much longer design, 32ft in the well, with no provision for baulks. By 24 September 1977 when it was photographed in Crewe locomotive works, this particular wagon had been transferred to departmental stock as CDB900918.* (Author).

ferent designs is not quite as bad as it appears at first sight, as many of the later diagrams are virtually re-issues of earlier ones to cover new construction fitted with roller-bearings.

As with previous tables the wheelbase for bogie vehicles is taken as distance between bogie centres. Constructionally the important feature of the well trolley wagon is that the load is carried on the well girders or on adjustable cross girders which bear on the main ones or on a combination of both, depending on the traffic. The well floor plays little or no part in load bearing, to the extent that many designs have no floor at all.

Wheel wagons

The wheel wagon is possibly the most specialised type of wagon to be built by British Railways, being designed for the transport of large wheels such as those used with pithead winding gear. The first examples were not ordered until 1958 and only five examples were built. The 10ton type to diagram 880 was something like a double bolster wagon with twin baulks and a large hole in the floor. In contrast the 20ton type, diagram 881, was a bogie design with adjustable cross-beams sitting on raised girders which ran the full length of the wagon.

Departmental wagons

All the specially-constructed wagons so far have been designed for traffic use, but there remains a series of five diagrams issued to cover special wagons for departmental use. All are 20ton four-wheeled trolleys covering 30 vehicles in total. Two of the diagrams, 900 and 902, are for trolleys with removable buffing struts, code named Loriots, also applied to the two examples of diagram 901 without such struts. The solitary example of diagram 903 is coded Flatrol SB and is equipped with three timber baulks, built up over one axle to form a packing block. It seems likely that it was used as a crane runner. The final diagram, 904, is virtually the Flatrol MVV (page 512 of the same book) designated for departmental use.

Chapter 12

Containers

At first sight it may seem rather unusual to include containers in a book about wagons. Nevertheless, there is a certain logic in so doing since they are in effect detachable wagon bodies. The Railway Executive certainly saw containers in this light because container orders were included in the wagon lot scheme right from the very start. A special diagram book was set up for containers, following that for the specially constructed wagons. In considering container flat wagons in Chapter 2 we commented on the fact that the Ideal Stocks Committee paid virtually no attention to container traffic during its deliberations. To be sure, its remit did not mention containers specifically but the omission was surprising nonetheless.

Containers were treated slightly differently from wagons in that a special numbering scheme was devised for them. It was more comprehensive than the system for wagons in that it comprised a one-, two- or three-letter prefix to the running number together with a builder suffix which for BR-built containers was B. As with wagons, running numbers were allocated in blocks according to container type. Amongst the railway companies there was a high degree of standardisation in container design resulting from the fact that containers as we know them arrived rather late in the day. British Railways containers followed pre-nationalisation designs very closely, so much so that in many cases construction was still to RCH drawings a long time after 1948.

Table 3 in Chapter 1 shows how container stocks rose from 20,000 in 1948 until they exceeded 50,000 at the end of the 1950s only to decline steadily as railway freight traffic ebbed away. Even so, it is interesting to compare these figures with those for wagons as a whole. In spite of heavy container withdrawals, stocks at the end of 1967 were still over 50% greater than they had been on vesting day, while wagon stocks had declined from 1,223,634 to 466,623 over the same period. Put another way, there was one container for every fifteen wagons at the end of 1967 compared with one for every sixty-five wagons twenty years previously.

Before reviewing container designs it is worth noting that container construction tended to be handled by workshops other than those building wagons. Many British Railways containers were built at Earlestown after that works had ceased to produce wagons, while Cowlairs works eked out its last years of existence with container work. Even Bromsgrove wagon repair shops built a batch of containers, and Ulster Transport Authority also built some for BR. Some of the more specialist designs were produced by firms such as E. R. Foden, a name one would not expect to find in a lot list.

A Type

We shall deal with container types in the order in which they appear in the diagram book. As with the other two diagram books pages were allocated in blocks for each type. The arrival of Freightliner containers disrupted the pattern somewhat but they will be excluded, as has been done with their wagons, as being outwith the compass of this volume.

The A type container in its various forms measures approximately 7ft 6in long, 7ft wide and 8ft high. There are doors at one end only, and capacity of the three main types is either 322 cu ft or 329 cu ft. The original designs were rated at three tons, a figure later increased by one ton. Apart from minor dimensional differences in some cases the three principal types vary only in methods of construction. Diagram 1 had sides and doors of tongue-and-groove boarding, with a pressed-steel end. In diagram 3 the end is also built of tongue-and-groove while diagram 2 is another all-wood design, this time employing ¾in plywood panels for the outer skin. As Appendix 4 shows most A

Plate 139. *Container Type A. Diagram 3/001. When considering containers we shall continuously refer to the materials used — principally tongue-and-groove boarding, plywood or metal — and the presence or absence of pressed-steel corrugated ends. Here we have the 3ton (later increased to 4ton) capacity A size container with tonge-and-groove boarding and corrugated end. It was easily the most popular A type diagram, with over 3,800 examples built. Millerhill, 27 July 1968.* (Author).

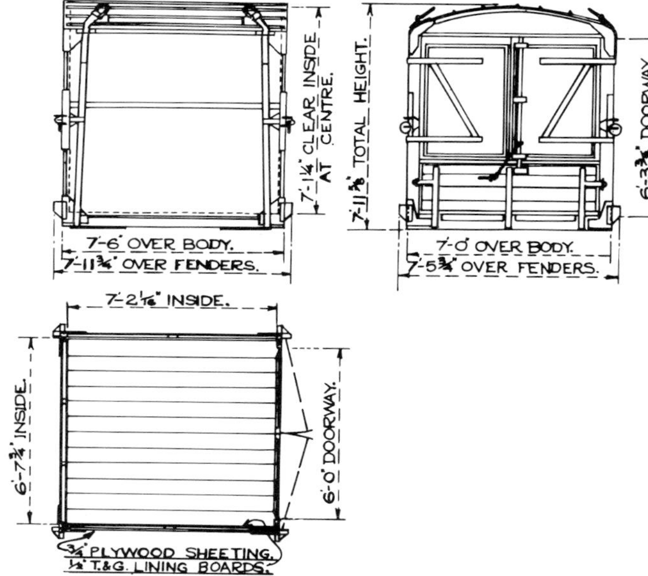

LOT	~~2068~~	2124	2056
QTY	~~50~~	50	60
Nos	~~A61B TO A110B~~	A291B TO A340B	A1B TO A60B
Dg.No.	RCH. 2063.		R.C.H. 2063
CARR. CAP. TONS.	~~3~~	3	3
CUB CAP CU. FT.	~~322~~	322	322
TARE		1T. 1C.	1T 2C 1Q

Figure 88. *Container Type A. Diagram 3/002. In contrast, only 110 examples of this plywood version were built. The lot details are exactly as they appear on the diagram. The containers A61B to A110B were never built, as is indicated by the erasure of lot 2068.*

type containers were built to diagram 1.

In addition to these three main designs there were three experimental designs for A type containers. Willerby Engineering produced two plastic containers on wooden pallets, allocated diagram 4, together with a single example in fibreglass to diagram 5. Cowlairs works also built a dozen containers in light alloy to diagram 6 but none of these designs ever saw large-scale production.

B Type and variants

B Type

As a general guide, the B type and its variants such as the BC, BD and BK types is an A type container but rather more than twice as long. Typical capacity is 724 cu ft compared with 322 cu ft for the A type.

There are two designs of B type container, both having doors at one end only. The principal one, diagram 49, has tongue-and-groove boarding for sides and doors, together with a pressed-steel end. Although the diagram does not say so specifically, one assumes that the other B type design, diagram 47, was of light-alloy construction since Park Royal, well-known for building bus bodies, handled the order. The missing diagram 48 was originally intended to cover lot 2833 but before entering traffic the sixty containers therein were reclassified BC and allocated diagram 100.

BD Type

The BD container was the most widely used type on British Railways, being in effect the general purpose merchandise container. It differs from the B type in having, in addition to doors at one end, double side doors as well. Capacity varied around 720 cu ft and load was four tons. The development of the BD type parallels that of the A type almost exactly. There were three main production types

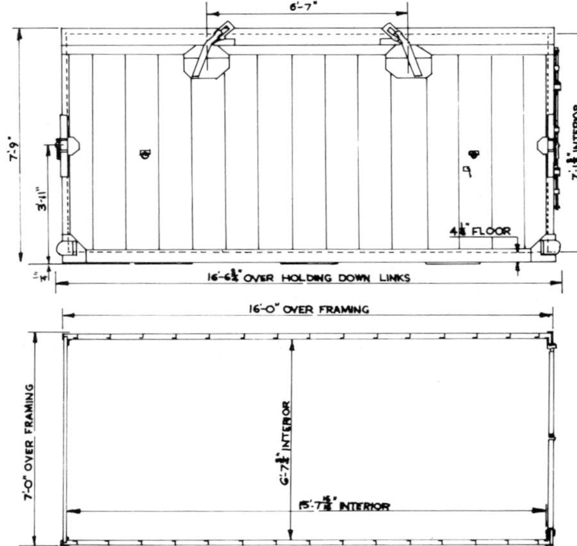

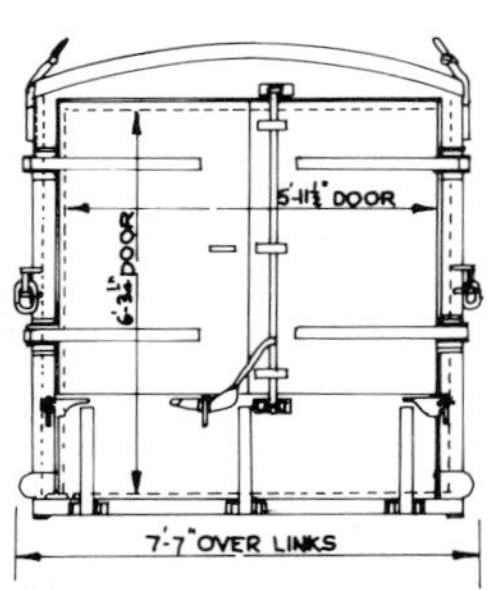

Figure 89. *Container Type B. Diagram 3/047. The B type container was in effect a double-length A type and like the A type had doors at one end only. This diagram was a little unusual in that it called for light alloy construction, a material that did not find widespread acceptance until Freightliner containers came along.*

Plate 140. *Container Type B. Diagram 3/049. According to the diagram these 325 containers were constructed of tongue-and-groove boarding with pressed-steel ends, yet quite clearly B55549B is built of plywood panels, and the lot book gives no indication of amendments. Millerhill, 27 July 1968.* (Author).

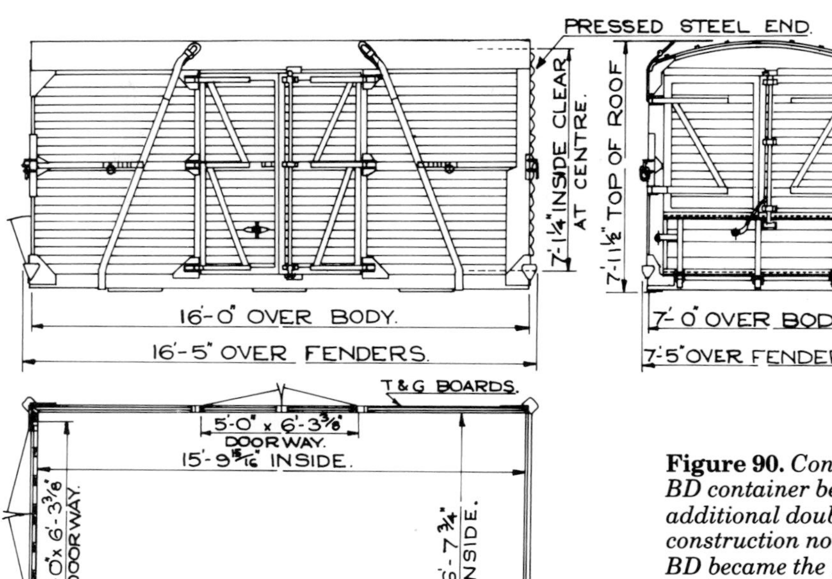

Figure 90. *Container Type BD. Diagram 3/050. The BD container began as a variation of the B type with additional double doors each side. In the end construction not only exceeded that of the B type but the BD became the most numerous of all container types.*

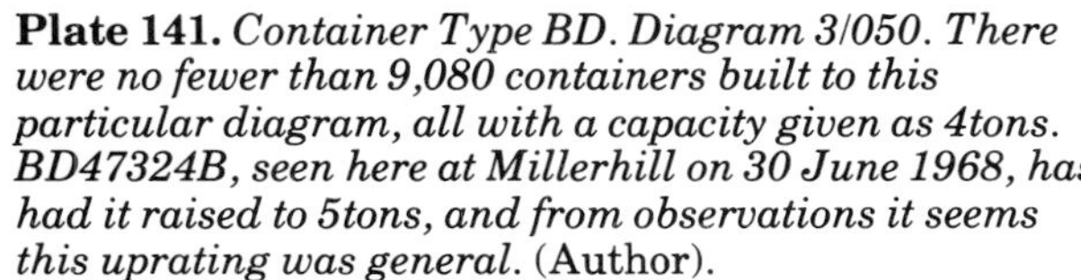

Plate 141. *Container Type BD. Diagram 3/050. There were no fewer than 9,080 containers built to this particular diagram, all with a capacity given as 4tons. BD47324B, seen here at Millerhill on 30 June 1968, has had it raised to 5tons, and from observations it seems this uprating was general.* (Author).

Plate 142. *Container Type BD, Diagram 3/050. Although at first sight BD48683B is a normal BD type container, a closer examination will show that there are no lifting shackles on the roof; unlike the containers illustrated up to now, it is not secured to the wagon with chains. In fact, both the container and the wagon have been modified to the Speedfreight system. Millerhill, 5 April 1969.* (Author).

followed by a series of experimental versions. The production designs showed the same permutations of tongue-and-groove boarding, plywood panels and ends of pressed-steel that were used with the A type, and again the one with steel ends was the most common.

After production of three lots the plywood panelled version, diagram 51, was not repeated. Likewise only three lots were produced to diagram 52, a design using tongue-and-groove boarding for both sides and ends. Of these three lots only the first was built to diagram 52 in its entirety; the remaining two batches were both parts of larger orders for BD containers of which the majority were produced with pressed-steel ends to diagram 50. Production of this latter type continued from 1949 right through to 1958, by which time no less than 10,080 examples had been completed. Apart from the final 400 built by contractors, all the others had come from former LMS railway works at Earlestown, St Rollox and Wolverton.

The remaining BD containers were all experi-

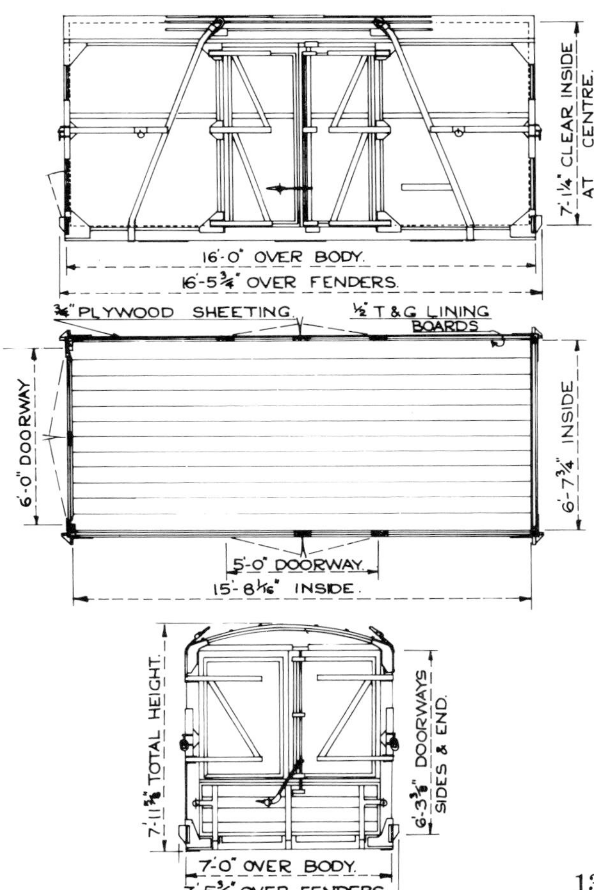

Figure 91. *Container Type BD. Diagram 3/051. In contrast to the thousands of BD containers built of tongue-and-groove boarding only three lots of the plywood version were built, all part of the 1949 programme.*

Plate 143. *Container Type BD (fibreglass construction). Diagram 3/054. From the late 1950s onwards British Railways investigated numerous new container types and the use of new construction materials. BD4304B was one of a batch of six containers made of fibreglass. The diagram shows them as having roller shutter doors, and certainly BD4305B was so equipped at one time, but by 27 July 1968 at Millerhill when this photograph was taken BD4304B had acquired hinged doors.* (Author).

Plate 144. *Light alloy container Type A. Diagram not known. Continuing the theme of the development of special containers, this picture taken at Niddrie (Edinburgh) on 5 June 1962 illustrates three of a group of containers built for McVitie & Price biscuit traffic from Gorgie East. We know from the running numbers that the wagons are Conflat ABs to diagram 1/077, but we have not been able to identify the containers any further.* (Author).

mental designs built in limited quantities. The single example to diagram 53 was a light-alloy design while diagram 54 featured fibreglass construction combined with roller shutters. The containers of both designs were smaller than the normal BD type. Those to the two remaining BD designs were also smaller and were insulated as well. Diagram 55 never progressed beyond the building of a single prototype and although four lots were produced to diagram 56 construction in total comprised no more than ten examples.

BA Type

The cessation of the BD type building programme in 1958 followed by the production of small numbers of new designs indicates that British Railways was looking for a replacement container for general service. This suggestion would seem to be confirmed by the production of forty larger BA type containers in 1961. They were a much improved design in light alloy with end doors and sliding side doors. Their capacity was increased to 810 cu ft; diagram 75 was allotted. They were followed by thirteen similar containers to diagram 76 although this order was in fact scaled down from the original twenty-five. The important point about all these containers, which were intended for Speedfreight services, was that they abandoned the hook-and-shackle fitting which had up to then been the standard method of securing containers to the host wagons in favour of a system of pins which where located in pockets on the wagon chassis, the forerunner of the system which was to become standard with the Freightliner concept. In fact the way things turned out the BA type as such was superseded by the Freightliner container and never saw large-scale production. Page 79 of the container diagram book covered a single container flat built at Temple Mills.

BC Type

We have already noted that the B type containers of lot 2833 were re-designated as BC type and appeared as diagram 100. It seems that the BC type, used for the carriage of bicycles, was in effect a B type fitted with racks to hold seventy-six cycles but could also be used for general merchandise. There were two diagrams, page 100 for those with pressed-steel ends and 101 for those having ends of tongue-and-groove boarding. No plywood version seems to have been produced.

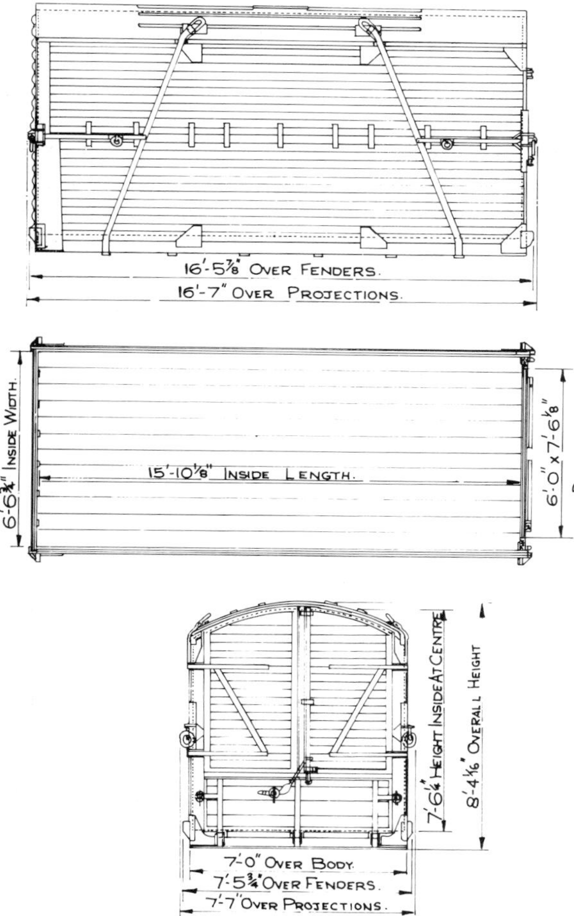

Figure 92. *Container Type B and BC. Diagram 3/100. In spite of the options in the title all containers to this diagram were built as type BC. Externally there was no difference, but internally the BC was fitted with racks to carry seventy-six bicycles. In later years many BCs were converted to Bs by the removal of these fittings.*

BK Type

The BK type was another variant of the B type and like it had doors at one end only. It was intended for furniture transport and as such was equipped with internal slats for securing webbing straps. There were again three diagrams, pages 125, 126 and 127, but all were for plywood designs without pressed-steel ends. There were minor dimensional differences between each design.

BM Type

In Chapter 5 we showed how few meat vans had been built by British Railways, indicating that in the event most rail-borne meat went in containers.

Plate 145. *Container Type BM. Diagram 3/150. The BM container was in effect a variant of the BD type, the principal external difference being louvred vents on sides and ends, and internally the provision of bars and hooks for the carriage of fresh meat. With the reduction in such traffic some BM containers were converted to BDs. Kirkcaldy, 24 June 1961.* (Author).

The BM type was used for fresh meat leaving the FM for frozen or chilled meat. For this traffic (ie fresh meat) hooks and bars were fitted, and louvred vents were built into the sides and ends. There were four diagrams, pages 150 to 153. Apart from minor dimensional differences the odd man out was diagram 152 which covered a single lot of forty containers of plywood construction with boarded floors. The other designs all had outer shells of tongue-and-groove boarding and floors covered with aluminium plate.

BP Type

Of the sixty BP type containers we have little information beyond that given in Appendix 4. They were of 1½tons capacity, but we have never seen a diagram nor have any examples been noted in traffic.

FM Type

Although production of BM containers for conveyance of fresh meat reached the respectable total of 1,305 this was easily exceeded by the 3,885 containers built for frozen meat traffic. In general terms the FM was an insulated version of the BD container, slightly smaller in length and equipped with bars and meat hooks. Diagrams 200, 201 and 204 covered designs with an outer skin of tongue-and-groove boarding, while (and this may not be

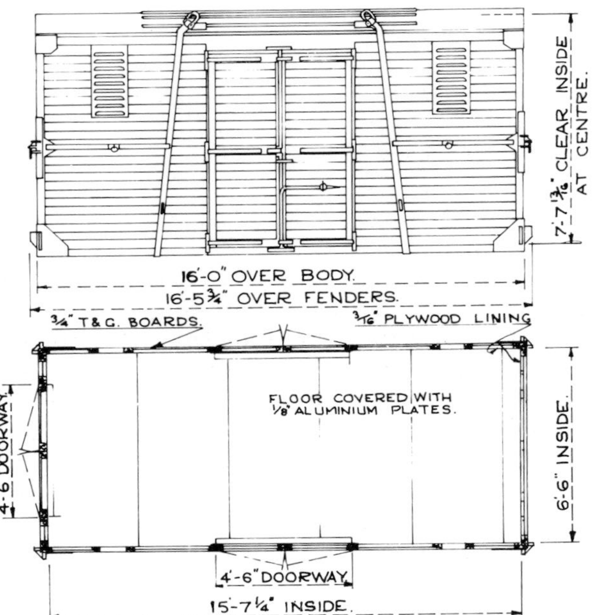

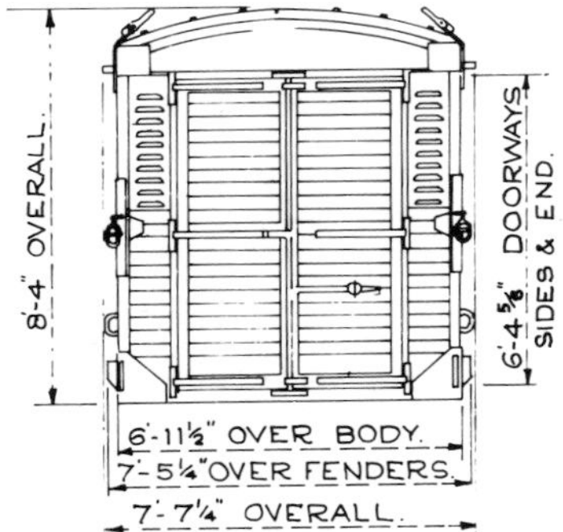

Figure 93. *Container Type BM. Diagram 3/150. Another feature of the BM type, as the diagram shows, was the provision of aluminium plates to cover the floor. A comparison with Figure 90 shows that the BMs to this diagram were approximately six inches taller than the BD, to accommodate hanging carcases.*

Plate 146. *Container Type BM. Diagram 3/153. For the last two batches of Bm containers a new diagram 3/153 was raised. There were minor differences, like the repositioning of the label holder and the use of rubbber fenders, but the principal one was that the new design was about three inches lower. Symington, 13 June 1959.* (Author).

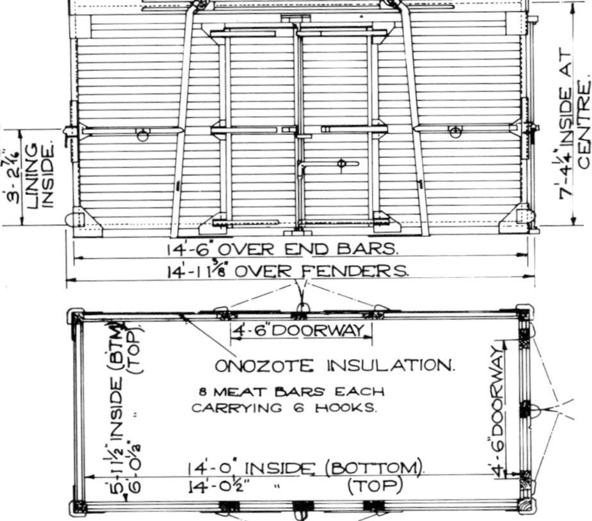

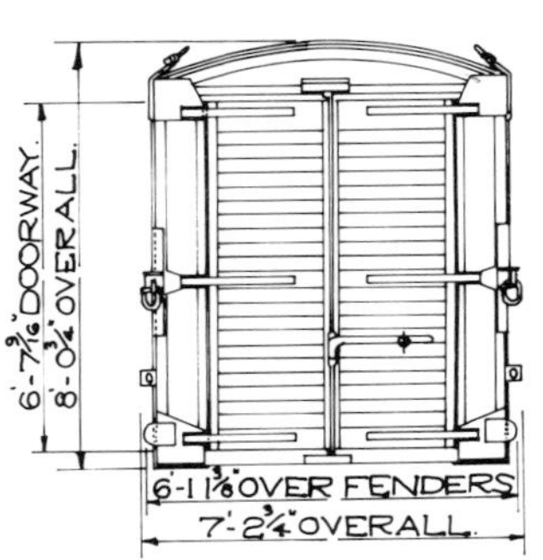

Figure 94. *Meat Container Type FM. Diagram 3/201. The title tells only part of the story because the BM type was also a meat container. The FM was in fact an insulated container for the conveyance of frozen meat, hence the thicker insulated sides, ends, floor and roof, and the absence of louvres.*

Plate 147. *Meat Container Type FM. Diagram 3/205. While numbers of the smaller insulated containers carried user liveries, their use on the larger FM type was relatively rare. Nevertheless it was not unknown for them to do so. Falkirk (Springfield) 4 May 1959.* (Author).

unexpected) 202, 203 and 205 were for designs using plywood panels. Pressed-steel ends were not used. Beyond that there are changes in insulating materials and other small changes. In effect, as time went on and designs developed one diagram superseded its predecessor.

A Type and variants

CA and FA Types

The thirteen CA type containers of diagram 210 seem to be a halfway house between the traditional container and the Freightliner version. Like the BA type they had Speedfreight fastenings, and could also be used on Freightliner wagons as well as on suitably modified Conflat A wagons. They were 27ft long, and although of 8ft width they were only 7ft 4⅝in overall height. Beyond a single lot the design was not repeated. The two diagrams for FA containers, namely pages 230 and 231, represent the insulated versions of the BA container (diagrams 75 and 76) with which they share the same external dimensions. Diagram 230, like the diagrams of the BA designs, shows a container with lifting brackets at 9ft 9in centres whereas on diagram 231 Freightliner lifting brackets are also fitted. So while the BA and the first FA designs show a break away from the traditional container concept in not having crane loops but instead having lifting brackets, the CA design (diagram 210) and the later FA one (diagram 231) go one step further away by also making provision for Freightliner loading.

AF Type and variants

The next groups of diagrams covered a series of highly-insulated containers, basically A size, of types AF and variants, with diagram numbers between 250 and 300. The first of these containers to be ordered was a batch of one hundred AF type to diagram 250, in effect a plywood-panelled A type with nine inches of insulation all round, which reduced capacity to 193 cu ft. A further 200 were to

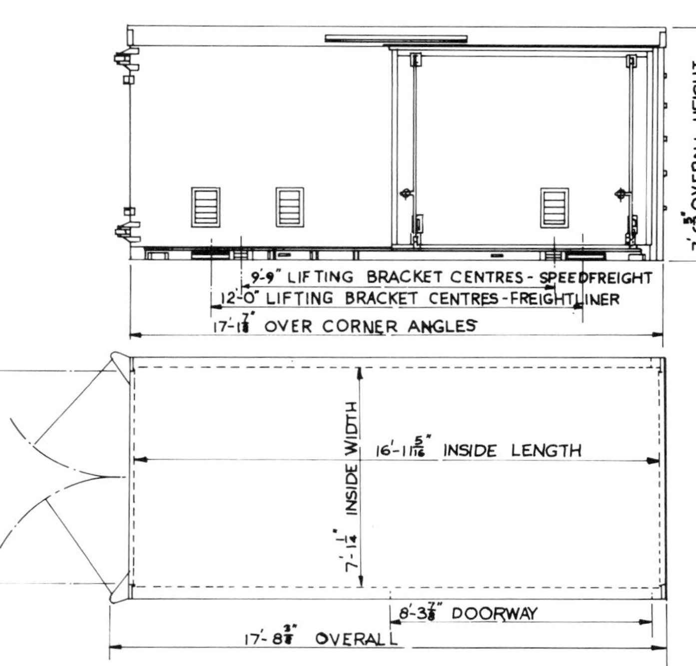

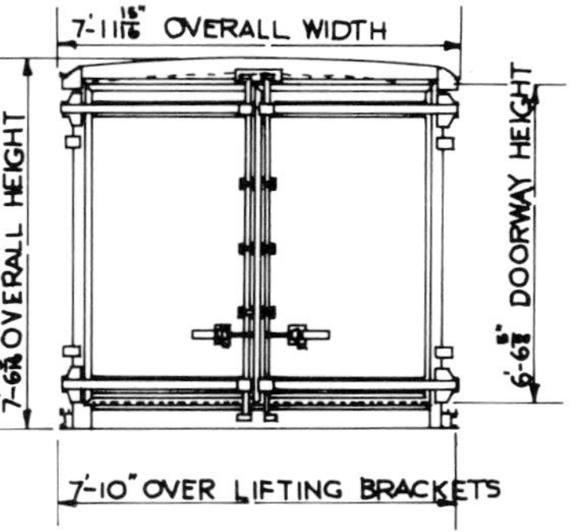

Figure 95. *Container Type FA (insulated). Diagram 3/231. The caption to Plate 142 referred to the move away from securing containers by chains, towards the Speedfreight system. These FA containers marked a further step forward in that they could also be used on Freightliner services.*

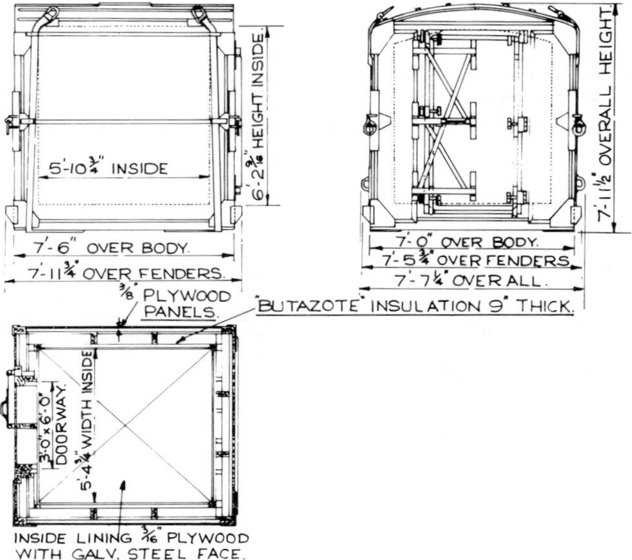

Figure 96. *Container Type AF. Diagram 3/250. The AF container was a highly insulated type (compare the thickness of insulation with Figure 94) used for carriage of frozen foods and ice cream. There were later variants, principally the AFU fitted with eutectic plates and the AFP with dry ice bunkers.*

be built to this design, but before the first lot had been completed it was decided that nine of them should be fitted with eutectic plates. A new lot number was issued for the nine together with a new diagram, page 251, of which they became the sole examples. For later batches insulation material was changed from Butazote to Onazote, thus giving rise to two new diagrams, 252 and 253, the latter covering AFU containers which were AFs with eutectic plates. Diagram 254 covered a single AFU Pallet container which began life as an experimental AFP numbered AFP79997B before emerging as AFU65800B. As such it was the prototype for the eighty-five AFU Pallet containers of diagram 255. While these were being produced British Railways also designed an AF variant having dry ice bunkers in the roof. It was designated the AFP type covered by diagrams 256 and 257.

The diagrams above covered containers that were basically the same shape as the A type. The AFC type on the other hand was much longer being 12ft 11½in over the body compared with the 7ft 6in of the AFs and AFUs. Four were built, two to diagram 260 and another two, with slightly different lifting shackles, to diagram 261 but the type never entered quantity production.

AX, AFX and F Types

The AX type was an extremely well insulated container (the X is believed to be a mnemonic for 'extremely') for the carriage of liquid carbon dioxide. In contrast to all other A types it was virtually a top loading tank with five two-inch layers of insulation and clad in tongue-and-groove boards. Only one diagram was issued (page 275). The AFX type was a conventional insulated container, mid-way in size between the A and AFC designs. The F type to diagram 375 was also something of an odd man out, but whereas the AFXs were built by British Railways as part of the 1953 programme the Fs were almost certainly an unexecuted Southern Railway order taken over by BR.

RY Type

Tucked in among all these insulated containers were six RY type containers to diagram 374. All were built by Ulster Transport Authority for British Railways. It is believed they were used for rayon traffic between Courtaulds factories in Northern Ireland and England, but this has not been confirmed.

Type L and variants

Under this heading come a group of rather odd-looking container designs, all intended for the carriage of bulk material. There are eight diagrams, pages 400 and 450 to 456. Of these, the LD type containers to diagram 400 had a most unusual appearance and were in effect portable dolomite hoppers which were carried in pairs on 21ton Conflat LDs.

The L type bulk limestone containers were a little more conventional in appearance, but this did not prevent the reviewer of a commercial model once describing them as 'transformers'. Be that as it may, the L type container proved to be a most popular one with some 6,386 being built, all to diagram 450. In contrast, the remaining designs were built in penny numbers. The fourteen LG type bulk flour containers to diagram 451 were in effect A types loaded through manholes in the roof and discharged through bottom outlets. The eight LGs to the very similar diagram 453 were in fact just that. The diagram even quotes the numbers of the containers concerned.

Diagram 452 covered seven LF bulk flour containers built by Duramin Engineering, while 454 related to three LP type containers built by Met-

Plate 148. *Container Type AX. Diagram 3/275. The AX container was developed to carry liquid carbon dioxide, for which purpose no less than ten inches of insulation was provided all round. The sheet covering the top of this example was not a normal feature and probably points to damage to the top of the bunker. Millerhill, 27 July 1968.* (Author).

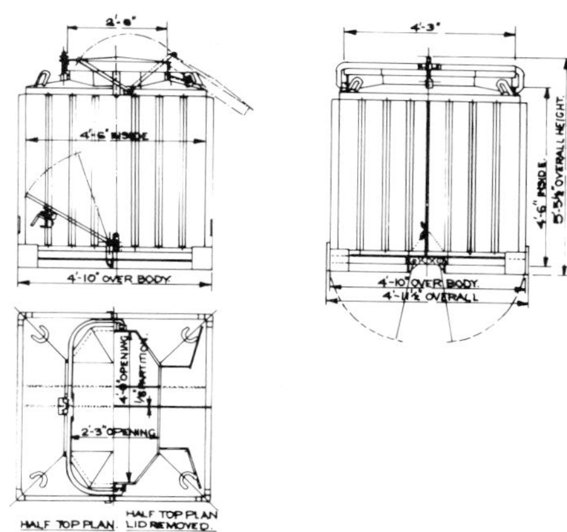

Figure 98. *Container Type L. Diagram 3/450. Likewise, the L type container, used principally for carriage of limestone, required special wagons, this time the Conflat Ls. Three of these containers loaded on such a wagon are illustrated in Plate 25.*

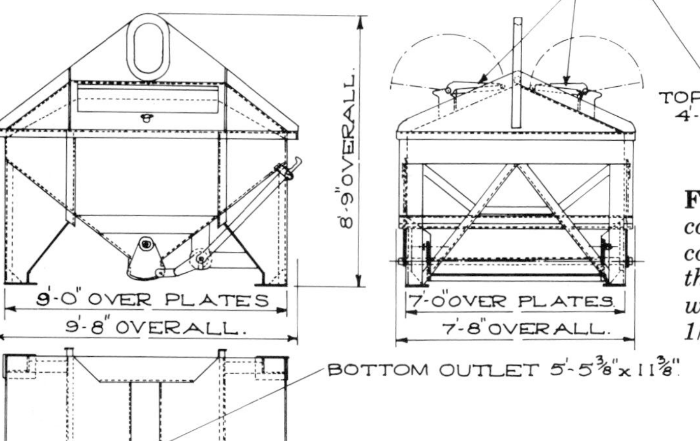

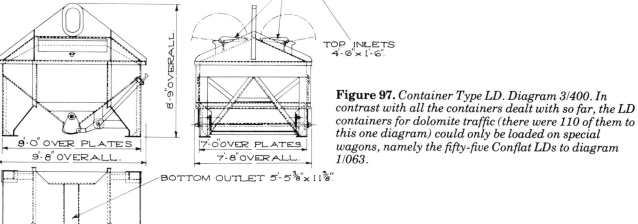

Figure 97. *Container Type LD. Diagram 3/400. In contrast with all the containers dealt with so far, the LD containers for dolomite traffic (there were 110 of them to this one diagram) could only be loaded on special wagons, namely the fifty-five Conflat LDs to diagram 1/063.*

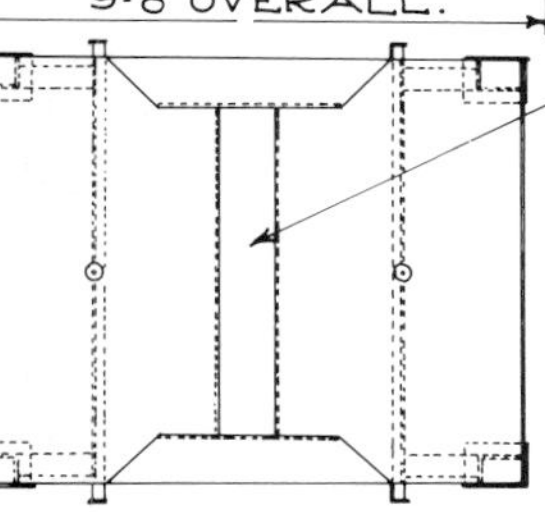

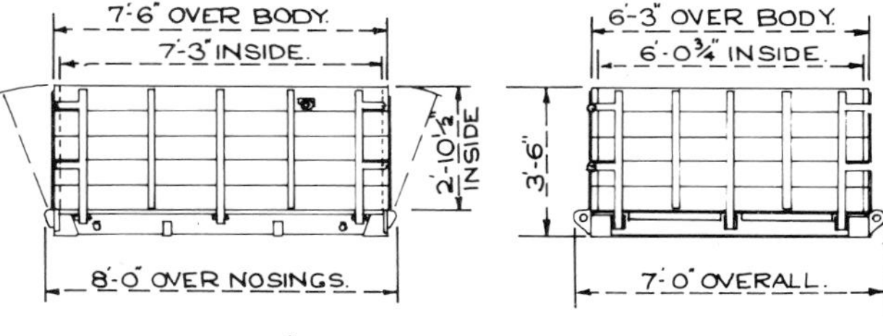

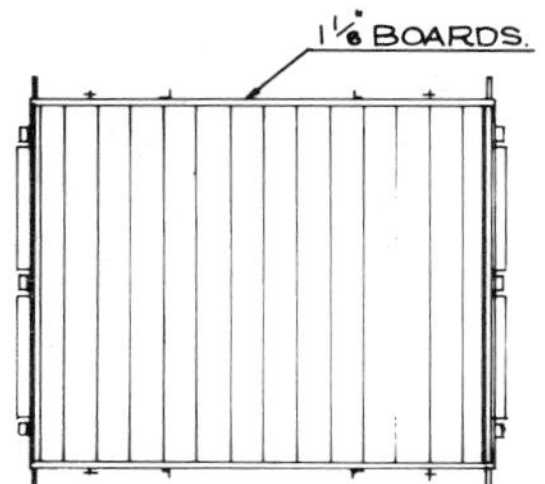

Figure 99. *Container Type C. Diagram 3/500. Although right from the beginning container schemes allowed for open designs, the type never achieved the popularity of the closed A and B styles and their variants. Even so, the three principal open designs, the 2¼ton H, this 3ton C and the larger 4ton D under British Railways alone ran to 6,975 examples.*

ropolitan-Cammell. From here the story becomes a little confusing. The lot book records that the fifteen LS containers of lot 3447 originally were all classed as being of type LP but were re-designated LS before entering traffic. As such they were the only LS containers built and page 78 of the wagon diagram book covers six 22ton container flat wagons to carry LS containers. Yet less than a year after the LF/LP/LS containers had entered traffic we find the firm of Carmichael building six similar type LT containers and we have observed at least three of these wagons coded Conflat LT and loaded with the LT containers. Whether the LS had a very short life we cannot say.

Open containers

The next pages of the diagram book cover various sizes of open container of differing shapes and dimensions and with varying combinations of door arrangements, all of which can be roughly described as open wagons without undergear. The C type, admittedly, would make a very small wagon even by British standards as its interior dimensions were a mere 6ft 0¾in by 7ft 0in but its boarded construction was strongly reminiscent of a wagon body. Capacity was 126 cu ft. There was a single diagram, page 500, and all 790 examples were built at Earlestown.

The next size, the D type, was very much more like an open wagon with its six-plank sides and side doors, also having one end door and the fixed end being secured with tee stanchions. Again there was but a single diagram, page 550. No Cs or Ds were built after 1954. This applies also to the DX type, a derivative of the D having detachable sides and end doors. A single lot was ordered and diagram 599 was allocated. Between these two types there are two other diagrams, page 560 for the DA type and page 565 covering the DL. Both were built on an experimental basis, single lots of twenty and two containers respectively.

The other main open type of container was the H, designed originally for building materials with the H being a mnemonic for 'hod'. It was even smaller than the C type with a 42.7 cu ft or 46 cu ft capacity. The first two lots were to diagram 600 with the others to diagram 602. There is no record of diagram 601 having been used. Before the advent of the Freightliners two other open container diagrams were issued. They were pages 640 and 641 for the BOO Speedfreight type but only six were built.

Plate 149. *Container Type LT. Diagram 3/456. With one exception; the remaining container diagrams covered relatively few examples of containers built for special traffics. These LT containers were one such case, there being six of them ordered for liquid malt traffic. Photographed at Millerhill on 5 April 1969 when they were painted light green with black lettering.* (Author).

Other types

Up to this point in the diagram book we have been dealing in the main either with established container types covered by Railway Clearing House drawings or with later developments of these types. The remaining diagrams represent British Railways concepts added as new designs appeared. The Grab Type Container — its official description — of page 650 appeared in 1950. Only four were built (and one of these was to different dimensions) and their running numbers had no type prefix. They were followed in 1954 by 220 S type containers to diagram 660, an almost cubic container with double side doors. A number of these, if not all, were used for the carriage of sundries traffic by rail and ship to the Scottish islands which suggests that the S may have stood for 'Sundries' or 'Shipment'.

The next group of diagrams relate to the small-wheeled SW type of container which was in effect a small covered trolley designed for travel inside a van, unlike all other containers which were conveyed on flat trucks or in open wagons. British Railways were prepared to convey the SW type by passenger train as well as by goods train if required. The first diagram, page 670, covered 1,785 containers supplied by the Tyneside Truck Com-

Plate 150. *Container Type S. Diagram 3/660. Likewise, the S type containers were built specifically for sundries traffic for transfer from rail to steamer at the Clyde ports. A trainload of them is seen here at College Goods station Glasgow on 12 October 1954, loaded with traffic for Dunoon and Rothesay.* (British Railways).

pany, although according to the lot book they were of German manufacture. They were superseded by a similar design to diagram 669 but supplied by Youngmans. Eastleigh works also built two experimental models to diagram 672 while Willerby Plastics built a further ten to diagram 671. These latter, although built in 1957, were not taken into stock until May 1959.

Diagrams 700 to 704 all relate to Type T Tote Bin containers built by Pressoturn Limited. The basic design was that of a metal box or canninster with a nine-inch diameter filler aperture on the top and a discharge door along the bottom of one side. There were different sizes, hence the five diagrams, with capacities ranging from 42 cu ft to 95 cu ft.

The remaining container diagrams cover a series of unrelated types built in small quantities. Some may have been special designs for individual customers, but most seem to have been experimental ideas tested by building sample batches. E. R. Foden, the motor lorry builders, were responsible for all containers of diagrams 720 to 723. They may have been a joint venture by the firm and British Railways but we have no evidence to support this view. The MJ containers to diagram 720 were for the conveyance of malt whilst the eighteen open containers of type MC and diagram 721 were designed for brick traffic. Neither lot book nor diagram book gives any information regarding the intended loads of the Bulkrane MA and MB types of pages 722 and 723. Fodens also built the single MD type open container of diagram 727.

Diagrams 724, 725 and 728 all covered Bulkrane Cement containers. The two MU type examples of diagram 724 were built by Interconsult (London) Ltd, which may have been agents rather than makers, while the ten MVs to diagram 725 were made by Dalzell Electric Welding, which later became Holmes & Alexandra. The same firm also built the remaining two MV type containers to diagram 730.

Diagrams 728 and 729 were for Bulkrane containers for the conveyance of liquids. The MR type, diagram 728 was a 950 gallon insulated design, while the almost identical MP type to diagram 729 had no insulation which increased its capacity to 1,030 gallons. All this last group of containers appears to have been experimental designs overtaken by the advent of the Freightliner.

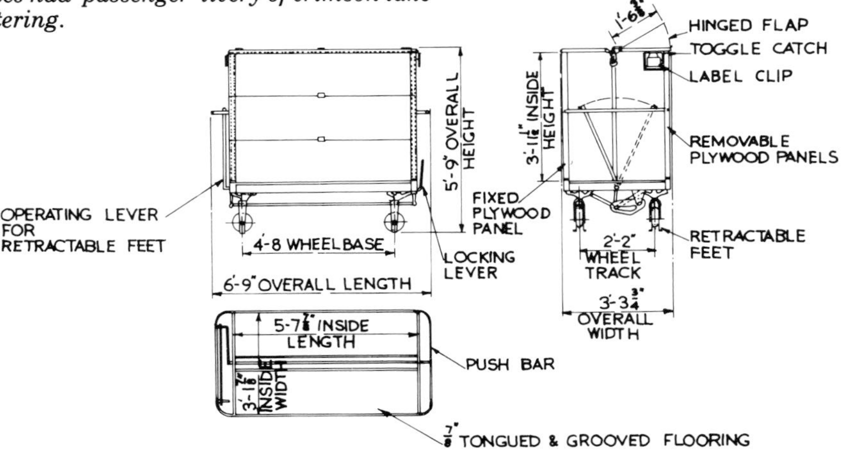

Figure 100. *Container Type SW. Diagram 3/669. The exception to the statement that remaining containers were built in small quantities was the small-wheeled SW type. Over 7,500 of them were built. It is believed that all examples had 'passenger' livery of crimson lake with cream lettering.*

Chapter 13

Apocrypha

Trends

If one accepts that history is best written with the benefit of hindsight, then by the same token recent happenings are best left for another generation of historians to cover. Thus the history of modern British Railways freight stock — and for this purpose 'modern' was taken to be synonymous with air-braked stock and all that goes therewith — is only in the early stages of evolution and the main theme in this book stops with the construction from new of the final vacuum-braked wagons.

But British Rail — for this chapter we shall use the current title — is still in the freight business and is still using wagons. Just because the narrative stops it does not mean that the action ceases as well. Yet this is not a time to write a definitive work on present-day rolling stock, and this final chapter has no such pretensions. Instead it is a broad review of trends over more recent years and should be regarded as no more than that.

Plate 151. *Bogie petroleum tanker — Shell & BP. The oil companies were some of the first to appreciate the high payloads attainable with bogie vehicles where the only limitation is the axle loading when the wagon is fully laden. This is one of a batch built by Metropolitan-Cammell in 1966.* (British Railways).

To carry the story forward let us look first at the wagon fleet. In Chapter 1 we left it in 1967 with 466,623 wagons in stock, the figure having dropped from 1,223,634 on 1 January 1948. Table 4 opposite shows how stocks have been reduced still further since that date. Once again it is the old story of increased road competition which has made inroads into rail traffic, especially in the general merchandise sector.

The raw figures of numbers of freight vehicles by themselves do not tell the full story for two reasons. First, the reduction in numbers has been offset to some degree by an increase in carrying capacity. This is a trend which has been apparent since nationalisation. With the introduction of long-wheelbase air-braked wagons having a gross loaded weight of 45tonnes, even though such vehicles are relatively few in number, the reduction in the total carrying capacity of the wagon fleet has not been so great as might be expected. Allied to this, although it has had no influence on the design of wagons, has been the introduction of the TOPS computer-based wagon control system. It has improved wagon utilisation to the point where fewer vehicles are needed to handle the traffic on offer, so allowing the withdrawal of wagons surplus to requirements.

A reduction in the numbers of railway-owned wagons has also been caused by the introduction of increasing numbers of privately-owned vehicles, a trend which has been actively encouraged by British Rail. Among the advantages of the arrangement are that it does not tie up BRB capital. Instead it is the user's money which is tied up in rolling stock, often of a specialised nature, and the user in turn feels more committed to use rail transport. One side effect of this policy has been the virtual cessation by British Rail of production of wagons for specialised traffics. The availability of government grants for terminal facilities has also accelerated this process.

Table 4 British Rail Wagons — Traffic Stock

Year	*Opening Stock*	*Additions (1)*	*Withdrawals*	*Transfers (+ or −)*	*Closing Stock*	*Hired Wagons At Year End (2)*	*Brake Vans At Year End (3)*	*Average Capacity per Wagon (tons)*
1967	551,422	1,590	85,862	−527	466,623	—	—	16·64
1968	466,623	2,120	31,673	+342	437,412	—	—	16·82
1969	437,412	1,228	22,924	+116	415,832	—	—	17·01
1970	415,832	1,180	45,157	−938	370,917	—	—	17·31
1971	370,917	41	68,320	−511	302,127	1,226	—	17·97
1972	302,127	2	32,949	−628	268,552	1,882	(4,878)(4)	18·46
1973	265,556(4)	383	17,707	+450	248,682	2,177	4,760	18·93
1974	248,682	759	8,937	+925	241,429	2,331	4,719	19·05
1975	241,429	1,504	26,857	+291	216,367	2,331	4,654	19·69
1976	216,367	1,715	32,103	+1021	187,000	2,331	4,172	20·33
1977	187,000	1,344	21,545	+136	166,935	2,331	3,797	21·01
1978	166,935	1,750	18,397	+83	150,371	2,311	3,698	21·70
1979	150,371	1,519	14,378	+77	137,589	2,283	3,485	22·14
1980	137,589	1,341	20,206	+783	119,501	186	2,946	22·81

1) Additions cover new vehicles built in railway workshops and by outside builders. In 1974 twenty-one wagons were built by outside builders, and in 1975 the figure was 129. All other wagons were built in railway workshops.
2) For 1971 and 1972 the figures for hired wagons are not included in the closing stock figures. For 1973 onwards they are.
3) The figures for brake vans include 'other vehicles' – presumably diesel brake tenders. Where figures are shown they are *in addition* to the closing stock figures.
4) From 1973 there was a change in accounting policy which explains the difference between the closing stock figure for 31 December and the opening stock figure for 1 January 1973. The inclusion of hired wagons from this date has been explained, as has the separate showing of brake vans. On this basis it is therefore assumed that the 268,552 wagons in stock at 31 December 1972 included 4,878 brake vans, but this has not been confirmed.

Plate 152. *Bulk grain hopper — BRT 6045 was an early example of the leased wagon arrangement in more recent years. When introduced, the wagons in this whole fleet were noticeable for their distinctive liveries. Millerhill, 27 July 1968.* (Author).

The elimination of steam traction undoubtedly helped to raise average freight train speed which in its turn has affected wagon design and development. The most noticeable advance has been the introduction of air-braked stock, the air brake being much more efficient than vacuum brake. In passing one can look back at the way the Ideal Stocks Committee twenty years earlier agonised over whether or not to advocate the wholesale adoption of the *vacuum* brake and considered it to be just too radical a step, but in their defence, if defence there need be, it can be pointed out that not only do vacuum-braked wagons still exist on British Rail but wagons with hand brakes only are by no means extinct.

Along with air brakes there have been far-reaching developments in wagon design to the point where the modern four-wheeled wagon is a most complex vehicle with braking, buffing, coupling and suspension systems of advanced design far removed from the standard 12ton, 17ft 6in underframe with its 10ft wheelbase which was built in its thousands in the early years of British Railways. The suspension system has been evolved after considerable study by the Railway Technical Centre at Derby.

At the same time as new wagon designs have been appearing there has been some application of air brakes to existing designs, sometimes accompanied by a general refurbishment. This has taken two forms. First of all there has been in a few instances some building of new wagons to which air brake rather than vacuum brake has been fitted. The 40ton Sealion bogie ballast hopper wagon is a case in point, being essentially an update of the

Plate 153. *Open wagon — Steetley Company. The company operates a number of wagons, most of which it owns. This example is one of a batch of twenty-four type PSA, numbered PR25500 to PR25523 owned by Procor and on hire to Steetley. This and the two previous examples illustrate that the modern private-owner wagon, which as well as being a significant part of the British wagon fleet, is a far cry from the old wood coal wagon. Burrelton, 4 June 1982.* (Author).

Plate 155. *High capacity coal wagon. Diagram 1/156. Since this photograph was taken as long ago as 1968 we have deliberately chosen to use the contemporary diagram name and number for what is now the HAA. The picture has been selected to show that the merry-go-round hopper has been with us for some time, but mainly to illustrate the original name and livery with lettering in black on the sides. Millerhill, 30 June 1968.* (Author).

vacuum-braked Walrus. Alongside this there has been the partial rebuilding of existing wagons with air brakes and here the former Vanwides and Pipe wagons are notable examples.

The final noteworthy design trend has been the re-bodying of existing wagons. In Chapter 3 this treatment of 16ton mineral wagons was dealt with, but there has also been some fitting of new mineral wagon bodies to 17ft 6in underframes which have a 10ft wheelbase. The other principal wagon type to receive this treatment is the 21ton hopper wagon, an example being shown in Plate 158.

Plate 154. *Container Type D. Diagram 3/550. As Tables 3 and 5 reveal, the container population of British Railways declined from over 50,000 at the start of 1960 to 311 at the end of 1979. There are almost certainly none now in stock. Scenes such as this, recorded at Wolverton in 1974, show the reason.* (Author).

Private-owner wagons

It is not intended to cover privately-owned wagons in depth, rather to devote a few paragraphs to them since they now form such an important part of the wagon fleet.

In 1948 the private-owner wagon also formed an important part of the fleet, but the situation has changed completely since those days. Then the major component was a stock of half a million wooden coal wagons. Today coal is the one commodity that is transported exclusively in railway-

Table 5 Privately Owned Wagons Running on BR

Year	*Number in Service*	*Year*	*Number in Service*	*Year*	*Number in Service*
1967	Not quoted	1972	19,000	1977	18,527
1968	25,300	1973	18,000	1978	18,438
1969	19,600	1974	18,418	1979	18,676
1970	19,000	1975	18,647	1980	18,752
1971	19,000	1976	18,400		

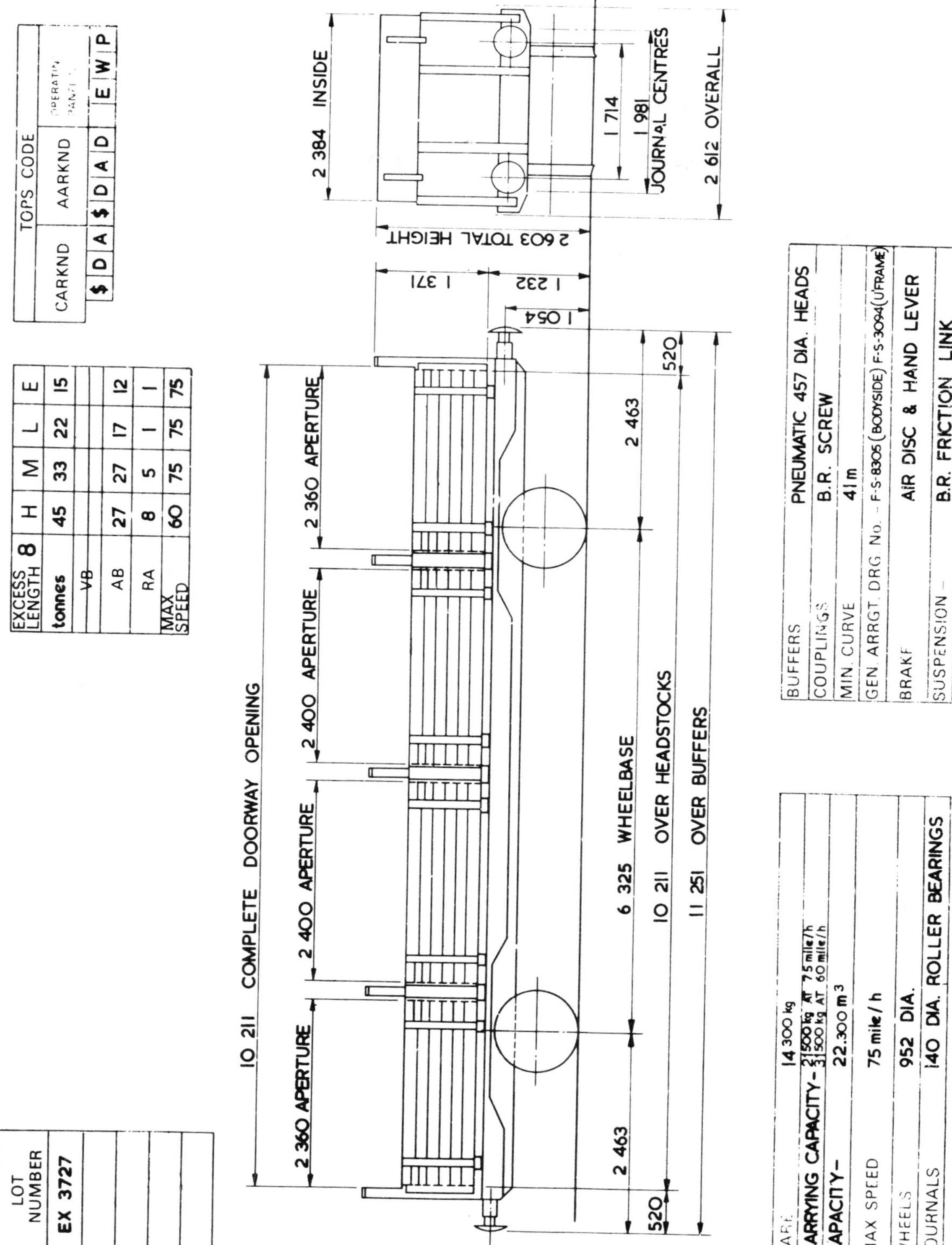

Figure 101. *Tube wagon (45tonnes glw). Diagram SD001A. This is included to give some idea of a typical diagram of the post-TOPS era and makes interesting comparison with Figure 2 on page 19. Although the layout is typical, the content is unique as it covers the solitary wagon (100043) converted from Open AB, later OAA, to a steel carrier as discussed on page 162.*

Plate 156. *Van (45tonnes* glw*). Diagram VA001A. This illustration is selected to portray a feature rather than a particular vehicle, in this case the bauxite red livery with the British Rail double arrow symbol and twin COV AB panels as applied late in 1969. Even so it is an excellent picture of the suspension as applied to the first air-braked vans. Almost certainly photographed at Derby early in 1970.* (British Railways).

owned wagons. Petroleum products have traditionally been carried in privately-owned tank wagons and this remains true today. The biggest change has taken place in the field of general merchandise and minerals, with the employment of specially-constructed wagons for such traffics as roadstone, fertilisers, cement and cars.

The other feature of the private-owner wagon scene has been the re-emergence of the wagon leasing organisation. To maximise a return on investment owners have frequently opted for wagons which can run regularly at high speeds over long distances with minimal maintenance. The resultant vehicles are inevitably a far cry from the wooden coal wagon and in consequence are costly to buy. A leasing arrangement, often with the wagon builder acting as lessor, frequently makes economic sense and is therefore popular with users having regular traffic flows.

TOPS codes and diagrams

We have already referred to the introduction of TOPS (Total Operations Processing System), the computer-based wagon control system, as a factor in reducing the number of wagons in service through improved utilisation. As so often happens with such systems it coincided with a lot of other changes for which, in the popular imagination at least, it will doubtless get the blame. To control wagons in use on British Rail it was first necessary to set up a computer master file containing details of every wagon in stock. Whether this step was the cause or the result is really immaterial, but around this time a number of far-reaching changes were introduced, which are dealt with briefly below.

Numbering

Each wagon in use on British Rail was allocated a TOPS number, be it BR or privately-owned. This consists of an alphabetic prefix identifying the owner (if other than BR) followed by the fleet number. Up until this time all railway-owned

Plate 157. *Steel carrying wagon. Diagram SP001A. The SPA type is discussed on page 165 but is included here to show a current Railfreight livery of flame red bodywork, white lettering and black solebars. Photographed at Tees Yard Spring 1981.* (D. Larkin).

wagons had a single-character prefix (see page xx) which was itself prefixed by D for wagons in departmental stock. A new series of British Rail running numbers has been introduced which omits the alpha prefix and examples will be found in the illustrations to this chapter. This is an entirely separate series so that wagon 200550 is an air-braked van coded VAA (qv post) from lot 3840 of 1974 whilst B200550 was a 21ton end door wagon from lot 2190 of 1951 which may still be in service alongside 200550.

For privately-owned wagons the prefixes were mnemonic, such as, for example PR for wagons owned by Procor Ltd. At initial registration distinctive yellow plates were fixed to the solebars and one interesting side effect of the system was that for the first time it was accurately known by British Rail just how many wagons were running on the system. An examination of Table 4 will show that from 1974 onwards the number of privately-owned wagons in service is quoted accurately rather than to the nearest hundred as was the previous practice.

Codes

Along with a standardised numbering system TOPS has brought about a system of universal codes for different wagon types, with the actual codes painted on each wagon. At the beginning of the British Railways era only specially-constructed wagons carried their code names and although telegraphic code names existed for all types and were shown on diagrams (see Figure 2) in practice they were little used. As described in Chapter 10 the use of code names for Engineer's wagons became widespread. Code names began to appear on Bogie Bolsters and steel-carrying wagons such as Pipes and Tubes and we also got them on more specialised merchandise wagons such as Hybars and Shocvans but they never really caught on for ordinary opens and vans. In the late 1960s the scheme was extended and we got Vanfits and Vanwides and the like, but still there was little rationale behind coding.

Plate 158. *Hopper coal wagon. Code HTO. An example of a re-bodied and refurbished 21ton (now 21.5tonnes) hopper. Comparison with Plate 44 shows much cleaner body lines, heavier springs, Instanter couplings and roller-bearings. Dewsnap Yard. Spring 1981.* (D. Larkin).

Prior to TOPS we got some halfway house codes such as COV AB, HOP 21, and HOP32AB, this latter being used for 32ton air-braked merry-go-round hopper now coded HAA. With TOPS a series of three-letter codes has been introduced. The first letter identifies the type of wagon and letters have been allocated as follows:

- B =Bogie bolster, plate and rail wagons
- C =Brake vans, covered hopper wagons and gunpowder vans.
- F =Flat wagons including Conflats, Carflats and Freightliner wagons
- H =Hopper wagons
- I =Internationally-owned stock
- J =Coil wagons
- K =Coil wagons
- M =Mineral wagons
- O =Open merchandise wagons
- R =Runner wagons, barrier wagons and diesel brake tenders
- S =Steel-carrying wagons (non-bogie)
- U =Various unconverted vacuum-braked wagon types
- V =Vans
- X =Specially-constructed vehicles
- Y =Departmental wagons
- Z =Departmental wagons

The second letter identifies a group within, and the third covers the type of braking as follows:

- A =Air-braked
- B =Air-braked with vacuum brake through pipe
- O =Hand brake only
- P =Vacuum brake through pipe
- V =Vacuum brake
- X =Dual air and vacuum brakes

Plate 159. *Mineral wagon. Code MTV. An example of a new wagon design using redundant underframes. In this case the frames came from privately-owned rail tanks with the tanks being replaced by a new all-steel doorless body. Photographed at Shepherd's Lane Junction, London, winter 1979/80.* (D. Larkin).

In the late 1960s there was also an attempt to apply self-adhesive labels to wagon solebars giving standardised weights and braking information. This was not carried out in full, partly because of adhesion problems with the labels but also because once the TOPS system became operative all this information was held on the master file within the computer system. For this reason also at one time it was seriously considered having only the wagon number on the vehicle, but the idea was not proceeded with.

Diagrams

Along with the changes to wagon numbering and coding the introduction of TOPS also brought about changes to wagon diagrams and to the way diagrams were designated. Diagrams are no longer numbered as pages in a book; instead diagrams are related to the wagon type. Over and above the 'page' number each diagram also carries a wagon code which is effectively the traffic code with the addition of an extra character to accommodate type variants which are not relevant for operating purposes. Figure 101 shows an example of the actual codes in use. In this case a diagram has actually been drawn for SD001A but in some instances — as happened with the previous diagram series — diagrams have been issued without a drawing having been made.

Figure 101 may be taken as a typical post-TOPS diagram in the same way that figure 2 was typical of the original British Railways style. A comparison between the two reveals that the new style carries more textual information. Graphically the vehicle body is still represented by an accurate drawing but underframe detail remains minimal. Principal dimensions are still given, but are now quoted in millimetres.

Metrication — except for maximum speeds which are still quoted in miles per hour — is probably the most apparent change with capacities and braking force as well as dimensions now quoted in metric units. Details of equipment, capacity, speeds and weight are now formally presented in two standard boxes below the drawing while along with lot details and TOPS codes operating details are quoted. These are standardised according to whether the wagon is considered to be heavily, medium or lightly laden or empty. These are the details which were once shown on the self-adhesive labels referred to above.

Liveries

Wagon liveries in the pre-air-brake period had the merit that they were reasonably few in number even if in practice they were not well-maintained. Furthermore, by the late 1960s most of the BR wagon fleet was in the same livery style, with (vacuum) fitted wagons in red bauxite, unfitted wagons in grey and departmental stock in black. Since that period several new liveries have emerged on new wagons. Some, but by no means all, existing air-braked wagons have been repainted in the new styles. Along with this those few non air-braked wagons to receive attention have been repainted in red bauxite; as recently as April 1982 some CAO brake vans were noted fully repainted in this colour.

The most consistently applied new livery has been that of rail blue with white lettering applied to Freightliner wagons. To date this is the only livery these vehicles have borne.

The 32ton merry-go-round hopper wagons originally had the body sheeting of galvanised steel left unpainted whilst body framing was a dull bauxite. Solebars, running gear and body lettering were black. In more recent years body lettering has become white in a black panel while what appears to be aluminium paint has been applied to body sheeting.

Plate 160. *Ballast wagon Plaice. Code ZCV. Another new type, this time for Engineer's use, with new bodies on redundant underframes. These underframes came from Plate wagons, mostly British Railways built but some ex-LNER. Photographed at Carstairs, 8 May 1982.* (Author).

Plate 161. *20ton Bogie trolley. Diagram 2/510. At least that is how DB900304 began life in 1950. Thirty-two years later it had been given air brake through pipe, transferred to departmental stock and fitted with hydraulic lifting gear for use when renewing points and crossings. Carstairs, 8 May 1982.* (Author).

The next colour to be used was a maroon (deeper than the 1960s carriage crimson lake) given to a number of vans and open merchandise wagons as well as some hopper wagons and bogie steel carriers. Some vacuum-fitted wagons received this livery, principally longer wheelbase vans. Towards the end of the 1970s (it is believed coincident with the introduction of the air-braked Speedlink services) a further livery appeared using a colour called Flame Red, which appears to be very similar to the Poppy Red used by the National Bus Company. So far as is known Flame Red has only been applied to air-braked wagons where it is generally used in conjunction with a light grey to give a two-tone livery. Some departmental wagons have begun to appear in two-tone livery, this time of yellow and grey, replacing the previous olive green which itself replaced black.

As well as the liveries described above there have also been some experimental ones, all combining to give a very varied selection of wagon liveries seen throughout the system. Add to this a variety of symbols and lettering and the whole effect can best be described as kaleidoscopic and in direct contrast to the coaching stock fleet where rail blue ruled supreme.

Design developments

Sophistication is a word which has not only lost its original meaning, but in its modern context is often used very loosely to mean anything one step removed from the simple rather than something highly developed or refined. To refer to the British Rail air-braked wagon underframe as a piece of sophisticated design is to use the word truthfully in its present-day context. It is a far cry from the 5334mm (17ft 6in) type with its 3048mm (10ft) wheelbase standardised by British Railways soon after 1948. Furthermore, the most important changes are not simply ones of dimensions or even equipment, but are far more fundamental in that they go right back to the performance of a four-wheeled vehicle running at moderately high speeds.

With the concentration of railway design work at Derby and the setting up of the Railway Technical Centre a study team was put to work on this particular problem, and from its work have ema-

Plate 162. *50ton bogie trolley. Code XKB. Plate 130 illustrated an earlier design of Flatrol used for carrying nuclear waste. Some of the wagons currently in use for this traffic are former vacuum-braked wagons refurbished, but 550000 illustrated here was the first of a new design fitted with air brakes and vacuum through pipe. Photograph probably taken in January 1970.* (British Railways).

nated significant changes in wagon suspension systems. The results have been published in the railway technical press and a detailed consideration is outside the scope of this work, but to illustrate the depth of their studies one example may be quoted. On modern four-wheeled wagon underframes it has been found desirable to allow a degree of yaw into axle movement whereby the centre line of the axle is no longer constrained always to be at right angles to the centre line, in plan, of the wagon underframe, something that was previously considered to be unacceptable.

To prove the theories put forward by the Railway Technical Centre a train of air-braked vans with various differences in suspension systems was run for a period at high speeds between Berwick and Aberdeen (a main line relatively lightly used and yet noted for its curvature) to evaluate the systems. As the weeks went by it was interesting to see the train get shorter and shorter as one by one vans were stopped by defects, which was of course the object of the exercise. The end result of all this work has been the adoption of the Taperlite suspension which gives an excellent combination of a good ride at speed with reasonable first cost and reduced maintenance.

The improvements in freight rolling stock have not been confined solely to suspension systems. The use of plain bearings for journals has been abandoned in favour of roller-bearings while disc rather than clasp brakes are now normal. On all but the earliest designs of air-braked wagons buffers are pneumatic or hydraulic. Finally among the list of design improvements must be recorded what is most obvious, namely the increased length of air-braked stock, normally 10211mm (33ft 6in) over headstocks — quite a step up from 17ft 6in!

Plate 164. *Bogie steel carrying wagon. Code BDA. 1,201 former Bogie Bolster Ds, many of them originally fitted with hand brake only, have been converted to air braking and given new bogies in the process. The four solebar fittings are another addition, namely rachets which operate the load securing straps. These can be seen in use in the next illustration. Scunthorpe, winter 1980.* (D. Larkin).

Plate 163. *Van Code VEA. Reference to Plate 62 will reveal the origins of this van. By June 1979 when it was photographed at Shepherd's Lane Junction, London, it had been refurbished, fitted with air brakes and repainted in maroon livery.* (D. Larkin).

Wagon designs

Rather than look at all new wagon designs as a single group, for ease of treatment they will be split into three groups covering vacuum-braked developments, air-braked derivatives and air-braked designs *per se*.

Plate 165. *Bogie steel carrying wagon. Code XVA. Another conversion, this time from former Trestle ED wagons. Air brakes and new bogies have been fitted. The livery is interesting in that while solebars and all below are black the trestle is red. Scunthorpe, winter 1980.* (D. Larkin).

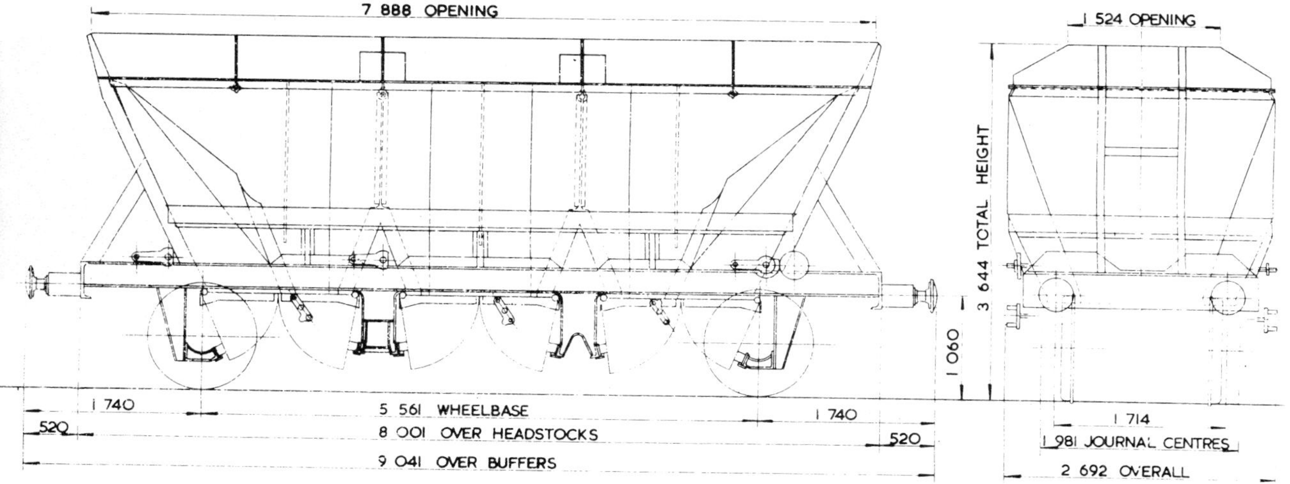

Figure 102. *Hopper coal wagon. Diagram HA001A. In contrast with the merry-go-round hopper illustrated in Plate 155 this diagram shows the version with side sheets extended to give a 32.5tonne capacity. It was diagram 1/156 in the old series. In passing, one may remark that the standard of draughtsmanship is higher than usual.*

Vacuum-braked developments

While it is true to state that no more vacuum-braked wagons have been built, such a statement borders on the semantic. It would mean more to say that no new vacuum-braked underframes have been built, although this does not invalidate the previous statement. What has taken place has been some re-bodying of existing wagons, together with the development of new body styles, which have been applied to redundant underframes. The procedure was not unknown in earlier years and examples have been quoted in previous chapters.

In Chapter 3 for example we referred to the re-bodying of 16ton mineral wagons on existing 9ft wheelbase underframes. The process was later carried one step further using vacuum-fitted underframes of redundant merchandise wagons with a 10ft wheelbase. The welded style of body has been used throughout. This refurbishing of mineral wagons has not been confined to 16ton wagons alone for there was a similarly extensive programme to deal with 21ton hopper wagons. In most cases the re-bodied wagons can be recognised by their cleaner body lines, but some rebuilds appear to have rivetted bodies. They were in fact assembled using Hucks patent bolts, a move caused by a shortage of skilled welders at Shildon works when the work was being done.

Along with new bodies it was decided to fit heavier (ten-leaf) springs to many refurbished hopper wagons with the object of increasing capacity to 25tonnes. Both vacuum-braked and hand-braked wagons were so dealt with, and being considered a new type two new number series were created, B340xxx for fitted vehicles, B345xxx and B346xxx for unfitted ones.

Rebuilding of the larger 21ton and 24½ton mineral wagons took the form of a new body style with but a single door at the left-hand end of each side.

Plate 166. *Hopper coal wagon. Code HBA. The HBA is a completely new design of air-braked hopper, but without automatic discharge facilities. Photographed at Hartlepool, autumn 1981.* (D. Larkin).

Plate 167. *Open goods wagon. Code OBA. This later open merchandise design still retains planked dropside doors, now increased to four per side, but features substantial raised ends. Scunthorpe, winter 1980/1.* (D. Larkin).

Plate 168. *Open goods wagon. Code OCA. The third open goods wagon design, seen here, was of all-steel construction. It reverted to three drop doors per side and the ends reverted to normal height.* (D. Larkin).

This design first appeared in the late 1970s, and both vacuum-fitted and unfitted examples were produced. As with the 21ton hopper wagons there was an introduction of ten-leaf springs with consequent uprating to 25tonnes capacity and renumbering of affected wagons, this time into the B290xxx range.

The final mineral wagon rebuilding covered a batch of 150 wagons for stone traffic, now coded MTV. The underframes were from privately-owned tank wagons and the new vehicles emerged in 1975. Like the former iron ore tippler and sand wagons, the bodies of these stone wagons have no doors.

Among departmental stock some 150 ZCV dropside ballast wagons were produced in 1979 and given the code name Plaice; again, redundant underframes were used. There have been numerous

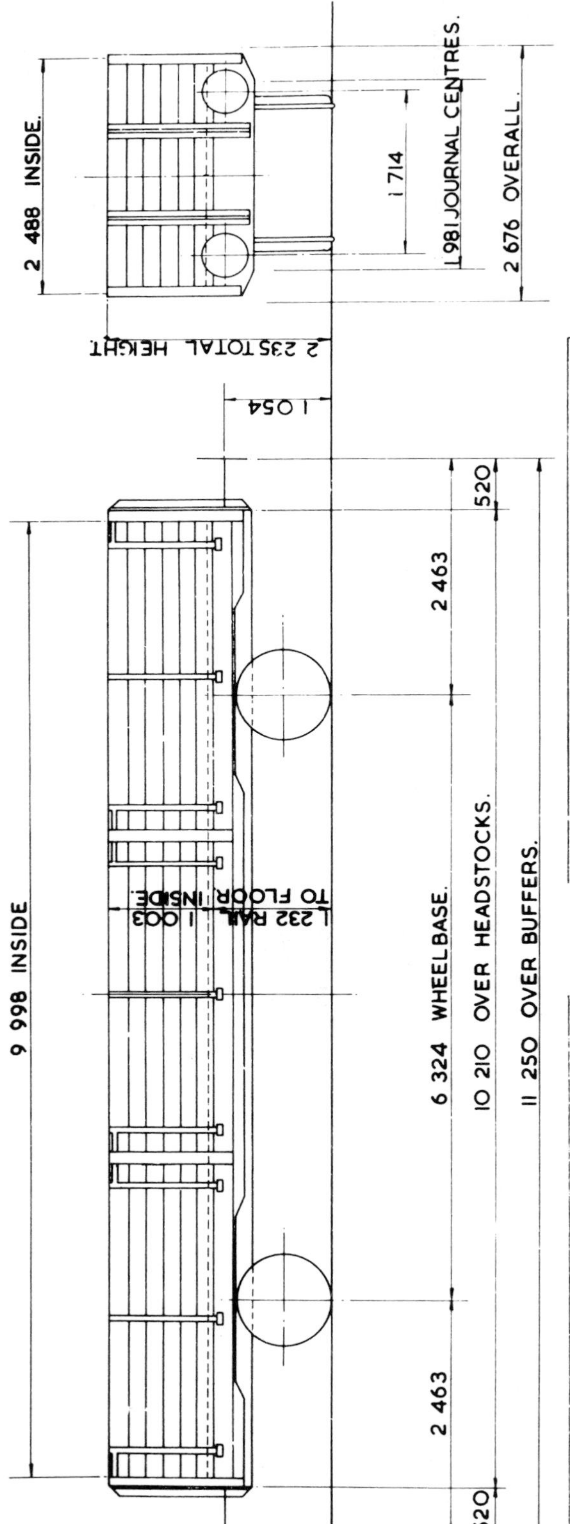

Figure 103. *Open goods wagon. Code AB. (45tonnes* glw.*) Diagram OA001A. This diagram (1/191 in the old series) covered the first group of air-braked open wagons to be built in 1971. On later designs using this underframe the wheelbase is quoted at 6325mm and length over headstocks is 10211mm.*

other conversions for none-revenue purposes plus other for traffic stock but the numbers have nearly always been small.

Air-braked derivatives

This section covers two separate groups of wagons. First there are vehicles which have been converted to air-brake operation, having previously had vacuum brakes. Secondly it deals with new wagon designs which are in effect air-braked updates of vacuum-braked designs. One example which effectively comes into both categories is the nuclear waste transporter wagon which we considered in Chapter 11 when dealing with specially constructed vehicles. There were originally 24 of these wagons, code lettered Flatrol MJ and fitted with vacuum brake. Some have been rebuilt with air brake and are now coded XKA. Since 1969 they have been joined by some newly-constructed wagons coded XKB and numbered from 550000 onwards. They are the only specially constructed wagons built new with air brakes.

So far as is known no open merchandise wagons have been rebuilt with air brakes, but a number of short (ie 10ft) wheelbase vans have been so treated. In the later 1960s and early 1970s numbers of vanfits and pallet vans were given air brakes, but the numbers involved were small. Most are now in departmental stock. Beginning in 1978 a number of vanwides were refurbished with roller-bearings and new springing and were given air brakes. One hundred and ten vans have been dealt with, and conversion of a further 230 is planned.

Air brakes have been applied to some service vehicle designs. One of the earliest batches of air-braked wagons to appear were the 50ton Whale bogie hopper ballast wagons of lot 3591. Although they had no direct vacuum-braked equivalent, they were virtually stretched versions of the 40ton Walrus. For further construction British Rail reverted to the 40ton design, the Sea Cows and Sea Lions being air-braked Walruses, but having either vacuum through pipe or full vacuum brake in addition.

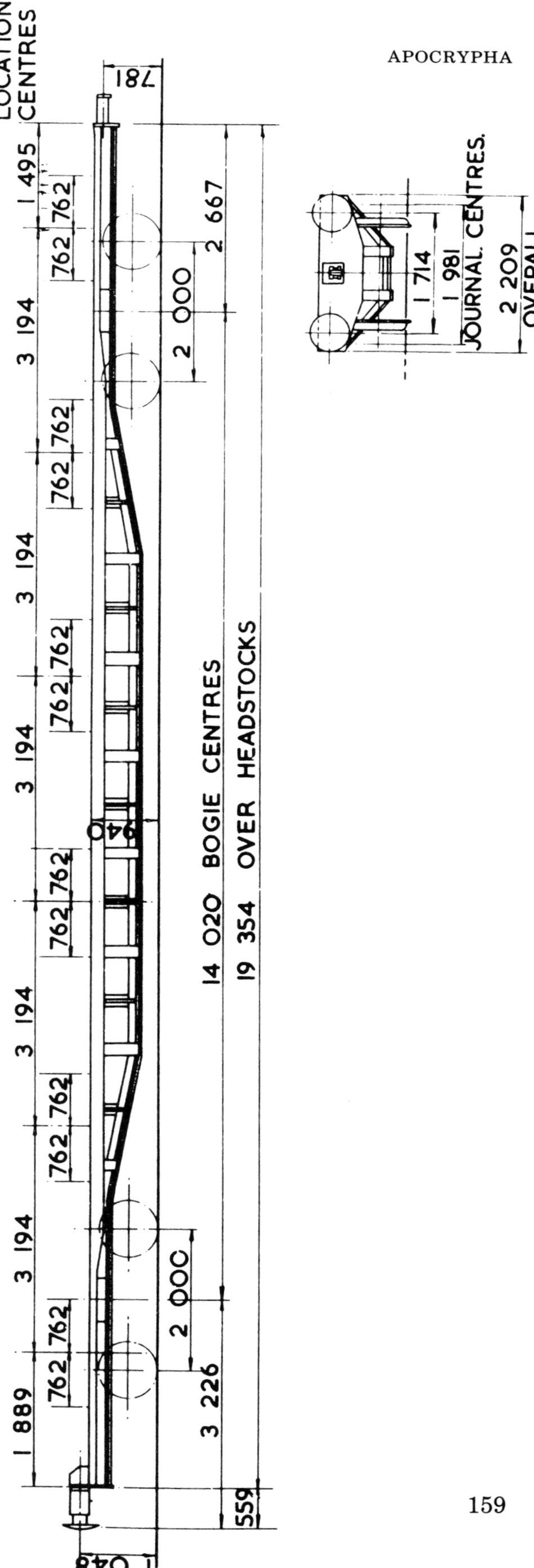

Figure 104. *Freightliner outer vehicle. Diagram FG004A. This diagram covers the first batch of 62ft 6in platform outer Freightliner wagons. As originally drawn there was also a plan view (diagram 1/082) which emphasised the complete absence of floor planking. (3.5mm — 1ft).*

Plate 169. *Freightliner outer vehicle. Code FGA. B601342 — note the running number on the headstock — was from a later batch than the eighteen covered by Figure 104, and had different securing arrangements. The tail lamp shield was a later modification to prevent draughts from extinguishing the tail lamp. This particular wagon has a standard draw hook but no shackle. Millerhill, 27 April 1968.* (Author).

When considering steel-carrying wagons in Chapter 8 we referred to the veritable plethora of conversions to deal with steel traffic, especially in coil form. There are parallels when looking at air-braked derivatives. A number of 22ton Plate wagons have been converted to air braking, also it is believed a number of Pipe wagons. Over and above these there have been conversions of some bogie designs. In certain cases this conversion has also involved the fitting of new bogies as well. The principal candidate has been the former Bogie Bolster D, now coded BDA, with some 1,201 examples numbered 950000 to 951200. In contrast only two Bogie Bolster Cs were converted (as BCAs 960000 and 960001) and both are now in departmental stock. Three further bogie designs renovated and fitted with air brakes and new bogies are the BPA (965000 to 965079 — formerly Boplate Es), BRA (967500 to 967649, formerly Borails) and XVA (990000 to 990050, formerly Trestle EDs).

Plate 170. *Freightliner inner vehicle. Code FFA. Again, one of the 62ft 6in platform type. It must be pointed out that the wagon does not have a solid floor but is in fact loaded with containers, the ones at the ends being flats. The vertical portion at the left-hand end belongs to the container and not the wagon. Millerhill, 27 April 1968.* (Author).

Air-braked designs

The search for a better design of wagon to replace the faithful 17ft 6in design began as long ago as 24 May 1960 when a WEC Minute authorised the production of six 'Long Low Experimental' 22ton wagons numbered B710250 to 710255 to which were assigned lot 3362. Although intended at first as vacuum-fitted wagons, from these six emerged the standard 6325mm (20ft 9in) wheelbase chassis which was to become the basis for all British Rail open wagons and vans.

Hoppers. The above notwithstanding, the most numerous kind of air-braked wagons, the mineral hoppers, use a 5561mm wheelbase underframe, 8001mm over headstocks. Following an agreement signed between British Railways and the CEGB which set up the merry-go-round system of delivering power station coal, construction began with lot 3495 authorised early in 1964, and has continued since with minor variations. Many of the earlier wagons have been given new body panels and over 10,600 are in service. Their code is HAA.

With their automatic unloading gear, their workings are confined to power stations where such facilities are available. For supplies of domestic coal to yards where no such unloading aids are provided the HBA hopper was introduced, the intention being to replace the old 21ton hopper designs. A prototype (lot 3881) and a production run

Figure 105. *Lowliner inner vehicle. Diagram FZ004A. Our copy of the diagram indicates that these wagons were originally diagram 1/128 in the old series and after that coded FF003A before being re-coded as above. On the equivalent outer vehicle there is a ramp at the buffer end which can be raised for loading and unloading.*

Figure 106. *Van (45tonnes* glw*). Diagram VA001A. This is the diagram for the van illustrated in Plate 156. From this it will be seen that the right-hand half of the side elevation is in fact a section through the van. The code for these vans is VAB indicating air brakes and vacuum brake through pipe.*

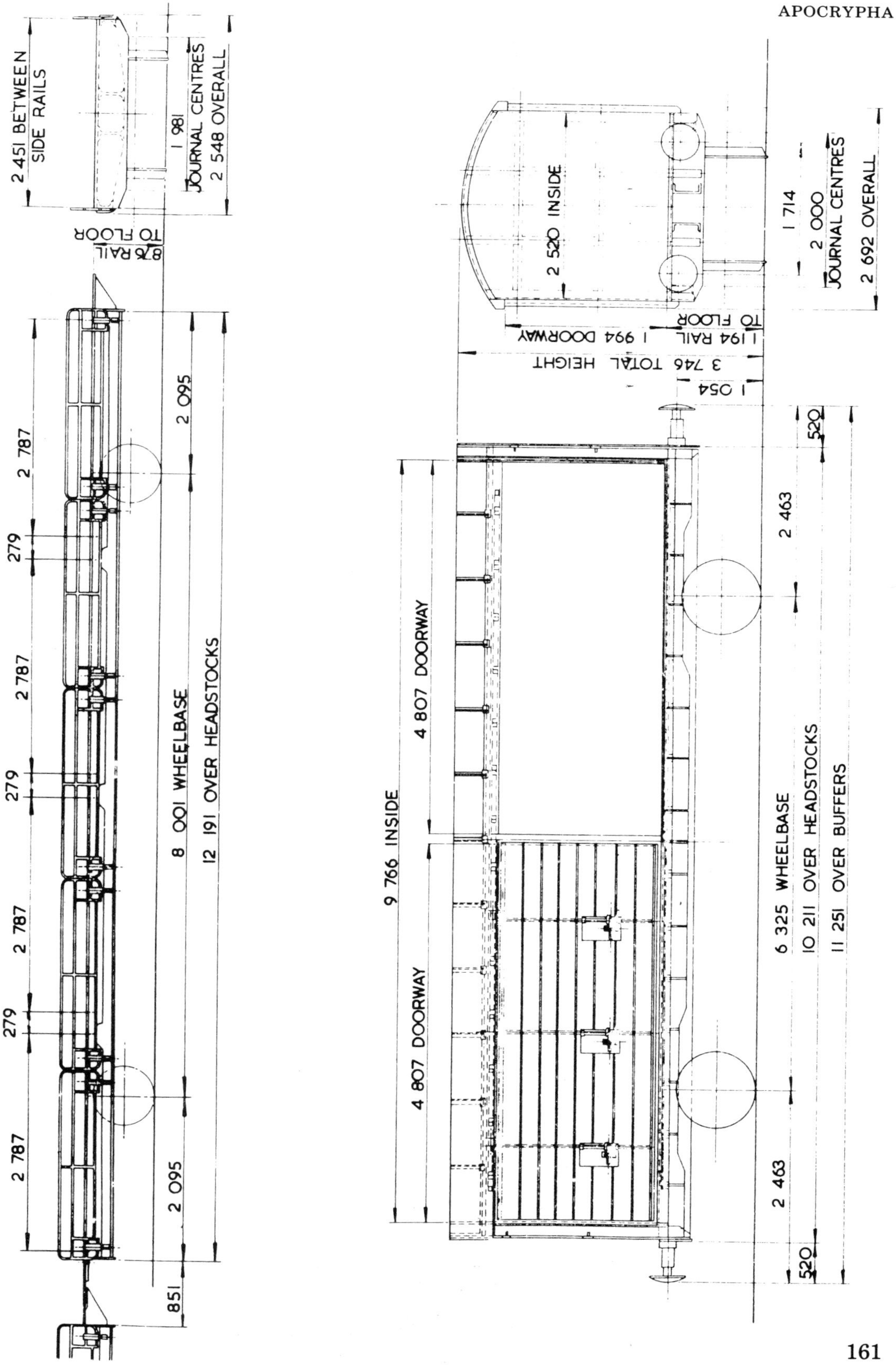

2 451 BETWEEN SIDE RAILS
1 981 JOURNAL CENTRES
2 548 OVERALL
876 RAIL TO FLOOR
2 787
279
2 787
279
2 787
279
2 787
8 001 WHEELBASE
12 191 OVER HEADSTOCKS
2 095
2 095
851

2 520 INSIDE
1 714
2 000 JOURNAL CENTRES
2 692 OVERALL
1 194 RAIL TO FLOOR
1 994 DOORWAY
3 746 TOTAL HEIGHT
1 054
520
2 463
9 766 INSIDE
4 807 DOORWAY
4 807 DOORWAY
6 325 WHEELBASE
10 211 OVER HEADSTOCKS
11 251 OVER BUFFERS
2 463
520

Plate 171. *Van (45tonnes* glw*). Code VBA. The date of this picture is 6 July 1971 and it was taken in the yard at Ashford Works when 200378 of lot 3726 had just been built and awaited painting.* (Author).

Plate 172. *Van (45tonnes* glw*). Code VDA. A comparison with the van in the previous illustration shows not only body variations — both doors and ends — but also detail changes in the underframe, especially the positioning of the handbrake lever. South Lambeth, winter 1980/1.* (D. Larkin).

of 1,998 (lot 3885) were built but there have been suspension problems and spring replacement is under way with improved vehicles re-coded HEA. There is also one derivative of the HAA, the CBA, originally the Covhop AB. It is basically the HAA with loading hatches provided in a permanent roof. Fifty-seven vehicles have been built in two lots.

General merchandise open wagons. The first air-braked open merchandise wagons did not appear until 1971 with one lot (3727) of one hundred vehicles numbered 100000 to 100099. Originally classed as Open AB they became OAA and were equipped with six-plank wood sides (with three-part drop doors) and steel ends. One wagon, 100043, was converted to a steel carrier with high rounded ends. It was first re-numbered 450000 and coded SDA and then later re-numbered again as 110000 and coded back among the opens as OBA.

Further OBAs, numbered 110001 to 110800 and built in two lots, 3909 and 3930, retained the high ends but have four-part, five-plank drop sides together with turnover bolsters on the floor and side stanchions. The second batch has Taperlite suspension, and earlier wagons are being brought up to this standard. Beginning with 400 wagons of lot 4014 numbered 112000 to 112399 delivered in 1981, current production is of an all-steel type coded OCA. The design is derived from the SPA and has turnover bolsters on the floor.

While the first *open* merchandise wagons may not have appeared until 1971, the first merchandise wagons to have air brakes were ordered at the beginning of 1964 when lot numbers were issued for the first Freightliner wagons. There were two designs, the shorter 42ft 6in platform type with buckeye couplers throughout, and the longer 62ft 6in platform design having screw couplers at the outer ends and bar couplers at the inner ends. With both types there was an outer vehicle with buffers at one end to couple with standard stock,

Plate 173. *Van (45tonnes* glw*). Code VGA. Although retaining the same basic underframe, this later van design shows even more changes, especially to the body. It also exhibits yet another livery style with sides being metal finish and ends red. Rochester, summer 1981.* (D. Larkin).

and an inner vehicle which coupled only with other Freightliner flats. A set of four wagons (two inner, two outer) was at first built to the 42ft 6in design, but the longer type went straight into production with an order for eighteen outer wagons (lot 3498, B601003 — B601020) and eighty-two inner ones (lot 3499, B602003 to B602084). All these wagons, of both lengths, are bogie vehicles using 812mm (2ft 8in) diameter wheels to give a platform of 940mm (3ft 1in) above rail level, which enables them to carry Freightliner or ISO containers. The longer wagons are coded FGA.

Lots 3713 (Outer) and 3714 (Inner) saw the emergence of the Lowliner, a four-wheeled version with floor height reduced to 876mm above rail level. Like the 62ft 6in Freightliner wagons there were screw couplers at the outer ends and bar couplers elsewhere. These wagons have passed to Freightliners Ltd and in so doing have joined the Freightliner containers which are owned by the same organisation. The only containers in British Railstock are the residue of traditional types which explains the very small container stock shown in Table 5.

Table 6 British Railways — Container Stock

Year	*Opening Stock*	*Additions (1)*	*Withdrawals*	*Closing Stock*
1967	31,969	2,855	3,786	31,038
1968	31,038	1,958	4,526	28,470
1969	17,368[2]	62	2,629	14,801
1970	14,801	79	2,927	11,953
1971	11,953	76	2,087	9,942
1972	9,942	63	3,231	6,774[3]
1973	6,814	52	1,827	4,999
1974	5,039	34	1,079	3,954
1975	3,994	21	2,150	1,825
1976	1,865	120	791	1,154
1977	1,194	24	183	995
1978	1,035	12	512	491
1979	531	—	220	311
1980	(4)	—	—	—

1) Additions cover new containers built in railway workshops (1967, 2,553; 1968, 1,842; 1970, 1), bought outside (1967, 259; 1968, 10; 1977, 1; 1978, 12) and transfers to stock (remainder).
2) The difference between the closing stock for 1968 and the opening stock for 1969 is the transfer of Freightliner containers.
3) From 1972 to 1979 there is a difference of forty between closing stock at year end and opening stock next year. This is caused by the existence of forty hired containers which, over this period, are not included in closing stock.
4) No figures given.

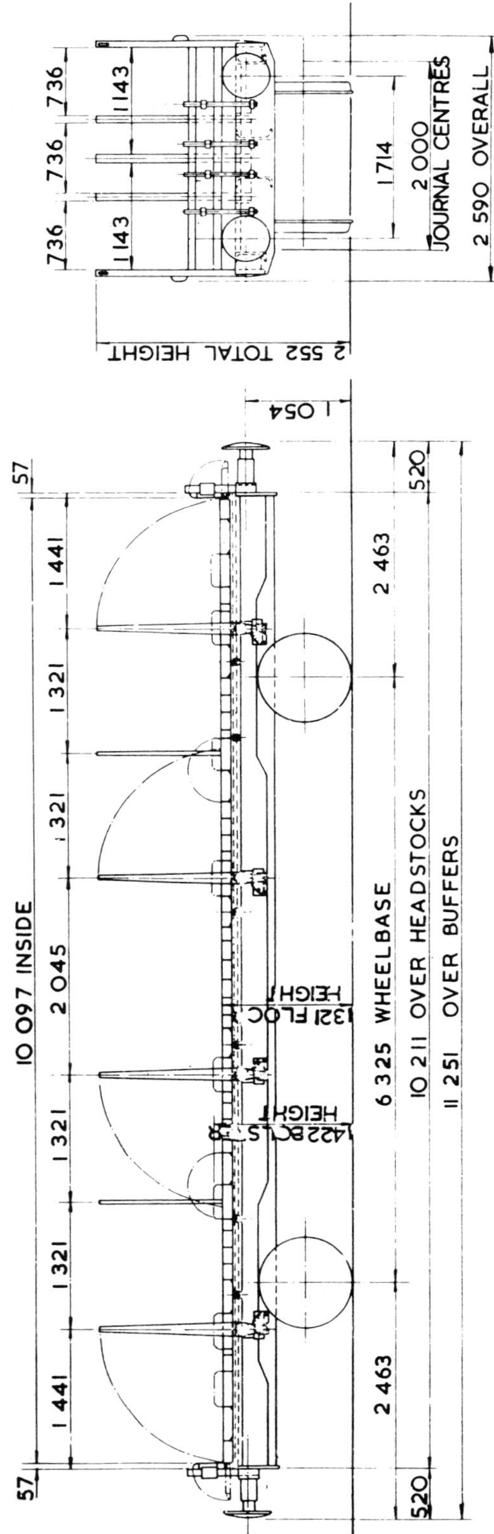

Figure 107. *Steel carrying wagon, Bogie Steel AB. Diagram SA001A. As stated in the text, these wagons have seen little use for steel carrying, in spite of the provision of turnover bolsters, drop ends and side stanchions.*

Plate 174. *Steel carrying wagon, Bogie Steel AB. Code SAA. This photograph was taken at Ashford on 6 July 1971. The particular wagon, 400126 of lot 3728, carried a 1970 building date and yet the floor appears to be temporary and there is as yet no sign of the turnover bolsters which were to be fitted later.* (Author).

General merchandise vans. Here the story is one of a surprising number of body variations all using the same standard underframe, albeit with suspension differences as previously described. The first 209 vans, 200000 to 200208 of lot 3685 of 1969, were followed by a further forty-one, numbered 200209 to 200249, in no less than six different lots. All 250 were originally coded COV AB and had all-steel bodies with flush doors opened by recessed handles. Along with later examples 200250 to 200324 and 200550 to 200649 they were originally to be coded VAA but now codes VAA, VAB, VBA and VBB are in use.

The missing numbers 200325 to 200549 cover two lots of centre-door vans at first coded COV CD but later changed to VCA. Beginning with 200650 to 200979 of lot 3855 a third type appeared, coded VDA, having differences in door placing along with ribbed ends. Two further lots brought the running numbers up to 201099 which were then followed by the incorrectly numbered 210100 to 210399. These should have been **201**100 to **201**300 but the error was allowed to stand.

The latest design, the VGA, appeared as a prototype in 1981 (lot 4007) and a production batch of

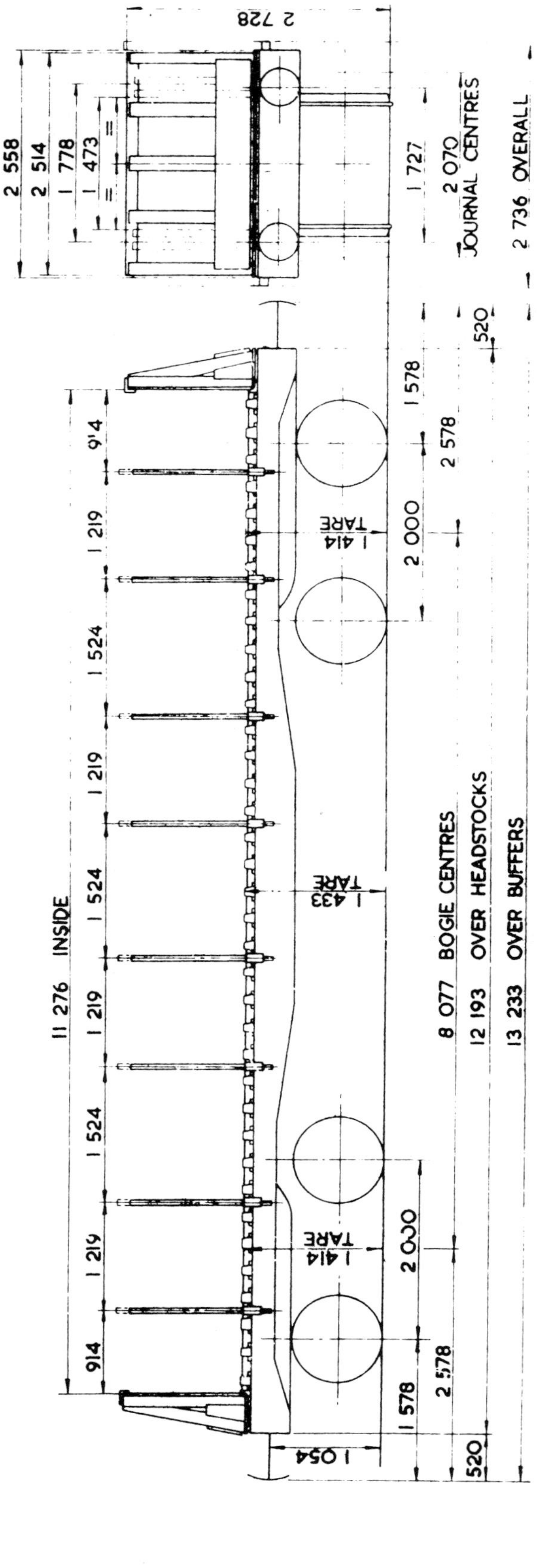

Figure 108. *Bogie steel carrier, Bogie Steel AB. Diagram BA001A. For some reason certain diagrams, and this is one, give a very skeletal impression of the buffers whereas others (cf Figure 107) show full detail. This diagram does clearly show the corrugated floor, which facilitates the loading and unloading of the vehicle by fork lift trucks.*

Plate 175. *Bogie steel carrier, Bogie Steel AB. Code BBA. Although modified to carry steel in coils this BBA has not been re-coded. Note the deeper frames compared with the BAB. Tees Yard, spring 1981.* (D. Larkin).

250 has been ordered. No special vans have been ordered but one COV CD (200376) was tried out as an insulated banana van in the 1970s. This, plus one van (200987) painted white in error and some vans with white roofs are the only variants to appear.

Steel carrying wagons. Some of the development of steel-carrying wagons has been covered already when looking at conversions of vacuum-braked vehicles but over and above these there have also been some entirely new designs, air-braked from the start. The story is somewhat complicated by changes in plans.

The first type to appear was the Steel AB, 300 vehicles built as one lot (3728) in 1971 and numbered 400000 to 400299. It was a four-wheeled design with turnover bolsters on the floor and hinged side stanchions. In spite of these fittings the class as a whole has spent most of the past eleven years running as barrier wagons and examples are being re-coded RBA, RBB, RRA or RRB. Some have been converted for coil traffic. However, if the Steel AB has had a chequered career it has at least done better than another steel-carrying design, the SEA. This was a proposed conversion to a four-wheeled wagon from the Bogie Bolster E, but the plan was cancelled before any of the first five proposed wagons were built.

The principal air-braked steel carrying wagon is the SPA of which 1,102 have been turned out, numbered 460000 to 461101. The first two appeared in 1977, to be followed by lot 3939 in 1980 and lot 3962 in 1981. Three-part drop sides and a corrugated floor are provided to facilitate loading and unloading by fork lift truck. A plan to convert one hundred Steel ABs to this type has not been carried out.

Three bogie designs had been produced, two of them in fair numbers but the largest, coded BLA, has only seen a prototype, 920000, built in 1976. Of the other two the smaller BAA/BAB was the first to appear under the name Bogie Steel AB. The first forty-nine, 900000 to 900048, came out in 1972 to be followed by a further 257 in four lots and numbered 900049 to 900305. Again, a corrugated floor and removable side stanchions are provided, this time along with high ends, a fishbelly underframe and French bogies. Some have been converted to carry coils and are coded BKA/BKB.

The larger version, the BBA, did not appear until 1975, with the prototype 910000. A further 449 have been built and are numbered in the range 910001 to 910591, less gaps for lots cancelled. Some have been modified for coil traffic but none has as yet been re-coded.

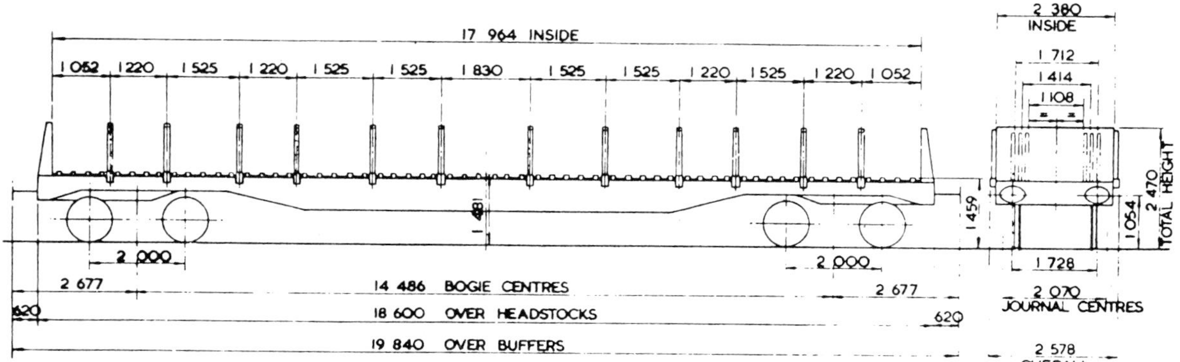

Figure 109. *Bogie steel carrier, Bogie Steel AB. Diagram BL001A. Finally the diagram for the solitary BLA, 920000, which is now in departmental stock.*

Appendix 1

16 ton All-steel Mineral Wagons (ex-Ministry of War Transport & Ministry of Transport)

This list is based on one issued by the Central Stock Registry (British Railways) on 15 November 1954. It gives wagon numbers and building contractors. There is no guarantee that all the wagons in a range passed into British Railways ownership. This same list also stated that there were '2 wagons numbered 26501-2-3' (*sic*). The diagram numbers quoted are based on observations and are in no way official. They attempt to assign lots of wagons to those diagrams in the BR Freight Stock diagram book against which no BR lots were built.

Numbering (inclusive)	*Diagram*	*Manufacturer*
B3002–4100	100	Metropolitan-Cammell C & W Co Ltd
B4101–4250		D. G. Hall
B4251–5652		Birmingham Railway C & W Co Ltd
B5653–5655		G. R. Turner Ltd
B5656–5665		Birmingham Railway C & W Co Ltd
B5666–6415		Gloucester C & W Co Ltd
B6431–8715	100	Charles Roberts & Co Ltd
B8816–9315		Birmingham Railway C & W Co Ltd
B9316–9565		R. Y. Pickering & Co Ltd
B9567–9930		Cravens Railway C & W Co Ltd
B9931–10460		Head Wrightson & Co Ltd
B10465–10860		R. Y. Pickering & Co Ltd
B10861–11520	100	G. R. Turner Ltd
B11521–11850	100	P. & W. McLellan Ltd
B11863–12750		Hurst Nelson & Co Ltd
B13001–17000	102	Royal Ordnance Factory, Woolwich
B17001–21000	102	Royal Ordnance Factory, Dalmuir
B21001–23000		Royal Ordnance Factory, Patricroft
B23001–23500		G. R. Turner Ltd
B23501–23750		Head Wrightson & Co Ltd
B23751–24000		R. Y. Pickering & Co Ltd
B24001–25000	102	Birmingham Railway C & W Co Ltd

Numbering (inclusive)	*Diagram*	*Manufacturer*
B25001–25500	102	Fairfields S & E Co Ltd
B25501–26000	101	Cambrian Wagon & Engineering Co Ltd
B26001–26500		Teesside Bridge & Engineering Ltd
B26501–27000		P. & W. McLellan Ltd
B27001–27500		Butterley Co Ltd
B27501–27750		Hurst Nelson & Co Ltd
B27751–28750	100	Charles Roberts & Co Ltd
B28751–29600		P. & W. McLellan Ltd
B29601–30250	103	Cambrian Wagon & Engineering Ltd
B30251–31650	102	Teesside Bridge & Engineering Ltd
B31651–31900		Derbyshire C & W Co Ltd
B31901–32550		Fairfields S & E Co Ltd
B32551–32700	103	Metropolitan-Cammell C & W Co Ltd
B32701–33000		G. R. Turner Ltd
B33001–33500		Birmingham Railway C & W Co Ltd
B33501–34000	102	Royal Ordnance Factory, Dalmuir
B34001–36500	102	Royal Ordnance Factory, Woolwich
B36501–37500		Royal Ordnance Factory, Dalmuir
B37501–38500	102	Royal Ordnance Factory, Woolwich
B38501–38580		Royal Ordnance Factory, Patricroft
B38581–39500		Royal Ordnance Factory, Dalmuir
B39501–41350	103*	Metropolitan-Cammell C & W Co Ltd
B41351–44350		Birmingham Railway C & W Co Ltd
B44351–45600		Butterley Co Ltd
B45601–46350	104	Derbyshire C & W Co Ltd
B46351–47550	104	Fairfields S & E Co Ltd
B47551–49050	105	Cambrian Wagon & Engineering Co Ltd
B49051–49800		Hurst Nelson & Co Ltd
B49801–51800	105	P. & W. McLellan Ltd
B51801–52800	100	Charles Roberts & Co Ltd
B52801–53700	105	G. R. Turner Ltd
B53701–55200	105	Gloucester C & W Co Ltd
B55201–57650		Royal Ordnance Factory, Dalmuir
B57651–61200	102	Royal Ordnance Factory, Woolwich
B61201–61700		Cravens Railway C & W Co Ltd
B61701–63000		Teesside Bridge & Engineering Co Ltd

*=also some to diagram 105.

Appendix 2

Running Numbers and original Lot Numbers

This Appendix gives the lot numbers to which all wagons (other than air braked ones) and all containers (other than Freightliner) were originally built. For wagons the B or DB prefix is omitted as are the prefixes and B suffixes for containers. For example, wagon B234567 was one of 1000 wagons B233949 to B234948 built as lot 2750.

RUNNING NUMBERS FROM	TO	LOT NO
64000	65499	2104
65500	66499	2105
66500	66999	2123
67000	67099	2160
67100	67499	2161
67500	67599	2162
67600	68099	2184
68100	68899	2210
68900	69199	2331
69600	70099	2221
70100	70399	2222
70400	70899	2223
70900	71599	2224
71600	72199	2225
72200	72599	2226
72600	73099	2227
73100	73599	2228
73600	73749	2229
73750	74149	2230
74150	74349	2231
74350	74449	2232
74450	74549	2242
74550	75199	2243
75200	77699	2250
77700	80199	2251
80200	82699	2252
82700	85199	2253
85200	87699	2254
87700	90199	2255
90200	92699	2256
92700	95199	2257
95200	97699	2258
97700	100199	2259
100200	101699	2290
101700	102299	2291
102300	103649	2292
103650	104249	2293
104250	104960	2294
104961	105660	2295
105661	106160	2296
106161	106960	2297
106961	108360	2298
108361	110360	2299
110361	112510	2300
112511	113910	2301
113911	114360	2302
114361	115610	2377
115611	116610	2378
116611	118210	2379
118211	120060	2380
120061	121260	2381
121261	122960	2382
122961	124810	2383
124811	125610	2384
125611	126860	2385
126861	129630	2386
129631	131160	2387
131161	132510	2388
132511	132860	2389
132861	134360	2390
134361	134860	2391
134861	136660	2463
136661	138360	2464
138361	139120	2473
139121	140120	2480
140121	141260	2502
141261	141360	2761
141361	142360	2485
142361	143360	2486
143361	143860	2508
143861	144260	2509
144261	144760	2510
144761	145093	2511
145094	145593	2512
145594	146093	2513
146094	146493	2514
146494	146993	2515
146994	147493	2516
147494	147960	2517
147961	148460	2518
148461	148827	2519
148828	149327	2520
149328	149994	2521
149995	150494	2522
150495	150994	2523
150995	151494	2524
151495	151994	2525
151995	152494	2526
152495	152994	2527
152995	153621	2528
153622	154221	2529
154222	154721	2530
154722	155221	2531
155222	155721	2547
155722	156221	2548
156222	156721	2549
156722	157221	2550
157222	157571	2567
157572	159071	2599
159072	159791	2906
159792	159891	3143
159892	160571	3143
160572	161518	2611
161519	162184	2612
162185	162684	2626
162685	163184	2627
163185	163851	2628
163852	164851	2629
164852	165351	2630
165352	165851	2631
165852	168351	2633
168352	170851	2634
170852	173351	2635
173352	175851	2636
175852	178351	2637
178352	179051	2639
179052	179451	2640
179452	180701	2653
180702	181951	2654
181952	183451	2663
183452	184951	2664
184952	185451	2666
185452	186451	2667
186452	187366	2669
187367	187866	2670
187867	188866	2674
188867	189866	2675
190000	190999	2286
191000	191299	2286
191300	192299	2286
192300	192599	2286
192600	194799	2286
194800	196999	2286
197000	197249	2287
197250	197324	2287
197325	197749	2287
197750	197849	2287
197850	198099	2287
198100	198599	2287
198600	198749	2287
198750	198891	2287
199000	199059	2288
199060	199099	2288
199100	199159	2288
199160	199219	2288
199220	199279	2288
199280	199307	2288
200000	200999	2190
201000	201499	2191
201500	201999	2192
202000	202499	2193
203000	203908	2676
203909	204999	2677
205000	205999	2678
206000	208499	2685
208500	210999	2686
211000	211999	2687
212000	212999	2698
213000	214299	2699
214300	214832	2700
214833	215765	2701
215766	217308	2702
217309	218308	2703
218309	219308	2711
219309	220808	2715
220809	222308	2716
222309	223058	2717
223059	223808	2718
223809	224808	2719
224809	225808	2720
225809	227308	2742
227309	228108	2743
228109	228708	2744
228709	228808	3053
228809	229208	3054
229209	229252	3054
229253	229308	3054
229309	230008	2745
230009	230708	2746
230709	231708	2747
231709	233248	2748
233249	233948	2749
233949	234948	2750
234949	236348	2751
236349	237848	2752
237849	238098	2756
238099	239008	2757
239009	241008	2788
241009	243008	2789
243009	244108	2790
244109	245358	2791
245359	245858	2792
246609	247608	2793
247609	248608	2794
248609	249608	2795
249609	250608	2796
250609	251608	2797
251609	253608	2798
253609	255608	2799
255609	256608	2800
256609	257608	2801
257609	258608	2802
258609	259608	2803
259609	260308	2804
260609	261308	2805
261309	261508	3178
261509	261714	2806
261715	262608	2806
262909	263158	3152
264209	265158	2808
265209	265708	2809
266209	266808	2810
266809	267008	2810
267209	267708	2811
267709	268708	2813
271209	272208	2814
273209	274208	2816
274209	275208	2817
275209	275708	2896
275709	276208	2897
276209	276708	2898
276709	277208	2899
277209	277808	2900
277809	278408	2901
278409	279408	2902
279409	279608	2903
279609	279658	2904
280000	280649	2460
280650	281149	2602
281150	282149	2600
282150	282769	3244
282770	282994	3302
282995	283129	3388
283130	283394	3427
310000	310999	3387
311000	311949	3390
312000	313499	3430
313500	314499	3438
314500	314999	3439
333000		2504
333001		2758
333002	333499	2609
333500	333699	3121
333700	334849	3221
334850	335594	3314
335595	335694	3315
335695	336234	3374
336235	336384	3425
336385	336932	3426
336933	337175	3437
337176	337753	3466
337754	338162	3525
338163	338262	3526
380000	380699	2274
380700	381499	2275
381500	381899	2310
381900	383139	2498
383140	383639	2601
383640	385139	2730
385140	385639	2844
385640	385667	3091
385668	385669	3091
385670	387089	3091
387090	388089	3324
388090	389089	3363
400000	400199	2038
400200	400499	2050
400500	401499	2129
401500	401749	2138
401750	401799	2139
402000	402249	2140
402250	402549	2282
402550	402899	2283
410000	410499	2052
410500	410999	2053
411000	411199	2054
411200	411549	2163
411550	411899	2164
411900	412049	2165
412050	412749	2166
412750	413249	2167
413250	413699	2168
413700	413949	2212
413950	414049	2330
414050	414249	2400
414250	414549	2401
414550	414849	2402
414850	415149	2403
415150	415949	2552
415950	416449	2713
416450	416749	2726
416750	417049	2727
417050	417549	2728
417550	419199	2731
419200	419249	2954
419250	419999	2932
420000	420699	2933
420700	421249	2934
421250	422249	2935
422250	422749	3013
423050	423549	3030
423550	424549	3031
424550	425349	3032
425350	425849	3033
425850	426149	3034
426150	426949	3035
426950	427399	3036
427400	428549	3037
428550	429049	3045
429350	429499	3158
429500	429649	3159
429650	429799	3160
429800	430799	3120
430800	433749	3157
435000	435999	2055
436000	436499	2148
436500	436999	2149
437000	437499	2150
437500	437899	3002
438000	438899	2733
438900	439499	3001
439500	439699	3142
439700	440049	3189
445000	445099	2040
445100	445149	2130
445150	445419	2962
446000	446029	2312
447000	447399	2039
447400	447499	2169
447500	447599	2198
447600	447649	2343
447650	447699	2474
447700	447799	2603
447800	447899	2732
447900	448349	2859
448350	448649	3003
448650	449199	3122
450000	450399	2107
450400	451399	2194
451400	451499	2313
451500	451699	2413
451700	451899	2340
451900	452199	2420
452200	452399	2461
452400	452599	2467
452600	452899	2729
452900	453449	2998
455500	455579	3465
456000	456199	2858
456200	456349	2999
457100	457199	2061
457200	457596	2108
457597	458596	2235
458597	459596	2236
459597	460396	2351
460397	460596	2430
460597	460996	2352
460997	461596	2488
461597	461608	3138
461609	461616	2668
461617	461996	3140
461997	462116	2724
462117	462246	2724
462447	462526	3141
462527	462686	3242
462707	462796	3243
462797	462846	3322
462847	463036	3365
474800	474824	2152
475000	475049	2082
475050	477049	2128
477050	477649	2153
477650	479149	2179
479150	480649	2195
480650	482149	2196
482150	483649	2197
483650	483749	2061
483750	483792	2314
483793		2314
483794	483999	2314
484000	484149	3026
484150	484199	3070
484750	485249	2315
485250	485999	2415
486000	486749	2462
486750	487719	2341
487720	488749	2342
488750	490249	2361
490250		2366
490251	490749	2366
491700	492199	2723
492200	492699	2834
492700	493899	2396
493900	494769	2397
494770	494919	2409
494920	495269	2409
495270	495519	2468
495520	495969	2704
495970	496619	2479
496620	497169	2469
497620	498019	2484
498020	499019	2551
502000	507549	3153
510000	510049	3494
530000	530576	3108
530577	530738	3384
540901		3457
540902	540907	3458
550000	550499	2907
550500	551449	2907
551600	552949	3145
553000	553499	2909
553500	553999	2910
554000	554429	2911
554430	554899	2912
554900	554999	2912
555000	555249	2913
555250	555749	3144
556050	557049	2915
557050	557599	2915
557750	558749	3146
558750	559749	3146
560200	561199	2917
561200	562199	2918
562200	562799	2919
562800	569299	2920
569300	576299	2921
576300	583299	2922
583300	587299	2923
587300	590299	2923
590300	591499	2992
591500	592199	2993
592200	592699	3076
592700	593199	3042
593200	593699	3043
593700	594199	3058
594200	594349	3062
594350	594749	3219
595150	595499	3063
595500	595699	3063
700000	700499	2688
700500	700999	2836
701000	701499	2837
701500	702499	2853
702500	703499	2854
703500	704499	2869
704500	705499	2971
705500	706199	2972
706200	706699	2984
706700	707199	2985
707200	708199	3024
708200	709199	3025
709200	709549	3083
709550	709699	3163
709700	709949	3084
709950	710249	3096
710250		3362
710251		3362
710252		3362
710253		3362
710254		3362
710255		3362
715000	715019	2579
715020	715039	2851
720000	720049	2031
720050	720249	2032
720250	720424	2033
720425	720924	2154
720925	721224	2155
721225	721324	2156
721325	721824	2180
721825	722424	2317
722425	723274	2416
723275	723524	2650
723525	723774	2445
723775	724024	2546
724025	724274	2705
724275	724674	2776
724675	724973	2839
724975	725274	2983
725275	725674	3082
725675	725874	3232
725875	726124	3275
726125	726224	3383
726255	726524	3429
730000	730099	2048
730100	730499	2049
730500	730919	3288
730920	730999	3332
731000	731099	2127
731100	731389	2204
731390	731489	2328

731490	731589	2457
731590	732039	2554
732040	732389	2740
732390	733039	2867
733040	733219	3226
733220	733239	3258
733240	733459	3332
733500	733999	2671
734000	734299	2764
734300	734559	2973
734560	734607	3097
734608	734848	3097
734849		3463
735000	735199	2106
735200	735399	2125
735400	735799	2266
735800	736299	2323
736300	737099	2493
737100	737599	2500
737600	737999	3107
738000	738039	2398
738040	738054	2638
738500	738872	2489
738873	738942	2870
739000	739499	2588
739500	739999	2589
740000	740299	2004
740300	740399	2046
740400	740599	2047
740600	740649	2305
740650	740699	2329
740700	740899	2458
740900	741099	2545
741100	741449	2712
741500	741559	2845
741560	741639	2846
741640	741669	2846
741670	741729	2846
741730	741749	3167
741750	741949	3335
743000	743099	2590
743100	743199	2697
743200	743299	2871
743300	743399	2974
743400	743574	3098
743575	743674	3195
743675	743874	3296
744000	744099	2446
744100	744599	2586
744620		2835
744621	744759	2857
744780	744879	3085
745057	745061	3715
745500	745549	2369
745550	745579	2466
745600	745647	3536
745648	745649	3548
745650	745664	3541
745665	745679	3542
745680	745699	3543
745700	745719	3544
745720	745731	3552
745732	745745	3553
745746	745759	3554
745760	745789	3562
745790	745803	3563
745804	745815	3564
745816	745845	3587
746000	746499	2157
746500	746749	2267
746750	746849	2986
747000	747149	2597
747500	747975	2988
747976	747999	3075
748000	748019	2088
748020	748049	2265
748050	748059	2587

748060	748109	2989
748110	748129	2770
748130	748149	2850
748150	748181	3283
748182	748187	3305
748188	748287	3283
748288	748347	3320
748348	748427	3321
748428	748460	3370
748468	748491	3479
748492		3550
748500	748502	2233
748503	748546	3312
748547	748576	3320
748577	748588	3326
748589	748656	3358
748657	748672	3485
748673	748697	3532
748698	748722	3533
748723	748747	3534
748748	748768	3535
748800	748817	2370
748818	748827	2537
748828	748830	2763
749000	749001	2041
749007	749009	2042
749010	749011	2395
749014		2043
749017		2278
749021	749022	2043
749023	749032	2073
749033	749034	2075
749035		2281
749036	749037	2394
749038	749040	2280
749041	749047	2393
749048		2423
749049		2424
749050	749053	2566
749054	749058	2649
749059	749065	2774
749066	749070	2946
749100	749101	2074
749200	749203	2044
749250		2239
749300	749305	2076
749306	749308	2621
749309	749314	3404
749350		2306
749370		2533
749400	749407	2077
749408	749411	2277
749412	749417	2427
749500		2112
749600	749609	2170
749650	749659	2240
749660	749679	2429
749750	749751	2410
749900	749909	2412
750000	751299	2001
751300	751799	2003
751800	752349	2013
752350	752789	2062
752790	753099	2063
753100	753199	2079
753200	753429	2083
753430	754429	2109
754430	755179	2134
755180	756679	2181
756680	758179	2182
758180	759179	2318
759180	760429	2319
760430	760679	2503
760680	760879	2347
760880	761343	2421
761344	761379	2538
761380	762179	2465

762180	762279	2470
762280	762429	2585
762430	763279	2595
763280		2696
763281	764030	2414
764301	764480	2541
764481	765480	2367
765481	766400	2422
766401	767600	2706
767601	769400	2707
769401	769634	2735
769636	769900	2735
769901	769950	2736
769951	770150	2784
770151	770650	2840
770651	771450	2841
771451	772200	2855
772201	772950	2856
772951	773250	2864
773251	773350	2961
773351	774450	2990
774451	775449	2991
775450		3218
775451	776150	3007
776151	776550	3011
776551	777350	3023
777351	778200	3086
778251	778750	3228
778751	779050	3191
779551	779850	3118
779851	780550	3109
780551	781750	3164
781751		3377
781752	782273	3310
782274	782523	3318
782524		3360
782525	782573	3378
782574	782853	3346
782854	782872	3373
782873	783872	3391
783873	784766	3392
784285	784290	3392
784773	784872	3421
784873	786872	3398
786873	787022	3413
787023	787097	3434
787098	787347	3472
787348	787394	3540
840001	840002	3455
840003	840052	3456
850000	850049	2014
850050	850099	2045
850100	850599	2158
850600	850999	2202
851000	851299	2348
851300	851599	2425
851600	852349	2471
852350	852499	2584
852500	852899	2737
852900	853599	2865
853600	854499	3008
854500	854500	3292
854501	854525	3216
854526	855000	3117
855001	855100	3224
855101	855150	3311
855551	855675	3347
870000	870099	2320
870100	870149	2417
870500	870589	3215
870590	870629	3371
870630	870759	3393
870670	870879	3431
872000	872199	2321
872200	872249	2418
873000	873023	3313
873024	873193	3323

873194	873199	3313
873200	873369	3361
873370	873419	3405
873420	873569	3406
873570	873719	3409
873720	873769	3460
873770		3467
873771	873792	3483
873794	873893	3497
873793		3491
873894	873915	3515
873916	873977	3516
875000	875199	2018
875200	875299	2084
875300	875549	2135
875550	875649	2472
875650	875749	2738
875750	875849	3009
880000	880079	2002
880080	880279	2015
880280	880429	2203
880430	880679	2346
880680	880729	2598
880730	880979	2739
880980	881129	2866
881130	881359	3010
881360	881609	3119
881610	882009	3209
882010	882236	3225
882237		3286
882238	882637	3290
884500	884514	3134
885000	885039	2009
885040	885089	2183
885090	885114	2447
885115	885139	2448
885140	885189	2656
885190	885309	2709
885310	885409	2925
885410	885509	2994
885510	885609	3166
885610	885659	3233
885660	885709	3234
886000	886009	2375
886010	886031	2376
886032	886081	2407
886082	886211	2408
886212	886261	2708
886262	886311	2767
886312	886341	2768
886342	886401	2842
886402	886461	2843
886462	886561	2987
886562	886686	3088
886687	886811	3089
886812	886921	3204
886922	886996	3289
887000	887019	2490
887020	887039	2499
887040	887064	2544
887065	887099	2689
887100	887119	2872
887120	887134	3099
887135	887159	3237
887800	887999	3177
888000		2679
888001	888110	2769
888111	888180	2863
888181	888280	3029
888281	888550	3156
888551	888580	3156
888581	888880	3175
888881	888980	3176
889000	889019	2848
889020	889029	3022
889100	889135	3090
889136	889143	3547

889200	889203	2849
890000	890149	2022
890150	891249	2036
891250	891399	2064
891400	891499	2070
891500	891749	2080
891750	891899	2086
891900	891499	2126
893000	893699	2269
893700	893949	2325
893950	894109	2426
894110	894199	2495
894200	894299	2501
900000	900009	2030
900010	900014	2354
900015	900019	2450
900020	900022	2613
900023	900026	2641
900027		2927
900028	900028	2927
900029	900030	2927
900031		2927
900032	900036	2927
900037	900042	2945
900043		2949
900044	900046	3199
900047	900048	2878
900100	900103	2218
900104		2452
900105	900107	2619
900108		2936
900109	900128	3252
900300	900309	2006
900310	900313	2304
900350		2219
900351		2453
900352		2620
900353	900354	3303
900355		2953
900400	900409	2005
900410	900414	2364
900415	900419	2451
900420	900422	2617
900423	900424	2948
900425	900428	3069
900429	900430	3266
900431	900436	3269
900437	900440	3270
900500	900503	2176
900504	900505	2572
900506		2573
900507	900508	2952
900509	900532	3300
900600	900601	2571
900602		2753
900603		2947
900675		2893
900700	900709	2356
900760		2357
900800	900809	2029
900810	900811	3272
900812	900813	3301
900900	900902	2454
900903	900905	2642
900906	900907	2879
900908	900910	2880
900911		2977
900912	900922	3102
900923	900924	3173
900925	900938	3192
901000	901005	2078
901006	901010	2360
901011	901013	2581
901014	901017	3193
901018	901021	3194
901022	901025	3241
901100	901101	2494
901102	901103	2647

901104	901105	2881
901106	901107	2978
901108	901109	3103
901150	901151	3074
901152	901152	3213
901200	901203	2582
901204		3016
901205		3273
901225	901226	3214
901260		2828
901261		3316
901400	901402	2177
901450		2574
901451		2950
901452		3018
901453		3111
901500	901509	2205
901510	901519	2355
901520	901530	3017
901531	901541	3112
901542	901576	3247
901600	901603	2175
901650		2575
901700	901701	2576
901702	901751	3309
901800	901801	2419
901850	901859	2877
902000	902005	2103
902006	902011	2491
902012	902024	2543
902025	902034	2646
902035	902037	2874
902038	902047	3071
902048	902049	3297
902500	902501	2570
902600		3251
902700	902702	3222
902703		3317
902800	902801	2173
902802		2568
902803		3020
902804		3110
902805	902810	3527
903265	903648	3066
903600	903624	2434
903649	903664	3124
903665	903683	3231
903684	903703	3410
904000	904016	2007
904017	904041	2189
904042	904081	2276
904082	904101	2324
904102	904104	2492
904105	904119	2592
904120	904122	2959
904123	904134	2976
904135	904144	3101
904145	904154	3254
904155	904157	3298
904500	904537	2187
904538	904565	2268
904566	904571	2449
904572	904629	2593
904630	904633	2594
904634	904641	2645
904642	904661	2693
904662	904674	2714
904675	904694	2876
904695	904709	3172
904710	904722	3198
905000	905019	2087
905020	905059	2475
905060	905071	2553
905072	905077	2591
905078	905087	2875
905088	905097	2975
905098	905116	3100
905117	905118	3197

906000	906005	2353
906006	906020	2644
906021		3019
906022	906026	3304
906800	906809	2632
906810	906816	3004
906817	906831	3123
907000	907001	2569
907100	907106	2008
907107	907113	2016
907200	907201	2943
907202	907207	2944
907208	907236	3044
907300	907301	2285
907302	907304	3151
907500	907501	2692
907502	907503	2873
907504	907505	2692
907506	907507	2873
908000	900808	2174
908009	908015	2622
908016	908019	2651
908020		2938
908021		3057
908022	908027	3171
908500	908509	2643
908510	908511	2721
908512		2924
908513		3041
908514	908519	3271
909000	909020	3165
909021	909047	3259
909048	909077	3299
909200	909205	3260
909300	909301	3518
909400	909401	3518
910000	910499	2034
910500	910999	2131
911000	911999	2783
912000	912999	2860
913000	913999	2861
914000	915999	3005
916000	917999	3006
918000	918495	3125
920000	920199	2020
920200	920399	2035
922000	922499	3060
922500	922699	3162
922700	922999	3200
923000	923099	3238
923100	923299	3341
923300	924399	3343
924400	924799	3397
924800	924899	3440
927000	927129	2979
927130	927199	3021
927200	927213	3028
927214	927399	3028
927400	927499	3104
927500	927599	3113
927600	927799	3246
927800	927999	3407
928000	928199	3408
930000	930249	2037
930250	930549	2132
930550	931049	2151
931050	931589	2199
931590	931749	2327
931750	931974	2476
931975	932824	2604
932825	933374	2734
933375	933874	2862
933875	934024	3128
934025	935524	3223
935525	936524	3338
940000	940049	2085
940050	940999	2308
941000	941149	2021

941150	941349	2211
941350	941416	2237
941417	941474	2238
941475	941554	2358
941555	941629	2487
941630	941779	2623
941780	941929	2624
941930	942029	2625
942030	942229	2691
942230	942329	2690
942330	942529	2787
942530	942679	2852
942680	942929	2882
943000	943099	2326
943100	943349	2406
943350	943509	2496
943510	943609	2539
943610	943859	2542
943860	943879	2583
943880	943880	2583
944310	944469	2616
944470	944519	2616
944520	944639	2616
944640	945379	3059
944740	944889	2759
944890	945189	2760
945190		2818
945191	945389	2818
945390	945790	2818
945791	945990	3155
946000	946049	2098
946050	946064	3263
946065	946074	3267
946075	946114	3268
946115	946209	3333
946210	946229	3334
947000	947049	2010
947050	947124	2133
947125	947174	2185
947175	947194	2344
947195	947234	2455
947235	947309	2618
947310	947349	2722
947350	947399	2930
947400	947559	3046
947560	947709	3055
947710	947859	3056
947860	948009	3229
948010	948134	3235
948135	948259	3236
948260	948409	3240
949000	949003	2209
949004	949004	2209
949005	949034	2209
949035	949049	3014
949050	949089	3015
949090	949129	3399
949130	949179	3450
949180	949185	3464
949186	949191	3478
949192	949197	3484
949198	949209	3513
949210	949219	3514
949501	949517	3359
949518	949537	3359
949538	949550	3359
949551	949608	3424
950000	950124	2025
950125	950249	2026
950250	950539	2051
950540	950541	2096
950542	950615	2099
950616	950865	2136
950866	951115	2137
951116	951275	2206
951276	951515	2207
951516	951715	2349

951716	951865	2350
951866	952005	2477
952006	952165	2478
952166	952515	2605
952516	952715	2606
952716	953115	2741
953116	953415	2868
953416	953675	3012
953676	954520	3129
954521	954997	3227
954998	955247	3394
964000	964004	3442
964005	964019	3443
964020	964028	3444
964029		3444
964030		3445
964031	964034	3445
964035	964037	3446
964038	964105	3448
964106	964111	3449
964112	964121	3500
965203	965216	3539
965217	965230	3539
965231	965243	3539
976000	976011	3752
982000	982149	2012
982150	982349	2264
983000	983309	2939
983376	983576	3039
983577	983626	3329
983627	983896	3331
983897	983920	3340
984000	984049	2942
984050	984249	3038
984250	984307	3048
984308	984549	3049
984550	984693	3050
984694	984993	3052
985000	985386	2362
985387	985646	2482
985647	985885	2483
985886	986137	2884
986138	986339	2885
986340	986455	2886
986456	986555	2887
986556	986707	2777
986708	986777	2778
986778	986837	2779
986838	986959	2780
986960	986986	3051
987000	987079	2089
988000	988199	2090
988200	988418	3245
988419	988521	3282
988522	988596	3339
989000	989019	2428
989020	989071	2535
989072	989088	2928
989089	989238	3170
989239	989288	3256
989289	989588	3330
989589	989638	3348
990000	990049	2120
990050	990099	2121
990100	901399	2200
990400	990689	2345
990690	990858	2940
990859	990958	2941
991000	991020	2065
991021	991140	2091
991141	991300	2241
991301	991320	2102
991321	991864	3168
992000	992023	2027
992024	992034	2117
992035	992056	2118
992057	992116	2178
992117	992196	2188

992197	992246	2214
992247	992830	2284
992381	992480	2405
992481	992530	2411
992531	992590	2682
992591	992650	2683
992651	992710	2775
992711	992858	2819
992859	993058	2820
993059	993148	2821
993149	993309	2822
993310	993470	2823
993471	993507	2824
993508	993566	2929
993567	993634	3255
993700	993701	2028
993702	993708	2172
993709	993712	2186
993713	993726	2431
993727	993756	2536
993757	993783	2657
993784	993809	2782
993810	993815	2119
993816	993856	2931
993857	993904	3040
993905	993920	3150
993921	993940	3285
994000	994089	2217
994090	994200	2895
994201	994310	2937
994311	994391	3047
994392	994421	3264
994422	994467	3265
994468		3291
994469	994472	3342
994500	994536	2322
994537	994716	2404
994717	994858	2507
994859	994999	2614
995000	995049	2215
995250	995252	2883
995500	995514	2081
995515	995524	2093
996000	996024	2011
996025	996099	2216
996100	996151	2363
996152	996213	2399
996214	996308	2534
996309	996362	2615
996363	996420	2894
996421	996518	2926
996519	996597	3065
996598	996677	3067
996700	996724	2094
996725	996794	2208
996795	996803	2208
996804	996881	3261
996882	996921	3262
996922	996969	3284
996970	996994	3352
996995	997019	3353
997300	997305	2608
997400	997401	2456
997500	997535	2201
997536	997540	2481
997541	997542	2773
997600	997633	2271
997634	997647	2309
997648		2497
997649	997669	2540
997700	997726	2272
997727	997746	2459
997900		2097
998000	998002	2095
998003	998005	2270
998006	998006	2951
998007	998010	2980
998011	998012	3149

998013	998014	3201
998015	998029	3257
998050		3077
998051	998053	3114
998070	998073	3709
998100	998101	2532
998102	998122	2725
998500		2122
998509	998510	3412
998900	998901	2220
998910	998912	2371
998913	998925	2372
998926	998391	2825
998932	998938	3354
998940	998954	2781
998955	998992	3139
998993	998996	3401
999000	999008	3700
999009	999012	3716
999501	999504	3093
999505		3094
999506		3095
999507		3248
999508	999509	3379

CONTAINERS

1	60	2056
161	290	2116
291	340	2124
341	450	2141
451	680	2244
681	1210	2335
1211	1310	2374
1311	1545	2436
1546	1965	2555
1966	2565	2658
2566	2915	2829
2916	3315	2958
3316	3465	2963
3466	3565	2981
3566	3840	2995
3841	3842	3368
3843		3403
3844	3851	3435
3852	3855	3470
4000	4224	2017
4225	4299	2057
4300		3220
4301	4306	3274
4307		3382
4309	4310	3496
4311	4350	3436
4351	4353	3549
4365	4444	2100
4445	4494	2101
4495	5124	2143
5125	5419	2213
5420	5689	2246
5690	6239	2333
6240	6474	2373
6475	6674	2437
6675	7384	2437
7385	7794	2556
7795	7994	3161
7995		3471
7996	7999	3493
8000	8029	2059
8030	8059	2060
8060	8139	2334
8140	8554	2438
8555	8684	2557
8685	9134	2830
9135	9184	2996
9185	9434	3105
9700	9709	2262
9710	9775	2444

9776	9875	2577
9876	9890	2680
9891	9950	2833
10000	10014	2071
10015	10114	2114
10115	10234	2234
10235	10274	2261
10275	10359	2311
10360	10594	2505
10595	10714	2564
10715	10914	2889
10915	11154	2982
11155	11304	3106
12000	12251	2067
12252	12351	2115
12352	12611	2147
12612	12826	2263
12827	12911	2432
12912	13066	2303
13067	13216	2336
13217	13416	2359
13417	13566	2365
13567	13796	2435
13797	13896	2435
13897	14096	2558
14097	14286	2578
14287	14536	2660
14537	14736	2672
14737	14986	2681
15000	15049	2142
15050	15074	2245
15075	15104	2506
15105	15204	2610
15205	15239	2665
16000	16090	2159
16091	16099	2289
16100	16179	2260
16180	16299	2273
16300	16319	2565
16320	16369	2673
16370	16429	2890
16430	16469	2891
16470	16489	3250
16490	16491	3357
16492	16493	3357
16494	16499	3428
16500	16516	2443
17000		2307
17001	17079	2332
17080	17109	2563
17110	17115	3474
17250		2433
17251	18249	2392
18250	19749	2652
19750	19959	2832
19960		3325
19961	19962	3336
19963	19974	3337
19975	19977	3375
19978	19983	3376
19984	19998	3447
20000	20099	2024
20100	20199	2111
20200	20399	2144
20400	20579	2247
20580	20709	2337
20710	20759	2439
20760	20789	2559
21000	21049	2066
21050	21249	2113
21250	21389	2145
21390	21804	2248
21805	22384	2338
22385	22604	2440
22605	22974	2560
22975	22994	3369
23000		3476
23001	23005	3476

23500	23501	3561
24000	24249	2019
24250	24999	2023
25000	25049	2072
25050	25149	2110
25150	25199	2146
25200	25549	2249
25550	25909	2339
25910	26909	2441
27000	27003	2171
27004	27021	3349
27022	27033	3355
27034	27045	3356
27046	27057	3366
29000	29499	2442
29500	30299	2562
40000	40549	2964
40550	41149	3078
46000	46449	2659
46450	46949	2785
46950	47549	2786
47550	47999	2966
48000	48549	2969
48550	49099	2970
49100	49449	3064
49450	49749	3079
49750	50149	3080
50150	50449	3131
50450	50799	3132
50800	50999	3169
51000	51012	3461
51013	51025	3475
55525	55699	2965
55700	55849	2888
55850	55899	3174
58000	58099	3072
58500	58523	3451
58524	58539	3452
58540	58559	3459
59500	59799	2831
59800	59999	2892
60000	60399	2997
60400	60649	3137
60650	60656	3468
60657	60661	3469
65000	65174	2648
65175	65199	2766
65200	65399	2967
65400	65599	3068
65600	65799	3136
65800		2956
65801	65835	3179
65836	66135	3180
66136	66315	3181
66316	66415	3249
66416	66445	3277
66446	66481	3278
68000	68899	2762
68900	69679	2968
69680	70719	3073
70180	70779	3081
71080	71161	3135
71162	71609	3380
71610	71975	3389
74000	74005	3319
74006	74007	3350
74018	74019	3351
74020	74029	3351
74030	74031	3372
74032	74033	3396
74034		3411
77000	78199	3133
78200	78999	3190
79000	79003	2771
79004	79083	2772
79084	79533	2955
79534	79583	2957
79584	79593	3148

79594	79949	3190
79950		2754
79951	79955	2755
79998		2826
79999		2694
80000	83643	3190
83644	84093	3280
84094	84593	3281
84594		3367
84595	84596	3386
84598	84620	3420
88000	88149	2561
89001	89050	3294
89051	89250	3295
89251	89500	3294
89501	89550	3293
89561	89585	3279
89586	89611	3287
89612	89631	3306
89632	89643	3307
89644	89713	3328
89714	89763	3381
89764	89869	3385
89870	89887	3395
89888	89917	3422
89918	89927	3423
89928	89977	3462
90001	90055	3453
90056	90088	3517
90101	90116	3454
90201	90234	3477
90235	90318	3481
90320	90339	3482
90340	90346	3517
94998		2827
94999		2695
95000	95023	2662
95024	95219	2684

Appendix 3

Lot Numbers and original Diagrams

This Appendix gives the lot number and appropriate diagram for all wagons (other than air-braked) and all containers (other than Freightliner). Where there are multiple entries against a lot the reader should refer to Appendix 4 for details. For example, vehicles of lot 2345 were built to the diagram on p.572 of the Freight Stock diagram book.

Lot	Diag.
2001	1/200
2002	1/240
2003	1/204
2004	1/460
2005	1/511
2006	2/510
2007	2/240
2008	2/001
2009	1/270
2010	1/490
2011	1/640
2012	1/565
2013	1/204
2014	1/206
2015	1/240
2016	2/001
2017	3/050
2018	1/230
2019	3/600
2020	1/416
2021	1/470
2022	1/350
2023	3/602
2024	3/500
2025	1/505
2026	1/503
2027	1/581
2028	1/596
2029	3/730
2030	2/512
2031	1/031
2032	1/031
2033	1/031
2034	1/400
2035	1/415
2036	1/350
2037	1/430
2038	1/142
2039	1/150
2040	1/160
2041	1/325
2042	1/325
2043	1/325
2043	1/325
2044	1/325
2045	1/201
2046	1/461
2047	1/461
2048	1/445
2049	1/445
2050	1/140
2051	1/500
2052	1/141
2053	1/141
2054	1/141
2055	1/161
2056	3/002
2057	3/051
2059	3/125
2060	3/125
2061	1/033
2061	1/016
2062	1/202
2063	1/202
2064	1/351
2065	1/570
2066	3/550
2067	3/375
2070	1/350
2071	3/150
2072	3/600
2073	1/327
2074	1/302
2075	1/326
2076	1/300
2077	1/329
2078	2/513
2079	1/203
2080	1/352
2081	1/620
2082	1/032
2083	1/205
2084	1/231
2085	1/471
2086	1/352
2087	2/241
2088	1/090
2089	1/566
2090	1/567
2091	1/568
2093	1/620
2094	1/641
2095	2/900
2096	1/501
2097	1/631
2098	1/480
2099	1/502
2100	3/051
2101	3/051
2102	1/570
2103	2/170
2104	1/106
2105	1/111
2106	1/061
2107	1/001
2108	1/017
2109	1/204
2110	3/602
2111	3/500
2112	1/328
2113	3/550
2114	3/150
2115	3/200
2117	1/580
2118	1/580
2119	1/595
2120	1/569
2121	1/571
2122	1/630
2123	1/111
2124	3/002
2125	1/061
2126	1/352
2127	1/446
2128	1/037
2129	1/142
2130	1/160
2131	1/400
2132	1/430
2133	1/491
2134	1/232
2135	1/230
2136	1/504
2137	1/506
2138	1/142
2139	1/142
2140	1/142
2141	3/001
2142	3/275
2143	3/050
2144	3/500
2145	3/550
2146	3/602
2146	3/200
2148	1/162
2149	1/162
2150	1/162
2151	1/430
2152	1/018
2153	1/034
2154	1/035
2155	1/035
2156	1/036
2157	1/071
2158	1/207
2159	3/250
2160	1/104
2161	1/104
2162	1/104
2163	1/143
2164	1/143
2165	1/143
2166	1/143
2167	1/143
2168	1/143
2169	1/150
2170	1/301
2171	3/650
2172	1/596
2173	2/030
2174	2/002
2175	2/681
2176	2/514
2177	2/660
2178	1/581
2179	1/039
2180	1/040
2181	1/208
2183	1/208
2183	1/271
2184	1/106
2185	1/490
2186	1/597
2187	2/242
2188	1/580
2189	2/240
2190	1/110
2191	1/107
2192	1/107
2193	1/107
2194	1/002
2195	1/041
2196	1/041
2197	1/041
2198	1/151
2199	1/431
2200	1/572
2201	1/431
2202	1/209
2203	1/241
2204	1/447
2205	2/680
2206	1/504
2207	1/504
2208	1/641
2208	1/488
2209	1/401
2209	1/406
2209	1/401
2210	1/106
2211	1/472
2212	1/143
2213	3/052
2214	1/582
2215	1/621
2216	1/640
2217	1/639
2218	2/516
2219	2/517
2220	1/648
2221	1/109
2222	1/109
2223	1/108
2224	1/108
2225	1/108
2226	1/108
2227	1/108
2228	1/109
2229	1/108
2230	1/108
2231	1/108
2232	1/108
2233	1/038
2234	3/150
2235	1/019
2236	1/019
2237	1/472
2238	1/472
2239	1/333
2240	1/304
2241	1/570
2242	1/104
2243	1/104
2244	3/001
2245	3/275
2246	3/050
2247	3/500
2248	3/550
2249	3/602
2250	1/108
2251	1/108
2252	1/108
2253	1/108
2254	1/108
2255	1/108
2256	1/108
2257	1/108
2258	1/108
2259	1/108
2260	3/250
2261	3/152
2262	3/100
2263	3/202
2264	1/565
2265	1/091
2266	1/062
2267	1/072
2268	2/243
2269	1/353
2270	2/900
2271	1/471
2272	1/622
2273	3/250
2274	1/180
2275	1/180
2276	2/240
2277	1/329
2278	1/330
2280	1/331
2281	1/330
2282	1/144
2283	1/144
2284	1/583
2285	2/070
2286	1/112
2286	1/112
2286	1/112
2286	1/112
2286	1/112
2286	1/112
2287	1/100
2287	1/100
2287	1/100
2287	1/100
2287	1/100
2287	1/100
2287	1/100
2288	1/113
2288	1/113
2288	1/113
2288	1/113
2288	1/113
2288	1/113
2289	3/251
2290	1/108
2291	1/108
2292	1/109
2293	1/108
2294	1/108
2295	1/108
2296	1/108
2297	1/109
2298	1/108
2299	1/109
2300	1/108
2301	1/108
2302	1/108
2303	3/202
2304	2/515
2305	1/460
2306	1/303
2307	3/400
2308	1/471
2309	1/471
2310	1/181
2311	3/151
2312	1/182
2313	1/003
2314	1/043
2314	1/042
2314	1/042
2315	1/039
2317	1/040
2318	1/208
2319	1/208
2320	1/250
2321	1/251
2322	1/638
2323	1/062
2324	2/245
2325	1/353
2326	1/471
2327	1/431
2328	1/447
2329	1/460
2330	1/146
2331	1/114
2332	3/400
2333	3/050
2333	3/052
2334	3/126
2335	3/003
2336	3/201
2337	3/500
2338	3/550
2339	3/602
2340	1/002
2341	1/146
2342	1/047
2343	1/151
2344	1/490
2345	1/572
2346	1/242
2347	1/208
2348	1/209
2349	1/506
2350	1/506
2351	1/019
2352	1/019
2353	2/390
2354	2/512
2355	2/682
2356	2/733
2357	2/732
2358	1/472
2359	3/202
2360	2/731
2361	1/041
2362	1/572
2363	1/642
2364	2/511
2365	3/202
2366	1/041
2366	1/047
2367	1/208
2369	1/046
2370	1/332
2371	1/633
2372	1/633
2373	3/050
2374	3/003
2375	1/210
2376	1/210
2377	1/108
2378	1/108
2379	1/108
2380	1/108
2381	1/108
2382	1/108
2383	1/108
2384	1/109
2385	1/108
2386	1/109
2387	1/108
2388	1/108
2389	1/108
2390	1/108
2391	1/108
2392	3/450
2393	1/334
2394	1/334
2395	1/334
2396	1/044
2397	1/044
2398	1/063
2399	1/640
2400	1/146
2401	1/146
2402	1/145
2403	1/145
2404	1/638
2405	1/584
2406	1/471
2407	1/210
2408	1/210
2409	1/045
2409	1/044
2410	1/307
2411	1/585
2412	1/306
2413	1/003
2414	1/208
2415	1/039
2416	1/040
2417	1/250
2418	1/251
2419	2/470
2420	1/002
2421	1/208
2422	1/213
2423	1/336
2424	1/338
2425	1/209
2426	1/353
2427	1/337
2428	1/573
2429	1/305
2430	1/019
2431	1/597
2432	3/202
2433	3/450
2434	2/491
2435	3/202
2435	3/203
2436	3/001
2437	3/052
2437	3/050
2438	3/126
2439	3/500
2440	3/550
2441	3/602
2442	3/602
2443	3/300
2444	3/101
2445	1/048
2446	1/004
2447	1/271
2448	1/271
2449	3/246
2450	2/512
2451	2/524
2452	2/516
2453	2/517
2454	2/735
2455	1/490
2456	1/490
2457	1/447
2458	1/460
2459	1/622
2460	1/115
2461	1/002
2462	1/039
2463	1/108
2464	1/108
2465	1/208
2466	1/046
2467	1/002
2468	1/047
2469	1/049
2470	1/208
2471	1/209
2472	1/233
2473	1/111
2474	1/151
2475	2/244
2476	1/431
2477	1/506
2478	1/506
2479	1/047
2480	1/111
2481	1/431
2482	1/572
2483	1/572
2484	1/044
2485	1/109
2486	1/109
2487	1/472
2488	1/019
2489	1/064
2490	1/260
2491	2/171
2492	2/245
2493	1/062
2494	3/734
2495	1/353
2496	1/473
2497	1/643
2498	1/183
2499	1/260
2500	1/062
2501	1/353
2502	1/111
2503	1/208
2504	1/148
2505	3/151
2506	3/275
2507	1/645
2508	1/108
2509	1/108
2510	1/108
2511	1/108
2512	1/108
2513	1/108
2514	1/108
2515	1/108
2516	1/108
2517	1/109
2518	1/109
2519	1/108
2520	1/108
2521	1/108
2522	1/108
2523	1/108
2524	1/108
2525	1/108
2526	1/108
2527	1/108
2528	1/108
2529	1/108
2530	1/108
2531	1/108
2532	1/632
2533	1/000
2534	1/642
2535	1/573
2536	1/597
2537	1/335
2538	1/211
2539	1/473
2540	1/473
2541	1/208
2542	1/473
2543	2/171
2544	1/260
2545	1/460
2546	1/040
2547	1/108
2548	1/108
2549	1/108
2550	1/108
2551	1/039
2552	1/146
2553	2/244
2554	1/448
2555	3/001
2556	3/050
2557	3/126
2558	3/204
2559	3/500
2560	3/550
2561	3/599
2562	3/602
2563	3/400
2564	3/151
2565	3/253
2566	1/334
2567	1/109
2568	2/031
2569	2/071
2570	2/172
2571	2/521
2572	2/520
2573	2/522
2574	2/661
2575	2/683
2576	2/684
2577	3/100
2578	3/203
2579	1/055
2581	2/736
2582	2/750
2583	1/473
2583	1/475
2584	1/209
2585	1/212
2586	1/004
2587	1/091
2588	1/065
2589	1/065
2590	1/051
2591	2/248
2592	2/245
2593	2/243
2594	2/246
2595	1/208
2597	1/179
2598	1/242
2599	1/117
2600	1/115
2601	1/181
2602	1/115
2603	1/151
2604	1/431
2605	1/506
2606	1/506
2608	1/619
2609	1/148
2610	3/275
2611	1/108
2612	1/108
2613	2/512
2614	1/645
2615	1/644
2616	1/473
2616	1/474
2616	1/475
2617	2/511
2618	1/490
2619	2/516
2620	2/517
2621	1/300
2622	2/002
2623	1/472
2624	1/472
2625	1/472
2626	1/108
2627	1/108
2628	1/108
2629	1/108
2630	1/108
2631	1/108
2632	2/072
2633	1/108
2634	1/108
2635	1/108
2636	1/108
2637	1/108
2638	1/063
2639	1/108
2640	1/108
2641	2/512
2642	2/735
2643	2/001
2644	2/391
2645	2/254
2646	2/171
2647	2/734
2648	3/252
2649	1/334
2650	1/050
2651	2/002
2652	3/450
2653	1/108
2654	1/108
2656	1/271
2657	1/597
2658	3/001
2659	3/050
2660	3/204
2662	3/660
2663	1/108
2664	1/108
2665	3/275
2666	1/109
2667	1/109
2668	1/020
2669	1/109
2670	1/108
2671	1/066
2672	3/205
2673	3/253
2674	1/108
2675	1/108
2676	1/108
2677	1/108
2678	1/108
2679	1/273
2680	3/100
2681	3/203
2683	1/586
2683	1/586
2684	3/660
2685	1/108
2686	1/108
2687	1/108
2688	1/067
2689	1/260
2690	1/472
2691	1/472
2692	2/150
2693	2/243
2694	3/000
2695	3/000
2696	1/229
2697	1/051
2698	1/108
2699	1/108
2700	1/108
2701	1/108
2702	1/108
2703	1/108
2704	1/049
2705	1/052
2706	1/208
2707	1/208
2708	1/210
2709	1/271
2711	1/108
2712	1/462
2713	1/146
2714	2/247
2715	1/108
2716	1/108
2717	1/108
2718	1/108
2719	1/108
2720	1/108
2721	2/001
2722	1/490
2723	1/039
2724	1/024
2724	1/022
2725	1/632
2726	1/146
2727	1/145
2728	1/145
2729	1/002
2730	1/183
2731	1/146
2732	1/151
2733	1/163
2734	1/432
2735	1/213
2735	1/213
2736	1/211
2737	1/209
2738	1/233
2739	1/242
2740	1/448
2741	1/504
2742	1/108
2743	1/108
2744	1/108
2745	1/108
2746	1/108
2747	1/108
2748	1/108
2749	1/108
2750	1/108
2751	1/108
2752	1/108
2753	2/523
2754	3/374
2755	3/374
2756	1/108
2757	1/108
2758	1/148
2759	1/475
2760	1/474
2761	1/116
2762	3/450
2763	1/335
2764	1/068
2766	3/253
2767	1/210
2768	1/210
2769	1/272
2770	1/092
2771	3/670
2772	3/670
2773	1/431
2774	1/334
2775	1/586
2776	1/050
2777	1/572
2778	1/572
2779	1/572
2780	1/572
2781	1/634
2782	1/597
2783	1/400
2784	1/211
2785	3/050
2786	3/050
2787	1/472
2788	1/108
2789	1/108
2790	1/108
2791	1/108
2792	1/108
2793	1/108
2794	1/108
2795	1/109
2796	1/108
2797	1/108
2798	1/108
2799	1/108
2800	1/108
2801	1/108
2802	1/108
2803	1/108
2804	1/108
2805	1/108
2806	1/108
2808	1/108
2809	1/108
2810	1/108
2810	1/108
2811	1/109
2813	1/108
2814	1/108
2816	1/108
2817	1/108
2818	1/475
2818	1/475
2818	1/474
2819	1/587
2820	1/587
2821	1/587
2822	1/587
2823	1/587
2824	1/587
2825	1/633
2826	3/000
2827	3/000
2828	2/737
2829	3/001
2830	3/127
2831	3/205
2832	3/450
2833	3/100
2834	1/039
2835	1/005
2836	1/067
2837	1/067
2839	1/050
2840	1/208
2841	1/208
2842	1/210
2843	1/210
2844	1/183
2845	1/462
2846	1/462
2846	1/462
2846	1/462
2848	1/291
2849	1/292
2850	1/092
2851	1/055
2852	1/472
2853	1/067
2854	1/067
2855	1/213
2856	1/213
2857	1/005
2858	1/099
2859	1/151
2860	1/400
2861	1/401
2862	1/432
2863	1/272
2864	1/211
2865	1/209
2866	1/242
2867	1/448
2868	1/506
2869	1/067
2870	1/068
2871	1/051
2872	1/260
2873	2/150
2873	2/150
2874	2/171
2875	2/248
2876	2/243
2877	2/450
2878	3/528
2879	2/743
2880	3/745
2881	2/751
2882	1/472
2883	1/622
2884	1/572
2885	1/572
2886	1/572
2887	1/572
2888	3/049
2889	3/151
2890	3/252
2891	3/253
2892	3/205
2893	2/519
2894	1/646
2895	1/645
2896	1/108
2897	1/108
2898	1/108

Appendix 4

Details of all wagons and containers built to British Railways order up to 1970 but excluding air braked wagons and Freightliner containers. The description is that given in the original series of diagram books. It is preceded by the diagram number in the form of diagram book number/page within that book: Book 1 is the freight diagram book; Book 2 covers specially constructed wagons; Book 3 is for containers. There then follows details of the wagons or containers built or rebuilt to that diagram in the form of lot number, brakes, quantity, running numbers, programme, builder, comments. For containers capacity, in tons, replaces brake details. Where no lot number is given, (eg with conversions) none was allocated or the lot number is not known.

The original braking details are given in the form of a key as follows; space = unfitted; p = vacuum brake through pipe only; v = automatic vacuum brake; w = Westinghouse brake or through pipe; x = v + w.

The quantity is the quantity built. A bracketed figure indicates the quantity converted. The last entry under a diagram is the total built or converted for that diagram.

The programme given is that to which the lot was finally built. Spaces indicate no programme was specified.

The name of the builder is given in an abbreviated form in most cases.

The notes are intended to provide a means of identification or give further information where this is known. In many cases they are from notes in the lot book which are themselves incomplete. For example, diagram 1/334 tanks are variously described as being for 'Bass' or 'Bass Ratcliff & Gretton'. Both are taken as recorded.

All vehicles are assumed to be four-wheeled unless otherwise stated. Where wagons are referred to as 'bogie vehicles' either in the description or notes this means each vehicle has two four-wheeled bogies again unless stated otherwise.

Notes refer to all vehicles or containers to that diagram unless there is an indication to the contrary.

1/001 13ton Lowfit - Lettered Lowfit

Lot		Qty	Numbers	Year	Builder	Notes
2107	v	400	B450000-450399	1950	Wolverton	Wood body; Originally unfitted.
Total		400				

1/002 13ton Low Goods Wagon - Lettered Lowfit

Lot		Qty	Numbers	Year	Builder	Notes
2194	v	1000	B450400-451399	1951	Shildon	All lots have steel body.
2340	v	200	B451700-451899	1952	Shildon	
2420	v	300	B451900-541299	1952	Shildon	
2461	v	200	B452200-452399	1952	Shildon	This lot originally to diagram 6
2467	v	200	B452400-452599	1953	Shildon	
2729	v	300	B452600-452899	1955	Shildon	This lot originally to diagram 6
2998	v	550	B452900-453449	1957	Shildon	
Total		2750				

1/003 13ton Pig Iron Wagon - Lettered Pig Iron

Lot		Qty	Numbers	Year	Builder	Notes
2313		100	B451400-451499	1952	Derby	Originally 'Low goods, fixed sides & ends'.
2413		200	B451500-451699	1952	Derby	
Total		300				

1/004 20ton Pig Iron Wagon - Lettered Pig Iron

Lot		Qty	Numbers	Year	Builder	Notes
2446		100	B744000-744099	1953	Derby	
2586		500	B744100-744599	1954	Derby	
Total		600				

1/005 30ton Hot Pig Iron Wagon

Lot		Qty	Numbers	Year	Builder	Notes
2835		1	B744620	1956	Shildon	Prototype
2857		139	B744621-744759	1956	Shildon	
Total		140				

1/007 20ton Pig Iron Wagon - Lettered Pig Iron

Lot		Qty	Numbers	Year	Builder	Notes
3085		100	B744780-744879	1958	Derby	Clasp type hand brake
Total		100				

1/016 13ton Medium Goods

Lot		Qty	Numbers	Year	Builder	Notes
2061		100	B457100-457199	1949	Ashford	Part lot - see diagram 33 also.
Total		100				

1/017 13ton Medium Goods Wagon

Lot		Qty	Numbers	Year	Builder	Notes
2108		397	B457200-457596	1950	Wolverton	Originally 400 ordered. 3-plank.
Total		397				

1/018 13ton Shock Absorbing Wagon for Glass Traffic

Lot		Qty	Numbers	Year	Builder	Notes
2152	v	25	B474800-474824	1949	Shildon	3-plank bodies.
Total		25				

1/019 13ton Medium Goods Wagon

Lot		Qty	Numbers	Year	Builder	Notes
2235	v	1000	B457597-458596	1951	Ashford	Steel bodies. Drop sides & ends.
2236	v	1000	B458597-459596	1951	Ashford	
2351	v	800	B459597-460396	1952	Ashford	(Lot 2351 amended to 'steel side doors').
2352	v	400	B460597-460996	1952	Ashford	
2430	v	200	B460397-460596	1952	Ashford	
2488	v	600	B460997-461596	1952	Ashford	
Total		4000				

1/020 13ton Pallet Brick Wagon - Lettered Palbrick A

Lot		Qty	Numbers	Year	Builder	Notes
2668	v	8	B461609-461616	1954	Ashford	Converted from diagram 19.
Total		8				

1/021 16ton Pallet Brick Wagon Lettered Palbrick B

Lot		Qty	Numbers	Year	Builder	Notes
3138	v	12	B461597-461608	1954	Ashford	With lots 2668 & 3140 originally 400 wagons
Total		12				

1/022 16ton Pallet Brick Wagon - Lettered Palbrick B

Lot		Qty	Numbers	Year	Builder	Notes
2724	v	430	B462117-462246	1955	Ashford	Part lot. Remainder to diagram 24.
Total		430				

1/023 13ton Pallet Brick Wagon - Lettered Palbrick A

Lot		Qty	Numbers	Year	Builder	Notes
3140	v	380	B461617-461996	1954	Ashford	461874 varies slightly
Total		380				

1/024 16ton Pallet Brick Wagon - Lettered Palbrick B

Lot		Qty	Numbers	Year	Builder	Notes
2724	v	20	B461997-462116	1955	Ashford	Part lot. Remainder to diagram 22.
3141	v	80	B462447-462526	1956	Ashford	
Total		100				

1/025 16ton Pallet Brick Wagon - Lettered Palbrick C

Lot		Qty	Numbers	Year	Builder	Notes
3242	v	160	B462527-462686	1959	Ashford	All lots have roller bearings
3322	v	50	B462797-462846	1960	Ashford	
3365	v	190	B462847-463036	1961	Ashford	
Total		400				

1/026 16ton Pallet Brick Wagon - Lettered Palbrick B

Lot		Qty	Numbers	Year	Builder	Notes
3243	v	90	B462707-462796	1959	Ashford	Roller bearings
Total		90				

1/027 Shellcase Wagon

Lot		Qty	Numbers	Year	Builder	Notes
		(22)	?		(Currock)	Converted from Palbrick B wagons

1/028 Ale Pallet Wagon

Lot		Qty	Numbers	Year	Builder	Notes
		(54)	?			Converted from diagram 448

1/031 13ton Shock Absorbing Wagon

Lot		Qty	Numbers	Year	Builder	Notes
2031	v	50	B720000-720049	1948	Shildon	Steel bodies all lots
2032	v	200	B720050-720249	1949	Shildon	
2033	v	175	B720250-720424	1949	Shildon	
Total		425				

1/032 13ton High Goods Wagon

Lot		Qty	Numbers	Year	Builder	Notes
2082	v	50	B475000-475049	1949	Swindon	Wood bodies, no side rails.
Total		50				

1/033 13ton High Goods Wagon

Lot		Qty	Numbers	Year	Builder	Notes
2061		100	B483650-483749	1949	Ashford	Part lot. See diagram 16 also.
Total		100				

1/034 13ton High Goods Wagon

Lot		Qty	Numbers	Year	Builder	Notes
2153		600	B477050-477649	1950	Ashford	Wood bodies. No side rail.
Total		600				

1/035 13ton Shock Absorbing Wagon

Lot		Qty	Numbers	Year	Builder	Notes
2154	v	500	B720425-720924	1950	Ashford	5-plank bodies, steel ends
2155		300	B720925-721224	1950	Ashford	
Total		800				

1/036 13ton Shock Absorbing Wagon with Sheet Support Rail

Lot		Qty	Numbers	Year	Builder	Notes
2156		100	B721225-721324	1950	Ashford	5-plank bodies, steel ends
Total		100				

1/037 13ton High Goods Wagon

Lot		Qty	Numbers	Year	Builder	Notes
2128	v	2000	B475050-477049	1950	Shildon	Steel body
Total		2000				

1/038 13ton Brick Wagon - Lettered Experimental Brick Wagon

Lot		Qty	Numbers	Year	Builder	Notes
2233		3	B748500-748502	1950	Wolverton	4-plank sides, steel ends.
Total		3				

1/039 13ton High Goods Wagon with Sheet Support Rail - Lettered Hybar

Lot		Qty	Numbers	Year	Builder	Notes
2179	v	1500	B477650-479149	1951	Derby	5-plank sides, corrugated ends.
2315	v	500	B484750-485249	1952	Derby	
2415	v	750	B485250-485999	1952	Derby	
2462	v	750	B486000-486749	1953	Derby	
2551	v	1000	B498020-499019	1954	Ashford	
2723	v	500	B491700-492199	1955	Ashford	
2834	v	500	B492200-492699	1956	Ashford	
3026	v	150	B484000-484149	1957	Ashford	
Total		5650				

1/040 13ton High Goods Wagon with Sheet Support Rail Lettered Shock

Lot		Qty	Numbers	Year	Builder	Notes
2180	v	500	B721325-721824	1951	Derby	5-plank sides, corrugated ends.
2317	v	600	B721825-722424	1952	Derby	
2416	v	850	B721425-723274	1952	Derby	
2546	v	250	B723275-724024	1955	Derby	
Total		2200				

1/041 13ton High Goods Wagon

Lot		Qty	Numbers	Year	Builder	Notes
2195	v	1500	B479150-480649	1951	Shildon	Steel bodies
2196	v	1500	B480650-482149	1951	Shildon	
2197	v	1500	B482150-483649	1951	Shildon	
2341	v	970	B486750-487719	1952	Shildon	
2361	v	1500	B488750-490249	1951	B'ham R C & W	
2366		499	B490251-490749	1952	Shildon	Part lot. 1 off to diagram 47.
Total		7469				

1/042 13ton High Goods Wagon

Lot		Qty	Numbers	Year	Builder	Notes
2314	v	43	B483750-483792	1952	Derby	Wood bodies with reinforced ends.
2314	v	206	B483794-483999	1952	Derby	
Total		249				

1/043 13ton High Goods Wagon

Lot		Qty	Numbers	Year	Builder	Notes
2314	v	1	B483793	1952	Derby	Steel body, no curb rail. Part lot, see diagram 42 above.
Total		1				

1/044 13ton High Goods Wagon

Lot		Qty	Numbers	Year	Builder	Notes
2396	v	1200	B492700-493899	1951	Gloster	5-plank sides & corrugated ends all lots.
2397	v	870	B493900-494769	1951	Pickering	Part lot, see diagram 45.
2409		350	B494920-495269	1952	Ashford	
2484	v	400	B497620-498019	1953	Ashford	
Total		2820				

1/045 13ton High Goods Wagon

Lot		Qty	Numbers	Year	Builder	Notes
2409		150	B494770-494919	1952	Ashford	5-plank sides & ends. Part lot, see diagram 44.
Total		150				

1/046 13ton Soda Ash Wagon - Lettered Soda Ash.

Lot		Qty	Numbers	Year	Builder	Notes
2369		50	B745500-745549	1952	Shildon	Steel bodies, sheet support rails.
2466		30	B745550-745579	1952	Shildon	
Total		80				

1/047 13ton High Goods Wagon

Lot		Qty	Numbers	Year	Builder	Notes
2342	v	1030	B487720-488749	1952	Shildon	Steel bodies, no curb rail, all (lots.
2366		1	B490250	1952	Shildon	Part lot, see diagram 41.
2468	v	250	B495270-495519	1953	Shildon	
2479	v	650	B495970-496619	1953	Shildon	
Total		1931				

1/048 13ton Shock Absorbing Wagon Lettered Shock

Lot		Qty	Numbers	Year	Builder	Notes
2445	v	250	B723525-723774	1954	Derby	5-plank sides & corrugated ends.
Total		250				

1/049 13ton High Goods Wagon with Sheet Support Rail

Lot		Qty	Numbers	Year	Builder	Notes
2469	v	550	B496620-497169	1953	Shildon	Steel body, no curb rail.
2704	v	450	B495520-495969	1953	Shildon	
Total		1000				

1/050 12ton High Goods Wagon Lettered Shock

Lot		Qty	Numbers	Year	Builder	Notes
2650	v	250	B723275-723524	1953	Derby	Originally 13tons. Wood sides, corrugated ends.
2776	v	400	B724275-724674	1956	Derby	
2839	v	299	B724675-724973	1956	Derby	
2983	v	300	B724975-725274	1957	Derby	
Total		1249				

1/051 13ton China Clay Wagon

Lot		Qty	Numbers	Year	Builder	Notes
2590		100	B743000-743099	1954	Swindon	Wood body, end door
2697		100	B743100-743199	1955	Swindon	
2871		100	B743200-743299	1956	Swindon	
2974	v	100	B743300-743399	1957	Swindon	
3098	v	175	B743400-743574	1958	Swindon	
3195	v	100	B743575-743674	1959	Swindon	
3296	v	200	B743675-743874	1960	Swindon	
Total		875				

1/052 12ton High Goods with Sheet Support Rail - Lettered Shock

Lot		Qty	Numbers	Year	Builder	Notes
2705	v	250	B724025-724274	1955	Derby	Wood sides, corrugated ends.
Total		250				

1/055 21ton High Goods Wagon with Sheet Support Bar

Lot		Qty	Numbers	Year	Builder	Notes
2579	x	20	B715000-715019	1954	Lancing	For Continental traffic
2851	x	20	B715020-715039	1956	Lancing	
Total		40				

1/056 12ton High Goods with Sheet Support Lettered Shock

Lot		Qty	Numbers	Year	Builder	Notes
3082	v	400	B725275-725674	1958	Derby	Wood sides, corrugated ends.
3232	v	200	B725675-725874	1959	Derby	
3275	v	250	B725875-726124	1959	Derby	
Total		850				

1/057 12ton High Goods Shock Absorbing Lettered Shocroof A

Lot		Qty	Numbers	Year	Builder	Notes
3383	v	100	B726125-726224	1961	Derby	Roller bearings
Total		100				

1/058 20ton Shock Absorbing Wagon fitted with Nylon Hood

Lot		Qty	Numbers	Year	Builder	Notes
3429	v	300	B726255-726524	1962	Derby	Roller bearings
Total		300				

1/059 Conflat I. S. O.

Lot		Qty	Numbers	Year	Builder	Notes
	?	(100)	various		?	Converted from ex-LMS, ex-LNE and British Railways built Lowmacs.
Total		(100)				

1/060 Conflat P - 22ton Wagon for conveyance of 'BD' & 'A' type Containers

Lot		Qty	Numbers	Year	Builder	Notes
	v	(60)	various		?	60 Plate wagons converted.
Total		(60)				

1/061 13ton Container Flat Wagon Lettered Conflat A

Lot		Qty	Numbers	Year	Builder	Notes
2106	v	200	B735000-735199	1950	Wolverton	
2125	v	200	B735200-735399	1950	Swindon	
Total		400				

1/062 12ton Container Flat Wagon Lettered Conflat A

Lot		Qty	Numbers	Year	Builder	Notes
2266	v	400	B735400-735799	1951	Swindon	Diagram shows short (1ft 6ins) buffers.
2323	v	500	B735800-736299	1952	Swindon	
2493	v	800	B736300-737099	1953	Swindon	
2500	v	500	B737100-737599	1953	Swindon	
Total		2200				

1/063 21ton Container Flat Wagon (for Dolomite Containers) Lettered Conflat LD

Lot		Qty	Numbers	Year	Builder	Notes
2398		40	B738000-738039	1952	Swindon	
2638		15	B738040-738054	1954	Swindon	
Total		55				

1/064 14ton Container Flat Wagon Lettered Conflat L

Lot		Qty	Numbers	Year	Builder	Notes
2489	v	373	B738500-738872	1953	Ashford	Diagram shows short (1ft 6ins) buffers
Total		373				

1/065 12ton Container Flat Wagon - Lettered Conflat A

Lot		Qty	Numbers	Year	Builder	Notes
2588	v	500	B739000-739499	1954	Swindon	3ft gap in sides, also 1ft 6ins buffers
2589	v	500	B739500-739999	1954	Swindon	
Total		1000				

1/066 14ton Container Flat Wagon - Lettered Conflat L

Lot		Qty	Numbers	Year	Builder	Notes
2671	v	500	B733500-733999	1955	Ashford	
Total		500				

1/067 11ton Container Flat Wagon - Lettered Conflat A

Lot		Qty	Numbers	Year	Builder	Notes
2688	v	500	B700000-700499	1955	Swindon	* 3ft gap in sides and 1ft 6ins (buffers all lots.
2836	v	500	B700500-700999	1956	Derby	*
2837	v	500	B701000-701499	1956	Derby	*
2853	v	1000	B701500-702499	1956	Ashford	#
2854	v	1000	B702500-703499	1956	Ashford	#
2869	v	1000	B703500-704499	1956	Swindon	
Total		4500				

Note:- Lot book gives capacity as 12tons (*) or 11/12tons (#).

1/068 14ton Conflat Wagon - Lettered Conflat L

Lot		Qty	Numbers	Year	Builder	Notes
2764	v	300	B734000-734299	1955	Swindon	
2870	v	70	B738873-738942	1956	Swindon	
2973	v	260	B734300-734559	1957	Swindon	)
3108	v	577	B530000-530576	1958	Ashford	(These lots have screw couplings.
3384	v	162	B530577-530738	1961	Derby	)
Total		1369				

1/069 13ton Container Flat Wagon (Lettered Conflat A)

Lot		Qty	Numbers	Year	Builder	Notes
2971	v	1000	B704500-705499	1957	Swindon	* All lots have gap in body sides, oleo-pneumatic buffers and roller bearings.
2972	v	700	B705500-706199	1957	Swindon	
2984	v	500	B706200-706699	1957	Derby	+
2985	v	500	B706700-707199	1957	Derby	+
3024	v	1000	B707200-708199	1957	Ashford	+
3025	v	1000	B708200-709199	1957	Ashford	+
3083	v	350	B709200-709549	1958	Derby	
3084	v	250	B709700-709949	1958	Wolverton	
3096	v	300	B709950-710249	1958	Swindon	
3097	v	241	B734608-734848	1958	Swindon	Part lot, see diagram 70.
3107	v	400	B737600-737999	1958	Ashford	
3153	v	5550	B502000-507549	1958	Pressed Steel	%
3163	v	150	B709550-709699	1958	Central Wagon	
Total		11941				

Note:- Lot book gives capacity as 11tons (*), 12tons (+) or 12/13tons (%).

1/070 13ton 14ton Container Flat Wagon (Lettered Conflat A)

Lot		Qty	Numbers	Year	Builder	Notes
3097	v	48	B734560-734607	1958	Swindon	Part lot, see diagram 69. B734560-3 & 570-4 were 14ton, others 13ton.
Total		48				

1/071 13ton Open Sand Wagon

Lot		Qty	Numbers	Year	Builder	Notes
2157		500	B746000-746499	1950	Ashford	Steel body
Total		500				

1/072 13ton Open Sand Wagon - Lettered Sand

Lot		Qty	Numbers	Year	Builder	Notes
2267		250	B746500-746749	1951	Swindon	Steel body, Morton brake.
Total		250				

1/073 13ton Steel Sand Wagon

Lot		Qty	Numbers	Year	Builder	Notes
2986	v	100	B746750-746849	1957	Derby	Wheelbase now 10ft, hydraulic buffers.
Total		100				

1/075 35ton Container Flat, Bogie, Condor

Lot		Qty	Numbers	Year	Builder	Notes
3494	v	50	B510000-510049		Ashford	See Plate 28.
Total		50				

1/076 12ton Container Flat Wagon - Lettered Conflat B

Lot		Qty	Numbers	Year	Builder	Notes
	v	(50)	?		?	Pipe wagons modified for Birds Eye traffic.
Total		(50)				

1/077 13ton Container Flat Wagon (to carry Light Alloy Container Type 'A')

Lot		Qty	Numbers	Year	Builder	Notes
	v	(5)	See note.		?	Conflat AB converted from diagram 69, Nos B505113,506116,506192, 507046 & 709671.
Total		(5)				

1/078 22ton Container Flat Wagon to Carry LS Type Container

Lot		Qty	Numbers	Year	Builder	Notes
	v	(6)	See note		?	Converted from diagram 434, Nos B935623,935725,935880,935933, 936228 & 936405.
Total		(6)				

1/079 24ton Container Flat Wagon

Lot		Qty	Numbers	Year	Builder	Notes
3463	v	1	B734849		Temple Mills	There may have been other vehicles.
Total		1				

1/085 20ton Salt Wagon

Lot		Qty	Numbers	Year	Builder	Notes
3134	v	15	B884500-884514	1957	Derby	Side discharge. Originally diagram 274
Total		15				

1/088 10ton Carflat

Lot		Qty	Numbers	Year	Builder	Notes
3532	v	25	B748673-748697		Cowlairs	Redundant carriage underframes, no diagram available. There were probably variations between lots.
3533	v	25	B748698-748722		Ashford	
3534	v	25	B748723-748747		Horwich	
3535	v	21	B748748-748768		Derby	
3541	v	15	B745650-745664		Ashford	
3542	v	15	B745665-745679		Cowlairs	
3543	v	20	B745680-745699		Horwich	
3544	v	20	B745700-745719		Derby	
3548	v	2	B745648-745649		Horwich	
3550	v	1	B748492		St Rollox	
3552	v	12	B745720-745731		Derby	
3553	v	14	B745732-745745		St Rollox	
3554	v	14	B745746-745759		Horwich	
3562	v	30	B745760-745789		Derby	
3563	v	14	B745790-745803		St Rollox	
3564	v	12	B745804-745815		Barassie	
Total		265				

1/089 10ton Carflat A

Lot		Qty	Numbers	Year	Builder	Notes
3479	v	24	B748468-748491		Cowlairs	Notes as above.
3485	v	16	B748657-748672		Cowlairs	
Total		40				

1/090 12ton Open Carriage Truck

Lot		Qty	Numbers	Year	Builder	Notes
2088		20	B748000-748019	1949	Swindon	2-plank sides.
Total		20				

1/091 12ton Open Carriage Truck Lettered Carfit 'A'

Lot		Qty	Numbers	Year	Builder	Notes
2265	v	30	B748020-748049	1951	Swindon	Slatted sides.
2587	v	10	B748050-748059	1954	Swindon	
2989	v	50	B748060-748109	1957	Wolverton	
Total		90				

1/092 20ton Open Carriage Truck Lettered Carfit 'C'

Lot		Qty	Numbers	Year	Builder	Notes
2770	x	20	B748110-748129	1955	Ashford	For Continental Traffic. Lot book states Ashford for these.
2850	x	20	B748130-748149	1956	Eastleigh	
Total		40				

1/093 10ton Carriage Truck Lettered Carflat

Lot		Qty	Numbers	Year	Builder	Notes
3283	v	112	B748150-748181 & B748188-748287*	1959	Swindon	Again redundant carriage underframes. *= Less 20 gaps; see diagram 97, lot 3283.
3326	v	12	B748577-748588	1959	Doncaster	
Total		124				

1/094 10ton Carriage Truck Lettered Carflat A

Lot		Qty	Numbers	Year	Builder	Notes
3305	v	6	B748182-748187	1959	Gorton	Again redundant carriage underframes
3312	v	44	B748503-748546	1959	Gorton	
3320	v	60	B748288-748347	1959	Central Wagon	
3320	v	30	B748547-748576	1959	Central Wagon	
3321	v	80	B748348-748427	1960	Wm Rigley	
Total		220				

1/095 10ton Carriage Truck Lettered Carflat

Lot		Qty	Numbers	Year	Builder	Notes
3358	v	68	B748589-748656	1960	Swindon	Redundant carriage underframes, dimensions vary.
Total		68				

1/096 10ton Container Flat Conflat BP

Lot		Qty	Numbers	Year	Builder	Notes
3370	v	33	B748428-748460	1960	Cowlairs	For pallet loads, originally Carflat P. Buckeye couplers. Records say 30 converted but 33 numbers were issued
Total		33				

1/097 10ton Carriage Truck Lettered Carflat

Lot		Qty	Numbers	Year	Builder	Notes
3283	v	20	B748159,748162, B748163,748166, B748169,748175, B748188,748191, B748193,748196, B748199,748204, B748219,748221, B748232,748237, B748246,748261, B748267,748276.	1959	Swindon	There is confusion in the records over lot 3283. It appears that 20 vehicles were modified from diagram 93 to diagram 97 (and not vice versa) during conversion from redundant carriages.
Total		20				

1/098 Match Wagon

Lot	Qty	Numbers	Year	Builder	Notes
2999	150	B456200-456349	1957	Shildon	Diagram later used for 21ton mineral wagons re-bodied.
Total	150				

1/099 Match Wagon

Lot	Qty	Numbers	Year	Builder	Notes
2858	200	B456000-456199	1956	Shildon	Diagram later used for 16ton mineral wagons re-bodied.
Total	200				

1/100 16ton End Door Wagon. All Steel Rivetted Body

Lot	Qty	Numbers	Year	Builder	Notes
2287	250	B197000-197249	1950	Earlestown	Lot 2287 was for wagons purchased from the French Government and reconditioned but the diagram almost certainly covers ex-M.O.T. and ex-M.W.T. wagons taken over by British Railways as well.
2287	250	B197850-198099	1950	Earlestown	
2287	500	B198100-198599	1950	Earlestown	
2287	142	B198750-198891	1950	Earlestown	
2287	75	B197250-197324	1950	New Cross Gate	
2287	425	B197325-197749	1050	New Cross Gate	
2287	100	B197750-197849	1950	New Cross Gate	
2287	125	B198600-198749	1950	New Cross Gate	
Total	1867				

1/101 16ton End Door Wagon All Steel Rivetted Body

1/102 16ton End Door Wagon All Steel Welded Body

1/103 16ton End Door Wagon All Steel Rivetted Body

) These diagrams, along with 104
) and 105 almost certainly cover
) ex-M.O.T & ex-M.W.T. wagons taken
) over by British Railways and for
) which, other than the five lots
) shown against diagram 104, no
lots were issued. See text.

1/104 16ton End Door Wagon All Steel Welded Body

Lot	Qty	Numbers	Year	Builder	Notes
2160	100	B67000-67099	1950	Fairfields	Design incorporates two flap doors
2161	400	B67100-67499	1950	Derbyshire	
2162	100	B67500-67599	1950	Cambrian	
2242	100	B74450-74549	1950	G R Turner	
2243	650	B74550-75199	1950	Fairfields	
Total	1350				

1/105 16ton End Door Wagon All Steel Rivetted Body — See notes for diagram 101.

1/106 16ton End Door Wagon All Steel: Welded Body

Lot	Qty	Numbers	Year	Builder	Notes
2104	1500	B64000-65499	1950	Derby	Probably ex-LMS design
2184	500	B67600-68099	1950	Derby	
2210	800	B68100-68899	1951	Derby	
Total	2800				

1/107 21ton End Door Wagon. All Steel Welded Body

Lot	Qty	Numbers	Year	Builder
2191	500	B201000-201499	1950	P W McLellan
2192	500	B201500-201999	1950	Chas Roberts
2193	500	B202000-202499	1950	Birmingham
Total	1500			

1/108 16ton End Door Wagon All Steel Welded Body

The principal 16ton design, very similar to diagram 106 except that bottom doors are now omitted. The diagram states that double brakes were fitted but this is doubtful.

Lot		Qty	Numbers	Year	Builder
2223		500	B70400-70899	1950	Birmingham
2224		700	B70900-71599	1950	P W McLellan
2225		600	B71600-72199	1950	Teesside B&E
2226		400	B72200-72599	1950	Butterley
2227		500	B72600-73099	1950	Head Wrightson
2229		150	B73600-73749	1950	G R Turner
2230		400	B73750-74149	1950	Derbyshire
2231		200	B74150-74349	1950	Fairfields
2232		100	B74350-74449	1950	Cravens
2250		2500	B75200-77699	1950	Pressed Steel
2251		2500	B77700-80199	1950	Pressed Steel
2252		2500	B80200-82699	1950	Pressed Steel
2253		2500	B82700-85199	1950	Pressed Steel
2254		2500	B85200-87699	1950	Pressed Steel
2255		2500	B87700-90199	1950	Pressed Steel
2256		2500	B90200-92699	1950	Pressed Steel
2257		2500	B92700-95199	1950	Pressed Steel
2258		2500	B95200-97699	1950	Pressed Steel
2259		2500	B97700-100199	1950	Pressed Steel
2290		1500	B100200-101699	1951	Birmingham
2291		600	B101700-102299	1951	Butterley
2293		600	B103650-104249	1951	Cravens
2294		711	B104250-104960	1951	Derbyshire
2295		700	B104961-105660	1951	Fairfields
2296		500	B105661-106160	1951	Gloucester
2298		1400	B106961-108360	1951	P W McLellan
2300		2150	B110361-112510	1951	Chas Roberts
2301		1400	B112511-113910	1951	Teesside B&E
2302		450	B113911-114360	1951	G R Turner
2377		1250	B114361-115610	1952	Chas Roberts
2378		1000	B115611-116610	1952	Cravens
2379		1600	B116611-118210	1952	Head Wrightson
2380		1850	B118211-120060	1952	Gloucester
2381		1200	B120061-121260	1952	Butterley
2382		1700	B121261-122960	1952	Fairfields
2383		1850	B122961-124810	1952	Teesside B&E
2385		1250	B125611-126860	1952	Derbyshire
2387		1800	B129631-131160	1952	P W McLellan
2388		1350	B131161-132510	1952	Metro-Cammell
2389		350	B132511-132860	1952	G R Turner
2390		1500	B132861-134360	1952	Birmingham
2391		500	B134361-134860	1952	R Y Pickering
2463		1800	B134861-136660	1953	Derby
2464		1700	B136661-138360	1953	Derby
2508		500	B143361-143860	1953	Birmingham
2509		400	B143861-144260	1953	Butterley
2510		500	B144261-144760	1953	Butterley
2511		333	B144761-145093	1953	Cambrian
2512		500	B145094-145593	1953	Cambrian
2513		500	B145594-146093	1953	Cambrian
2514		400	B146094-146493	1953	Derbyshire
2515		500	B146494-146993	1953	Derbyshire
2516		500	B146994-147493	1953	Gloucester
2519		367	B148461-148827	1953	P W McLellan
2520		500	B148828-149327	1953	P W McLellan
2521		667	B149328-149994	1953	Metro-Cammell
2522		500	B149995-150494	1953	Metro-Cammell
2523		500	B150495-150994	1953	Metro-Cammell
2524		500	B150995-151494	1953	Chas Roberts
2525		500	B151495-151994	1953	Chas Roberts
2526		500	B151995-152494	1953	Chas Roberts
2527		500	B152495-152994	1953	Chas Roberts
2528		627	B152995-153621	1953	Teesside B&E
2529		600	B153622-154221	1953	Teesside B&E
2530		500	B154222-154721	1953	Teesside B&E
2531		500	B154722-155221	1953	Teesside B&E
2547		500	B155222-155721	1953	Metro-Cammell
2548		500	B155722-156221	1953	Metro-Cammell
2549		500	B156222-156721	1953	Metro-Cammell
2550		500	B156722-157221	1953	Metro-Cammell
2611		947	B160572-161518	1953	Teesside B&E
2612		666	B161519-162184	1953	Teesside B&E
2626		500	B162185-162684	1954	Derbyshire
2627		500	B162685-163184	1954	Derbyshire
2628		667	B163185-163851	1953	Cambrian
2629		1000	B163852-164851	1954	Cambrian
2630		500	B164852-165351	1954	P W McLellan
2631		500	B165352-165851	1954	P W McLellan
2633		2500	B165852-168351		Pressed Steel
2634		2500	B168352-170851		Pressed Steel
2635		2500	B170852-173351		Pressed Steel
2636		2500	B173352-175851		Pressed Steel
2637		2500	B175852-178351		Pressed Steel
2639		700	B178352-179051	1953	Butterley
2640		400	B179052-179451	1954	Butterley
2653		1250	B179452-180701	1954	Derby
2654		1250	B180702-181951	1954	Derby
2663		1500	B181952-183451	1954	Metro-Cammell
2664		1500	B183452-184951	1954	Metro-Cammell
2670		500	B187367-187866	1954	Derby
2674		1000	B187867-188866	1954	Gloucester
2675		1000	B188867-189866	1954	Chas Roberts
2676		909	B203000-203908	1953	Birmingham
2677		1091	B203909-204999	1954	Birmingham
2678		1000	B205000-205999	1954	Birmingham
2685		2500	B206000-208499		Pressed Steel
2686		2500	B208500-210999		Pressed Steel
2687		1000	B211000-211999		Pressed Steel
2698		1000	B212000-212999	1954	Birmingham
2699		1300	B213000-214299	1954	Cambrian
2700		333	B214300-214832	1954	Hurst Nelson
2701		933	B214833-215765	1954	P W McLellan
2702		1543	B215766-217308	1954	Metro-Cammell
2703		1000	B217309-218308	1954	Teesside B&E
2711		1000	B218309-219308	1955	Derby
2715		1500	B219309-220808	1955	Birmingham
2716		1500	B220809-222308	1955	Birmingham
2717		750	B222309-223508	1955	Gloucester
2718		750	B223059-223808	1955	Gloucester
2719		1000	B223809-224808	1955	Chas Roberts
2720		1000	B224809-225808	1955	Chas Roberts
2742		1500	B225809-227308	1955	Teesside B&E
2743		800	B227309-228108	1955	Butterley
2744		600	B228109-228708	1955	Cambrian
2745		700	B229309-230008	1955	Derbyshire
2746		700	B230009-230708	1955	Hurst Nelson
2747		1000	B230709-231708	1955	P W McLellan
2748		1540	B231709-233248	1955	Metro-Cammell
2749		700	B233249-233948	1954	R Y Pickering
2750		1000	B233949-234948	1955	Cravens
2751		1400	B234949-236348	1955	Fairfields
2752		1500	B236349-237848	1955	R Y Pickering
2756		250	B237849-238098	1955	G R Turner
2757		910	B238099-239008	1955	Central Wagon
2788		2000	B239009-241008	1956	Birmingham
2789		2000	B241009-243008	1959	Birmingham
2790		1100	B243009-244108	1956	Butterley
2791		1250	B244109-245358	1959	Cambrian
2792		500	B245359-245858	1959	Cambrian
2793		1000	B246609-247608	1956	Derbyshire
2794		1000	B247609-248608	1956	Gloucester
2796		1000	B249609-250608	1956	P W McLellan
2797		1000	B250609-251608	1956	P W McLellan
2798		2000	B251609-253608	1956	Metro-Cammell
2799		2000	B253609-255608	1959	Metro-Cammell
2800		1000	B255609-256608	1956	Chas Roberts
2801		1000	B256609-257608	1959	Chas Roberts
2802		1000	B257609-258608	1956	Teesside B&E
2803		1000	B258609-259608	1956	Teesside B&E
2804		700	B259609-260308	1956	Birmingham
2805		700	B260609-261308	1957	Birmingham
2806	v	206	B261509-261714	1957	Cambrian
2806		894	B261715-262608	1957	Cambrian
2808		950	B264209-265158	1957	Derbyshire
2809		500	B265209-265708	1957	Derbyshire
2810	v	600	B266209-266808	1957	Gloucester
2810		200	B266809-267008	1957	Gloucester
2813		1000	B267709-268708	1957	Metro-Cammell
2814		1000	B271209-272208	1957	Chas Roberts
2816		1000	B273209-274208	1957	Teesside B&E
2817		1000	B274209-275208	1957	Teesside B&E
2896		500	B275209-275708	1956	Central Wagon
2897		500	B275709-276208	1956	Central Wagon
2898		500	B276209-276708	1956	Cravens
2899		500	B276709-277208	1956	Cravens
2900		600	B277209-277808	1959	Fairfields
2901		600	B277809-278408	1959	Fairfields
2902		1000	B278409-279408	1956	R Y Pickering
2903		200	B279409-279608	1959	G R Turner
2904		50	B279609-279658	1957	G R Turner
2906		720	B159072-159791	1957	P W McLellan
2907	v	500	B550000-550499	1957	Birmingham
2907		950	B550500-551449	1957	Birmingham
2909		500	B553000-553499	1957	Central Wagon
2910		500	B553500-553999	1957	Central Wagon
2911		430	B554000-554429	1957	Cravens
2912	v	470	B554430-554899	1957	Cravens
2912		100	B554900-554999	1957	Cravens
2913		250	B555000-555249	1957	Fairfields
2915	v	1000	B556050-557049	1957	Metro-Cammell

Lot		Qty	Numbers	Year	Builder	Notes
2915		500	B557050-557599	1957	Metro-Cammell	
2917		1000	B560200-561199	1957	R Y Pickering	
2918		1000	B561200-562199	1957	R Y Pickering	
2919		600	B562200-562799	1957	Teesside B&E	
2920		6500	B562800-569299		Pressed Steel	
2921		7000	B569300-576299	1956	Pressed Steel	
2922		7000	B576300-583299	1957	Pressed Steel	
2923		4000	B583300-587299	1957	Pressed Steel	
2923	v	3000	B587300-590299	1957	Pressed Steel	
3053		100	B228709-228808	1955	Cambrian	
3054		400	B228809-229208	1959	Cambrian	
3054	v	44	B229209-229252	1959	Cambrian	
3054		56	B229253-229308	1959	Cambrian	
3058		500	B593700-594199	1957	Teesside B&E	
3062	v	150	B594200-594349	1957	Butterley	
3063	v	350	B595150-595499	1957	Derbyshire	
3063		200	B595500-595699	1957	Derbyshire	
3143		100	B159792-159891	1958	P W McLellan	
3143	v	680	B159892-160571	1958	P W McLellan	
3144	v	500	B555250-555749	1957	Teesside B&E	
3152		250	B262909-263158	1958	Cambrian	
3178	v	200	B261309-261508	1957	Butterley	
3219		400	B594350-594749	1957	Butterley	
Total		206444				

1/109 16ton End Door Wagon All Steel: Rivetted Body

Lot		Qty	Numbers	Year	Builder	Notes
2221		500	B69600-70099	1950	Hurst Nelson	The rivetted version of diagram 108
2222		300	B70100-70399	1950	Gloucester	
2228		500	B73100-73599	1950	Cambrian	
2292		1350	B102300-103649	1951	Cambrian	
2297		800	B106161-106960	1951	Hurst Nelson	
2299		2000	B108361-110360	1951	Metro-Cammell	
2384		800	B124811-125610	1952	Hurst Nelson	
2386		2500	B126861-129630	1952	Cambrian	
2485		1000	B141361-142360	1953	Ashford	
2486		1000	B142361-143360	1953	Ashford	
2517		467	B147494-147960	1953	Hurst Nelson	
2518		500	B147961-148460	1953	Hurst Nelson	
2567		350	B157222-157571	1954	Ashford	
2666		500	B184952-185451	1953	Hurst Nelson	
2667		1000	B185452-186451	1954	Hurst Nelson	
2669		915	B186452-187366	1954	Ashford	
2795		1000	B248609-249608	1959	Hurst Nelson	
2811		500	B267209-267708	1957	Hurst Nelson	
Total		15982				

1/110 21ton End Door Wagon. AllSteel Rivetted Body

Lot		Qty	Numbers	Year	Builder	Notes
2190		1000	B200000-200999	1950	Metro-Cammell	
Total		1000				

1/111 16ton End Door Wagon. All Steel Welded Body

Lot		Qty	Numbers	Year	Builder	Notes
2105		1000	B65500-66499	1950	Derby	Minor differences of diagram 108.
2123		500	B66500-66999	1951	Derby	
2473		760	B138361-139120	1953	Shildon	
2480		1000	B139121-140120	1953	Shildon	
2502		1140	B140121-141260	1953	Shildon	
Total		4400				

1/112 16ton Open Wagon Lettered Min

Lot		Qty	Numbers	Year	Builder	Notes
2286		1000	B190000-190999	1950	Earlestown	Ex-French Government. Metro-Cammell design re-conditioned by British Railways
2286		1000	B191300-192299	1950	Earlestown	
2286		2200	B192600-194799	1950	Earlestown	
2286		300	B191000-191299	1950	New Cross Gate	
2286		300	B192300-192599	1950	New Cross Gate	
2286		2182	B194800-196999	1950	New Cross Gate	
Total		6982				

1/113 16ton End Door Wagon: All Steel: Rivetted Body

Lot		Qty	Numbers	Year	Builder	Notes
2288		60	B199000-199059	1950	Earlestown	Ex-French Government. Hurst Nelson design re-conditioned by British Railways
2288		60	B199160-199219	1950	Earlestown	
2288		60	B199220-199279	1950	Earlestown	
2288		40	B199060-199099	1950	New Cross Gate	
2288		60	B199100-199159	1950	New Cross Gate	
2288		25	B199280-199307	1950	New Cross Gate	
Total		305				

1/114 16ton End Door Wagon. All Steel. Welded Body

Lot		Qty	Numbers	Year	Builder	Notes
2331	v	100	B68900-68999	1951	Derby	Vacuum fitted version of diagram 111. Balance of order was built
2331		200	B69000-69199	1951	Derby	

1/114 24½ton End Door Wagon All Steel Welded Body

Lot		Qty	Numbers	Year	Builder	Notes
2460		650	B280000-280649	1953	Shildon	
2600		1000	B281150-282149	1954	Shildon	
2602		500	B280650-281149	1954	Shildon	
Total		2150				

1/116 16ton End Door Wagon Aluminium Body - Rivetted

Lot		Qty	Numbers	Year	Builder	Notes
2761		100	B141261141360	1953	Shildon	
Total		100				

1/117 16ton End door Wagon All Steel Welded Body

Lot		Qty	Numbers	Year	Builder	Notes
2599		1500	B157572-159071	1954	Shildon	Minor differences of diagram 108 but diagram shows Morton Brake
2992		1200	B590300-591499	1957	Derby	
2993		700	B591500-592199	1957	Derby	
3042		150	B592700-592849	1957	Central Wagon	
3042	v	350	B592850-593199	1957	Central Wagon	
3043		500	B593200-593699	1957	Central Wagon	
3076	v	500	B592200-592699	1957	Derby	
3145	v	1350	B551600-552949	1957	Pressed Steel	
3146	v	1000	B557750-558749	1957	Pressed Steel	
3146		1000	B558750-559749	1957	Pressed Steel	
Total		8250				

1/118 24½ton Side and End Door Wagon

Lot		Qty	Numbers	Year	Builder	Notes
3244		620	B282150-282769	1959	Ashford	Roller bearings & self contained buffers.
3302		225	B282770-282994	1960	Ashford	
3388		135	B282995-283129	1961	Shildon	
3427		265	B283130-283394	1962	Shildon	
Total		1245				

1/119 21ton Mineral Wagon

Lot		Qty	Numbers	Year	Builder	Notes
3387	v	1000	B310000-310999	1961	Shildon	Roller bearings, hydraulic buffers & manual changeover vacuum brake.
3438	v	1000	B313500-314499	1962	Shildon	
3439	v	500	B314500-314999	1962	Derby	
Total		2500				

1/120 21ton Mineral Wagon

Lot		Qty	Numbers	Year	Builder	Notes
3390	v	950	B311000-311949	1961	Derby	As diagram 119 but with S.A.B. vacuum brake.
3430	v	1500	B312000-313499	1962	Derby	
Total		2450				

1/121 22ton Conflat P for I.S.O. Containers

Lot		Qty	Numbers	Year	Builder	Notes
?		(8)	B933090,933221, B933289,933750, B933846,935594, B935915,936368.		?	Converted from diagram 60.
Total		(8)				

1/130 10ton Carriage Truck (with Removable Sides) Lettered Carflat

Lot		Qty	Numbers	Year	Builder	Notes
3536	v	4	B745639-745640		Swindon	Redundant carriage underframes
3536	v	4	B745642-745647		Swindon	
Total		8				

1/131 10ton Carriage Truck (End Loading) Lettered Carflat

Lot		Qty	Numbers	Year	Builder	Notes
3536	v	39	B745600-745638		Swindon	Redundant carriage underframes
3536	v	1	B745641		Swindon	
Total		40				

1/132 10ton Carriage Truck

Lot		Qty	Numbers	Year	Builder	Notes
3588	v					No details available
3589	v					
Total		?				

1/133 10ton Carriage ruck - End Loading

Lot		Qty	Numbers	Year	Builder	Notes
3587	v	30	B745816-745845		?	Redundant carriage underframes
Total		30				

1/134 10ton Carriage Truck

Lot		Qty	Numbers	Year	Builder	Notes
3715	v	5	B745057-745061		?	Redundant carriage underframes
Total		5				

1/140 13ton Hopper Coal Wagon

Lot		Qty	Numbers	Year	Builder	Notes
2050		300	B400200-400499	1949	Faverdale	Wood body, wood solebars.
Total		300				

1/141 21ton Hopper Coal Wagon

Lot		Qty	Numbers	Year	Builder	Notes
2052		500	B410000-410499	1949	Cravens	Steel body, brake blocks one side.
2053		500	B410500-410999	1949	Head Wrightson	
2054		200	B411000-411199	1949	Teesside B&E	
Total		1200				

1/142 13ton Hopper Coal Wagon

Lot		Qty	Numbers	Year	Builder	Notes
2038		200	B400000-400199	1949	Shildon	Steel body, bottom doors wood.
2129		1000	B400500-401499	1950	Shildon	
2138		250	B401500-401749	1950	Fairfields	
2139		250	B401750-401799	1950	R Y Pickering	
2140		250	B402000-402249	1950	Cravens	
Totla		1950				

1/143 21ton Hopper Coal Wagon

Lot		Qty	Numbers	Year	Builder	Notes
2163		350	B411200-411549	1950	Cravens	Minor differences from diagram 141
2164		350	B411550-411899	1950	Head Wrightson	
2165		150	B411900-412049	1950	Teesside B&E	
2166		700	B412050-412749	1950	Birmingham	
2167		500	B412750-413249	1950	Metro-Cammell	
2168		450	B413250-413699	1950	Head Wrightson	
2212		250	B413700-413949	1949	Butterley	
Total		2750				

1/144 13ton Hopper Coal Wagon

Lot		Qty	Numbers	Year	Builder	Notes
2282		300	B402250-402549	1951	R Y Pickering	¼" higher than diagram 142
2283		350	B402550-402899	1951	Fairfields	
Total		650				

1/145 21ton Hopper Coal Wagon

Lot		Qty	Numbers	Year	Builder	Notes
2402		300	B414550-414849	1952	Hurst Nelson	Again minor differences, Morton brake, body probably rivetted.
2403		300	B414850-415149	1952	Metro-Cammell	
2727		300	B416750-417049	1955	Hurst Nelson	
2728		500	B417050-417549	1955	Metro-Cammell	
Total		1400				

1/146 21ton Hopper Coal Wagon

Lot		Qty	Numbers	Year	Builder	Notes
2330		100	B413950-414049	1952	Shildon	Welded body and 20ton standard hand lever brake, all lots.
2400		200	B414050-414249	1952	Butterley	
2401		300	B414250-414549	1952	Cravens	
2552		800	B451150-451949	1954	Shildon	
2713		500	B415950-416449	1955	Shildon	
2726		300	B416450-416749	1955	Cravens	
2731		1650	B417550-419199	1955	Shildon	
2932		750	B419250-419999	1956	Birmingham	
2933		700	B420000-420699	1956	Cravens	
2934		550	B420700-421249	1959	Fairfields	
2935		1000	B421250-422249	1956	Metro-Cammell	
2954		50	B419200-419249	1955	Shildon	This lot adapted for grain traffic between Millwall Dock & Welwyn GC.
3013		500	B422250-422749	1957	Fairfields	
3030		500	B423050-423549	1957	Birmingham	
3031		1000	B423550-424549	1957	Cravens	
3032		800	B424550-425349	1957	Gloucester	
3033		500	B425350-425849	1957	Head Wrightson	
3034		300	B425850-426149	1957	Head Wrightson	
3035		800	B426150-426949	1957	Hurst Nelson	
3036		450	B426950-427399	1957	Metro-Cammell	
3037		1150	B427400-428549	1957	Chas Roberts	
3045		500	B428550-429049	1957	Standard	
3157		2950	B430800-433749	1958	Pressed Steel	
3158		150	B429350-429499	1958	Birmingham	
3159		150	B429500-429649	1958	Gloucester	
3160		150	B429650-429799	1958	Hurst Nelson	
Total		16800				

1/148 24½ton Hopper Coal Wagon

Lot		Qty	Numbers	Year	Builder	Notes
2504		1	B333000	1953	Shildon	Both 333000 & 333001 described as prototypes, former at first considered to be to diagram 147 but amended before delivery.
2609		498	B333002-333499	1954	Shildon	
2758		1	B333001	1955	Ashford	
3121		200	B333500-333699	1958	Shildon	
3221		1150	B333700-334849	1959	Shildon	
3314		745	B334850-335594	1960	Shildon	
3374		540	B335695-336234	1960	Shildon	
3437		243	B336933-337175	1962	Shildon	
Total		3378				

1/149 21ton Hopper Coal Wagon

Lot		Qty	Numbers	Year	Builder	Notes
3120		1000	B429800-430799	1958	Shildon	Roller bearings & self-contained buffers. 100 vacuum piped.
Total		1000				

1/150 20ton Hopper Coke Wagon

Lot		Qty	Numbers	Year	Builder	Notes
2039		400	B447000-447399	1949	Shildon	Body & raves all steel.
2169		100	B447400-447499	1950	Teesside B&E	
Total		500				

1/151 20ton Hopper Coke Wagon

Lot		Qty	Numbers	Year	Builder	Notes
2198		100	B447500-447599	1951	Shildon	End raves replaced by sheeting
2343		50	B447600-447649	1952	Shildon	
2474		50	B447650-447699	1953	Shildon	
2603		100	B447700-447799	1954	Shildon	
2732		100	B447800-447899	1955	Shildon	
2859		450	B447900-448349	1956	Shildon	
3003		300	B448350-448649	1957	Shildon	
Total		1150				

1/152 20ton Hopper Coke Wagon

Lot		Qty	Numbers	Year	Builder	Notes
3122		550	B448650-449199	1958	Shildon	No raves, full height sheeting. 250 welded, 300 rivetted. 279 have vacuum pipe.
Total		550				

1/153 20ton Hopper Coal Wagon

Lot		Qty	Numbers	Year	Builder	Notes
3315	v	100	B335595-335694	1960	Shildon	Disc brake. Lot book gives lot 3315 as 24½ton & lot 3425 as 24ton
3425	v	150	B336235-336384	1962	Shildon	
Total		250				

1/154 24½ton Hopper Coal Wagon

Lot		Qty	Numbers	Year	Builder	Notes
3426		548	B336385-336932	1962	Shildon	
Total		548				

1/155 24½ton Hopper Coal Wagon

Lot		Qty	Numbers	Year	Builder	Notes
3466		578	B337176-337753		Shildon	
3525		409	B337754-338162		Pressed Steel	
3526		100	B338163-338262		Shildon	
Total		1087				

1/158 20ton Hopper Coke Wagon Fitted with Sheet Support Bar

Lot		Qty	Numbers	Year	Builder	Notes
3122		(21)	?		Shildon	21 vehicles of lot 3122 built with sheet support but no numbers given
Total		(21)				

1/160 25ton Ironstone Wagon

Lot		Qty	Numbers	Year	Builder	Notes
2040		100	B445000-445099	1949	Shildon	Hopper wagon with brake handles across ends.
2130		50	B445100-445149	1950	Shildon	
Total		150				

1/161 22ton Hopper Ironstone Wagon

Lot		Qty	Numbers	Year	Builder	Notes
2055		1000	B435000-435999	1949	Chas Roberts	Double brake
Total		1000				

1/162 24ton Hopper Ironstone Wagon - Lettered Iron Ore

Lot		Qty	Numbers	Year	Builder	Notes
2148		500	B436000-436499	1950	Birmingham	Diagram 161 updated
2149		500	B436500-436999	1950	Cambrian	
2150		500	B437000-437499	1950	Chas Roberts	
Total		1500				

1/163 25½ton Ironstone Hopper Wagon

Lot		Qty	Numbers	Year	Builder	Notes
2733		900	B438000-438899	1955	Shildon	
3001		600	B438900-439499	1957	Shildon	
Total		1500				

1/164 33ton Hoppered Ironstone Wagon

Lot		Qty	Numbers	Year	Builder	Notes
2962	v	270	B445150-445419	1956	Shildon	
Total		270				

1/165 24ton Ironstone Hopper Wagon Lettered 24T Ironstone

Lot		Qty	Numbers	Year	Builder	Notes
3142	v	200	B439500-439699	1957	Shildon	Diagram 163 vacuum fitted
Total		200				

1/166 25½ton Ironstone Hopper Wagon Lettered 25½T Ironstone

Lot		Qty	Numbers	Year	Builder	Notes
3189		350	B439700-440049	1959	Shildon	Roller bearings. 121 with vacuum pipe.
Total		350				

1/167 33½ton Ironstone Wagon Lettered Iron Ore

Lot		Qty	Numbers	Year	Builder	Notes
3002	v	400	B437500-437899	1957	Shildon	Hopper wagons
Total		400				

1/175 30ton Clinker Wagon

Unknown number converted from ironstone wagons; no further details known

1/179 25ton Anhydrite Wagon Lettered Anhydrite

Lot		Qty	Numbers	Year	Builder	Notes
2597	v	150	B747000-747149	1954	Shildon	Hopper wagons
Total		150				

1/180 27ton Ironstone Wagon Lettered Iron Ore <u>Tippler</u>

Lot		Qty	Numbers	Year	Builder	Notes
2274		700	B380000-380699	1951	Cravens	Double brake, not hoppered.
2275		800	B380700-381499	1951	Head Wrightson	
Total		1500				

1/181 27ton Ironstone Wagon Lettered Iron Ore <u>Tippler</u>

Lot		Qty	Numbers	Year	Builder	Notes
2310		400	B381500-381899	1951	Derby	Minor differences of diagram 180.
2601		500	B383140-383639	1954	Shildon	
Total		900				

1/182 56ton Iron Ore Wagon Lettered Iron Ore

Lot		Qty	Numbers	Year	Builder	Notes
2312	v	30	B446000-446029	1951	Shildon	Bogie wagons, side discharge.
Total		30				

1/183 27ton Iron Ore Wagon Lettered Iron Ore Tippler

Lot		Qty	Numbers	Year	Builder	Notes
2498		240	B381900-383139	1953	Shildon	Body 4" shallower than diagram 180
2730		1500	B383640-385139	1953	Shildon	
2844		500	B385140-385639	1956	Derby	
2988		476	B747500-747975	1957	Derby	
3075		24	B747976-747999	1957	Derby	This lot had Hoffman boxes.
3324		1000	B387090-399089	1960	Derby	
Total		3740				

1/184 27ton Iron Ore Wagon Lettered Iron Ore Tippler

Lot		Qty	Numbers	Year	Builder	Notes
3091		1028	B385640-385667	1958	Derby	B385640-386639 were 26ton, the rest were 27ton. There were minor dimensional differences within the batch.
3091	v	2	B385668-385669	1958	Derby	
3091		420	B385670-387089	1958	Derby	
Total		1450				

1/185 26ton Ironstone Wagon Lettered Iron Ore Tippler

Lot		Qty	Numbers	Year	Builder	Notes
3363	v	1000	B388090-389089	1960	Derby	Roller bearings.
Total		1000				

1/190 Adaptor Wagon for Ro-Railer

Lot		Qty	Numbers	Year	Builder	Notes
3457	v	1	B540901		Pressed Steel	
3458	v	6	B540902-540907		York	
Total		7				

1/200 Goods Van

Lot		Qty	Numbers	Year	Builder	Notes
2001	v	1300	B750000-751299	1949	Wolverton	12ton ventilated, LMS design, ply body
Total		1300				

1/201 12ton Goods Van Shock Absorbing

Lot		Qty	Numbers	Year	Builder	Notes
2045		50	B850050-850099	1948	Faverdale	LNE design.
Total		50				

1/202 12ton Goods Van

Lot		Qty	Numbers	Year	Builder	Notes
2062		440	B752350-752789	1949	Ashford	Southern Rly design.
2063	v	310	B752790-753099	1949	Ashford	
Total		750				

1/203 12ton Goods Van

Lot		Qty	Numbers	Year	Builder	Notes
2079	v	100	B753100-753199	1949	Swindon	GWR design
Total		100				

1/204 Goods Van

Lot		Qty	Numbers	Year	Builder	Notes
2003	v	500	B751300-751799	1949	Wolverton	12ton ventilated, LMS design, planked body.
2013	v	550	B751800-752349	1949	Wolverton	
2109	v	1000	B753430-754429	1950	Wolverton	
Total		2050				

1/205 12ton Goods Van

Lot		Qty	Numbers	Year	Builder	Notes
2083		230	B753200-753429	1949	Swindon	Diagram 203 unfitted.
Total		230				

1/206 12ton Goods Van Lettered Shocvan

Lot		Qty	Numbers	Year	Builder	Notes
2014	v	50	B850000-850049	1949	Wolverton	Shock absorbing, LMS design, planked body.
Total		50				

1/207 12ton Goods Van Lettered Shocvan

Lot		Qty	Numbers	Year	Builder	Notes
2158	v	500	B850100-850599	1950	Ashford	Shock absorbing, ply body.
Total		500				

1/208 12ton Ventilated Goods Van

Lot		Qty	Numbers	Year	Builder	Notes
2181	v	1000	B755180-756679	1951	Wolverton	British Railways standard design.
2182	v	2000	B756680-758179	1951	Wolverton	
2318	v	1000	B758180-759179	1952	Wolverton	
2319	v	1250	B759180-760429	1952	Wolverton	
2347	v	200	B760680-760879	1952	Faverdale	
2367	v	1000	B764481-765480	1952	Faverdale	
2414	v	750	B763281-764030	1952	Wolverton	
2421	v	464	B760880-761343	1952	Faverdale	
2465	v	800	B761380-762179	1952	Wolverton	
2470	v	100	B762180-762279	1953	Faverdale	
2503	v	250	B760430-760679	1952	Wolverton	
2541	v	450	B764301-764480	1953	Wolverton	
2595	v	850	B762430-763279	1954	Wolverton	
2706	v	1200	B766401-767600	1955	Wolverton	
2707	v	1800	B767601-769400	1955	Wolverton	
2840	v	500	B770151-770650	1956	Wolverton	
2841	v	800	B770651-771450	1956	Wolverton	
2990	v	1100	B773351-774450	1957	Wolverton	
2991	v	999	B774451-775449	1957	Wolverton	For B775450 see diagram 216
3086	v	850	B777351-778200	1958	Wolverton	
3164	v	1200	B780551-781750	1958	Chas Roberts	
3228	v	500	B778251-778750	1958	Wolverton	
Total		19063				

1/209 12ton Goods Van Lettered Shocvan

Lot		Qty	Numbers	Year	Builder	Notes
2202	v	400	B850600-850999	1951	Faverdale	Shock absorbing version of diagram 208.
2348	v	300	B851000-851299	1952	Faverdale	
2425	v	300	B851300-851599	1952	Ashford	

Lot		Qty	Numbers	Year	Builder	Notes
2471	v	750	B851600-852349	1953	Faverdale	
2584	v	150	B852350-852499	1954	Faverdale	
2737	v	400	B852500-852899	1955	Faverdale	
2865	v	700	B852900-853599	1956	Faverdale	
Total		3000				

1/210 24ton Covered Hopper Van Lettered Covhop

Lot		Qty	Numbers	Year	Builder	Notes
2375		10	B886000-886009	1952	Derby	This lot 'For catalyst'
2376		22	B886010-886031	1952	Derby	) These two lots 'For Sodium Tri-
2407		50	B886032-886081	1952	Derby	) polyphosphate'.
2408		130	B886082-886211	1952	Derby	This lot 'For Soda Ash'.
2708		50	B886212-886261	1955	Derby	
2767		50	B886262-886311	1955	Derby	
2768		30	B886312-886341	1955	Derby	
2842		60	B886342-886401	1956	Derby	
2843		60	B886402-886461	1956	Derby	
2987		100	B886462-886561	1957	Derby	
3088		125	B886562-886686	1958	Derby	
3089		125	B886687-886811	1958	Derby	
3204	p	110	B886812-886921	1959	Derby	
3215	p	90	B870500-870589	1958	Chas Roberts	
3289	p	75	B886922-886996	1960	Derby	
3393	p	130	B870630-870759	1961	Ashford	B870744 has vacuum brake & Girling disc brakes.
3431	v	120	B870670-870879	1962	Ashford	Disc brakes but B870879 is piped only.
Total		1337				

1/211 12ton Ventilated Goods Van Lettered Palvan

Lot		Qty	Numbers	Year	Builder	Notes
2536	v	36	B761344-761379	1952	Faverdale	Doors at LH ends of body
2736	v	50	B769901-769950	1955	Faverdale	
2784	v	200	B769951-770150	1956	Faverdale	
2864	v	300	B772951-773250	1956	Faverdale	
3011	v	400	B776151-776550	1957	Faverdale	
3118	v	300	B779551-779850	1958	Faverdale	
3191	v	300	B778751-779050	1959	Faverdale	
3310	v	522	B781752-782273	1960	Wolverton	
3346	v	280	B782574-782853	1961	Wolverton	
Total		2388				

1/212 12ton Ventilated Goods Van Lettered - Margarine

Lot		Qty	Numbers	Year	Builder	Notes
2585	v	150	B762280-762429	1954	Faverdale	As diagram 208 apart from branding and oleo buffers.
Total		150				

1/213 12ton Ventilated Goods Van

Lot		Qty	Numbers	Year	Builder	Notes
2422	v	920	B765481-766400	1952	Faverdale	Ply sides & doors
2735	v	234	B769401-769634	1955	Faverdale	
2735	v	265	B769636-769900	1955	Faverdale	B769635 became B882237, lot 3286
2855	v	750	B771451-772200	1956	Ashford	
2856	v	750	B772201-772950	1956	Ashford	
3007	v	700	B775451-776150	1957	Faverdale	
3023	v	80	B776551-777350	1957	Ashford	
Total		3699				

1/214 12ton End Door Covered Goods Wagon

Lot		Qty	Numbers	Year	Builder	Notes
2961	v	100	B773251-773350	1957	Wolverton	Doors at one end only, no side doors.
Total		100				

1/215 12ton Pallet Shock Absorbing Wagon

Lot		Qty	Numbers	Year	Builder	Notes
3292	v	1	B854500	1960	Derby & Wolverton	Experimental lot 9001: Planked sides..
Total		1				

1/216 Goods Van with Roller Shutters for Pallet Traffic

Lot		Qty	Numbers	Year	Builder	Notes
3218	v	1	B775450	1957	Wolverton	See lot 2991, diagram 208.
Total		1				

1/217 12ton Ventilated Goods Van

Lot		Qty	Numbers	Year	Builder	Notes
3391	v	1000	B782873-783872	1962	Wolverton	Double sliding doors.
3392	v	894	B783873-784766	1962	Derby	
3421	v	100	B784773-784872	1962	Wolverton	This lot had translucent roofs.
Total		1994				

1/218 12ton Goods Van (Shock Absorbing)

Lot		Qty	Numbers	Year	Builder	Notes
3008	v	900	B853600-854499	1957	Faverdale	Duplex buffers
3109	v	700	B779851-780550	1958	Ashford	Hydraulic buffers
3117	v	475	B854526-855000	1958	Faverdale	Hydraulic buffers
Total		2075				

1/219 12ton Covered Goods Van (Ventilated) Lettered Palshocvan

Lot		Qty	Numbers	Year	Builder	Notes
3216	v	25	B854501-854525	1958	Faverdale	Roller bearings, doors at LH end.
3311	v	50	B855101-855150	1960	Wolverton	
3347	v	125	B855551-855765	1961	Wolverton	
Total		200				

1/220 12ton Goods Van (Shock Absorbing)

Lot		Qty	Numbers	Year	Builder	Notes
3224	v	100	B855001-855100	1959	Faverdale	Ply body, hydraulic buffers.
Total		100				

1/221 12ton Ventilator Goods Van Lettered Palvan

Lot		Qty	Numbers	Year	Builder	Notes
3318	v	250	B782274-782253	1960	Derby	4 sliding doors each side
Total		250				

1/222 10ton Ventilated Goods Van Lettered Palvan for Glass Bottle Traffic

Lot		Qty	Numbers	Year	Builder	Notes
3360	v	1	B782524	1961	Wolverton	20ft 11ins body with 4 sliding doors each side
Total		1				

1/223 14ton Ventilated Goods Van Lettered - Palvan

Lot		Qty	Numbers	Year	Builder	Notes
3373	v	19	B782854-782872	1960	Wolverton	20ft body with 4 hinged doors each side
3377	v	1	B781751	1961	Wolverton	
Total		20				

1/224 12ton Ventilated Goods Van

Lot		Qty	Numbers	Year	Builder	Notes
3398	v	1000	B784873-786872	1961	Pressed Steel	As diagram 213 but with oleo buffers.
Total		1000				

1/225 10ton Ventilated Goods Van Lettered Palvan for Glass Bottle Traffic

Lot		Qty	Numbers	Year	Builder	Notes
3378	v	49	B782525-782573	1961	Wolverton	1in longer than diagram 222.
Total		49				

1/227 20ton Ferry Van

Lot		Qty	Numbers	Year	Builder	Notes
3413	x	150	GB786873-787022	1961	Pressed Steel	For continental traffic
3472	x	250	GB787098-787347		Ashford	
Total		400				

1/228 Road Railer Van

Lot		Qty	Numbers	Year	Builder	Notes
3455	v	2	B840001-840002		Pressed Steel	
3456	v	50	B840003-840052		Pressed Steel	
Total		52				

1/229 20ton Pallet Van

Lot		Qty	Numbers	Year	Builder	Notes
2696	v	1	B763280		Faverdale	Prototype with 20ft body.
Total		1				

1/230 Goods Van Lettered Fruit

Lot		Qty	Numbers	Year	Builder	Notes
2018	v	200	B875000-875199	1949	Wolverton	12ton LMS design, ply sides
2135	v	250	B875300-875549	1950	Faverdale	
Total		450				

1/231 12ton Fruit Van - Lettered Fruit

Lot		Qty	Numbers	Year	Builder	Notes
2084	v	100	B875200-875299	1949	Swindon	GWR design with planked & louvred sides.
Total		100				

1/232 12ton Fruit Van - Lettered Fruit

Lot		Qty	Numbers	Year	Builder	Notes
2134	v	750	B754430-755179	1950	Faverdale	LNE design with ply sides & louvred ends.
Total		750				

1/233 12ton Ventilated Fruit Van Lettered Fruit

Lot		Qty	Numbers	Year	Builder	Notes
2472	v	100	B875550-875649	1953	Faverdale	As diagram 213 but with air scoops on body sides & internal shelves.
2738	v	100	B875650-875749	1955	Faverdale	
3009	v	100	B875750-875849	1957	Faverdale	
Total		300				

1/234 12ton Ventila ed Goods Van

Lot		Qty	Numbers	Year	Builder	Notes
3392	v	6	B784285-784290	1962	Derby	Shuttered louvres in doors.
Total		6				

1/235 22ton Pallet Van

Lot		Qty	Numbers	Year	Builder	Notes
3362	v	1	B710250		Ashford	35ft body, roller bearings. B710250 originally Long Low experimental wagon.
3434	v	75	B787023-787097	1962	Ashford	
3540	v	47	B787348-787394		Ashford	
Total		123				

1/240 Banana Van

Lot		Qty	Numbers	Year	Builder	Notes
2002	v	80	B880000-880079	1949	Wolverton	10tons, LMS design with 9ft wheelbase & steam heat
2015	v	200	B880080-880279	1949	Wolverton	
Total		280				

1/241 Banana Van Lettered Banana

Lot		Qty	Numbers	Year	Builder	Notes
2203	v	150	B880280-880429	1951	Faverdale	8tons, 9ft wheelbase, steam heat.
Total		150				

1/242 Banana Van Lettered Banana

Lot		Qty	Numbers	Year	Builder	Notes
2346	v	250	B880430-880679	1952	Faverdale	As above but 10ft wheelbase
2598	v	50	B880680-880279	1954	Faverdale	
2739	v	250	B880730-880979	1955	Faverdale	
2866	v	150	B880980-881129	1956	Faverdale	
Total		700				

1/243 Banana Van Lettered Banana

Lot		Qty	Numbers	Year	Builder	Notes
3010	v	230	B881130-881359	1957	Faverdale	8tons, diagonal bracing added.
Total		230				

1/244 Banana Van Lettered Banana

Lot		Qty	Numbers	Year	Builder	Notes
3119	v	250	B881360-881609	1958	Faverdale	As above but with 2ft 0½in buffers
Total		250				

1/246 12ton Banana Van Lettered Banana

Lot		Qty	Numbers	Year	Builder	Notes
3209	v	400	B881610-882009	1959	Wolverton	No steam heating
3225	v	227	B882010-882236	1959	Faverdale	
3286	v	1	B882237	1955	Faverdale	See diagram 213 for B882237
3290	v	400	B882238-882637	1960	Wolverton	
Total		1028				

1/247 20ton Pallet Wagon for I.C.I. Palletised Fertilizer Traffic

Lot		Qty	Numbers	Year	Builder	Notes
		(1)	B935439			Converted from Platefit
Total		(1)				

1/249 23ton Wagon for Conveyance of Refined Sugar

Lot		Qty	Numbers	Year	Builder	Notes
		(27)	?			Converted from Covhops.
Total		(27)				

1/250 10ton Ventilated Meat Van Lettered - Meat for Fresh Meat

Lot		Qty	Numbers	Year	Builder	Notes
2320	v	100	B870000-870099	1952	Wolverton	Side vents plus four each end.
2417	v	50	B870100-870149	1952	Wolverton	
Total		150				

1/215 10ton Insulated Meat Van Lettered - Insul Meat

Lot		Qty	Numbers	Year	Builder	Notes
2321	v	200	B872000-872199	1952	Wolverton	No vents
2418	v	50	B872200-872249	1952	Wolverton	
Total		250				

1/255 Fish Van

30125 v ? Faverdale — Ex coaching stock taken into freight stock.

1/256 Fish Van

30442 v ? — Ex coaching stock taken into freight stock.

1/260 11ton Gunpowder Van Lettered Gunpowder

Lot		Qty	Numbers	Year	Builder	Notes
2490		20	B887000-887019	1953	Swindon	9ft wheelbase, sttel body & roof
2499		20	B887020-887039	1953	Swindon	
2544		25	B887040-887064	1954	Lancing	
2689	v	35	B887065-887099	1955	Swindon	
2872		20	B887100-887119	1956	Swindon	
Total		100				

1/261 11ton Gunpowder Van

Lot		Qty	Numbers	Year	Builder	Notes
3099	v	15	B887120-887134	1958	Swindon	Wheelbase now 10ft, hydraulic buffers.
3237	v	25	B887135-887159	1959	Swindon	
Total		40				

1/270 20ton Hopper Grain Van

Lot		Qty	Numbers	Year	Builder	Notes
2009		40	B885000-885039	1949	Derby	All steel, LMS design.
Total		40				

1/271 20ton Hopper Grain Van - Lettered Grain

Lot		Qty	Numbers	Year	Builder	Notes
2183		50	B885040-885089	1951	Derby	As above but end portholes omitted
2447		25	B885090-885114	1953	Derby	
2448		25	B885115-885139	1953	Pressed Steel	
2656		50	B885140-885189	1954	Pressed Steel	
2709		120	B885190-885309	1955	Pressed Steel	
2925		100	B885310-885409	1956	Pressed Steel	
2994		100	B885410-885509	1957	Pressed Steel	
3233	p	50	B885610-885659	1959	Derby	
3234	p	50	B885660-885709	1959	Derby	
Total		570				

1/272 20ton Hopper Cement Wagon

Lot		Qty	Numbers	Year	Builder	Notes
2769	v	110	B888001-888110	1955	Shildon	Presflos. Buffer lengths & couplings vary between lots.
2863	v	70	B888111-888180	1956	Shildon	
3029	v	100	B888181-888280	1957	Metro-Cammell	20 branded 'Bulk Salt' this lot.
3156	v	270	B888281-888550	1958	Mtero-Cammell	
3156	v	30	B888551-888580	1958	Metro-Cammell	These 30 branded 'Bulk Salt'.
3175	v	300	B888581-888880	1958	Central	
3176	v	100	B888881-888890	1958	Butterley	
3177	v	200	B887800-887999	1958	Gloucester	
3323	v	170	B873024-873193	1960	Gloucester	
3361	v	170	B873200-873369	1961	Gloucester	
3406	v	150	B873420-873569	1961	Gloucester	
3409	v	150	B873570-873719	1961	Gloucester	
3497	v	100	B873794-873893		Central	This lot rated 22tons
Total		1920				

1/273 20ton Hopper Cement Wagon

Lot		Qty	Numbers	Year	Builder	Notes
2679	v	1	B888000	1953	Shildon	Prototype Presflo
Total		1				

1/274 20ton Prestwin Air Discharge Wagon

Lot		Qty	Numbers	Year	Builder	Notes
3313	v	24	B873000-873023	1960	Metro-Cammell	
3313	v	6	B873194-873199	1960	Metro-Cammell	
3467	v	1	B873770		R Y Pickering	
Total		31				

1/275 20ton Hopper Grain Van

Lot		Qty	Numbers	Year	Builder	Notes
3166		100	B885510-885609	1958	Chas Roberts	Lot book says vacuum brake was fitted
Total		100				

1/276 23ton Calcium Carbide Wagon Lettered Carbide of Calcium

Lot		Qty	Numbers	Year	Builder	Notes
3371	v	40	B870590-870629	1960	Powell-Duffryn	Twin cylindrical silos
Total		40				

1/277 20ton Prestwin Wagon

Lot		Qty	Numbers	Year	Builder	Notes
3405	v	50	B873370-873419	1961	Metro-Cammell	Increased capacity
3460	v	50	B873270-873769		Central	
Total		100				

1/278 17ton Fly Ash Wagon

Lot		Qty	Numbers	Year	Builder	Notes
3483	v	22	B873771-873792		Shildon	Development of Presflo design
Total		22				

1/279 21ton Fly Ash Wagon

Lot		Qty	Numbers	Year	Builder	Notes
3491	v	1	B873793		Darl'n (Loco)	Larger version of diagram 278
3515	v	22	B873894-873915		Shildon	)
3516	v	62	B873916-873977		Ashford	) These 2 lots have disc brakes.
Total		85				

1/281 17ton Fly Ash Wagon

Lot		Qty	Numbers	Year	Builder	Notes
	v	(1)	B873082			One wagon ex lot 3323 converted
Total		(1)				

1/290 Bocar

Lot		Qty	Numbers	Year	Builder	Notes
3090	v	36	B889100-889135	1958	Wolverton	5ton. Used redundant carriage underframes with roof, ends & open sides.
Total		36				

1/291 14ton Motor Car Van for Continental Ferry Service

Lot		Qty	Numbers	Year	Builder	Notes
2848	x	20	B889000-889019	1961	Lancing	Similar to carriage lot 30189 (CCT)
3022	x	10	B889020-889029	1957	Lancing	
Total		30				

1/292 14ton Scenery Van for Continental Ferry Service

Lot		Qty	Numbers	Year	Builder	Notes
2849	x	4	B889200-889203	1955	Eastleigh	Similar to carriage lot 30417 etc (GUV)
Total		4				

1/293 5ton Carriage Truck Bocar P

Lot		Qty	Numbers	Year	Builder	Notes
3547	v	8	B889136-889143		Derby	Believed to be similar to diagram 290.
Total		8				

1/300 40ton Bogie Tank Wagon (Rubber Latex)

Lot		Qty	Numbers	Year	Builder	Notes
2076	v	6	B749300-749305	1949	Derby	Tanks owned by H Diaper & Co.
2621	v	3	B749306-749308	1954	Derby	
3404	v	6	B749309-749314	1961	Earlestown	
Total		15				

1/301 Tank Wagon (Ethylene Oxide)

Lot		Qty	Numbers	Year	Builder	Notes
2170	p	10	B749600-749609	1955	Grazebrook	
Total		10				

1/302 Tank Wagon for Beer

Lot		Qty	Numbers	Year	Builder	Notes
2074	v	2	B749100-749101	1949	Derby	Steam heating through pipe.
Total		2				

1/303 Cable-Compound Tank

Lot		Qty	Numbers	Year	Builder	Notes
2306	v	1	B749350	1951	Derby	12tons, 6 wheeled. Tank by Andrew Barclay.
Total		1				

1/304 20ton Tank for Class 'A' Liquids.

Lot		Qty	Numbers	Year	Builder	Notes
2240	v	10	B740660-749679	1952	Ashford	
Total		10				

1/305 20ton Tank Wagon for Class 'A' Liquids (for Continental Traffic)

Lot		Qty	Numbers	Year	Builder	Notes
2429	w	20	B749660-749679	1952	Ashford	Tanks by Hurst Nelson.
Total		20				

1/306 Tank Wagon for Conveyance of Propane & Butane

Lot		Qty	Numbers	Year	Builder	Notes
2412		10	B749900-749909	1952	Lancing	20ton. Tanks by M & W Grazebrook.
Total		10				

1/307 20ton Class 'B' Tank Wagon

Lot		Qty	Numbers	Year	Builder	Notes
2410		2	B749750-749751	1952	Chas Roberts	For unrefined oils for Townson Tankers, Oldham.
Total		2				

1/325 Demountable Tank Wagon

Lot		Qty	Numbers	Year	Builder	Notes
2041	v	2	B749000-749001	1949	Shildon	Beer;) Tanks owned by Aitchisons
2042	v	3	B749007-749009	1949	Shildon	Beer;) of Edinburgh
2043	v	1	B749014	1949	Shildon	Beer;) Tanks owned by BR but
2043	v	2	B749021-749022	1949	Shildon	Beer;) hired to Younger
2044	v	4	B749200-749203	1949	Shildon	Cyder;
Total		12				

1/326 Demountable Tanks For Beer

Lot		Qty	Numbers	Year	Builder	Notes
2075	v	2	B749033-749034	1949	Derby	Steam heating through pipe.
Total		2				

1/327 Demountable Tank for Beer

Lot		Qty	Numbers	Year	Builder	Notes
2073	v	10	B749023-749032	1949	Derby	Steam heating through pipe.
Total		10				

1/328 Demountable Tanks for Paint & Varnish

Lot		Qty	Numbers	Year	Builder	Notes
2112	v	1	B749500	1949	Swindon	Tanks (4) owned by I. C. I.
Total		1				

1/329 Demountable Tank for Silicate of Soda

Lot		Qty	Numbers	Year	Builder	Notes
2077	v	8	B749400-749407	1949	Derby	
2277	v	4	B749408-749411	1951	Shildon & Derby	
Total		12				

1/330 Demountable Tank for Beer

Lot		Qty	Numbers	Year	Builder	Notes
2278	v	1	B749017	1951	) Shildon &	Steam heating through pipe. Both
2281	v	1	B749035	1951	) Derby	wagons for Truman Hanbury & Buxton
Total		2				

1/331 Demountable Tank for Beer

Lot		Qty	Numbers	Year	Builder	Notes
2280	v	3	B749038-749040	1951	Shildon & Derby	Bass & Co
Total		3				

1/332 Chassis for Road Rail Tank

Lot		Qty	Numbers	Year	Builder	Notes
2370	v	18	B748800-748817	1951	Swindon	Tanks owned by Guinness
Total		18				

1/333 Demountable Tank for Lemon Hart Rum

Lot		Qty	Numbers	Year	Builder	Notes
2239	v	1	B749250	1951	Derby	Probably conveyed water
Total		1				

1/334 Demountable Tank for Beer

Lot		Qty	Numbers	Year	Builder	Notes
2393	v	7	B749041-749047	1951	Earlestown	) Beer for Bass. Tanks built by
2394	v	2	B749036-749037	1951	) Shildon &	) Butterfields of Shipley.
2395	v	2	B749010-749011	1951	) Derby	)
2566	v	4	B749050-749053	1954	Earlestown	Bass Ratcliff & Gretton
2649	v	5	B749054-749058	1954	Earlestown	Bass Ratcliff & Gretton
2774	v	7	B749059-749065	1955	Earlestown	Bass
2946	v	5	B749066-749070	1956	Earlestown	Bass
Total		32				

1/335 Chassis for Road Rail Tank

Lot		Qty	Numbers	Year	Builder	Notes
2537	v	10	B748818-748827	1953	Faverdale	6 wheeled vehicles with tanks privately owned by Guinness.
2763	v	3	B748828-748830	1955	Swindon	
Total		13				

1/336 Chassis for Demountable Beer Tank

2423 v 1 B749048 1952 Shildon John Aitcheson & Co.
Total 1

1/337 Demountable Tank for Sodium Silicate

2427 v 6 B749412-749417 1952 Earlestown Second hand underframes used
Total 6

1/338 Demountable Tank for Beer

2424 v 1 B749049 1952 Shildon Truman Hanbury & Buxton - spare tank made.
Total 1

1/339 Demountable Tank for Ammonia Liquor

v (5) B708811,709786 B736740,702143 Chassis converted from Conflats.
Total (5) B707235

1/340 Demountable Tank Wagon - Anhydrous Dimethylamine Transport Tank

(2) B504916,503934 Chassis converted from Conflats
Total (2)

1/341 Chassis for Road Rail Tank

v (1) M707007 Converted from ex-LMS wagon to diagram 59.
Total (1)

1/342 Demountable Tanks for Liquified Ammonia

v ? ? Chassis converted from Conflats
Total ?

1/343 Demountable Tank Wagon - Anhydrous Dimethylamine Transport Tank

? ? Believed to be a Conflat conversion.

1/350 12ton Cattle Wagon

2022 v 150 B890000-890149 1949 Derby LMS design. Steam pipe fitted.
2036 v 1100 B890150-891249 1949 Shildon & Derby
2070 v 100 B891400-891499 1949 G R Turner
Total 1350

1/351 12ton Cattle Wagon

2064 v 150 B891250-891399 1949 Ashford SR design
Total 150

1352 12ton Cattle Wagon

2080 v 250 B891500-891749 1949 Swindon GWR design
2086 v 150 B891750-891899 1949 Swindon
2126 v 600 B891900-892499 1950 Swindon
Total 1000

1/353 8ton Cattle Wagon

2269 v 700 B893000-893699 1951 Swindon BR standard design
2325 v 250 B893700-893949 1952 Swindon
2426 v 160 B893950-894109 1952 Swindon
2495 v 90 B894110-894199 1952 Swindon
2501 v 100 B894200-894299 1953 Swindon
Total 1300

1/354 8 & 12ton Cattle Wagons Converted for use on Dover - Dunkerque Ferry Service from Pages 352 & 353.

v (40) Various 14 8ton & 26 12ton wagons.
Total (40)

1/400 13ton Single Bolster Wagon. Steel Body: Wood Floor.

2034 500 B910000-910499 1949 Shildon
2131 500 B910500-910999 1950 Shildon
2783 1000 B911000-911999 1956 Shildon
2860 1000 B912000-912999 1956 Shildon
Total 3000

1/401 42ton Strip Coil Wagon Lettered Stripcoil

2209 35 B949000-949034 1950 Swindon Bogie vehicles - all converted to diagram 407
Total 35

1/401 Single Bolster Wagon

2861 1000 B913000-913999 1956 Shildon Second issue of diagram. 13tons.
Total 1000

1/402 13ton Single Bolster Wagon

3005 2000 B914000-915999 1957 Shildon Hydraulic buffers
3006 2000 B916000-917999 1957 Shildon
Total 4000

1/403 42ton Strip Coil Wagon

3014 v 15 B949035-949049 1957 Head Wri'tson Bogie vehicles
Total 15

1/404 56ton Strip Coil Wagon

3015 v 40 B949050-949089 1959 Head Wri'tson Bogie vehicles. Later uprated to 60ton & fitted with nylon hoods.
Total 40

1/405 13ton Single Bolster Wagon

3125 v 496 B918000-918945 1958 Shildon All believed to have been twinned in 1964 - see diagram 438.
Total 496

1/406 42ton Strip Coil Wagon

2209 v (1) B949004 One wagon converted from diagram 401 & later further converted as below
Total (1)

1/407 42ton Strip Coil Wagon (Hot Coil)

2209 v (35) B949000-949034 One wagon, and subsequently all of lot 2209 converted to this diagram
Total (35)

1/408 57ton Slab Wagon

3359 v 20 Between B949501 1961 Swindon Part lot. See diagrams 417 & 419 Random numbers in range
Total 20 & B949550

1/409 16ton Strip Coil Wagon Converted from 16ton Min. Wagons to BR Diags. Nos 108 & 117

v (200) See note Between B160007 & B595476
Total (200)

1/410 26ton Twin Sets

v (?) ? Converted from Lowfits
Total (?)

1/411 45ton Slab Coil Wagon

3424 v 58 B949551-949608 1962 Swindon Bogie vehicles. Roller bearings
Total 58

1/412 21ton Strip Coil Wagon Lettered Coil A

3450 v 50 B949130-949179 Derby With sheet support rails
Total 50

1/413 60ton Strip Coil Wagon

3399 v 40 B949090-949129 1961 Swindon Bogie vehicles. Roller bearings
Total 40

1/414 24ton Strip Coil Wagon fitted with Nylon Hood

3464 v 6 B949180-949185 Derby Roller bearings
3478 v 6 B949186-949191 Derby
3484 v 24 B949192-949197 Derby
3513 v 12 B949198-949209 Derby
3514 v 10 B949210-949219 Derby
Total 58

1/415 21ton Double Bolster Wagon

2035 200 B920200-920399 1949 Shildon Removable bolsters
Total 200

1/416 21ton Double Bolster Wagon

2020 200 B920000-920199 1949 Wloverton Floor ½in higher than diagram 415. 81 built without bolsters.
Total 200

1/417 57ton Slab Wagon -(Single Tier Loading - 6 Slabs)

3359 v 17 Between B949501 1961 Swindon Part lot. Random numbers within range
Total 17 & 949550

1/418 22ton Twin Bolster Wagon -(Converted from WD 11ton Ramp Wagons)

3419 44 W162500-162543 22 sets each of two wagons.
Total 44

1/419 57ton Slab Wagon -(Single Tier Loading - 8 Slabs)

3359 v 13 Between B949501 1961 Swindon Part lot. Random numbers within range
Total 13 & 949550

1/420 15ton Open Timber Truck

3465 v 80 B455500-455579 Ashford
Total 80

1/421 44ton Strip Coil Wagon with Nylon Hood (Ex WD Warflat)

3414 v 30 W16000-160254 Part lot. Random numbers within range.
Total 30

1/422 24ton Strip Coil Wagon Converted from 20ton Pig Iron Wagon to BR Diagram 7.

(?) ? Number of vehicles not known
Total (?)

1/423 20ton Strip Coil Wagon Converted from 20ton Pig Iron Wagon to BR Diagram 4.

(?) ? Number of vehicles not known
Total (?)

1/424 24ton Strip Coil Wagon Ex 22ton Plate Wagon

(25) ? Between B931170 & 936516
Total (25)

1/425 50ton Flat Wagon (Ex Warflat) for the Conveyance of Coil Strip Loaded with Plate Width Vertical

3414 v (10) W160006-160250 Part lot. Random numbers within range.
Total (10)

1/426 Diagram of (sic) 44ton Strip Coil Wagon with Nylon Hood (Ex WD Warflat)
3414 v (20) W160089-161057 Part lot. Random numbers within range. Note that according to the lot book one wagon is from lot 3417 and 14 from lot 3416
Total (20)

1/428 30ton Strip Coil Wagon for the Conveyance of Steel Coil in Stillages Ex 30ton Pig Iron Wagon

(10) Ex lot 2857, diagram 5.
Total (10)

1/429 21ton 'Rod Coil' wagon

Lot		Qty	Numbers	Year	Builder	Notes
		(?)				Ex 22ton Double Bolster wagons. Number of vehicles unknown
Total		(?)				

1/430 22ton Plate Wagon

Lot		Qty	Numbers	Year	Builder	Notes
2037		250	B930000-930249	1949	Shildon	
2132		300	B930250-930549	1950	Shildon	
2151		500	B930550-931049	1950	G R Turner	
Total		1050				

1/431 22ton Plate Wagon

Lot		Qty	Numbers	Year	Builder	Notes
2199		540	B931050-931589	1951	Shildon	¼in higher than diagram 430.
2201		36	DB997500-997535	1951	Shildon	This lot for S&T Dept.
2327		160	B931590-931749	1952	Shildon	
2476		225	B931750-931974	1953	Shildon	
2481		5	DB997536-997540	1953	Shildon	This lot for S&T Dept.
2604		850	B931975-932824	1954	Shildon	
2773		2	DB997541-997542	1955	Shildon	This lot - Code name Winkle.
Total		1818				

1/432 22ton Plate Wagon - Lettered Plate

Lot		Qty	Numbers	Year	Builder	Notes
2734	v	550	B932825-933374	1955	Shildon	Vacuum braked version of diag.431
2862	v	500	B933375-933874	1956	Shildon	
3128	v	150	B933875-934024	1958	Faverdale	
Total		1200				

1/433 22ton Wagon for Conveyance of 'BD' &'A' Type Containers

Lot		Qty	Numbers	Year	Builder	Notes
	v	(?)				Converted from diagram 430
Total		(?)				

1/434 22ton Plate Wagon

Lot		Qty	Numbers	Year	Builder	Notes
3223	v	1500	B934025-935524	1959	Shildon	Isothermos boxes or roller bearings
3338	v	1000	B935525-936524	1961	Shildon	
Total		2500				

1/435 24ton 'D' Coil Wagon

Lot		Qty	Numbers	Year	Builder	Notes
	v	(71)	?			Converted from Plate wagons
Total		(71)				

1/436 25ton Zinc Ingot Wagon

Lot		Qty	Numbers	Year	Builder	Notes
		(1)	B311047			Converted from 21ton mineral lot 3390.
Total		(1)				

1/437 26ton Twin Sets

Lot		Qty	Numbers	Year	Builder	Notes
		(?)	?			Converted from Conflat 'A'
Total		(?)				

1/438 26ton Twin Sets

Lot		Qty	Numbers	Year	Builder	Notes
		(?)	?			Converted from Single Bolster wagons
Total		(?)				

1/439 22ton Timber Wagon

Lot		Qty	Numbers	Year	Builder	Notes
	v	(?)	?		Barassie	Converted from Conflat 'P', diagram 60
Total		(?)				

1/442 16ton Strip Coil Wagon - Lettered Coil P

Lot		Qty	Numbers	Year	Builder	Notes
		(?)	?			Converted from Pallet Brick wagons diagram 25.
Total		(?)				

1/443 16ton Strip Coil Wagon - Lettered Coil P

Lot		Qty	Numbers	Year	Builder	Notes
		(?)	?			Converted from Pallet Brick wagons diagrams 22 & 24.
Total		(?)				

1/444 30ton Strip Coil Wagon

Lot		Qty	Numbers	Year	Builder	Notes
		(?)	?			Converted from Hot Pig Iron wagons diagram 5.
Total		(?)				

1/445 20ton Tube Wagon Lettered - Tube

Lot		Qty	Numbers	Year	Builder	Notes
2048		100	B730000-730099	1949	Faverdale	LNE design. Full length doors.
2049	v	400	B730100-730499	1949	Faverdale	
Total		500				

1/446 22ton Tube Wagon Lettered Tube

Lot		Qty	Numbers	Year	Builder	Notes
2127		100	B731000-731099	1950	Swindon	GWR design. Trussed underframe.
Total		100				

1/447 22ton Steel Tube Wagon - Lettered Tube

Lot		Qty	Numbers	Year	Builder	Notes
2204		290	B731100-731389	1951	Faverdale	30ft 6ins long, corrugated ends.
2328		100	B731390-731489	1952	Swindon	
2457		100	B731490-731589	1953	Wolverton	
Total		490				

1/448 22ton Tube Wagon - Lettered Tube

Lot		Qty	Numbers	Year	Builder	Notes
2554		450	B731590-732039	1954	Faverdale	32ft long, corrugated ends.
2740	v	350	B732040-733289	1955	Faverdale	
2867	v	650	B732390-733039	1956	Faverdale	
3226	v	180	B733040-733219	1959	Faverdale	
3288	v	420	B730500-730919	1960	Derby	
3332	v	80	B730920-730999	1961	Derby	
3332	v	220	B733240-733459	1961	Derby	
Total		2350				

1/449 22ton Tube Wagon for Continental Traffic Lettered Tube (Batten)

Lot		Qty	Numbers	Year	Builder	Notes
3258	x	20	B733220-733239	1959	Faverdale	32ft long, corrugated ends.
Total		20				

1/450 13ton Rod Coil Wagon

Lot		Qty	Numbers	Year	Builder	Notes
		(?)	?			Converted from 13ton Hyfits, diagram 32.
Total		(?)				

1/452 12ton Strip Coil Wagon Coil Q

Lot		Qty	Numbers	Year	Builder	Notes
		(?)	?			Converted from Palbrick wagons, diagram 23.
Total		(?)				

1/453 60ton Slab Coil agon Coil T

Lot		Qty	Numbers	Year	Builder	Notes
		(29)	?			Converted from diagrams 417 & 419.
Total		(29)				

1/460 13ton Pipe Wagon

Lot		Qty	Numbers	Year	Builder	Notes
2004		300	B740000-740299	1949	Derby	21ft 6ins long. Originally 12tons.
2305		50	B740600-740649	1951	Cambrian	
2329		50	B740650-740699	1952	Swindon	
2458		200	B740700-740899	1953	Wolverton	
2545		200	B740900-741099	1954	Wolverton	
Total		800				

1/461 13ton Pipe Wagon

Lot		Qty	Numbers	Year	Builder	Notes
2046	v	100	B740300-740399	1949	Faverdale	As diagram 460 but vacuum fitted.
2047	v	200	B740400-740599	1949	Faverdale	
Total		300				

1/462 12ton Pipe Wagon Lettered : Pipefit

Lot		Qty	Numbers	Year	Builder	Notes
2712	v	350	B741100-741449	1955	Wolverton	As diagram 461 but with short buffers and reduced capacity.
2845	v	60	B741500-741559	1956	Wolverton	
2846	v	80	B741560-741639	1956	Wolverton	These described as 'High Goods'
2846	v	30	B741640-741669	1956	Wolverton	
2846	v	60	B741670-741729	1956	Wolverton	
3070	v	50	B484150-484199	1957	Wolverton	
3335	v	200	B741750-741949	1961	Wolverton	
Total		830				

1/463 12ton Pipe Wagon Lettered Pipefit

Lot		Qty	Numbers	Year	Builder	Notes
3167	v	20	B741730-741749	1958	Wolverton	Hydraulic buffers
Tot l		20				

1/470 42ton Bogie Bolster Truck Code - Bogie Bolster D

Lot		Qty	Numbers	Year	Builder	Notes
2021		150	B941000-941149	1949	Derby	52ft long
Total		150				

1/471 30ton Bogie Bolster Truck. Lettered - Bogie Bolster C

Lot		Qty	Numbers	Year	Builder	Notes
2085		50	B940000-940049	1948	Swindon	45ft long
2271		34	DB997600-997633	1951	Swindon	This lot for S&T Dept.
2308		950	B940050-940999	1951	Metro-Cammell	
2309		14	DB997634-997647	1951	Metro-Cammell	This lot for S&T Dept.
2326		100	B943000-943099	1952	Swindon	
2406		250	B943100-943349	1952	Metro-Cammell	
Total		1398				

1/472 42ton Bogie Bolster Lettered Bogie Bolster D

Lot		Qty	Numbers	Year	Builder	Notes
2211		200	B941150-941349	1950	Teesside B&E	Stanchions & bolsters higher than on diagram 470.
2237		67	B941350-941416	1951	Lancing	
2238		58	B941417-941474	1951	Swindon	
2358		80	B941475-941554	1952	Lancing	
2487		75	B941555-941629	1953	Lancing	
2623		150	B941630-941779	1954	Teesside B&E	
2624		150	B941780-941929	1954	Cravens	
2625		100	B941930-942029	1954	R Y Pickering	
2690		100	B942230-942329	1955	Teesside B&E	
2691		100	B942030-942229	1955	Swindon	
2787		200	B942330-942529	1956	Teesside B&E	
2852		150	B942530-942679	1956	Lancing	
2882		250	B942680-942929	1956	Swindon	
2979		130	B927000-927129	1957	Swindon	
3021		70	B927130-927199	1957	Eastleigh	
3028		14	B927200-927213	1957	Teesside B&E	Part lot. Remainder to diag. 476.
3104	v	100	B927400-927499	1958	Swindon	
3113	v	100	B927500-927599	1958	Lancing	
Total		2094				

1/473 30ton Bogie Bolster Truck

Lot		Qty	Numbers	Year	Builder	Notes
2496		160	B943350-943509	1953	Swindon	As diagram 471 but heavier journals.
2539		100	B943510-943609	1953	Metro-Cammell	
2540		21	DB997649-997669	1953	Metro-Cammell	User dept. not specified.
2542		250	B943610-943859	1954	Swindon	
2583		200	B943860-944059	1954	Metro-Cammell	Part lot. Remainder to diag. 475.
2616		160	B944310-944469	1954	Birmingham	Part lot. Remainder to diags. 474 & 475.
Total		891				

1/474 30ton Bogie Bolster Truck Lettered - Bogie Bolster C

Lot		Qty	Numbers	Year	Builder	Notes
2616		50	B944470-944519	1954	Birmingham	Stanchions & Bolsters higher than on diagram 473
2760		300	B944890-945189	1955	Birmingham	
2818		401	B945390-945790	1956	Metro-Cammell	Part lot. Remainder to diag. 475
Total		751				

1/475 30ton Bogie Bolster Wagon - Bogie Bolster 'C'

Lot		Qty	Numbers	Year	Builder	Notes
2583		250	B944060-944309	1954	Metro-Cammell	Similar to diag 474 but heavier journals
2616		120	B944520-944639	1954	Birmingham	
2759		150	B944740-944889	1955	Metro-Cammell	
2818		1	B945190	1955	Metro-Cammell	
2818		199	B945191-945389	1956	Metro-Cammell	
Total		720				

1/476 42ton Bogie Bolster Lettered Bogie Bolster D

Lot		Qty	Numbers	Year	Builder	Notes
3028		186	B927214-927399	1957	Teesside B&E	Bolster positions differ from diag. 470, otherwise similar.
Total		186				

1/477 30ton Bogie Bolster

Lot		Qty	Numbers	Year	Builder	Notes
3059		100	B944640-945379	1957	Teesside B&E	Cast steel bogies. Some lots have roller bearings also.
3060		500	B922000-922499	1957	Metro-Cammell	
3155	v	200	B945791-945990	1958	Metro-Cammell	
3162	v	200	B922500-922699	1958	Metro-Cammell	
3200	v	300	B922700-922999	1959	Swindon	
3238	v	100	B923000-923099	1959	Swindon	
3341		200	B923100-923299	1961	Swindon	
3397		400	B924400-924799	1961	Metro-Cammell	
Total		2000				

1/478 42ton Bogie Bolster Lettered Bogie Bolster D

Lot		Qty	Numbers	Year	Builder	Notes
3246	v	200	B927600-927799	1959	Lancing	
Total		200				

1/479 30ton Bogie Bolster E

Lot		Qty	Numbers	Year	Builder	Notes
3343	v	1100	B923300-924399	1961	Ashford	
3440	v	100	B924800-924899	1962	Ashford	
Total		1200				

1/480 40ton Bogie Bolster Truck Lettered Borail WE

Lot		Qty	Numbers	Year	Builder	Notes
2098		50	B946000-946049	1949	Swindon	Lot book notes: 'Special bogie bolster... now described as Bogie Bolster C'.
Total		50				

1/481 50ton Bogie Bolster Lettered Borail WG

Lot		Qty	Numbers	Year	Builder	Notes
3263	p	15	B946050-946064		Standard	62ft long.
Total		15				

1/482 50ton Borail for Conveyance of Prestressed Concrete Beams Lettered Borail C.

Lot		Qty	Numbers	Year	Builder	Notes
3267	v	10	B946065-946074	1959	Derby	62ft long. Roller bearings
3334	v	20	B946210-946229	1961	Derby	
Total		30				

1/483 50ton Bogie Bolster Lettered Borail MB or Borail EB

Lot		Qty	Numbers	Year	Builder	Notes
3268	v	10	B946075-946114	1959	Derby	As above but raised bolsters.
3333	v	95	B946115-946209	1961	Derby	
Total		105				

1/484 42ton Bogie Bolster Lettered Bogie Bolster D

Lot		Qty	Numbers	Year	Builder	Notes
3407	v	200	B927800-927999	1961	Powell-Duffryn	As dia. 478 but with roller bearings.
3408	v	200	B928000-928199	1961	Chas Roberts	
Total		400				

1/485 50ton Bogie Bolster B Converted from Warflat

Lot		Qty	Numbers	Year	Builder	Notes
3414		225	W160000-160254			Less gaps. Some vacuum fitted. See also diagrams 421, 425, 426 & 427.
Total		225				

1/486 30ton Bogie Bolster B Converted from Warwell A

Lot		Qty	Numbers	Year	Builder	Notes
3415		40	W160800-160839			Some vacuum fitted.
Total		40				

1/487 35ton Bogie Bolster A Converted from Rectank

Lot		Qty	Numbers	Year	Builder	Notes
3418		5	W162000-162004			
Total		5				

1/488 40ton Bogie Rail Wagon

Lot		Qty	Numbers	Year	Builder	Notes
2208	v	9	B996795-996803	1950	Cravens	Part lot, see also diagram 641. 10vehicles of GWR lot 1305 also to this diagram
Total		9				

1/489 30ton Bogie Bolster Truck BBQ for Conveyance of Steel Pipes.

Lot		Qty	Numbers	Year	Builder	Notes
		(?)	?			Converted from diagram 477.
Total		(?)				

1/490 42ton Bogie Plate Wagon Code Boplate E

Lot		Qty	Numbers	Year	Builder	Notes
2010		50	B947000-947049	1949	Derby	52ft long. Drop sides
2185		50	B947125-947174	1951	Derby	
2344		20	B947175-947194	1952	Shildon	
2455		40	B947195-947234	1953	Derby	
2456		2	DB997400-997401	1953	Derby	For S&T Dept. Codename Whelk
2618		75	B947235-947309	1954	Cambrian	
2722		40	B947310-947349	1955	Cambrian	
2930		50	B947350-947399	1956	Cambrian	
3046		160	B947400-947559	1957	Cambrian	
3055		150	B947560-947709	1957	Hurst Nelson	
3056		150	B947710-947859	1957	R Y Pickering	
3235	v	125	B948010-948134	1959	Derby	
3236	v	125	B948135-948259	1959	Derby	
Total		1037				

1/491 42ton Bogie Plate Wagon

Lot		Qty	Numbers	Year	Builder	Notes
2133		75	B947050-947124	1950	Shildon	
Total		75				

1/492 42ton Bogie Plate Wagon - Lettered Boplate E

Lot		Qty	Numbers	Year	Builder	Notes
3229	v	150	B947860-948009	1958	Ashford	Roller bearings
3240	v	150	B948260-948409	1958	Ashford	
Total		300				

1/493 30ton Bogie Bolster 'H'

Lot		Qty	Numbers	Year	Builder	Notes
		(?)	?			Converted from diagram 477
Total		(?)				

1/500 20ton Goods Brake Van

Lot		Qty	Numbers	Year	Builder	Notes
2051	v	290	B950250-950539	1949	Faverdale	LNER design
Total		290				

1/501 10ton Goods Brake Van

Lot		Qty	Numbers	Year	Builder	Notes
2096		2	B950540-950541	1949	Swindon	GWR design for Pontnewynydd line.
Total		2				

1/502 20ton Goods Brake Van

Lot		Qty	Numbers	Year	Builder	Notes
2099		74	B950542-950615	1949	Swindon	GWR design
Total		74				

1/503 20ton Goods Brake Van

Lot		Qty	Numbers	Year	Builder	Notes
2026		125	B950125-950249	1949	Derby	LMS design
Total		125				

1/504 20ton Goods Brake Van

Lot		Qty	Numbers	Year	Builder	Notes
2136	p	250	B950616-950865	1950	Faverdale	LNER design
2206	p	160	B951116-951275	1951	Faverdale	
2207		240	B951276-951515	1951	Faverdale	
2741	v	400	B952716-953115	1955	Faverdale	
Total		1050				

1/505 20ton Goods Brake Van

Lot		Qty	Numbers	Year	Builder	Notes
2025	p	125	B950000-950124	1949	Derby	LMS design
Total		125				

1/506 20ton Goods Brake Van

Lot		Qty	Numbers	Year	Builder	Notes
2137		250	B950866-951115	1950	Faverdale	BR standard design
2349	v	200	B951516-951715	1952	Faverdale	
2350		150	B951716-951865	1952	Faverdale	
2477		140	B951866-952005	1953	Faverdale	
2478	v	160	B952006-952165	1953	Faverdale	
2605		350	B952166-952515	1954	Faverdale	
2606	v	200	B952516-952715	1954	Faverdale	
2868	v	300	B953116-953415	1956	Faverdale	
3012	v	260	B953416-953675	1957	Faverdale	Regional allocation no longer used
3129	v	845	B953676-954520	1958	Faverdale	
Total		2855				

1/507 20ton Goods Brake Van

Lot		Qty	Numbers	Year	Builder	Notes
3227	p	477	B954521-954997	1959	Faverdale	Roller bearings
3394	p	250	B954998-955247	1961	Faverdale	
3402		(6)	L580-585		Ashford	Built for LTE & not taken into BR stock
Total		727				

1/550 Inspection Saloon

Lot		Qty	Numbers	Year	Builder	Notes
3093	v	4	DB999501-999504	1957	Wolverton	LMS lot 1432. 32ton bogie vehicles
Total		4				

1/551 Inspection Saloon

Lot		Qty	Numbers	Year	Builder	Notes
3094	v	1	DB999505	1958	Wolverton	32ton bogie vehicle
Total		1				

1/552 Inspection Saloon

Lot		Qty	Numbers	Year	Builder	Notes
3095	v	1	DB999506	1958	Swindon	Bogie vehicles
3379	v	2	DB999508-999509	1959	Swindon	
Total		3				

1/555 Diesel Brake Tender

Lot		Qty	Numbers	Year	Builder	Notes
3446	v	3	DB964035-964037		Cowlairs	35½ton bogie vehicles
3448	v	68	DB964038-964105		York	
3500	v	10	DB964112-964121		York	
Total		81				

1/556 Diesel Brake Tender

Lot		Qty	Numbers	Year	Builder	Notes
3442	v	5	DB964000-964004		Derbyshire	35½ton bogie vehicles
3443	v	15	DB964005-964019		Central	
3444	v	9	DB964020-964028		Standard	Part lot
3445	v	4	DB964031-964034		Marcroft	Part lot
Total		33				

1/557 Diesel Brake Tender

Lot		Qty	Numbers	Year	Builder	Notes
3444	v	1	DB964029		Standard	Part lot. 35½ton bogie vehicles
3445	v	1	DB964030		Marcroft	Part lot
Total		2				

1/558 Diesel Brake Tender

Lot		Qty	Numbers	Year	Builder	Notes
3449	v	6	DB964106-964111		Stratford	37½tons bogie vehicles
Total		6				

1/565 12ton Ballast Wagon

Lot		Qty	Numbers	Year	Builder	Notes
2012		150	DB982000-982149	1949	Wolverton	Code Sole. Wood dropsides & ends
2264		200	DB982150-982349	1950	Fairfields	
Total		350				

1/566 10ton Ballast Wagon - Lettered Starfish

Lot		Qty	Numbers	Year	Builder	Notes
2089		80	DB987000-987079	1949	Swindon	Steel body, drop sides.
Total		80				

1/567 14ton Ballast Wagon - Lettered Ling

Lot		Qty	Numbers	Year	Builder	Notes
2090		200	DB988000-988199	1948	Swindon	Steel body, drop sides.
Total		200				

1/568 20ton Ballast Wagon - Lettered Tunney

Lot		Qty	Numbers	Year	Builder	Notes
2091		120	DB991021-991140	1949	Swindon	Steel body, drop sides.
Total		120				

1/569 20ton Ballast & Sleeper Wagon

Lot		Qty	Numbers	Year	Builder	Notes
2120		50	DB990000-990049	1948	Butterley	Code Gudgeon. Wood body & 'Chaldron' buffers.
Total		50				

1/570 20ton Ballast Wagon Lettered Lamphrey

Lot		Qty	Numbers	Year	Builder	Notes
2065	v	21	DB991000-991020	1949	Lancing	Steel body, drop sides & ends.
2102	v	50	DB991301-991320	1949	Ashford	
2241	v	160	DB991141-991300	1951	Butterley	
Total		231				

1/571 20ton Ballast & Sleeper Wagon

Lot		Qty	Numbers	Year	Builder	Notes
2121		50	DB990050-990099	1949	Butterley	Code Pilchard. Bogie vehicles
Total		50				

1/572 20ton Sleeper & Ballast Wagon Lettered Grampus

Lot		Qty	Numbers	Year	Builder	Notes
2200		300	DB990100-990399	1951	Shildon	Steel body, drop sides & ends.
2345		290	DB990400-990689	1952	Shildon	
2362		387	DB985000-985386	1951	Butterley	
2482		260	DB985387-985646	1953	Shildon	
2483		239	DB985647-985885	1953	Shildon	
2777		152	DB986556-986707	1955	Butterley	
2778		70	DB986708-986777	1955	Cambrian	
2779		60	DB986778-986837	1955	Derbyshire	

Lot		Qty	Numbers	Year	Builder	Notes
2780		122	DB986838-986959	1955	Gloucester	
2884		252	DB985886-986137	1954	Butterley	
2885		202	DB986138-986339	1954	Gloucester	
2886		116	DB986340-986455	1954	Cambrian	
2887		100	DB986456-986555	1954	Derbyshire	
2940		169	DB990690-990858	1956	Cambrian	
2941		100	DB990859-990958	1956	Derbyshire	
2942		50	DB984000-984049	1956	Gloucester	
3038		200	DB984050-984249	1957	Cambrian	
3048		58	DB984250-984307	1957	Butterley	
3049		242	DB984308-984549	1957	Butterley	
3050		144	DB984550-984693	1957	Derbyshire	
3051		27	DB986960-986986	1957	Derbyshire	
3052		300	DB984694-984993	1957	Gloucester	
3245	v	219	DB988200-988418	1959	Ashford	
Total		4059				

1/573 14ton Ballast Side Tipping Wagon Lettered Mermaid

Lot		Qty	Numbers	Year	Builder	Notes
2428		20	DB989000-989019	1952	Metro-Cammell	
2535		52	DB989020-989071	1953	Metro-Cammell	
2928		17	DB989072-989088	1956	Metro-Cammell	
Total		89				

1/574 20ton Sleeper Ballast Wagon Lettered Grampus

Lot		Qty	Numbers	Year	Builder	Notes
3168	v	544	DB991321-991864	1958	Pressed Steel	Vacuum fitted version of diag. 572
3282	v	103	DB988419-988521	1959	Shildon	
3339	v	75	DB988522-988596	1961	Shildon	
Total		722				

1/575 14ton Ballast Side Tipping Wagon Lettered Mermaid

Lot		Qty	Numbers	Year	Builder	Notes
3170	v	150	DB989089-989238	1959	Metro-Cammell	Vacuum fitted version of diag. 573 Some lots have hydraulic buffers.
3256	v	50	DB989239-989288	1959	Mttro-Cammell	
3330	v	300	DB989289-989588	1960	Metro-Cammell	
3348	v	50	DB989589-989638	1961	Metro-Cammell	
Total		550				

1/580 25ton Hopper Ballast Wagon

Lot		Qty	Numbers	Year	Builder	Notes
2117		11	DB992024-992034	1948	Metro-Cammell	Code Trout. 3 bottom doors.
2118		22	DB992035-992056	1948	Metro-Cammell	
2188		80	DB992117-992196	1950	Metro-Cammell	
Total		113				

1/581 25ton Hopper Ballast Wagon

Lot		Qty	Numbers	Year	Builder	Notes
2027		24	DB992000-992023	1949	Teesside B&E	Code Trout. 4 bottom doors - 2 each side.
2178		60	DB992057-992116	1950	Metro-Cammell	
Total		84				

1/582 20ton Hopper Ballast Wagon Lettered Herring

Lot		Qty	Numbers	Year	Builder	Notes
2214	v	50	DB992197-992246	1950	Metro-Cammell	
Total		50				

1/583 17ton Hopper Ballast Wagon Lettered Mackerel

Lot		Qty	Numbers	Year	Builder	Notes
2284	v	134	DB992247-992380	1951	Metro-Cammell	
Total		134				

1/584 20ton Hopper Ballast Wagon lettered Herring

Lot		Qty	Numbers	Year	Builder	Notes
2405	v	100	DB992381-992480	1952	Metro-Cammell	Despite code, similar to diag. 573
Total		100				

1/585 40ton Hopper Ballast Wagon Lettered Walrus

Lot		Qty	Numbers	Year	Builder	Notes
2411	v	50	DB992481-992530	1952	Metro-Cammell	Bogie wagons
Total		50				

1/586 19ton Hopper Ballast Wagon Lettered Catfish

Lot		Qty	Numbers	Year	Builder	Notes
2682	v	60	DB992531-992590	1953	Metro-Cammell	Longer & lower than diagram 584.
2683	v	60	DB992591-992650	1954	Metro-Cammell	
2775	v	66	DB992651-992710	1955	Metro-Cammell	
2929	v	59	DB993508-993566	1959	Metro-Cammell	
3039	v	201	DB983376-983576	1957	Metro-Cammell	
3331	v	270	DB983627-983896	1960	Metro-Cammell	
Total		716				

1/587 24ton Hopper Ballast Wagon Lettered Dogfish

Lot		Qty	Numbers	Year	Builder	Notes
2819	v	148	DB992711-992858	1959	Chas Roberts	Enlarged version of diagram 586
2820	v	200	DB992859-993058	1959	Metro-Cammell	
2821	v	90	DB993059-993148	1959	Chas Roberts	
2822	v	161	DB993149-993309	1959	Metro-Cammell	
2823	v	161	DB993310-993470	1959	Metro-Cammell	
2824	v	37	DB993471-993507	1959	Metro-Cammell	
2939	v	310	DB983000-983309	1959	Chas Roberts	
3255	v	68	DB993567-993634	1959	Shildon	
3329	v	50	DB983577-983626	1960	Shildon	
3340	v	24	DB983897-983920	1961	Shildon	
Total		1249				

1/588 24ton Hopper Ballast Wagon Modified for Conveyance of Slag

Lot		Qty	Numbers	Year	Builder	Notes
	v	(221)	?			Wagons from diagram 587 modified.
Total		(221)				

1/595 12ton Ballast Plough Brake Van

Lot		Qty	Numbers	Year	Builder	Notes
2119		6	DB993810-993815	1948	Metro-Cammell	Code Shark. Ploughs within wheel-base.
Total		6				

1/596 16ton Ballast Plough Brake Van

Lot		Qty	Numbers	Year	Builder	Notes
2028		2	DB993700-993701	1949	Derby	Code Shark. Ploughs outwith wheel-base.
2172		7	DB993702-993708	1950	R Y Pickering	
Total		9				

1/597 20ton Ballast Plough Brake Van

Lot		Qty	Numbers	Year	Builder	Notes
2186	v	4	DB993709-993712	1951	Derby	Code Shark. Heavier version of diagram 596.
2431	v	14	DB993713-993726	1952	Birmingham	
2536		30	DB993727-993756	1953	Birmingham	
2657		27	DB993757-993783	1954	Birmingham	
2782		26	DB993784-993809	1955	Birmingham	
2931		41	DB993816-993856	1959	Birmingham	
3040		48	DB993857-993904	1957	Birmingham	
3150		16	DB993905-993920	1958	Birmingham	
Total		206				

1/598 20ton Ballast Plough Brake Van

Lot		Qty	Numbers	Year	Builder	Notes
3285	v	20	DB993921-993940	1960	Central	Code Shark. Roller bearings.
Total		20				

1/617 Tank Wagon for Traction Oil 14tons.

Lot		Qty	Numbers	Year	Builder	Notes
3700		9	DB999000-999008			Purchased second hand from Shell-Mex & BP.
Total		9				

1/618 Tank Wagon for Traction Oil GLW 33½tons.

Lot		Qty	Numbers	Year	Builder	Notes
3716		4	DB999009-999012			Purchased second hand from Shell-Mex & BP
Total		4				

1/619 12ton Low Sided Wagon (For S&T Engineer)

Lot		Qty	Numbers	Year	Builder	Notes
2608		6	DB997300-997305	1954	Wolverton	Code ? 3-plank drop side wagons.
Total		6				

1/620 14ton Sleeper Wagon

Lot		Qty	Numbers	Year	Builder	Notes
2081		15	DB995500-995514	1949	Swindon	Code Minnow. 4-plank open.
2093		10	DB995515-995524	1949	Swindon	
Total		25				

1/621 12ton Sleeper Wagon for Engineers Dept.

Lot		Qty	Numbers	Year	Builder	Notes
2215		50	DB995000-995049	1950	Butterley	Code Haddock. 3-plank drop side.
Total		50				

1/622 14ton Rail Wagon

Lot		Qty	Numbers	Year	Builder	Notes
2272		27	DB997700-997726	1951	Swindon	Code Whiting. 2-plank open. This lotfor S&T
2459		20	DB997727-997746	1953	Wolverton	
2883		3	DB995250-995252	1956	Swindon	
Total		50				

1/623 Independent Snow Plough

Lot		Qty	Numbers	Year	Builder	Notes
3539	v	41	DB965203-965243		Cowlairs, Eastleigh & Swindon	Steam locomotive tenders modified.
Total		41				

1/624 Crane Flat Wagon

Lot		Qty	Numbers	Year	Builder	Notes
		3	DB998511,998513,			No lot number allocated. Probably purchased along with cranes.
Total		3	DB998515			

1/625 Crane Flat Wagon

Lot		Qty	Numbers	Year	Builder	Notes
		4	DB998501-998504			No lot number allocated. Probably purchased along with cranes.
Total		4				

1/626 Crane Match Wagon

Lot		Qty	Numbers	Year	Builder	Notes
		4	DB998505-998508			No lot number allocated. Probably purchased along with cranes.
		3	DB998512,998514, DB998516			
Total		7				

1/628 50ton Bogie Rail Wagon Lettered Salmon

Lot		Qty	Numbers	Year	Builder	Notes
3352	p	25	DB996970-996994	1961	Pow'l-Duffryn	As diagram 637 but with side rails.
Total		25				

1/629 20ton Water Tank

Lot		Qty	Numbers	Year	Builder	Notes
3354	p	7	DB998932-998938	1960	R Y Pickering	Purchased from Wilkinsons Wagons.
Total		7				

1/630 Crane Match Wagon (For 36ton Breakdown Crane)

Lot		Qty	Numbers	Year	Builder	Notes
2122	v	1	DB998500	1949	Shildon	
Total		1				

1/631 Shunting Truck

Lot		Qty	Numbers	Year	Builder	Notes
2097	p	1	DB997900	1949	Swindon	
Total		1				

1/632 14ton Refuse Wagon Lettered - Sludge

Lot		Qty	Numbers	Year	Builder	Notes
2532		2	DB998100-998101	1954	Ashford	4 compartments with side doors.
2725		21	DB998102-998122	1955	Ashford	
Total		23				

1/633 14ton Creosote Wagon

Lot		Qty	Numbers	Year	Builder	Notes
2371		3	DB998910-998912	1950	Chas Roberts	3190 gallon tank
2372		13	DB998913-998925	1951	Chas Roberts	
2825		6	DB998926-998931	1959	Chas Roberts	
Total		22				

1/634 20ton Tank for Conveyance of Marine Fuel Oil

Lot		Qty	Numbers	Year	Builder	Notes
2781		15	DB998940-998954	1959	R Y Pickering	5415 gallon tank
Total		15				

1/635 13ton Flat Wagon for Diesel Units

Lot		Qty	Numbers	Year	Builder	Notes
3077	v	1	DB998050	1957	Ashford	Removable centre hood, probably second-hand underframes
3114	v	3	DB998051-998053	1958	Ashford	
Total		4				

1/636 22ton Creosote Wagon

Lot		Qty	Numbers	Year	Builder	Notes
3139	v	38	DB998955-998992	1958	Chas Roberts	4880 gallon tank
3401	v	4	DB998993-998996	1960	Chas Roberts	
Total		42				

1/637 50ton Bogie Rail Wagon Lettered Salmon

Lot		Qty	Numbers	Year	Builder	Notes
3261	p	78	DB996804-996881	1959	Wolverton	As diagram 628 without side rails.
3262	p	40	DB996882-996921	1958	Wolverton	) Some of these lots may have been
3284	p	48	DB996922-996969	1960	Wolverton	) to diagram 628.
3353	p	25	DB996995-997019	1961	Head-Wrightson	
Total		191				

1/638 50ton Bogie Rail, Sleeper, Ballast & General Utility Wagon Lettered Sturgeon

2322	37	DB994500-994536	1951	Head-Wrightson	66ft 1in long 3-plank drop side.
2404	180	DB994537-994716	1952	Head-Wrightson	
Total	217				

1/639 40ton Rail Sleeper & Ballast Wagon Lettered Dolphin

2217	90	DB994000-994089	1950	Head-Wrightson	6ins shorter than diagram 638
Total	90				

1/640 50ton Bogie Rail Wagon (Engineers Dept) Code Salmon

2011	25	DB996000-996024	1949	Derby	As diagram 637 but with planked floor
2216	75	DB996025-996099	1950	Teesside B&E	
2399	62	DB996152-996213	1952	Teesside B&E	
Total	162				

1/641 40ton Bogie Rail Wagon (Engineers Dept) Lettered - Oyster

2094	25	DB996700-996724	1949	Swindon	See also diagram 488
2208	70	DB996725-996794	1950	Cravens	
Total	95				

1/642 50ton Bogie Rail Wagon Lettered Salmon

2363	52	DB996100-996151	1951	Head-Wrightson	Raised bolsters.
2534	95	DB996214-996308	1953	Head-Wrightson	
Total	147				

1/643 30ton Bogie Bolster Wagon Lettered Shrimp

2497	1	DB997648	1953	Lancing	3-plank drop sides & bolsters.
Total	1				

1/644 50ton Bogie Rail Wagon Lettered Salmon

2615	54	DB996309-996362	1954	Turner	Similar to diagram 637
Total	54				

1/645 50ton Bogie Rail Sleeper - Ballast Lettered Sturgeon 'A'

2507	142	DB994717-994858	1953	Head-Wrightson	Similar to diagram 638
2614	141	DB994859-994999	1954	Head-Wrightson	
2895	111	DB994090-994200	1955	Head-Wrightson	
Total	394				

1/646 50ton Bogie Rail Wagon Lettered Salmon

2894	58	DB996363-996420	1955	Turner	Similar to diagram 637
2926	98	DB996421-996518	1956	Turner	
3065	79	DB996519-996597	1957	Teesside B&E	
3067	80	DB996598-996677	1957	Turner	
Total	315				

1/647 50ton Bogie Rail Sleeper - Ballast Lettered Sturgeon 'A'

2937		110	DB994201-994310	1956	Head-Wrightson	Bolsters & stanchions removable.
3047		81	DB994311-994391	1957	Head-Wrightson	
3264	p	30	DB994392-994421	1959	Lancing	
3265	p	46	DB994422-994467	1959	Lancing	
3291	p	1	DB994468	1960	Lancing	
3342	p	4	DB994469-994472	1961	Lancing	
Total		272				

1/648 Overhead Line Maintenance Vehicle

2220	w	2	DB998900-998901	1950	E E Bagley	Self-propelled diesel vehicles.
Total		2				

1/649 Dynamometer Car

	v	1	DB999500		Doncaster	Originally DE320041, later re-numbered. Ordered 1938, built 1951.
Total		1				

1/653 Flats for Conveyance of Re-inforced Concrete

3752	12	DB976000-976011		St Rollox	Ex-Bogie Bolster Ds modified.

Experimental Vehicle - No Details Available

	1	B724974		Derby	Originally part lot 2839
Total	1				

20ton Tank for Conveyance of Cement in Bulk

2533	1	B749370	1953	Shildon	Built 1953, broken up 1954
Total	1				

22ton Long Open Experimental

3362	v	5	B710251-710255		Ashford	For B710250 see diagram 235. Different body fittings to each vehicle.
Total		5				

Track Recording Coach

3248	v	1	DB999507		P R Wickham	No details known.
Total		1				

Adaptor Wagon for Electric Carriages

3412	2	DB998509-998510		Temple Mills	No details known.
Total	2				

2/001 40ton Armour Plate Truck Lettered Arm EL, WE

2008		7	B907100-907106	1949	Derby	Bogie wagons
2016		7	B907107-907113	1949	Derby	
2643		10	B908500-908509	1954	Cambrian	
2721		2	B908510-908511	1955	Cambrian	
2924		1	B908512	1956	Cambrian	
3041		1	B908513	1957	Cambrian	
3271	p	6	B908514-908519	1958	Standard	Arm AB this lot.
Total		34				

2/002 55ton Armour Plate Truck Lettered Arm ET, MD, WF

2174	9	B908000-908008	1950	Teesside B&E	Bogie Wagons
2622	7	B908009-908015	1954	Teesside B&E	
2651	4	B908016-908019	1955	Teesside B&E	
2938	1	B908020	1956	Teesside B&E	
3057	1	B908012	1957	Teesside B&E	
Total	22				

2/003 55ton Armour Plate Truck Lettered Arm ET

3171	p	6	B908022-908027	1958	Teesside B&E	Piped version of diagram 2
Total		6				

2/030 35ton Boiler Wagon Lettered Boiler EG

2173	2	B902800-902801	1950	Hurst Nelson	Bogie wagons. Trussed underframe.
Total	2				

2/031 35ton Boiler Wagon Lettered Boiler EF

2568	1	B902802	1954	Lancing	Bogie wagons. Girder underframe.
3020	1	B902803	1957	Eastleigh	
Total	2				

2/032 35ton Boiler Wagon Lettered Boiler EF

3110	p	1	B902804	1961	Ashford	Piped version of diagram 31.
Total		1				

2/033 290ton Boiler Wagon Lettered Boiler EB

3527	v	6	B902805-902810		Ashford	Diagrams 2/033, 2/034 & 2/035 cover the 150ton and 290ton boiler wagons. The 290ton wagon consists
Total		6				

of two pairs of 6axle wagons (24 axles in all) each pair being two wagons joined with an equalizing beam. For the 150ton version equalizing beams are not used but match wagons 902809 & 902810 are attached to make two complete 150ton wagons.

2/070 60ton Bogie Flat Wagon Lettered Flat EQ

2285	2	B907300-907301	1951	Fairfields	Six wheeled bogies
Total	2				

2/071 30ton Flat Wagon Lettered Flat EL

2569	2	B907000-907001	1954	Lancing	Bogie Vehicles
Total	2				

2/072 12ton Flat Wagon Lettered Flat ED

2632	10	B906800-906809	1954	Shildon
3004	7	B906810-906816	1957	Shildon
3123	15	B906817-906831	1958	Shildon
Total	32			

2/073 50ton Flat Wagon Lettered Flat WC (ex Warflat)

3416	60	W161000-161059			Bogie vehicles. Some vaccum fitted.
Total	60				

2/074 45ton Flat Wagon Lettered Flat ET

2943	2	B907200-907201	1959	R Y Pickering	Bogie vehicles
2944	6	B907202-907207	1959	R Y Pickering	
3044	29	B907208-907236	1957	R Y Pickering	
Total	37				

2/075 60ton Bogie Flat Wagon Lettered Flat EQ

3151	p	3	B907302-907304	1958	Fairfields	Six wheeled bogies
Total		3				

2/150 40ton Girder Wagon Set Lettered Girder WG

2692	2	B907500-907501	1961	Swindon	A set originally comprised a pair of single ended wagons semi-permanently coupled and given one number. Each wagon was later given its own number so that although the number of wagons became eight there were still only four sets.
2692	2	B907504-907505	1961	Swindon	
2873	2	B907502-907503	1959	Swindon	
2873	2	B907506-907507	1959	Swindon	
Total	8				

100ton Bogie Set Lettered Conger

3709	4	DB998070-998073		Ashford	For use in pairs.
Total	4				

2/170 12ton Glass Wagon Lettered - Glass WC

2103	6	B902000-902005	1949	Swindon	GWR design. 21ft 6ins long.
Total	6				

2/171 12ton Glass Truck Lettered Glass MD

2491	6	B902006-902011	1953	Swindon	LMS design. 26ft long.
2543	13	B902012-902024	1954	Swindon	
2646	10	B902025-902034	1955	Swindon	4 lettered Glass EP
2874	3	B902035-902037	1956	Swindon	Lettered Glass WE
3071	10	B902038-902047	1957	Swindon	5 lettered Glass EP
Total	42				

2/172 30ton Glass Wagon Lettered Glass EO

2570	2	B902500-902501	1954	Lancing	Bogie Vehicles
Total	2				

2/173 12ton Glass Truck Lettered - Glass EP

3297	p	2	B902048-902049	1960	Swindon	Piped version of diagram 171
Total		2				

2/240 21ton Lowmac Lettered Lowmac MR

2007		17	B904000-904016	1949	P W McLellan	
2189		25	B904017-904041	1950	P W McLellan	
2276		40	B904042-904081	1951	P W McLellan	
3254	p	10	B904145-904154	1959	Shildon	Lettered Lowmac AB
Total		92				

2/241 15ton Lowmac Lettered Lowmac WE

2087	20	B905000-905019	1949	Swindon
2975	10	B905088-905097	1957	Swindon

2/242 25ton Lowmac Lettered Lowmac EP, Lowmac SC

2187 v 38 B904500-904537 1950 P W McLellan
Total 38

2/243 25ton Lowmac Lettered Lowmac WP, Lowmac ER

2268 28 B904538-904565 1951 Swindon Last 8 Lowmac ER
2593 58 B904572-904629 1954 Swindon 44 Lowmac ER, rest Lowmac MS
2693 20 B904642-904661 1955 Swindon Lowmac MS
2876 20 B904675-904694 1956 Swindon Lowmac MS
Total 126

2/244 14ton Lowmac Lettered - Lowmac EK

2475 40 B905020-905059 1953 Shildon
2553 12 B905060-905071 1954 Shildon
Total 52

2/245 20ton Lowmac Lettered - Lowmac WN

2324 20 B904082-904101 1952 Swindon
2492 3 B904102-904104 1953 Swindon
2592 15 B904105-904119 1954 Swindon Lowmac ET
Total 38

2/246 25ton Lowmac Lettered Lowmac WBB

2449 v 6 B904566-904571 1953 Teesside B&E Lowmac ES
2594 v 4 B904630-904633 1954 Swindon
Total 10

2/247 25ton Lowmac Lettered Lowmac EU

2714 w 13 B904662-904674 1955 Derbyshire For Continental working
Total 13

2/248 15ton Lowmac Lettered Lowmac WV

2591 v 6 B905072-905077 1954 Swindon
2875 v 10 B905078-906087 1956 Swindon
3100 v 19 B905098-905116 1958 Swindon
3197 v 2 B905117-905118 1959 Swindon This lot had roller bearings.
Total 37

2/249 20ton Lowmac Lettered Lowmac EO

2959 v 3 B904120-904122 1956 Teesside B&E
Total 3

2/250 20ton Lowmac Lettered Lowmac MU

2976 v 12 B904123-904134 1957 Swindon
Total 12

2/252 20ton Lowmac

3101 v 10 B904135-904144 1958 Swindon Lowmac SG
3298 v 3 B904155-904157 1960 Swindon Lowmac MU
Total 13

2/253 25ton Lowmac

3172 v 15 B904695-904709 1958 Derbyshire First 10 Lowmac MS, others Lowmac SH
3198 v 13 B904710-904722 1959 Swindon First 6 Lowmac MS, others Lowmac WP
Total 28

2/254 25ton Lowmac Lettered Lowmac SF

2645 w 8 B904634-904641 1954 Derbyshire For Continental working.
Total 8

2/293 12½ton Two Tier Car Transporter Lettered Tierwag

3269 v 6 B909200-909205 1959 Newton Chambers Bogie vehicles
Total 6

2/294,295 Articulated Car Transport Cartic 4 (32tons)

3518 v 2 B909300-909301 Ashford
3518 v 2 B909400-909401 Ashford
Total 4

These 4 vehicles form an articulated unit with diagram 294 covering the outer vehicles (300/1) and 295 the inner ones. The lot book suggests that they may originally have been to Non-passenger diagram No 821.

2/390 20tons High Machine Trolley Lettered - Hymac 'EP'

2353 6 B906000-906005 1952 Lancing
Total 6

2/391 21ton Hymac Lettered - Hymac EX

2644 15 B906006-906020 1954 Hurst Nelson
Total 15

2/392 20ton Hymac Lettered Hymac EP

3019 1 B906021 1957 Eastleigh Virtually identical to diagram 391.
Total 1

2/393 21ton Hymac Lettered - Hymac EX

3304 v 5 B906022-906026 1960 Lancing Vacuum fitted version of diag.391.
Total 5

2/440 38ton Rectank Wagon Lettered Rectank EC Rectank WC

3165 p 21 B909000-909020 1958 Butterley Bogie vehicles
3259 p 27 B909021-909047 1959 Cambrian
3299 p 30 B909048-909077 1960 Swindon Lettered Rectank MD
Total 78

2/450 12ton Roll Wagon Lettered Roll WC

2877 10 B901850-901859 1956 Swindon
Total 10

2/470 135ton Transformer Trolley Lettered Transformer MC

2419 2 B901800-901801 1952 Head-Wrightson 12-axle vehicle 89ft long.
Total 2

2/490 21ton Trestle Wagon Lettered Trestle EA

(23)
Total (23)

Converted from diagrams 1/415 & 1/416 and numbered between B920001 & B920361.

2/491 42ton Trestle Wagon Lettered - Trestle ED

2434 25 B903600-903624 1950 Teesside B&E Bogie vehicles
3066 24 B903625-903648 1957 Teesside B&E
Total 49

2/492 21ton Trestle Wagon Lettered Trestle EA, Trestle AA.

3124 v 16 B903649-903664 1958 Shildon Vacuum fitted version of diagram 490. Lot book indicates they were new vehicles, not conversions.
Total 16

2/493 42ton Trestle Wagon Lettered - Trestle ED

3231 v 19 B903665-903683 1959 Derby Vacuum fitted version of diagram 491
Total 19

2/494 42ton Trestle Wagon Lettered - Trestle AB

? (10)
Total (10)

Converted from diagram 1/472 numbered between B942030 & 942751.

2/495 42ton Trestle Wagon Lettered Trestle ED

3410 v 20 B903684-903703 1961 Chas Roberts As diagram 493 but with roller bearings.
Total 20

2/496 50ton Trestle Plate Wagon (Ex Warflat) Lettered Trestle EH

3417 35 W161500-161534 Bogie vehicles, some vacuum fitt
Total 35

2/510 20ton Bogie Trolley Lettered Flatrol MSS

2006 10 B900300-900309 1949 Derby With baulks.
Total 10

2/511 40ton Bogie Lettered Flatrol MHH

2005 10 B900400-900409 1949 Derby With baulks.
2364 5 B900410-900414 1950 Head Wrightson
2617 3 B900420-900422 1954 Head Wrightson
Total 18

2/512 20ton Four Wheeled Trolley Lettered Flatrol MVV

2030 10 B900000-900009 1949 Derby With baulks.
2354 5 B900010-900014 1952 Lancing
2450 5 B900015-900019 1953 Derby
2613 3 B900020-900022 1954 Derby
2641 4 B900023-900026 1955 Derby
2945 6 B900037-900042 1956 Lancing
Total 33

2/513 40ton Bogie Trolley Lettered - Flatrol WX

2078 6 B901000-901005 1949 Swindon
Total 6

2/514 50ton Bogie Trolley Lettered - Flatrol EZ

2176 4 B900500-900503 1950 P W McLellan With baulks.
2952 2 B900507-900508 1959 Lancing
Total 6

2/515 20ton Bogie Trolley Lettered - Flatrol MUU

2304 4 B900310-900313 1950 Cambrian With baulks.
Total 4

2/516 20ton Four Wheeled Trolley Lettered Flatrol EAB

2218 4 B900100-900103 1950 Fairfields With baulks.
2452 1 B900104 1953 Fairfields
2619 3 B900105-900107 1954 Fairfields
2936 1 B900108 1956 Fairfields
Total 9

2/517 25ton Bogie Trolley Lettered Flatrol ED

2219 1 B900350 1951 Fairfields With baulks.
2453 1 B900351 1953 Fairfields
2620 1 B900352 1954 Fairfields
Total 3

2/518 35ton Bogie Trolley Lettered Flatrol EN

2947 w 1 B900603 1959 R Y Pickering For Continental traffic?
Total 1

2/519 120ton Trolley Wagon Lettered Flatrol EAA

2893 1 B900675 1955 Head-Wrightson 12-axle vehicle, with baulks. Only the understructure & bogies were new, the rest being ex-LNER diagra 134.
Total 1

2/520 50ton Bogie Trolley Lettered Flatrol EX

2572 2 B900504-900505 1954 Lancing
Total 2

2/521 30ton Trolley Wagon Lettered Flatrol EL

2571 w 2 B900600-900601 1954 Lancing Bogie vehicles, with baulks. Modified to run on the Continent.
Total 2

2/522 50ton Trolley Wagon Lettered Flatrol EY

2573 1 B900506 1954 Lancing Bogie vehicle, with beams.
Total 1

2/523 30ton Trolley Wagon R.I.V. Lettered Flatrol EL

2753 w 1 B900602 1955 Lancing Bogie vehicle, with beams.
Total 1

2/524 40ton Bogie Trolley Lettered Flatrol ET & MHH

2451 5 B900415-900419 1953 Head Wrightson With baulks.
2948 2 B900423-900424 1954 Head Wrightson These lettered ET, the rest MHH
3069 4 B900425-900428 1957 Head Wrightson
Total 11

2/525 20ton Four Wheeled Trolley Lettered Flatrol SB

2927 w 1 B900027 1956 Lancing With baulks, for Continental working
2927 w 2 B900029-900030 1956 Lancing Part lot. For rest see diagram 533.
2927 w 5 B900032-900036 1956 Lancing
Total 8

2/526 25ton Bogie Trolley Lettered Flatrol EV

2953 1 B900355 1959 Lancing With baulks. Vacuum & Westinghouse through pipes for Continental working.
3303 2 B900353-900354 1960 Lancing
Total 3

2/527 20ton Four Wheeld Trolley (R.I.V.) Lettered Flatrol EG

2949 w 1 B900043 1959 Lancing With baulks.
Total 1

2/528 20ton Four Wheeled Trolley Lettered Flatrol WW

2878 p 2 B900047-900048 1959 Swindon
3199 p 3 B900044-900046 1959 Swindon
Total 5

2/529 40ton Bogie Well Wagon Lettered Flatrol MDD

3266 p 2 B900429-900430 1959 Teesside B&E With rail sections adjustable to suit gauge & wheelbase of vehicle.
Total 2

2/530 21ton Flatrol Wagon Lettered Flatrol EAC

3252 x 20 B900109-900128 1959 Shildon With baulks.
Total 20

2/531 40ton Bogie Trolley Lettered Flatrol MCC

3269 p 6 B900431-900436 1958 Standard 6-wheel bogies. For conveyance of nuclear flasks
3270 p 4 B900437-900440 1959 Standard
Total 10

2/532 50ton Flatrol Lettered Flatrol NJ

3300 v 24 B900509-900532 1960 Swindon
Total 24

2/533 20ton Four Wheel Trolley Lettered Flatrol SBC

2927 w 1 B900028 1956 Lancing With baulks. Part lot, see diagram 525 for remainder.
2927 w 1 B900031 1956 Lancing
Total 2

2/660 20ton Propellor Trolley Lettered Protrol ED

2177 3 B901400-901402 1950 G R Turner Bogie vehicles, with baulks.
Total 3

2/661 40ton Trolley Wagon Lettered Protrol EG

2574 1 B901450 1954 Lancing Bogie vehicles, with beams.
3018 1 B901452 1957 Eastleigh
Total 2

2/662 40ton Trolley Wagon Lettered Protrol EG

2950 w 1 B901451 1956 Lancing Bogie vehicle, with beams, probably for Continental traffic.
Total 1

2/663 40ton Trolley Wagon Lettered Protrol EF

3111 p 1 B901453 1961 Ashford Bogie vehicle, with beams.
Total 1

2/680 40ton Bogie Trolley Lettered Trestrol MO

2205 10 B901500-901509 1950 Head Wrightson With trestles
Total 10

2/681 55ton Trestle Trolley Lettered Trestrol EC

2175 4 B901600-901603 1950 Teesside B&E 6-wheel bogies
Total 4

2/682 40ton Bogie Trolley Lettered Trestrol MO

2355 10 B901510-901519 1952 Lancing Slightly different from diag. 680
3017 11 B901520-901530 1957 Lancing
3112 p 11 B901531-901541 1958 Ashford Loco
3247 p 35 B901542-901576 1959 Ashford Loco Lettered Trestrol EO
3309 p 50 B901702-901751 1960 Derby Lettered Trestrol EO
Total 117

2/683 20ton Four Wheeled Trestle Trolley

2575 1 B901650 1954 Lancing Fixed trestles with chocks for circular plates.
Total 1

2/684 30ton Trestle Trolley Wagon Lettered Trestrol EN

2576 2 B901700-901701 1954 Lancing Bogie vehicles, fixed trestles.
Total 2

2/730 20ton Bogie Well Trolley Lettered Weltrol MC

2029 10 B900800-900809 1949 Derby With baulks.
Total 10

2/731 40ton Bogie Well Trolley Lettered - Weltrol MV

2360 5 B901006-901010 1950 Head Wrightson With baulks.
3241 4 B901022-901025 1960 Lancing
Total 9

2/732 30ton Bogie Well Trolley Lettered - Weltrol EC

2357 1 B900760 1952 Lancing With baulks.
Total 1

2/733 20ton Four Wheeled Trolley Lettered Weltrol MA

2356 10 B900700-900709 1952 Lancing With baulks.
Total 10

2/734 35ton Well Trolley Lettered Weltrol WW

2494 2 B901100-901101 1953 Swindon Bogie Vehicles
2647 2 B901102-901103 1955 Swindon
Total 4

2/735 25ton Bogie Well Trolley Lettered Weltrol WBB

2454 3 B900900-900902 1953 Swindon With baulks.
2642 3 B900903-900905 1955 Head-Wrightson
Total 6

2/736 40ton Well Trolley Wagon Lettered Weltrol EB

2581 3 B901011-901013 1954 Lancing Bogie vehicles, with baulks.
Total 3

2/737 120ton Weltrol WL

2828 1 B901260 1955 Teesside B&E 12-wheel bogies. Detachable side girders.
Total 1

2/738 50ton Weltrol EP (R.I.V.)

3074 w 2 B901150-901151 1956 Lancing 6-wheel bogies, with beams.
Total 2

2/739 25ton Weltrol WZ Steel Floor.

2977 p 1 B900911 1957 Swindon Bogie vehicle.
Total 1

2/740 25ton Trolley Wagon Lettered Weltrol EL

3173 p 2 B900923-900924 1958 Butterley Bogie vehicles, with beams.
Total 2

2/741 25ton Weltrol WP Wood Floor

3102 p 11 B900912-900922 1958 Swindon Bogie vehicles.
3192 p 14 B900925-900938 1960 Swindon
Total 25

2/742 50ton Weltrol WJ

3213 p 1 B901152 1960 Swindon Bogie vehicle
Total 1

2/743 25ton Weltrol Steel Floor

2879 p 2 B900906-900907 1959 Swindon Bogie vehicles
Total 2

2/744 65ton Weltrol WH

3214 p 2 B901225-901226 1960 Swindon Bogie vehicles.
Total 2

2/745 25ton Weltrol WZ Wood Floor

2880 p 3 B900908-900910 1959 Swindon Bogie vehicles.
Total 3

2/746 20ton Bogie Well Trolley Lettered - Weltrol MC

3272 p 2 B900810-900811 1959 Standard With baulks.
3301 p 2 B900812-900813 1960 Swindon
Total 4

2/747 35ton Weltrol WW

2978 p 2 B900106-901107 1960 Swindon Bogie vehicles
3103 p 2 B901108-901109 1958 Swindon
Total 4

2/748 40ton Weltrol

3193 p 4 B901014-901017 1957 Swindon Bogie vehicles, lettered Weltrol WGG
3194 p 4 B901018-901021 1961 Swindon Lettered Weltrol MV
Total 8

2/749 120ton Trolley Wagon Lettered Weltrol ENN

3316 1 B901261 1960 Darlington (N Rd) four 6-wheel bogies.
Total 1

2/750 55ton Bogie Well Trolley Wagon Lettered - Weltrol EJC

2582 x 4 B901200-901203 1959 Ashford 6-wheel bogies, with baulks, for Continental working.
3016 x 1 B901204 1957 Ashford
3273 x 1 B901205 1959 Ashford
Total 6

2/751 35ton Weltrol WW

2881	p	2	B901104-901105	1956	Swindon	Bogie vehicles. Diagram book looks on them as diagram 734.
Total		2				

2/880 10ton Wheel Wagon

3251	v	1	B902600	1959	Shildon	Code - Wheel EA
Total		1				

2/881 20ton Wheel Wagon Lettered Wheel EL

3222	p	3	B902700-902702	1959	Shildon	Bogie vehicles
3317	p	1	B902703	1960	Shildon	
Total		4				

2/900 20ton Trolley

2095		3	DB998000-998002	1949	Swindon	Code, Engineering Dept Loriot.
2270		3	DB998003-998005	1951	Swindon	
Total		6				

2/901 20ton Trolley Lettered Loriot

3201	p	2	DB998013-998014	1959	Swindon	Departmental version of diag. 528.
Total		2				

2/902 20ton Loriot Lettered Loriot

2980	p	4	DB998007-998010	1957	Swindon	
3149	p	2	DB998011-998012	1958	Swindon	
Total		6				

2/903 20ton Four Wheeled Trolley Lettered Flatrol SB

2951		1	DB998006	1956	Lancing	With end baulks.
Total		1				

2/904 20ton Flat Trolley

3257	p	15	DB998015-998029	1959	Lancing	No code quoted.
Total		15				

3/001 Container Type A

2116	3	180	A111-290B	1949	Wolverton	Boarded with pressed steel end.
2141	3	110	A341-450B	1950	Earlestown	
2244	3	230	A451-680B	1951	Earlestown	
2436	3	235	A1311-1545B	1953	Wolverton	
2555	3	420	A1546-1965B	1954	Earlestown	
2658	4	600	A1966-2565B	1955	Earlestown	
2829	4	350	A2566-2915B	1956	Earlestown	
2963	4	150	A3316-3465B	1956	Earlestown	
2964	4	550	A40000-40549B	1957	Earlestown	
2981	4	100	A3466-3565B	1957	Swindon	
2995	4	275	A3566-3840B	1957	Faverdale	
3078	4	600	A40550-41149B	1957	Earlestown	
Total		3800				

3/002 Container Type A

2056	3	60	A1-60B	1949	Faverdale	Plywood sides & ends
2124	3	50	A291-340B	1949	Wolverton	
Total		110				

3/003 Container Type A

2335	3	530	A681-1210B	1952	Wolverton	Boarded sides & ends
2374	3	100	A1211-1310B	1952	Eastleigh	
2958	4	400	A2916-3315B	1956	Cowlairs	
Total		1030				

3/004 Container Type A

3368	5	2	A3841-3842B		Willerby	Plastics material, no diagram available
Total		2				

3/005 Container Type A

3403	5	1	A3843B		Willerby	Experimental, assumed to be plastics.
Total		1				

3/006 Container Type A

3435	3	8	A3844-3851B	1961	Cowlairs	No diagram available
3470	3	4	A3852-3855B		Cowlairs	
Total		12				

3/047 'B' Type Container

3174	5	50	B55850-55899B	1958	Park Royal	Probably aluminium construction.
Total		50				

3/049 Container Type B

2888	4	150	B55700-55849B	1956	Swindon	Boarded with pressed steel end
2965	4	175	B55525-55699B	1957	Earlestown	
Total		325				

3/050 Container Type BD

2017	4	225	BD4000-4224B	1949	Earlestown	
2143	4	630	BD4495-5124B	1950	Earlestown	
2246	4	270	BD5420-5689B	1951	Earlestown	
2333	4	311	BD5690-6000B	1952	Earlestown	Part lot. Balance to diagram 52.
2333	4	89	BD6151-6239B	1952	Earlestown	
2373	4	235	BD6240-6474B	1952	Earlestown	
2437	4	710	BD6675-7384B	1953	Wolverton	Part lot. Balance to diagram 52.
2556	4	410	BD7385-7794B	1954	Earlestown	
2659	4	450	BD46000-46449B	1955	Earlestown	
2785	4	1500	BD46450-46949B	1956	Wolverton	
2786	4	600	BD46950-47549B	1956	Wolverton	
2966	4	450	BD47550-47999B	1957	Earlestown	
2969	4	550	BD48000-48549B	1957	Wolverton	
2970	4	550	BD48550-49099B	1957	Wolverton	
3064	4	350	BD49100-49449B	1957	St Rollox	
3079	4	300	BD49450-49749B	1957	Earlestown	
3080	4	400	BD49750-50149B	1957	Wolverton	
3131	4	300	BD50150-50449B	1957	St Rollox	
3132	4	350	BD50450-50799B	1958	St Rollox	
3161	4	200	BD7795-7994B	1958	Papworth	
3169	4	200	BD50800-50999B	1958	Mickleover	
Total		9080				

3/051 Container Type BD

2057	4	75	BD4225-4299B	1949	Earlestown	Plywood sides & ends. Diagram gives capacity as 5tons
2100	4	80	BD4365-4444B	1949	Swindon	
2101	4	50	BD4445-4494B	1949	Swindon	
Total		205				

3/052 Container Type BD

2213	4	295	BD5125-5419B	1949	Eastleigh	Boarded sides & ends. Diagram gives capacity as 5tons
2333	4	150	BD6001-6150B	1952	Earlestown	Part lot, see diagram 50.
2437	4	200	BD6475-6674B	1953	Wolverton	Part lot, see diagram 50.
Total		645				

3/053 Container Type BD

3220	5	1	BD4300B		Natl. Aluminium	Experimental, smaller size.
Total		1				

3/054 Container Type BD (Fibreglass Construction)

3274	5	6	BD4301-4306B		Mickleover	Smaller size, roller shutters.
Total		6				

3/055 'BD' Type Covered Pallet Container (Insulated)

3382	4½	1	BD4307B		Earlestown	Plywood sides & ends. Experimental.
Total		1				

3/056 BD Type Container Insulated

3471	7	1	BD7995B		Earlestown	Plywood sides & ends.
3493	7	4	BD7996-7999B		Earlestown	
3496	7	2	BD4309-4310B		Earlestown	
3549	7	3	BD4351-4353B		Horwich	
Total		10				

3/075 BA Type Container (Light Alloy)

3436	10	40	BA4311-4350B		Earlestown	End doors plus sliding door one side. Fork lift brackets, no crane shackles. Speedfreight service.
Total		40				

3/076 'BA' Type Container (Light Alloy)

3461	10	13	BA51000-51012B		Earlestown	Similar to diagram 75.
Total		13				

3/100 Container Type 'B' & 'BC'.

2262	4	10	BC9700-9709B	1951	Faverdale	Boarded sides & ends. The BC carrie 4tons or 76 bicycles. The design was to have been type 'B' (5tons) but all were built as BC type.
2577	4	100	BC9776-9875B	1954	Eastleigh	
2680	4	15	BC9876-9890B	1955	Eastleigh	
2833	4	60	B9891-9950B	1956	Wolverton	
3072	4	100	BC58000-58099B	1957	Eastleigh	
Total		285				

3/101 Container Type 'B' & 'BC'.

2444	4	66	BC9710-9775B	1953	Eastleigh	Similar to diagram 100
Total		66				

3/125 Container Type 'BK'

2059	4	30	BK8000-8029B	1949	Faverdale	Plywood sides & ends. For furniture
2060	4	30	BK8030-8059B	1949	Faverdale	
Total		60				

3/126 Container Type 'BK'

2334	4	80	BK8060-8139B	1952	Earlestown	Similar to diagram 125.
2438	4	415	BK8140-8554B	1953	Earlestown	
2557	4	130	BK8555-8684B	1954	Earlestown	
Total		625				

3/127 Container Type 'BK'.

2830	4	450	BK8685-9134B	1956	Earlestown	Similar to diagram 125.
2996	4	50	BK9135-9184B	1957	Faverdale	
3105	4	250	BK9185-9434B	1958	Swindon	
Total		750				

3/150 Container Type 'BM'.

2071	4	15	BM10000-10014B	1948	Earlestown	Fresh meat. Boarded sides & ends with louvres.
2114	4	100	BM10015-10114B	1949	Earlestown	
2234	4	120	BM10115-10234B	1950	R Y Pickering	
Total		235				

3/151 Container Type 'BM'.

2311	4	85	BM10275-10359B	1952	Swindon	Similar to diagram 150.
2505	4	235	BM10360-10594B	1953	Swindon	
2564	4	120	BM10595-10714B	1954	Earlestown	
2889	4	200	BM10715-10914B	1956	Swindon	
Total		640				

3/152 Container Type 'BM'.

2261	4	40	BM10235-10274B	1951	Faverdale	Plywood construction
Total		40				

3/153 Container Type 'BM'.

2982	4	240	BM10915-11154B	1957	Swindon	Similar to diagram 150
3106	4	150	BM11155-11304B	1958	Swindon	
Total		390				

3/170 Container Type 'BP'.

3451	1½	24	BP58500-58523B	1962	Cowlairs	For bulk powders
3452	1½	16	BP58524-58539B		Kerby Eng.	
3459	1½	20	BP58540-58559B		Cowlairs	
Total		60				

3/200 Container Type 'FM'.

2115	4	100	FM12252-12351B	1949	Wolverton	Insulated. For frozen meat. Boarded sides & ends.
2147	4	260	FM12352-12611B	1950	Wolverton	
Total		360				

3/201 Meat Container Type 'FM'.

2336	4	150	FM13067-13216B	1952	Wolverton	Similar to diagram 200
Total		150				

3/202 Meat Container Type 'FM'.

2263	4	215	FM12612-12826B	1951	Faverdale	Plywood sides & ends.
2303	4	155	FM12912-13066B	1951	Eastleigh	
2359	4	200	FM13217-13416B	1952	Eastleigh	
2365	4	150	FM13417-13566B	1952	Derby	
2432	4	85	FM12827-12911B	1951	Eastleigh	
2435	4	230	FM13567-13796B	1953	Faverdale	Part lot. See diagram 203
Total		1035				

3/203 Meat Container Type FM

2435	4	100	FM13797-13896B	1953	Faverdale	Similar to diagram 202.
2578	4	190	FM14097-14286B	1954	Eastleigh	
2681	4	250	FM14737-14986B	1955	Eastleigh	
Total		540				

3/204 Meat Container Type FM

2558	4	200	FM13897-14096B	1954	Earlestown	Similar to diagram 200
2660	4	250	FM14287-14536B	1955	Earlestown	
Total		450				

3/205 Meat Container Type FM

2672	4	200	FM14537-14736B	1955	Ashford	Similar to diagram 202
2831	4	300	FM59500-59799B	1956	Earlestown	
2892	4	200	FM59800-59999B	1956	Faverdale	
2997	4	400	FM60000-60399B	1957	Faverdale	
3137	4	250	FM60400-60649B	1958	Faverdale	
Total		1350				

3/210 27ft Covered Container Type CA Speedfreight.

3475	16	13	CA51013-51025B		Earlestown	Also usable on Freightliners.
Total		13				

3/230 FA Type Container (Insulated)

3468	10	7	FA60650-60656B		Earlestown	Insulated version of diagram 75.
Total		7				

3/231 FA Type Container (Insulated)

3469	10	5	FA60657-60661B		Earlestown	Similar to diagram 230.
Total		5				

3/250 Container Type AF

2159	3	91	AF16000-16090B	1950	Swindon	Highly insulated A type. Plywood body.
2260	3	80	AF16100-16179B	1951	Faverdale	
2273	3	120	AF16180-16299B	1951	Swindon	
Total		291				

3/251 Container Type AF Fitted with Eutectic Plates.

2289	3	9	AFU16091-16099B	1950	Swindon	Similar to diagram 250 but with eutectic plates.
Total		9				

3/252 Container Type AF

2648	3	175	AF65000-65174B	1955	Earlestown	Similar to diagram 250
2890	3	60	AF16370-16429B	1956	Swindon	
2967	3	200	AF65200-65399B	1957	Earlestown	
3068	3	200	AF65400-65599B	1957	Park Royal	
3136	3	200	AF65600-65799B	1958	Faverdale	
3180	3	300	AF65836-66135B	1958	Earlestown	
3181	3	180	AF66136-66315B	1958	Earlestown	
Total		1315				

3/253 Container Type "AFU" Fitted with Eutectic Plates

2565	3	20	AFU16300-16319B	1954	Earlestown	Similar to diagram 251
2673	3	50	AFU16320-16369B	1955	Swindon	
2766	3	25	AFU65175-65199B	1955	Earlestown	
2891	3	40	AFU16430-16469B	1956	Swindon	
Total		135				

3/254 Container Fitted with Eutectic Plates Type AFU Pallet

2956	3	1	AFU65800B	1958	Earlestown	Originally experimental container AFP79997. Floor rollers for pallet loading
Total		1				

3/255 Container Fitted with Eutectic Plates Type AFU Pallet

3179	3	35	AFU65801-65835B	1958	Earlestown	Similar to diagram 254
3250	3	20	AFU16470-16489B	1958	Earlestown	
3277	3	30	AFU66416-66445B	1959	Earlestown	
Total		85				

3/256 Container Type AFP

3249	4	100	AFU66316-66415B	1958	Swindon	Insulated type with dry ice bunkers.
3278	4	36	AFU66446-66481B	1959	Swindon	
Total		136				

3/257 Container Type AFP

3428	4	6	AFP16494-16499B		Mickleover	No diagram available
Total		6				

3/260 Container Type AFC

3357	4¾	2	AFC16490-16491B		Swindon	Part lot (experimental)
Total		2				

3/261 Container Type AFC

3357	4¾	2	AFC16492-16493B		Swindon	Part lot, see above
Total		2				

3/275 Container Type AX

2142	3	50	AX15000-15049B	1950	Earlestown	For Drikold, highly insulated.
2245	3	25	AX15050-15074B	1951	Earlestown	
2506	3	30	AX15075-15104B	1953	Swindon	
2610	3	100	AX15105-15204B	1954	Faverdale	
2665	3	35	AX15205-15239B	1955	Faverdale	
Total		240				

3/300 Container Type "AFX" Fitted with Eutectic Plates.

2443	3½	17	AFX16500-16516B	1953	Earlestown	Longer version of AFU type.
Total		17				

3/374 Container Type "RY"

2754	3.5	1	RY79950B	1954	Ulster T.A.	For rayon yarn traffic to N Ireland
2755	3.6	5	RY79951-79955B	1954	Ulster T.A.	
Total		6				

3/375 Container Type F

2067	3½	252	F12000-12251B	1948	Eastleigh	Insulated meat containers.
Total		252				

3/400 Container Type LD

2307	8	1	LD17000B	1951	Swindon	Covered hoppers for dolomite.
2332	8	79	LD17001-17079B	1952	Fairleede	
2536	6	30	LD17080-17109B	1953	Earlestown	
Total		110				

3/450 Container Type 'L'

2392	4	999	L17251-18249B	1951	Cravens	Covered hoppers for lime.
2433	4	1	L17250B	1951	Eastleigh	
2652	4	1500	L18250-19749B	1955	Cravens	
2762	4	900	L68000-68899B	1955	Earlestown	
2832	4	210	L19750-19959B	1956	Earlestown	
2968	4	780	L68900-69679B	1957	Earlestown	Some of this lot built at Wolverton
3073	4	500	L69680-70719B	1958	Earlestwon	
3081	4	600	L70180-70779B	1957	Earlestown	
3135	4	82	L71080-71161B	1958	Bentley Eng.	
3380	4	448	L71162-71609B	1961	Earlestown	
3389	4	366	L71610-71975B	1961	Earlestown	
Total		6386				

3/451 Container Type LG

3336	6	2	LG19961-19962B	1961	Doncaster	Covered hoppers for malt.
3337	6	12	LG19963-19974B	1961	Doncaster	
Total		14				

3/452 Container Type LF

3325	8	1	LF19960B	1959	Duramin	Cylindrical type for bulk flour.
3376	8	6	LF19978-19983B		Duramin	
Total		7				

3/453 Container Type LG

	4	(3)				Converted from A type containers to diagrams 1, 2 & 3 between A2-1501B
Total		(3)				

3/454 Container Type LP

3375	4	3	LP19975-19977B		Metro-Cammell	Experimental, diagram not available.
Total		3				

3/455 Container Type LS

3447	8	15	LS19984-19998B	1961	Carmichael	Originally type LP
Total		15				

3/456 Container Type LT

3474	8¼	6	LT17110-17115B		Carmichael	Cylindrical type.
Total		6				

3/500 Container Type C

2024	3	100	C20000-20099B	1949	Earlestown	Open type, planked body.
2111	3	100	C20100-20199B	1949	Earlestown	
2144	3	200	C20200-20399B	1950	Earlestown	
2247	3	180	C20400-20579B	1951	Earlestown	
2337	3	130	C20580-20709B	1952	Earlestown	
2439	3	50	C20710-20759B	1953	Earlestown	
2559	3	30	C20760-20789B	1954	Earlestown	
Total		790				

3/550 Container Type D

2066	4	50	D21000-21049B	1948	Eastleigh	Open type, planked body.
2113	4	200	D21050-21249B	1949	Earlestown	
2145	4	140	D21250-21389B	1950	Earlestown	
2246	4	415	D21390-21804B	1951	Eastleigh	
2338	4	580	D21805-22384B	1952	Earlestown	
2440	4	220	D22385-22604B	1953	Earlestown	
2560	4	370	D22605-22974B	1954	Earlestown	
Total		1975				

3/560 Container Type DA

3369	5	20	DA22975-22994B		Cowlairs	Open type, probably for Speedfreight services.
Total		20				

APPENDIX 4

3/565 Container Type DL

3561	10	2	DL23500-23501B		Darlington	No diagram available.
Total		2				

3/599 Container Type DX

2561	4	150	DX88000-88149B	1954	Earlestown	Open type, planked body.
Total		150				

3/600 Container Type H

2019	2¼	250	H24000-24249B	1949	Earlestown	Open type, planked body.
2072	2¼	50	H25000-25049B	1948	Earlestown	
Total		300				

3/602 Container Type H

2023	2¼	750	H24250-24999B	1949	Earlestown	Similar to diagram 600
2110	2¼	100	H25050-25149B	1949	Earlestown	
2146	2¼	50	H25150-25199B	1950	Earlestown	
2249	2¼	350	H25200-25549B	1951	Bromsgrove	
2339	2¼	360	H25550-25909B	1952	Earlestown	
2441	2¼	1000	H25910-26909B	1953	Earlestown	
2442	2¼	500	H29000-29499B	1953	Earlestown	
2562	2¼	800	H29500-30299B	1954	Earlestown	
Total		3910				

3/640 18ft Open Container Type BO - Speedfreight

3476	10	5	B23001-23005B		Earlestown	For fork lift loading
Total		5				

3/641 18ft Open Container Type BO - Speedfreight

3476	10	1	B23000B		Earlestown	Part lot, similar to diagram 640.
Total		1				

3/650 Grab Type Container

2171		4	27000-27003B	1950	Earlestown	Experimental, capacity 57 or 60cu ft.
Total		4				

3/660 Container Type "S"

2662	3	24	S95000-95023B	1954	Cowlairs	Side doors only, plywood construction
2684	3	196	S95024-95219B	1954	Earlestown	
Total		220				

3/669 Container Type SW

3190	1	800	SW78200-78999B	1958	Youngmans	Small wheeled container also available for passenger train traffic.
3190	1	356	SW79594-79949B	1958	Youngmans	
3190	1	3644	SW80000-83643B	1958	Youngmans	
3280	1	450	SW83644-84093B	1959	Youngmans	
3281	1	500	SW84094-84593B	1959	Youngmans	
Total		5750				

3/670 Container Type SW

2771	1	4	SW79000-79003B	1955	Tyne Truck	Similar to diagram 669. Believed to be of German manufacture.
2772	1	80	SW79004-79083B	1955	Tyne Truck	
2955	1	450	SW79084-79533B	1955	Tyne Truck	
2957	1	50	SW79354-79583B	1955	Tyne Truck	
3133	1	1200	SW77000-78199B	1958	Curzons	
3367	1	1	SW84594B	1961	Tyne Truck	
Total		1785				

3/671 Container Type SW

3148	1	10	SW79584-79593B	1959	Willerby	Possibly fibreglass construction.
Total		10				

3/672 Container Type SW

3386	1	2	SW84595-84596B		Eastleigh	Experimental. No diagram available.
Total		2				

3/673 Container Type SW

3420	1	23	SW84598-84620B		Eastleigh	Experimental. No diagram available.
Total		23				

3/700 Tote Bin Type T

3279	1¼	25	T89561-89585B	1959	Pressoturn	Small hoppers. Diagrams 700 to 704 cover different capacities of container which are all standard Pressoturn designs.
3287	1¼	26	T89586-89611B	1959	Pressoturn	
Total		51				

3/701 Tote Bin Type T

3295	1¼	200	T89051-89250B	1959	Pressoturn	
3306	1¼	20	T89612-89631B	1959	Pressoturn	
3307	1¼	12	T89632-89643B	1959	Pressoturn	
3381	1¼	50	T89714-89763B	1960	Pressoturn	
3395	1¼	18	T89870-89887B	1960	Pressoturn	
Total		300				

3/702 Tote Bin Type T

3293	1¼	50	T89501-89550B	1959	Pressoturn	
Total		50				

3/703 Tote Bin Type T

3294	1¼	50	T89001-89050B	1959	Pressoturn	
3294	1¼	250	T89251-89500B	1959	Pressoturn	
3328	1¼	70	T89644-89713B	1960	Pressoturn	
3385	1¼	106	T89764-89869B	1960	Pressoturn	
3422	1¼	30	T89888-89917B	1961	Pressoturn	
3423	1¼	10	T89918-89927B	1961	Pressoturn	
3453	1¼	55	T90001-90055B		Pressoturn	
3454	1¼	16	T90101-90116B		Pressoturn	
3462	1¼	50	T89928-89977B		Pressoturn	
Total		637				

3/704 Tote Bin Type T

3477	1¼	34	T90201-90234B		Pressoturn	
3481	1¼	84	T90235-90318B		Pressoturn	
3482	1¼	20	T90320-90339B		Pressoturn	
3517	1¼	33	T90056-90088B		Pressoturn	
3517	1¼	7	T90340-90346B		Pressoturn	
Total		178				

3/720 Container Type MJ

3319	4½	6	MJ74000-74005B	1960	Fodens	Diagrams 720 to 730 form a series of Bulkrane designs for different loads. It is understood that they were a joint project between Fodens and British Railwyas.
Total		6				

3/721 Brick Container Type MC

3349	5	18	MC27004-27021B	1960	Fodens	
Total		18				

3/722 Bulkrane 'MA' Type

3355	5½	12	MA27022-27033B	1960	Fodens	
Total		12				

3/723 Bulkrane 'MB' Type

3356	5½	12	MA27034-27045B	1960	Fodens	
Total		12				

3/724 Bulkrane Container Type MU Cement

3372	5½	2	MU74030-74031B	1960	Inter-Consult	
Total		2				

3/725 143cu ft Transportable Cement Silo Bulkrane MV

3351	5½	10	MV74020-74029B	1960	Dalzell El. Weld.	
Total		10				

3/726 Container MW Bulkrane

3350	3½	2	MW74006-74007B	1960	Mickleover	
Total		2				

3/727 Open Container 'MD'

3366	5¼	12	MD27046-27057B	1960	Fodens	
Total		12				

3/728 950gallon Bulkrane Container Type MR

3396	4½	2	MR74032-74033B	1960	Mickleover	
Total		2				

3/729 Bulkrane Container Type MP

3411	4¾	1	MP74034B	1960	Mickleover	
Total						

3/730 140cu ft Transportable Cement Silo Bulkrane MV

3351	5	2	MV74018-74019B	1960	Dalzell El. Weld.	
Total		2				

3/ Various Open & Covered Experimental Containers

2694		1	79999B		Swindon	No diagrams issued
2695		1	94999B		Swindon	
2826		1	EXP79998B		Swindon	
2827		1	Exp94998B		Swindon	
Total		4				

Index